ORACLE® *Oracle Press*™

Oracle Streams 11g Data Replication

About the Author

Kirtikumar Deshpande (Kirti) has over 29 years of experience in the information technology field. He has been working with Oracle products and technologies for over 15 years. Kirti co-authored the Oracle Press books *Oracle Wait Interface: A Practical Guide to Performance Diagnostics & Tuning* and *Oracle Performance Tuning 101* and received the "Oracle Author of the Year 2005" award from *Oracle Magazine* for the former. He has presented a number of technical papers at various Oracle user group meetings and conferences in the United States and abroad. Prior to joining Oracle Corporation, Kirti worked as an Oracle architect and a database administrator. He currently works as a Consulting Technical Manager with the Oracle Advanced Technology Solutions group, specializing exclusively in helping customers deploy high availability, disaster recovery, and replication solutions. He has designed and implemented complex Streams replication environments for several customers.

About the Contributor

Achala Deshpande has over 25 years of experience in the information technology field in various capacities. She has worked with Oracle technologies for the past 20 years, mainly designing and implementing database-driven interactive applications using PL/SQL, SQL, Pro*C, and J2EE. Currently, Achala works for a major airline in the United States as a Senior Software Engineer designing and developing rich Internet applications.

About the Technical Editors

Volker Kuhr is a Principal Service Delivery Engineer (SDE) for Oracle Corporation. Since 2000, Volker has worked in the line of database technology, after moving from Unix administration and C programming in the area of high-energy physics.

Starting initially within consulting for distributed databases (Advanced Replication, Streams, and OGG), Volker became a technical team leader for core technology, and eventually transitioned to Advanced Customer Support. Still working in this field, he has supported and assisted many Streams projects in Europe, the Middle East, and Africa.

Volker believes in sharing knowledge, and within the past decade he has lectured at colleges, presented at conferences, and provided instructional material. He holds a PhD in Science (Physics) from the University of Göttingen, Germany.

Lewis Kaplan, Technical Manager, Enterprise Solutions Group, Oracle Corporation, has been both a consultant in Advanced Technology Services and a developer in Server Technologies at Oracle. He was one of the principal developers of Oracle Streams and Logical Standby. Lewis is a co-inventor on two patents relating to replication methodology, as well as an internationally recognized expert in distributed technologies.

K. Gopalakrishnan (Gopal) is with the Enterprise Solutions Group at Oracle Corporation. With more than a decade of Oracle experience, Gopal has worked with a few of the biggest and busiest databases on the planet. A recognized expert in Oracle Real Application Clusters and Oracle Database Performance Tuning, he has solved vexing performance and scalability problems for banks, telcos, and e-commerce applications in more than 40 countries. Oracle Technology Network recognized him as an Oracle ACE.

Gopal is an award-winning co-author ("Oracle Author of the Year 2005," *Oracle Magazine*) of a bestselling Oracle Press performance tuning book, *Oracle Wait Interface: A Practical Guide to Performance Diagnostics & Tuning*. He also authored *Oracle Database 10g Real Application Clusters Handbook*.

ORACLE®   *Oracle Press*™

Oracle Streams 11g Data Replication

Kirtikumar Deshpande

McGraw Hill

New York   Chicago   San Francisco
Lisbon   London   Madrid   Mexico City   Milan
New Delhi   San Juan   Seoul   Singapore   Sydney   Toronto

The McGraw·Hill Companies

Cataloging-in-Publication Data is on file with the Library of Congress

Oracle Streams 11*g* Data Replication

1 2 3 4 5 6 7 8 9 0   QFR QFR   1 0 9 8 7 6 5 4 3 2 1 0

ISBN   978-0-07-149664-3
MHID   0-07-149664-5

Sponsoring Editor	**Contributor**	**Production Supervisor**
Lisa McClain	Achala Deshpande	George Anderson
Associate Acquisitions Editor	**Technical Editors**	**Composition**
Meghan Riley	Volker Kuhr, Lewis Kaplan,	Glyph International
Editorial Supervisor	K. Gopalakrishnan	**Illustration**
Janet Walden	**Copy Editor**	Glyph International
Project Manager	William McManus	**Art Director, Cover**
Vipra Fauzdar,	**Proofreader**	Jeff Weeks
Glyph International	Constance Blazewicz	**Cover Designer**
Acquisitions Coordinator	**Indexer**	Pattie Lee
Stephanie Evans	Jack Lewis	

To my father

Contents at a Glance

PART V
Appendixes

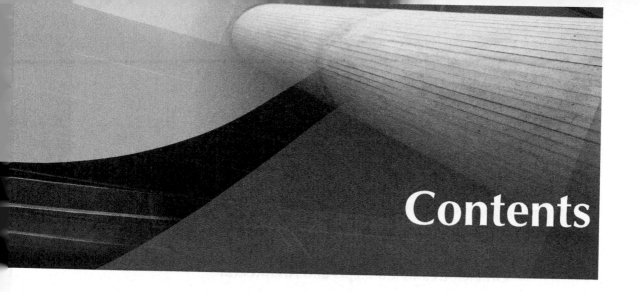

Contents

PART I
Introduction to Oracle Streams

PART II

Oracle Streams Concepts and Architecture

PART III

Oracle Streams Configuration

PART IV

Oracle Streams Management

Acknowledgments

y sincere thanks go to my technical editors, Dr. Volker Kuhr, Lewis Kaplan, and K. Gopalakrishnan, for their help in reviewing the book to make sure that the contents are correct and appropriate. Their suggestions and contributions have been very valuable.

I also sincerely thank Patricia McElroy, Distinguished Product Manager for Streams at Oracle Corporation. Over the years, first as a customer and then as an employee, I have conversed with Patricia numerous times when stumped with a Streams problem. Not only did she offer an appropriate solution, but she also explained in detail why and how the problem occurred. I have learned a lot from her. Pat, thank you very much for sharing the knowledge.

It was my pleasure to work with the people at McGraw-Hill: Lisa McClain, Meghan Riley, Stephanie Evans, Janet Walden, and Bill McManus. Thank you so much for your patience and for not losing hope that I would complete this book. For a number of reasons, it has taken longer than expected, but you did not give up. Thank you very much.

I would also like to thank my managers at Oracle Corporation, Inderpal Tahim and Michael Ervin, for their continued support and encouragement to write this book.

Sincere thanks to all of the DBAs, developers, and architects I have met at various Oracle conferences and at customer sites. The numerous discussions with them, and their intriguing questions, helped me explore Oracle Streams further. It was this interaction and feedback that became the motivation for this book.

This book would not have been possible without the support of my wife, Achala. It has been a long journey and Achala kept me going. Achala not only supported me morally and mentally, but also actively contributed to the book while taking care of the kitchen, house, and her full-time job. I am very grateful for her. Also, I thank our son, Sameer, for his understanding, when I could not be with him when he visited us during his school breaks.

Introduction

he need for data replication is steadily increasing as more businesses are using distributed environments for various reasons. Access to this data in real time is becoming a necessity to compete in the global market. Global data integrity and consistency in such environments are equally important. Oracle Streams addresses these requirements well.

Oracle Corporation introduced Streams in Oracle9i Database Release 2 as its flagship solution for data replication and information sharing among applications and databases in distributed environments. Oracle Streams provides a sophisticated, flexible, and robust infrastructure that meets a wide variety of data replication needs. Its flexibility over traditional solutions for data replication allows users to select a single information sharing solution that can be deployed faster and at lower cost.

Streams is an integral part of the Oracle database. You do not have to license it separately or install any additional software.

Some of the strong features and options available in Oracle Streams are

- Near real-time replication

- Data integrity (follows transaction boundaries)

- Automatic conflict resolution

- Data transformations

- Replication to multiple destinations from a single source

- N-way replication

- Detailed monitoring of the replication environment

- Extensive rule management

- Flexible configuration options and several configuration methods

In earlier Oracle releases, configuring and managing the Oracle Streams environment was somewhat complex. Several enhancements in Oracle Database 10*g* R2 made implementing, monitoring, and managing Streams very easy. Oracle Database 11*g* R2 takes the enhancements even further. With improvements in core Streams code, the replication performance has improved drastically. Also, management of complex Streams environments has become very easy.

Although the Oracle Streams product has been available since Oracle9*i* Database Release 2, there is a general lack of comprehensive literature. For a practicing DBA, there is not a single source that details how to configure the Streams environment or monitor and troubleshoot problems. For architects, a similar lack of concise information has deterred them from using Streams in their designs. This book attempts to fill this void by explaining the concepts behind the product. It offers practical advice from configuring to troubleshooting the Streams environment. As such, this book is a single source for Streams replication for DBAs, developers, and architects alike.

How to Use This Book

This book covers Streams from different perspectives, keeping in mind the needs of several different types of readers. Architects, developers, and DBAs will learn the concepts and get a good understanding of various Streams components. Also, DBAs will benefit from all the practical scripts and step-by-step instructions.

Very rarely would one read a technical book from cover to cover in one sitting. However, I urge all readers to begin by reading the first two chapters to get a good conceptual understanding of Streams. Thereafter, you can jump to any chapter to read about a specific Streams component or learn how to perform a specific task in Streams. For example, a practicing DBA who wants to set up a working Streams environment can jump straight to Chapter 8 and follow the step-by-step instructions to set up Streams. Or, because Oracle Enterprise Manager Grid Control 10.2.0.5 makes this job even easier, the DBA may want to check out Chapter 14 instead. Readers who are interested in learning more about apply process components can review Chapter 6. All readers will benefit from a detailed understanding of how rules are used in a Streams environment, which can be found in Chapter 3.

The book has 14 chapters and 5 appendixes, as described next.

Chapter 1: What Is Oracle Streams   This chapter introduces you to Oracle Streams replication. It discusses the Streams architecture and briefly explains various components. You should read this chapter to get familiar with its architecture and components.

Chapter 2: Using Oracle Streams   This chapter discusses how Streams replication can be configured to support various different requirements for replicated data. It also discusses how Streams technology can be leveraged to solve other business problems that do not necessarily need data replication.

Chapter 3: Streams Rules and Rule Sets   Oracle Streams uses rules and rule sets that control how data is captured and replicated. This chapter discusses what these rules are and how Streams uses them. Understanding of the rules is required when customizing a Streams environment that involves data transformations. You may skip this chapter until you have a working Streams environment. You can then review this chapter to get familiar with the rules and rule sets to understand how these work.

Chapter 4: Capture Process   This chapter discusses in detail how Streams captures the changes to replicate, the types of capture processes, the capture process components, and the capture process's configuration, requirements, and limitations. It also explains how to create capture processes in various Streams environments.

Chapter 5: Staging and Propagation Process   This chapter explains what queues are, how to create them, and how Streams uses them to propagate captured messages. It discusses what propagation is and how to create it to support various Streams environments.

Chapter 6: Apply Process   This chapter discusses in detail how Streams applies the changes to the destination tables and discusses the apply process's components, requirements, and limitations. It also discusses how to create the apply process and the various custom procedures that can be associated with it to handle errors, conflicts, or customization of data before that data is applied.

Chapter 7: Logical Change Records   The captured messages are internally formatted into Logical Change Records (LCRs). This chapter explains in detail what these LCRs are, what information they contain, and how to tap into that information. Accessing and modifying the LCR information will be required when customizing Streams to support business requirements. The chapter explains this by using a working example that demonstrates how to manipulate the LCR contents.

Chapter 8: Configuring Oracle Streams for Data Replication   After discussing the prerequisite tasks, this chapter describes in detail how to configure Streams replication. It discusses various different methods you can use. It also explains how to use the Oracle-provided APIs to configure simple Streams replication at various levels, such as the database, schema, and table levels. It discusses how to manually configure Streams replication using the supplied PL/SQL packages. Configuration of complex Streams replication in various topologies is also discussed. The example scripts in this chapter can be used to quickly create a simple Streams environment.

Chapter 9: Data Transformations   This chapter discusses Oracle-supplied procedures that transform contents in the LCR when the source and destination tables differ in definition and structure. It also explains, with examples, how to create your own data transformation functions and procedures to address your business requirements that cannot be met with Oracle-supplied procedures.

Chapter 10: Handling Data Conflicts   This chapter explains different types of data conflicts that may occur in a Streams environment. It discusses methods to avoid data conflicts and explains how to handle conflicts when they cannot be avoided. It explains how to use Oracle-provided conflict handler procedures to resolve the conflicts.

Chapter 11: Managing and Monitoring Streams Replication   This chapter discusses Streams management and monitoring tasks. The discussion includes how to start and stop Streams processes, how to change their parameters and other attributes, and how to monitor their status, state, and performance. It explains how to monitor transactions in a Streams environment. The chapter discusses the split and merge functionality and its management when there are multiple destinations for the same source database. The chapter also shows you how to install and use Streams Performance Advisor, which makes it very easy to monitor end-to-end Streams performance.

Chapter 12: Maintenance and Troubleshooting   This chapter discusses Streams maintenance and troubleshooting. The discussion includes how to modify existing Streams replication by adding new objects to replication, or remove existing objects or components. It also explains how to troubleshoot problems with Streams components and debug replication errors encountered by the apply process. The chapter shows you how to use the new Streams message tracking facility in troubleshooting replication problems. It also discusses how you can use the data comparison procedure to identify and correct data mismatches between the source and destination tables.

Chapter 13: Streams Performance Considerations   This chapter discusses common causes and problems that adversely affect replication performance. It discusses various techniques and configuration settings to improve overall Streams performance.

Chapter 14: Oracle Enterprise Manager Grid Control for Streams Replication   This chapter discusses how to use Oracle Enterprise Manager Grid Control 10.2.0.5 for configuring, managing, and monitoring the Streams replication environment.

Appendix A: Oracle Streams Best Practices   This appendix discusses Oracle's best practices for successfully deploying Streams replication.

Appendix B: Oracle Streams Replication in a RAC Environment   This appendix discusses additional details for Streams configuration that are specific to an Oracle RAC environment.

Appendix C: Streams Health Check Report   This appendix discusses how to create and use the Streams Health Check report to document, review, and troubleshoot your Streams environment.

Appendix D: Data Dictionary Views for Streams Replication   This appendix provides a list of data dictionary and dynamic performance views containing information about Streams components and processes and their performance.

Appendix E: References   This appendix provides a list of all the Oracle Corporation material used as references for this book.

PART
I

Introduction to
Oracle Streams

CHAPTER
1

What Is Oracle Streams

usinesses operating in a distributed environment typically maintain several databases instead of one large data store. As a result, sharing data between the distributed databases and applications becomes a necessity. Applications and users expect access to the data in near real time. Over a period of time, businesses find themselves using a variety of products and customized applications to share the information. Oracle Streams provides the single information sharing solution.

Simply put, Oracle Streams is the managed flow of information. This information flow can be from one application to another, one database to another, within the same application, or within the same database. The applications and databases can be on the same machine or can be far apart. The databases can all be Oracle databases with different Oracle releases, different platforms (homogeneous environment), or a combination of Oracle and non-Oracle databases such as DB2 or Microsoft SQL-Server (heterogeneous environment).

Oracle Streams provides a solid infrastructure for such information flow. Oracle introduced Streams as an information sharing solution in Oracle9*i* Database Release 2. It has since been enhanced and improved significantly. Oracle Streams offers a number of features to match your information sharing requirements.

In Oracle Streams, the smallest unit of shared information is called a *message*. A message can be captured from the changes made to the database, or it can be generated by an event in the database. Typically, this includes data changes from the insert, update, and delete operations on the tables in the database. In addition, it can be a Data Definition Language (DDL) operation such as adding, altering, or dropping a table, an index, or a schema. However, certain other changes made to the database, such as adding a data file, starting a backup, or taking a tablespace offline, are not candidates for sharing.

The message can also be created by the user application and put in the Streams information flow. These application messages are generated outside the database. For example, when an application wants to shutdown, it can send a message to other applications. The application programs simply use Streams infrastructure to send messages to other applications, which will receive the message and process it. The message that is written can then be propagated to other databases or applications. You can manage the message as it flows through Oracle Streams.

Using Oracle Streams, you can control what messages to capture, how to propagate those messages, and how to consume, or apply, those messages when they reach their intended destination. Oracle Streams can capture database changes as a result of Data Manipulation Language (DML) and DDL commands. You can have total control over the message and its contents at each step of the way. It is possible for you to modify data in these messages using supplied procedures or by writing your own procedures. Such powerful flexibility enables you to build robust distributed databases and applications, replicated systems, and other high-availability solutions.

Prior to Oracle Database 11*g*, Oracle Streams captured information in an asynchronous manner by scanning the database redo information. Oracle Database 11*g* offers you an additional feature of *synchronous capture*. With synchronous capture, Oracle Streams captures database DML changes as they happen, and not afterward from the redo logs. Oracle Streams does not use database triggers to capture such information.

Although Oracle Streams has numerous applications, such as message queuing, data protection, data warehouse loading, and so on, this book discusses data replication using Oracle Streams.

Oracle Streams is a standard and integrated feature of Oracle Database 11*g*. However, the Standard Edition of Oracle Database 11*g* offers synchronous capture as the only method to automatically capture database changes. In Standard Edition, asynchronous capture is not available. You must have Enterprise Edition for that. You do not need to install any additional software and you do not have to license Oracle Streams separately.

Information Flow in Oracle Streams

In a simplistic form, here is how a message, or a change, flows through Oracle Streams following the standard publish-subscribe model. First, the capture process of Oracle Streams captures the message. The message is reformatted by the capture process and placed (staged or queued) in a staging area, which is typically an in-memory structure, called the *Streams queue*. The capture process thus publishes the message to the Streams queue. The processes that read these messages from the Streams queue are called consumer processes. These processes need to register an interest in receiving messages from the Streams queue. In other words, the processes subscribe to receive the messages. These can also be referred to as subscriber processes. The consumer or subscriber can either be a Streams process, such as an apply process, or an external application process. From the Streams queue, a message can be read, or dequeued, by the local consumer that will process the message, or it can be propagated to another Streams queue on another system to be consumed by a consumer or an apply process, for example.

If the same message is not put in another Streams queue, then its flow in Oracle Streams ends. The message remains in the flow until consumed by all intended consumers.

Figure 1-1 depicts the Streams information flow.

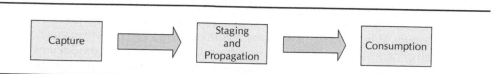

FIGURE 1-1. *Information flow in Oracle Streams*

The three major components responsible for the Streams information flow are

- Capture
- Staging and Propagation
- Consumption

In the Streams architecture, each of these major components has a few other subcomponents, processes, or configuration requirements. In Oracle Streams replication, these components coordinate automatic delivery of the message to its destination.

Architectural Overview of Oracle Streams

This section briefly reviews the Streams components, subcomponents, processes, configuration options, and configuration requirements. This will provide enough foundation for the in-depth discussion of how to configure and manage Streams replication environments in subsequent chapters.

Capture

As shown in Figure 1-1, the message flow begins at capture when Oracle Streams creates the message. Typically, the capture process, which is a database background process, creates the messages. This capture process is an asynchronous process that reads the redo log files to extract the database changes to create the messages. The synchronous capture process, available from Oracle Database 11g, uses a different mechanism to create the messages. The synchronous capture process captures the DML changes in real time to create the messages.

The messages are created in a particular data format and are called *Logical Change Records (LCRs)*. The messages created by the capture process are called *implicitly captured LCRs* and are enqueued into a buffer queue. The messages created by the synchronous capture process are also called implicitly captured LCRs but are enqueued into a persistent queue stored on the disk.

When messages are automatically captured, the process is referred to as *implicit capture*. The database that created the information contained in the message is called the *source database*.

Your external applications can also create messages in the LCR format, or your own format. When messages are created by user applications, the process is referred to as *explicit capture*. When you don't want to capture each and every change, you can specify which changes to capture. These instructions are called *rules* in the Streams environment. In other words, the Streams rules associated with the capture process determine which changes the capture process captures. Such rules can be created automatically or manually. You can modify existing rules or define your own rules.

Log-Based Capture

Oracle Streams utilizes the Log Miner functionality to mine database redo logs to capture changes made to the database. Using the redo log information to capture changes guarantees data recoverability from database crashes or media failures. You do not lose changes that you want to capture, as long as the redo logs (or archived logs) are available. The mined information from the redo logs is presented to the capture process to identify changes to capture and convert the change information into an LCR.

Local Capture

Typically, the capture process runs on the source database as a database background process. This is called the *local capture process*. It is local to the source database. It seamlessly scans, or mines, the in-memory redo log buffer, the online redo logs, and, when necessary, the archived logs to capture changes to the local database. The changes that satisfy the selection criteria defined by the capture rules are captured and converted into LCRs to be placed in an in-memory staging area called the Streams Pool. This is the default behavior of the local capture.

Downstream Capture

Oracle Streams also provides an option to capture changes for the source database by running the capture process on another database server. In this case, the log files are written to the remote database server in addition to the source database server. Oracle Streams leverages Log Transport Services, Oracle Data Guard functionality, to write logs to the remote server. The capture process on the remote server mines the logs from the source database and stages them locally. These changes can be applied to the remote database if its apply process is the subscriber to these changes; otherwise, the changes can be propagated to another staging area for consumption.

Downstream capture offers a couple of benefits. First, you can offload the process of capturing changes from the production database to another database. Second, since remote writing of the redo log files is achieved using Data Guard protection modes (maximum availability, maximum performance, maximum protection), you have a choice to select an appropriate mode for your environment. It is possible to use one remote database to capture changes from multiple source databases.

NOTE
The capture process does not capture certain types of DML and DDL changes. Changes made to SYS, SYSTEM, and CTXSYS schema are ignored.

Synchronous Capture

Introduced in Oracle Database 11*g*, synchronous capture operates differently. Instead of mining the redo information to capture changes, synchronous capture captures the changes to the table as a result of a DML statement. As soon as the table data changes, this change or message is captured in real time by the synchronous capture process and converted to an LCR. The LCR is then written to the disk queue instead of the in-memory staging area. In Oracle Database 11*g*, synchronous capture does not capture changes as a result of DDL statements. Synchronous capture can be a better option when you want to replicate low-volume DML activity on a small number of tables.

NOTE
Synchronous capture only captures DML changes.

Staging and Propagation

The captured LCRs must be made available to the subscribers and consumers. Oracle Streams achieves this by staging the LCRs for propagation.

Staging

All captured messages are stored in a staging area. The staging area is an in-memory buffer and is part of the system global area (SGA) of the database instance. Messages created by user applications are also stored in this staging area. The LCRs created by the synchronous capture process are not stored in the memory queue, but they are stored in a disk queue table.

The messages remain in the staging area until consumed by the subscribers. The subscriber can read the contents of the staging area to select messages of their interest. The subscriber can be an application, a staging area, or the apply process of a different database. The applications can explicitly dequeue, or read, the message from the staging area to consume it. If the subscriber to this staging area is an apply process, then the messages will be dequeued and applied by the apply process.

Propagation

Messages in one staging area can be propagated to another staging area in another database using database links over Oracle Net. Streams offers a great deal of flexibility in choosing how messages are routed. Rules can be applied during propagation to select which messages will be propagated to another staging area. You can modify existing propagation rules or define your own rules.

In some cases, the propagation may not be required. The messages can be dequeued by the consumer from the same staging area where the capture process created the message. In this case, the publisher and consumer processes run in the same database.

Directed Networks   Oracle Streams offers a capability to control how you propagate the messages within your network. Messages captured at one database can be published and propagated to or propagated through other databases anywhere in your network until they reach the intended subscriber or destination. This capability is referred to as *directed networks*.

Even if the source and the destination database do not have direct network communication, the messages can be directed though another, intermediary database that has network communication between the source and the destination database.

Figure 1-2 shows such a directed network. Messages from database A are sent to database C through database B. Database A propagates the message to the staging area in database B. Database B does not consume the messages locally, but only propagates those to the staging area in database C.

There could be more than one database in between A and C, or there could be more destinations than just database C.

Instead of sending the message to all destinations from the source database, the message can be sent only once to the intermediate database, which can send the same message to all the other destinations. The intermediate database simply forwards the contents of one Streams queue to another. This is called Queue Forwarding.

It is also possible to apply the message to the intermediate database and then capture it again using a capture process on the intermediate database to propagate it to other database. This is called Apply Forwarding.

Consumption

When a message is dequeued from the staging area, it is considered consumed. The apply process implicitly dequeues messages from the staging area. If the message is consumed by the apply process and applied to the objects in the database, then that database is called the *destination database*. The apply process runs locally on the destination database.

Your application, or process, can also explicitly dequeue messages from the staging area. The staging area can be local or remote to the user application.

Apply rules can determine which messages are dequeued and applied by the apply process at the destination database. By default, the apply process applies the

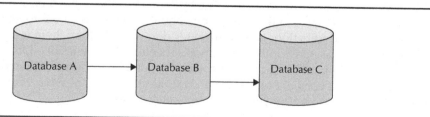

FIGURE 1-2.   *A directed network*

captured LCRs, but you can intercept and process these LCRs with your own PL/SQL procedure. The apply process can also dequeue the message from the buffer queue and enqueue it into a persistent queue for your application to process it.

Default Apply Process

The default apply process is configured as multiple database background processes on the destination database. By default, it automatically applies the captured LCRs for the DML and DDL changes from the source database. The apply process can detect any data conflicts when applying changes to the destination database.

In a heterogeneous environment, you can configure the apply process to send the message to the remote non-Oracle database using appropriate Oracle Transparent Gateways.

Custom Apply Process

A custom apply process is similar to the default apply process in its functionality. The customization gives you total control over how the apply process handles the LCRs. You write the custom PL/SQL procedure. In Oracle Streams, this user-created procedure is called the *apply handler procedure.*

The apply handler procedure can be common to all LCRs or it can selectively apply to certain LCRs. You can also define different apply handlers to process the type of the DML change. For example, you can define separate apply handlers for INSERT, DELETE, and UPDATE operations against the same table. You can then choose to ignore all delete statements at the destination database for selected tables. You can also modify the DELETE command in the LCR to an UPDATE command, so that the delete statement is changed to an update statement to update a column (a delete indicator, for example) in the destination table.

With such flexibility, you can implement customized replicated databases to address unique business and statutory requirements.

Conflict Detection and Resolution

By design, the apply process detects data conflicts when applying the change to the database. A conflict occurs when the data in the destination row does not match the corresponding data in the LCR when the apply process is trying to identify the row for an UPDATE or DELETE operation. The LCR contains the old and new values of the column that changed in the source row, and it expects old values to be present in the row at the destination. If the old values don't match, then there is a data conflict. In such cases, a conflict resolution procedure can be invoked, if needed. Oracle provides a number of prebuilt conflict handler procedures. You can use either the supplied conflict handler procedures as applicable, or write your own to resolve the conflict to satisfy your business requirements.

In case of unresolved conflicts or exceptions from the conflict handler procedure, the apply process puts the entire transaction into a persistent error queue. You can re-execute the error transaction after correcting the data conflict problem. If desired, you can also delete the error transaction if you resolved the conflict by some other means that does not require re-executing the error transaction.

Queues

Queues can be viewed as a storage location for messages. Applications can send messages to the queue and retrieve messages from the queue. When an application wants to communicate with some other application or process, it can leave a message in the message queue and then the other application will be able to retrieve the message from the queue.

Oracle Streams components use queues to exchange messages. Message queues offer a means of asynchronous communication in a failsafe manner for different processes or applications. The queues support operations to enqueue messages, to dequeue messages, and to propagate the messages to other queues or systems.

A message typically is made of two parts: the message control information and the content or payload. The content of the message can be of specific data type or can be raw data type. Oracle Streams has a very generic data type called ANYDATA. All LCRs must be staged in the ANYDATA queue.

The Oracle Streams Advanced Queuing feature supports messages of type ANYDATA or any abstract type. The main advantage of the ANYDATA queue is to allow applications to send messages of different types in the same queue. A queue can be persisted in the database using one or more tables.

Streams Tag

The redo information for all database changes contains a marker, or a tag. By default, the value of this tag field is NULL and it does not consume any space in the redo record. The data type of the tag field is RAW and its size limit is 2000 bytes. The tag field becomes part of the LCR when the capture process converts the redo information into an LCR.

Oracle Streams leverages this feature of the database to identify and track if a particular LCR was generated by a particular database. Such identification is mandatory when configuring bidirectional or multidirectional replication environments. Lack of such identification will cause the messages to recycle back to their original source database.

By default, the Streams rules for capture, propagate, and apply processes check the value of the tag field. LCRs with the tag field set to NULL are processed, while LCRs with a non-NULL value are discarded. The apply process on the destination database sets the tag field value to hexadecimal 00 (zero) when applying the change to the destination database. Thus, the redo information generated by the transactions executed by the apply process will have a non-NULL tag field. So, if there were a capture process for bidirectional replication, it will ignore the LCR for such a change made by the local apply process, thereby avoiding the change recycling.

You can also leverage this functionality to temporarily suspend replication of certain actions. You can modify the tag value for your session at the source database so that the capture process will ignore all the LCRs from the redo records generated in your session. Then, you may have to perform the same actions at the destination database to keep data in sync with the source database. You can reset the tag value for your session back to its original value to resume normal replication, or simply exit the session.

Rules and Rule Sets

Oracle Streams uses rules to control the message capture, message propagation, and message consumption. A rule is a database object, such as table or index. It is specified as a condition when configuring Streams components. The rule condition is similar to the WHERE clause of a SQL statement.

The rule has the following components:

- **Rule condition**   This is a combination of one or more expressions that returns a Boolean value (TRUE, FALSE, or NULL).

- **Evaluation context**   This defines external data that can be referenced by the rule while evaluating the rule condition. The external data can be a variable, table data, or both.

- **Action context**   This is optional information that is interpreted by the client of the rules engine while evaluating the rule condition. The capture, propagation, and apply processes are the clients of the rules engine.

Related rules are grouped together into a rule set, and a rule set is associated with a Streams component.

Oracle Streams supports two types of rule sets:

- **Positive rule set**   If the rule in a positive rule set evaluates to TRUE, then Streams will include the LCR for processing.

- **Negative rule set**   If the rule in a negative rule set evaluates to TRUE, then Streams will discard the LCR.

You can have both, positive and negative, rule sets defined for a Streams component. In such a case, the rule from the negative rule set is evaluated first. If it evaluates to TRUE, then the positive rule set is ignored, since the message will be discarded.

NOTE
The synchronous capture process can only have a positive rule set.

Oracle generates required rules and rule sets if you do not create them when configuring Streams replication. These are called system-generated rules and rule sets. For most simple replication environments, such system-generated rule and rule sets are sufficient. You can create your own rules and rule sets. You can modify system-generated rules to match your requirements.

Instantiation

When replicating table changes from the source database to the destination database, the destination database must contain the copy of the table. If the destination database does not contain the table, then it must be created, or *instantiated*, from the source database. There are a number of ways to instantiate the table. You can use Create Table As Select (CTAS), data pump, export/Import, transportable tablespaces, split mirror copies, or recovery manager (RMAN), depending on your environment and needs.

First, the table has to be prepared for instantiation at the source database. During the replication configuration, Oracle automatically prepares the tables for instantiation. You can also prepare the table for instantiation using supplied procedures. At this point, Oracle records the database system change number (SCN) and populates an internal Streams data dictionary with the global name of the database, the table name and its object number, the column name and column number, and so forth. Next, if the table did not exist at the destination, it must be created with contents from the source database. And lastly, the destination table's instantiation SCN must be set to the SCN from the source database. The data pump and export/import utilities can set the instantiation SCN for the table at the destination database when importing data. You can also use a supplied procedure to set the instantiation SCN for the tables in the destination database.

The instantiation SCN controls which LCRs containing database changes are applied to the destination database by the apply process and which LCRs are ignored. If the commit SCN in the LCR for the source table is greater than the instantiation SCN for the table in the destination database, then the apply process will apply the change to the table. Otherwise, the LCR will be ignored. Oracle will not report any warning or error when ignoring such LCRs.

LogMiner Data Dictionary

Oracle database processes use the database data dictionary to map object numbers, object version information, and internal column numbers to table names, column names, and column data types. The data dictionary is always kept in sync with the current database configuration.

The Streams capture process needs its own data dictionary because the current information in the database data dictionary might not apply to the redo information from the redo or archive log files that the capture process is reading. This information could have been generated first, and the database data dictionary could have changed before the capture process scanned the log file.

The data dictionary used by the capture process is called the LogMiner data dictionary. Oracle extracts the database data dictionary information in the redo logs when the very first capture process is created. The capture process, when started for the first time, reads this data dictionary information from the redo logs and creates the LogMiner data dictionary. The contents of this LogMiner data dictionary are maintained in internal LogMiner tables.

There can be multiple LogMiner data dictionaries for the source database. Multiple capture processes can share a common LogMiner data dictionary or each process can have its own LogMiner data dictionary.

NOTE
The synchronous capture process does not use the LogMiner data dictionary.

Streams Data Dictionary

Similar to the capture process, the propagation and apply processes need their own data dictionary to keep track of the object names and numbers from the source database. When objects are prepared for instantiation in the source database, information about the instantiation is written to the redo log along with object details. The capture process reads this information and populates what is called the Streams data dictionary in the database where it is running. For a local capture process, the Streams data dictionary will be in the source database, whereas for a downstream capture process, it will be in the downstream database. The Streams data dictionary is updated as and when objects are prepared for instantiation.

The propagation process requires the object mapping information in the Streams data dictionary from the source database when it evaluates rules to process the captured LCRs. Oracle automatically populates a local multi-version Streams data dictionary at each database that has the propagation process configured.

Similarly, the apply process requires object mapping information in the Streams data dictionary from the source database when it evaluates rules to process the captured LCRs. Oracle automatically populates a local multi-version Streams data dictionary at each destination database that has the apply process configured.

NOLOGGING and UNRECOVERABLE Operations

Oracle Streams captures database changes from the redo logs. When DML operations are performed with the NOLOGGING option, where applicable, the redo information is not generated. Using the UNRECOVERABLE option in the SQL*Loader direct path load also suppresses the redo generation. In these situations, the DML changes are not captured due to their obvious absence in the redo log. To replicate these changes successfully, you should avoid the use of the NOLOGGING and UNRECOVERABLE operations.

To ensure proper logging of changes made to tables, you may want to set FORCE LOGGING at the tablespace level or at the database level. Once this is set, Oracle will silently generate redo log information for all NOLOGGING and UNRECOVERABLE operations.

If you must use the NOLOGGING and UNRECOVERABLE operations for performance reasons on the source database, you will have to perform the same operations at the destination database to preserve data synchronization. Otherwise, the data mismatch at the destination database can result in apply process errors in subsequent DML operations.

Supplemental Logging

The database changes are recorded in the redo log with required information to perform database recovery in the event of an instance or media failure. Oracle Streams uses the same redo log information to create messages (LCRs) to apply to the destination database. The redo information contains the values for the columns that changed at the source database. This information may not always be sufficient to identify correctly the row in the destination table to apply the same change.

Supplemental logging is a process of recording additional column data into the redo log. The capture process inserts this additional information in the LCRs. The apply process uses this additional information to correctly identify the row to which to apply the change.

In situations where the application maintains data integrity outside the Oracle database, and the tables do not have primary key or unique constraints, it becomes necessary to configure adequate supplemental logging. Sometimes it requires supplemental logging of all columns in the table.

NOTE
Supplemental logging is always configured at the source database irrespective of the capture process location—local or downstream.

Supplemental logging can be configured at the database level or at the table level. At the database level, it can be configured to record additional information in the redo log to identify the rows in the redo log, or it can be configured to record the before and after values of specified types of columns, such as primary key columns, unique index columns, foreign key columns, or all columns of the table.

If a table does not have a primary key constraint or unique index, then it becomes necessary to identify a set of columns for supplemental logging.

At the table level, supplemental logging creates separate log groups containing the column names for each table. Such logging can be conditional or unconditional. *Conditional supplemental logging* records in the redo log the before image of all the specified columns only when one of those columns is updated. *Unconditional supplemental logging* records in the redo log the before image of all the specified columns regardless of whether or not any of the columns changed. Sometimes this is called "always logging." Unconditional logging is necessary for all the columns used for row identification.

NOTE
The synchronous capture process does not need supplemental logging information.

Logical Change Records

As mentioned earlier, the capture process reformats the information for the database change it captured from the log file. The reformatted message is called a Logical Change Record and represents the database change.

The following two types of LCR can be created by the capture process:

- **Row LCR** Each row LCR (sometimes called DML LCR) represents the change made to a single row. In addition, there could be multiple LCRs for a change made to a single column with a data type of LONG, LONG RAW, LOB, or XMLType stored as CLOB. Also, a single DML statement can affect multiple rows, causing creation of multiple LCRs.

- **DDL LCR** This LCR represents the change made by a DDL command.

These LCRs contain enough information to apply the change to the destination database. In addition, you can include extra information in the LCR for auditing and tracking purposes.

Although the LCR has an internal data format used by Oracle Streams, there are procedures to access and modify the information contained in the LCR.

Table Data Comparison

Oracle Database 11g includes procedures to compare and synchronize (merge) data in shared tables in a distributed and replicated environment. The procedures in the DBMS_COMPARISON package can be used to compare table data without interfering with other applications. These procedures allow you to compare data for the entire table or for data subsets or data ranges. The comparison can be done on a periodic basis or whenever needed. Data consistency can be checked at the row level or table level. The identified differences can be viewed, if there are any. These data differences could arise due to incomplete transactions, unrecoverable errors, and so forth. When data differences are found, the supplied procedures can be used to merge the differences and confirm that the table data mismatch is resolved.

Summary

Oracle Streams is an information sharing solution. It offers a robust and flexible infrastructure to manage information flow between Oracle and non-Oracle databases. Using the redo information, Oracle Streams can capture and easily replicate database changes seamlessly within your network. The Streams rules for capture, propagation, and apply processes offer customization to control the selection, routing, and consumption of messages to address your business needs. With the availability of synchronous capture, you can replicate data from databases using Oracle Database 11g Standard Edition. The downstream capture configuration can offload the log-mining process to another database to minimize load on the production system. Oracle Streams is an integrated feature of the Oracle Database software.

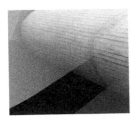

CHAPTER
2

Using Oracle Streams

eplicating data undoubtedly is the most common application of Oracle Streams. Because of its capability to transform the replicated data and its flexibility that enables administrators to customize the information flow, Streams is useful in addressing a number of business requirements.

One of the key benefits of Oracle Streams is that it can replicate data between different hardware platforms and Oracle database versions. This powerful feature enables you to migrate databases across hardware platforms with little or no downtime and no data loss. It also facilitates database, platform, and application upgrades without downtime.

In this chapter you will learn about a few other applications of Oracle Streams, particularly how it can be used for various data replication environments.

Data Replication

Oracle Streams facilitates sharing of objects and their data between multiple databases. A change made to these objects at any one database can be propagated to all other databases participating in the replication. Oracle Streams can capture and replicate DDL and DML changes made to tables. You can configure replication of such changes at the database, schema, or table level or even on subsets of data.

Oracle Streams supports replicating data to tables when tables differ in their structure or column data types. During replication, you can rename a schema, rename a table, rename a column, and add or remove a column in any component (capture, propagation, and apply).

Unidirectional (One-Way) Replication

Unidirectional replication is probably the most widely used method of Oracle Streams replication. It is also the easiest replication environment to configure. Two databases participate in the unidirectional replication. One acts as the source database and the other as the destination database. Changes made to the source database are replicated to the destination database. As shown in Figure 2-1, the user application makes changes to the data in database A. Those changes are propagated and applied to database B. This data is available to the read-only application accessing database B.

This configuration is useful when you need to offload routine but expensive read-only operations, such as complex queries or reporting jobs, to another database server. No changes to the replicated tables are allowed in the destination database. Only the apply user, typically the Streams administrator, applies the replicated changes to these tables. The local tables, if any, that are not replicated can be changed by the application and users.

When replicating the entire source database in a unidirectional replication, the configuration may appear to resemble the logical standby database of Oracle Data

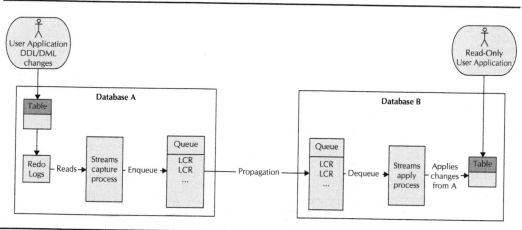

FIGURE 2-1.   *Unidirectional replication*

Guard. But unlike the logical standby database, the Streams replicated database is open in read-write mode and provides near real-time data to applications running in the replicated database. A new option in Oracle Database 11*g* Data Guard, called the active standby database, provides similar real-time data to applications while changes are applied to the database. However, the active standby database cannot have any tables in read-write mode for the applications.

Bidirectional Replication

In a two-database replication environment, changes can be made to either of the databases and replicated to the other database. Both databases capture local changes and propagate those to the apply process running on the other database. This is called *bidirectional replication*. It is simply two instances of unidirectional Streams replication active between two databases.

As shown in Figure 2-2, the user application makes changes to the data locally in database A and database B. Changes made to database A are applied to database B. Similarly, changes made to database B are applied to database A.

This configuration is useful when you need to keep the data in the local database closer to the applications and users. Such a configuration can also be useful to create a disaster recovery site with either an active/active or active/passive role for these databases.

In bidirectional replication, it is possible to change the same data at the same time in both the databases. Such a change can cause a data conflict when the apply process in the other database tries to apply the change. This will result in an apply error.

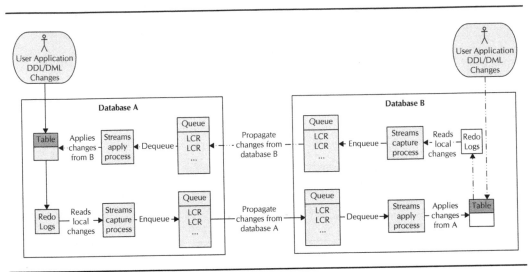

FIGURE 2-2. *Bidirectional replication*

To avoid such an error, you will need to implement update conflict handler procedures. Ideally, the data conflicts should be minimized or eliminated where possible, in application design. Oracle provides certain types of conflict handlers. If those are not sufficient to resolve the conflict, user-defined procedures can be used. Also, the use of Streams tags is required to avoid change recycling.

N-Way (Peer-to-Peer) Replication

N-way replication can be seen as an extension of bidirectional replication. In this configuration, more than two databases are involved. Each database is a source database for every other database and propagates the local changes to all other databases. Each database is also a destination database for every other database and applies changes from all other databases. With the use of Streams tags, the change is not sent to the originating source database.

Figure 2-3 shows such a configuration for three databases. The user applications make changes to the data in database A, database B, and database C. Changes made to database A are applied to databases B and C. Changes made to database B are applied to databases A and C. And, changes made to database C are applied databases A and B.

This configuration is useful when data resides in more than two databases in a distributed fashion, but applications and users need a unified view of the data.

Similar to bidirectional replication, N-way replication also needs adequate conflict handler procedures and use of Streams tags to avoid change recycling.

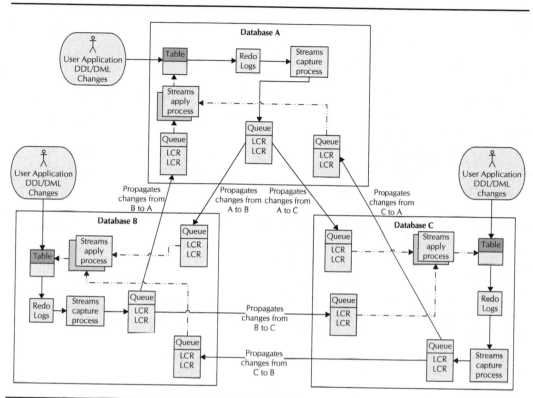

FIGURE 2-3. *N-way replication*

Hub-and-Spoke Replication

When data needs to be replicated to several secondary databases from one single primary database, Oracle Streams offers what is called a hub-and-spoke configuration.

In a hub-and-spoke configuration, one primary database maintains connection with all other databases. The primary database acts as the hub. All other databases act as spokes. Each spoke database does not directly communicate with other spoke databases. There is no connectivity between the individual spokes. All information must pass through the centralized hub in this architecture.

Two variations of the hub-and-spoke configuration are described next.

Read-Only Spokes

In this case, the hub, or primary database, replicates local changes to all the spoke databases. The spoke databases do not change replicated objects. For a single hub-and-spoke branch, this is similar to unidirectional replication.

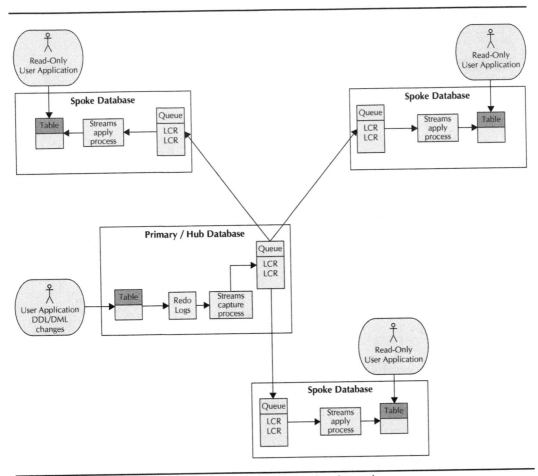

FIGURE 2-4. *Hub-and-spoke replication with read-only spokes*

Figure 2-4 shows a configuration with three spoke databases and a primary or hub database. The capture process in the hub database captures the local changes. These changes are propagated to all three spoke databases. The apply process running on each of the spoke databases applies the changes.

Read-Write Spokes

In this case, the hub and all the spoke databases change the replicated objects. These changes are replicated to the remaining databases by the hub database. The spoke database captures the local changes and propagates those to the hub database. The hub database applies those changes, and recaptures those to propagate to the remaining spoke databases.

The capture process in the hub database captures the local changes as well as changes made by the spoke database. It propagates the captured changes to the appropriate spoke databases. With the use of Streams tags, the change is not sent to the originating spoke database.

Figure 2-5 shows a configuration of hub-and-spoke replication with a hub and two spoke databases.

In addition, it is also possible to configure the hub database as the propagation hub for forwarding the changes from one spoke database to all others. The hub database does not apply these changes locally or capture any local changes. This is an example of queue forwarding while implementing N-way replication.

Such a configuration for N-way replication eliminates the complexity of connecting each database to every other database to replicate data. Figure 2-6 shows this configuration.

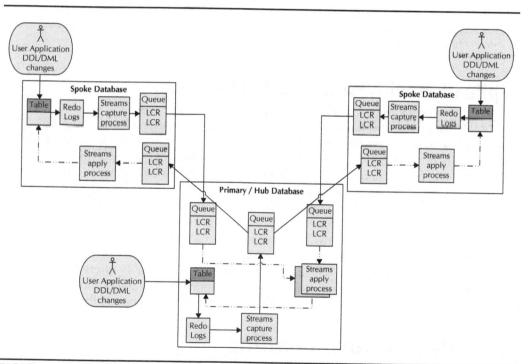

FIGURE 2-5. *Hub-and-spoke replication with read-write spokes*

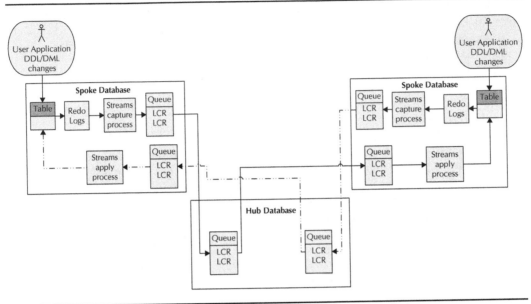

FIGURE 2-6. *Hub-and-spoke replication with queue forwarding hub*

Replication with Non-Oracle Databases

Oracle Streams provides mechanisms to share information between Oracle and non-Oracle databases. This heterogeneous exchange of information can be achieved using Oracle Gateways or using Java Messaging Service (JMS) client. These methods, however, may not adequately address the performance needs of the application systems. The replication latency and throughput requirements can be difficult to meet.

To improve performance and usability, Oracle Database 11*g* R2 introduced a new application programming interface (API) called XStream to send and receive data to and from an Oracle database. The API allows information sharing between Oracle databases and other systems. The other systems can be non-Oracle databases, file systems, or even client applications. The XStream interface is built on Oracle Streams infrastructure and offers the same flexibility and functionality offered by Oracle Streams. However, XStream is available as an additional database option and must be licensed separately. Discussion of XStream is outside the scope of this book.

Data Warehouse Loading

Data warehouses or data marts have become an integral part of many businesses. Data maintenance in these databases includes refreshing existing data and adding more data from transactional and operational databases. Typically these operations are performed on a routine basis and can be quite time consuming. This can be considered a different form of data replication because data is duplicated from several other databases.

Oracle Streams can be used to capture changes made to operational databases. These changes can be stored in an intermediate database before being processed and applied to the data warehouse. This eliminates the periodic data extraction process. Oracle Streams can also directly apply these changes to the destination tables in the data warehouse, keeping the data in those tables up to date.

Oracle Streams offers the flexibility to transform, reformat, and modify the data to suit the requirements of the data warehouse applications. This facilitates easy data loading of the data warehouse tables irrespective of the differences in the operational tables and data warehouse tables. Several data transformations are done automatically by Oracle Streams, such as transforming LONG to LOB. User-defined custom transformations can also be configured during the data loading operation.

Data Auditing

Oracle Streams can be configured to act as an auditing mechanism to track data changes. In this mode, you are not replicating the data but simply capturing the data changes. With its ability and flexibility to control what information can be captured, Oracle Streams offers a very simple but effective solution to track and monitor changes to sensitive and critical data.

You can audit the DML changes using the information in the DML LCRs. In addition to the schema, table, and column names and the old and new values of the columns, you can include in the LCR additional information about the change, such as the rowid of the row affected, the username of the person who performed the change, and the serial and session number in which the change took place. This information can be easily extracted from the LCR and stored in your own auditing tables.

Tracking and reporting DDL changes made to databases by DBAs, particularly in the absence of a strict code-control mechanism, can be challenging. And in many cases where fewer DBAs support a large number of databases, this can be a daunting task. You can configure Oracle Streams to only capture DDL changes and propagate those to another database that acts as a DDL Audit repository. The DDL LCRs provide all the information you need to identify the source database, the affected object name, and the date and time of the change. By including additional information in the LCR, you can also capture the username who made the change and the serial and session number in which the change was made.

Data Protection

Protecting the corporate data for business continuity in case of unforeseen disasters is of paramount importance to almost all businesses. In fact, data protection has now become one of the crucial requirements for numerous businesses in the global marketplace for whom even a few minutes of outage can adversely affect the revenue.

Oracle offers Data Guard to set up standby databases to solve data protection and business continuity problems. The logical standby (SQL Apply) configuration uses some of the same infrastructure of Oracle Streams. In case of a loss of the primary production database, the standby database can assume the role of the primary production database while the original database is being recovered.

Using Oracle Streams, you can create a remote copy of the production database. This copy is called a replica database, not a standby database. The replica database is a near real-time image of the production database and is open for read/write access. Changes from the production databases are replicated to the replica database. When the primary database becomes unavailable, you can direct the applications to use the replica database. With bidirectional Streams replication, you can synchronize the data from the replica database to the original production database as soon as it becomes available. Such a configuration provides required data protection for business continuity.

Message Queuing

The Advanced Queuing (AQ) component of Oracle Streams is an integrated messaging infrastructure. It supports all the standard features of a message queuing system.

Oracle Streams AQ allows the messages to be propagated from one queue to another in the same database or in the remote database. This allows the applications to communicate asynchronously in a distributed environment. An important feature of Oracle Streams AQ is that it provides transactional support to messages. Applications can manage data as well as messages in a single transaction.

Oracle Streams AQ allows the queues to be created in a database. It supports both point-to-point and publish-subscribe (or multiconsumer) models for these queues.

The queues can be configured to accept messages of a specific type or of the ANYDATA type. Messages of practically any type can be wrapped in an ANYDATA wrapper. Once created, the user applications can enqueue messages into the queue. These messages are then propagated to subscribing queues. The user application dequeues the messages upon receiving notification that the messages are available. These queues are persisted in internal database queue tables. A row in these underlying tables corresponds to a message in the queue.

Oracle Streams AQ allows the message to be routed based on message contents. In addition, rule-based content routing is also supported. The Oracle Streams AQ system supports message transformations to reformat the message before it is delivered to the subscriber.

Minimizing Downtime During Database Upgrades

As newer releases of Oracle Database are introduced, the support for older releases eventually comes to an end. The databases need to be upgraded to the newer release, often to stay supported, even if the applications do not utilize newer or improved features offered by the new release. During the upgrade process, the database running under the older release is transformed to the newer release. Taking an offline backup of the database is often recommended, and sometimes required, prior to the upgrade process, causing lengthy downtime for the applications.

In today's competitive and global business world, such downtimes are not well tolerated. The DBAs are asked the quintessential question, "How long will this take?" And the most common answers are "It depends" and "I don't know, I've never done that before." So, some DBAs try to extrapolate the downtime based on the upgrade process they conduct on their smallish test databases, while others attempt a dress rehearsal of the upgrade process with a full copy of the database.

Oracle Streams can considerably minimize, and in certain cases eliminate, the database downtime irrespective of the time it takes to perform such upgrades.

Using Streams in such cases involves configuring a single-source unidirectional replication environment. First, an empty destination database is created under the same Oracle release as the current source database. Then, Stream replication at the database level is configured between them. The applications continue using the current source database. Replication is then suspended by stopping the capture process at the source database, and the destination database is upgraded. Once the destination database upgrade is complete, the replication is resumed. All pending changes from the source database are replicated to the destination database. Once the destination database catches up with the source database, the source database is taken offline and applications are switched to use the destination database. Streams configuration from the destination database can be dropped.

The preceding process also can be used to minimize downtime when performing operating system upgrades or short-term application release cycles.

Minimizing Downtime During Maintenance Tasks

Similar to the database upgrade process, certain database maintenance tasks require unacceptable downtime. These tasks include migrating a database to a different hardware platform and operating system, changing a database to a different character set, making changes to schema objects to support enhancements to applications, and so on.

As described in the previous section, you can configure a single-source unidirectional Streams replication environment. The maintenance tasks can then be performed on the destination database while the applications continue using the source database. When the destination database catches up with the source database, the applications are switched to use the destination database, and the old source database is taken offline. Streams configuration from the destination database can be dropped.

Summary

Oracle Streams offers a versatile solution for data replication needs. It can be used in a number of replication scenarios. However, data replication is not the only application of Oracle Streams. With its flexible and easy-to-customize environment, it can be used to capture data changes for various business requirements. Its ability to capture database changes from redo and archived log files and replicate those across hardware platforms and Oracle database releases helps you minimize or eliminate downtime when performing database migrations and upgrades.

The Oracle Streams AQ component provides an integrated messaging infrastructure. In addition to the standard messaging features, it provides transactional support to the messages. Applications can manage data as well as the messages in a single transaction.

Oracle Streams is like a Swiss army knife; you can use it to solve a number of business problems. The list of possible applications of Oracle Streams discussed in this chapter is not exhaustive, so you might even find yet another application for it in your particular business.

PART
II

Oracle Streams Concepts
and Architecture

CHAPTER
3

Streams Rules
and Rule Sets

he Oracle database has a built-in rules engine, and the Streams components—capture, propagation, and apply—are clients of the rules engine and use rules to perform their tasks in the replication process. The clients perform an action when a certain condition is satisfied or an event occurs that is defined in the rule.

In Oracle Streams, rules and rule sets determine whether or not a change or a message is to be captured, propagated, and applied. It is possible to have no rule set defined for the Streams clients. In the absence of a rule set, all changes to the database are captured, propagated, and applied. However, when you want to replicate only a portion of the database, rules must be defined to capture the changes to interested database objects. In addition, if the replicated data needs any modification to the object name, schema name, data types, or contents, rules must be defined to achieve such transformations. Chapter 9 discusses such transformations.

This chapter discusses how rules and rule sets are defined and how Oracle Streams uses them.

Rules

Oracle Streams uses an in-built technology of the rules engine to control what changes are captured and how they are processed. A rule is an individual database object. It has three components: evaluation context, rule condition, and action context. The rule condition is mandatory. The Streams clients perform tasks based on evaluation of the rule condition. Typically, to evaluate a rule, the evaluation context is optional, but in Oracle Streams the evaluation context is required. Oracle provides a default evaluation context called SYS.STREAMS$_EVALUATION_CONTEXT and automatically creates the action context for the rule when needed.

The following sections discuss the three components of the rule and how Oracle Streams uses those components.

Evaluation Context

The evaluation context defines an external data that can be referenced by the rule while evaluating the rule condition. The external data can be a variable, table data, or both. In the Oracle Streams replication environment, the rules are evaluated based on the contents of the LCRs, and Oracle-provided evaluation context SYS.STREAMS$_EVALUATION_CONTEXT is used. This is the default evaluation context when creating rules for Streams replication.

STREAMS$_EVALUATION_CONTEXT defines two variables, DML and DDL, of type SYS.LCR$_ROW_RECORD and SYS.LCR$_DDL_RECORD, respectively. The following query shows this definition:

```
SQL> select evaluation_context_owner owner,
  2           evaluation_context_name  context_name,
  3           variable_name,
  4           variable_type
  5     from dba_evaluation_context_vars;
OWNER        CONTEXT_NAME                       VAR        VARIABLE_TYPE
----------   -------------------------------    --------   --------------------
SYS          STREAMS$_EVALUATION_CONTEXT                   SYS.ANYDATA
SYS          STREAMS$_EVALUATION_CONTEXT        DDL        SYS.LCR$_DDL_RECORD
SYS          STREAMS$_EVALUATION_CONTEXT        DML        SYS.LCR$_ROW_RECORD
```

The variable types LCR$_ROW_RECORD and LCR$_DDL_RECORD provide several subprograms and functions that can be used in the rule conditions. You can obtain a list of these by describing the types from a SQL session. The DBA_RULES view lists the defined evaluation context for the rule in the RULE_EVALUATION_CONTEXT_NAME column.

Rule Condition

A rule condition is a combination of one or more expressions that returns the rule evaluation result. It can be TRUE, FALSE, MAYBE, or UNKNOWN. The values other than TRUE or FALSE are possible because of optimization in the rule evaluation process. The following example shows a rule condition associated with a rule for a capture process. Here we want to capture the changes made to the DEPT table in the SCOTT schema residing in the DBXA.WORLD database. When this condition evaluates to TRUE, the LCR will be captured. The rule condition checks for the schema name, table name, and the source database name.

```
((((:dml.get_object_owner() = 'SCOTT' and
   :dml.get_object_name() = 'DEPT')) and
   :dml.get_source_database_name() = 'DBXA.WORLD' )
```

The rule condition uses the DML variable from the evaluation context described previously and three member functions from the LCR$_ROW_RECORD type. In the previous example, :dml.get_object_owner() is a call to the member function named GET_OBJECT_OWNER of LCR$_ROW_RECORD. Similarly, :dml.get_object_name() and :dml.get_source_database_name() call the member functions GET_OBJECT_NAME and GET_SOURCE_DATABASE_NAME, respectively.

Action Context

This is optional information that provides a context for the action taken by the client of the rules engine when the rule evaluates to TRUE or MAYBE. The action context is an array of name-value pairs and is of type SYS.RE$_NV_LIST. When evaluating the rule, the rules engine simply returns the action context to the client without interpreting it. The client uses the information to act upon it.

In Oracle Streams, a required action context is created automatically for the rule when a subset rule or rule-based transformation is defined for the Streams client. The rule-based transformation can be customized or declarative. The name-value pair consists of an internal function name beginning with STREAMS$_ or APPLY$_ and a value that is an ANYDATA instance.

For the custom rule-based transformation, the function name is STREAMS$_ TRANSFORM_FUNCTION or STREAMS$_ARRAY_TRANS_FUNCTION depending on whether the function is a one-to-one or one-to-many transformation function. The value is of type ANYDATA and contains the name of the user-defined PL/SQL function that performs the transformation.

For the declarative rule-based transformation, the function name is STREAMS$_ INTERNAL_TRANS, and for the subset rule, the function name is STREAMS$_ROW_ SUBSET. The value is of type ANYDATA in both cases and contains internal information to carry out these transformations.

The DBA_RULES view lists the defined action context for the rule in the RULE_ACTION_CONTEXT column.

Rule Sets

Rules are grouped together in rule sets. A rule set is associated with a Streams client. The rules engine evaluates a rule set as a whole. In the rule set, individual rules are internally joined by an OR operator. The rules engine stops the evaluation process as soon as one of the individual rule conditions evaluates to TRUE, and returns the result to the Streams client. You cannot control the sequence of rule evaluations in a rule set. This also means that if you have overlapping rules in the rule set, then which rule condition evaluates to TRUE is unpredictable. For example, if you have a table-level rule that does not replicate DELETE operations, and then you add a schema-level rule for the schema to which the table belongs, then you have created an overlapping condition. As soon as one of these rules evaluates to TRUE, the rule evaluation process stops. So, in this example, if the table rule evaluates first, the DELETE operation will not replicate. But, if the schema rule evaluates first, the DELETE operation will be replicated.

In Oracle Streams replication, there are two types of rule set: a positive rule set and a negative rule set.

Positive Rule Set

A rule set is considered to be a positive rule set when the rule in the rule set evaluates to TRUE and the Oracle Streams client performs its task. When you add rules to the Streams client using the procedures in the DBMS_STREAMS_ADM package, Oracle by default adds those to the positive rule set.

Let us consider an example. Suppose we want to replicate all DML and DDL changes made to all tables under the SCOTT schema in the DBXA.WORLD database.

To achieve this, we need rules for the capture process that will select all DML and DDL changes made to tables under the SCOTT schema. Assuming all other requirements and setup are in place for this replication, we will use the following PL/SQL procedure to create the required rule.

In the PL/SQL procedure, we add rules to the capture process to replicate DDL and DML changes made to all tables under the SCOTT schema. In here, we are only discussing the key parameters related to rule settings. The important thing to consider here is that the DDL and DML rule is being added to the capture process called DBXA_CAP. The parameter `inclusion_rule` is set to TRUE, and that is its default value. This setting instructs Oracle to add rules to the positive rule set associated with the capture process. If there is no positive rule set already assigned, Oracle creates one. The procedure is run under the Streams Administrator (STRMADMIN) account. The procedure displays the rule names that Oracle created to capture the DDL and DML changes using two optional out parameters. There is one rule each to capture DDL and DML changes.

```
SQL> declare
  2    l_dml_rule_name  varchar2(30);
  3    l_ddl_rule_name  varchar2(30);
  4  begin
  5    dbms_streams_adm.add_schema_rules (
  6        schema_name      => 'SCOTT',
  7        streams_type     => 'CAPTURE',
  8        streams_name     => 'DBXA_CAP',
  9        queue_name       => 'DBXA_CAP_Q',
 10        include_dml      => true,
 11        include_ddl      => true,
 12        inclusion_rule   => true,
 13        source_database  => 'DBXA.WORLD',
 14        dml_rule_name    => l_dml_rule_name,
 15        ddl_rule_name    => l_ddl_rule_name
 16        );
 17    dbms_output.put_line('DML Rule Name is: ' || l_dml_rule_name);
 18    dbms_output.put_line('DDL Rule Name is: ' || l_ddl_rule_name);
 19  end;
 20  /
DML Rule Name is: "STRMADMIN"."SCOTT13"
DDL Rule Name is: "STRMADMIN"."SCOTT14"
PL/SQL procedure successfully completed.
```

We run the following SQL query against the DBA_STREAMS_RULES view to see more information about the rules we just created:

```
SQL> select rule_name,
  2         rule_type,
  3         rule_set_type,
  4         rule_set_name,
```

```
  5          streams_type,
  6          streams_name
  7  from dba_streams_rules
  8  where rule_name in ('SCOTT13','SCOTT14');
```

RULE_NAME	RULE_TYPE	RULE_SET_TYPE	RULE_SET_NAME	STREAMS_TYPE	STREAMS_NAME
SCOTT14	DDL	POSITIVE	RULESET$_15	CAPTURE	DBXA_CAP
SCOTT13	DML	POSITIVE	RULESET$_15	CAPTURE	DBXA_CAP

We see that Oracle assigned both these rules, one to capture DDL changes and the other to capture DML changes, to the positive rule set named RULESET$_15. When the rules engine evaluates RULESET$_15, if one of these rules is TRUE, the capture process will enqueue the LCR for propagation.

Negative Rule Set

A rule set is considered to be a negative rule set when the rule in the rule set evaluates to TRUE and the Oracle Streams client discards the message and does not perform its task. You direct Oracle to add the rule to the negative rule set when adding rules to the Streams client using procedures in the DBMS_STREAMS_ADM package.

In our example in the positive rule set configuration, we set up rules to replicate DDL and DML changes made to all tables under the SCOTT schema. Now, let's assume that we do not want to replicate a table named BONUS. We can set up an additional rule that instructs the capture process to ignore changes made to the BONUS table. We run the following procedure to achieve this:

```
SQL> declare
  2     l_dml_rule_name  varchar2(30);
  3     l_ddl_rule_name  varchar2(30);
  4  begin
  5     dbms_streams_adm.add_table_rules (
  6          table_name        => 'SCOTT.BONUS',
  7          streams_type      => 'CAPTURE',
  8          streams_name      => 'DBXA_CAP',
  9          queue_name        => 'DBXA_CAP_Q',
 10          include_dml       => true,
 11          include_ddl       => true,
 12          inclusion_rule    => false,
 13          source_database   => 'DBXA.WORLD',
 14          dml_rule_name     => l_dml_rule_name,
 15          ddl_rule_name     => l_ddl_rule_name
 16          );
 17     dbms_output.put_line('DML Rule Name is: ' || l_dml_rule_name);
 18     dbms_output.put_line('DDL Rule Name is: ' || l_ddl_rule_name);
 19  end;
 20  /
```

```
DML Rule Name is: "STRMADMIN"."BONUS26"
DDL Rule Name is: "STRMADMIN"."BONUS27"
PL/SQL procedure successfully completed.
```

We used the ADD_TABLE_RULES procedure in the DBMS_STREAMS_ADM package to specify the table name. Notice the value for `inclusion_rule` is set to FALSE. This setting instructs Oracle to add rules for the BONUS table to the negative rule set associated with the capture process. If there is no negative rule set already assigned, Oracle creates one.

Now, let's run the following SQL query against the DBA_STREAMS_RULES view to see more information about the rules we just created:

```
SQL> select rule_name,
  2          rule_type,
  3          rule_set_type,
  4          rule_set_name,
  5          streams_type,
  6          streams_name
  7    from dba_streams_rules
  8   where rule_name in ('BONUS26','BONUS27');
```

RULE_NAME	RULE_TYPE	RULE_SET_TYPE	RULE_SET_NAME	STREAMS_TYPE	STREAMS_NAME
BONUS27	DDL	NEGATIVE	RULESET$_28	CAPTURE	DBXA_CAP
BONUS26	DML	NEGATIVE	RULESET$_28	CAPTURE	DBXA_CAP

Here we see that the negative rule set named RULESET$_28 contains both the rules, one to capture DDL changes and the other to capture DML changes, for the BONUS table.

The following query shows that the capture process named DBXA_CAP has both the positive and negative rule sets assigned. The positive rule set is at the schema level, and the negative rule set is at the table level. This is listed under the STREAMS_RULE_TYPE column.

```
SQL> select rule_set_name,
  2          rule_set_type,
  3          rule_type,
  4          rule_name,
  5          streams_rule_type
  6    from dba_streams_rules
  7   where streams_name = 'DBXA_CAP';
```

RULE_SET_NAME	RULE_SET_TYPE	RULE_TYPE	RULE_NAME	STREAMS_RULE_TYPE
RULESET$_15	POSITIVE	DDL	SCOTT14	SCHEMA
RULESET$_15	POSITIVE	DML	SCOTT13	SCHEMA
RULESET$_28	NEGATIVE	DDL	BONUS27	TABLE
RULESET$_28	NEGATIVE	DML	BONUS26	TABLE

NOTE
A Streams client, other than synchronous capture, can have both the positive and the negative rule sets. The synchronous capture can only have a positive rule set.

In this case, the capture process will first evaluate the negative rule set named RULESET$_28. It will evaluate to TRUE if the change belonged to the BONUS table by virtue of the rule condition. Since this is a negative rule set, and it has evaluated to TRUE, the capture process will discard this change. There is no reason to evaluate the positive rule set against this change. Thus, we have stopped replicating changes to the BONUS table in the SCOTT schema.

NOTE
If the Streams client has a negative rule set, then Oracle evaluates the negative rule set first. If it evaluates to TRUE, then the message is discarded without checking for the positive rule set. If the negative rule set does not evaluate to TRUE, then the positive rule set is evaluated, if present.

A rule can be part of one or more rule sets. A rule set can contain one or more rules. A Streams client can have at least one rule set, and at most two rule sets, with the exception of synchronous capture, which can only have one positive rule set.

The rule set evaluation flow is depicted in Figure 3-1. Notice the difference in the behavior of the Streams client when it does not have a rule set and when it has an empty (a rule set that has no rules) positive rule set.

Creating Rules and Rule Sets

In most Oracle Streams replication environments, creation of rules and rule sets can be automatic. You may not need to create them manually. Oracle-supplied procedures in the DBMS_STREAMS_ADM package automatically create required rules and rule sets. These are called system-created rules and rule sets. Oracle assigns system-generated names to these rules and rule sets. However, in situations where system-created rules are not sufficient, you must create your own rules and, optionally, rule sets. You can use the procedures in the DBMS_RULE_ADM package to create rules and rule sets. Rules and rule sets created using these procedures are called user-created rules and rule sets.

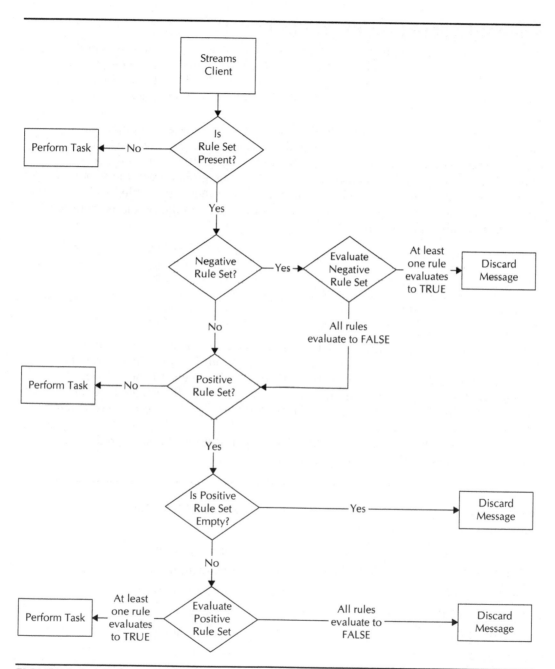

FIGURE 3-1.   *Rule set evaluation process*

System-Created Rules and Rule Sets

In most Oracle Streams replication environments, automatically created rules and rule sets are sufficient. In addition, Oracle provides a mechanism via which you can add your own rule conditions to the system-created rules. By default, all system-created rules use STREAMS$_EVALUATION_CONTEXT. You do not need to create a context separately.

The system-created rules and rule sets have a system-generated name. The names are unique. The rule set name is of the form RULESET$_*n*, where *n* is a number. The rule name is of the form OBJNAME*n*, where OBJNAME is the name of the object—such as the database name for rules at the global level, the schema name for rules at the schema level, or a table name for rules at the table level—and *n* is a number. The following output from our example in the previous section shows this naming convention:

```
RULE_SET_NAME    RULE_SET_TYPE   RULE_TYPE   RULE_NAME   STREAMS_RULE_TYPE
---------------  -------------   ---------   ---------   -----------------
RULESET$_15      POSITIVE        DDL         SCOTT14     SCHEMA
RULESET$_15      POSITIVE        DML         SCOTT13     SCHEMA
RULESET$_28      NEGATIVE        DDL         BONUS27     TABLE
RULESET$_28      NEGATIVE        DML         BONUS26     TABLE
```

Notice the column STREAMS_RULE_TYPE, which tells us whether the rule is defined at the schema level or at the table level. In addition, you can see that the DDL and DML rules share the same rule set whether the rule set is positive or negative. In this example, the rules and rule sets are automatically created by Oracle when we use the ADD_SCHEMA_RULES and ADD_TABLE_RULES procedures in the DBMS_STREAMS_ADM package.

Table 3-1 lists the procedures in the DBMS_STREAMS_ADM package that automatically create rules for specified Streams clients.

Procedure Name	Streams Client Name
ADD_GLOBAL_PROPAGATION_RULES	Propagation
ADD_GLOBAL_RULES	Capture, Apply
ADD_SCHEMA_PROPAGATION_RULES	Propagation
ADD_SCHEMA_RULES	Capture, Apply
ADD_SUBSET_PROPAGATION_RULES	Propagation
ADD_SUBSET_RULES	Capture, Apply
ADD_TABLE_PROPAGATION_RULES	Propagation
ADD_TABLE_RULES	Capture, Apply

TABLE 3-1. *DBMS_STREAMS_ADM Procedures for System-Created Rules*

Streams Rule Condition

In addition to the system-created names for the rules, Oracle also creates an appropriate rule condition for each of the rules. The contents of the rule condition depend on the procedure used in creating it. For example, the ADD_SCHEMA_RULES procedure will create a rule condition that will check for the defined schema name when creating rules for capture and apply processes. Similarly, the ADD_SCHEMA_PROPAGATION_RULES procedure will do the same when creating rules for the propagation process. Going back to our earlier example, we can list the rule conditions for the capture rules created for the SCOTT schema using the following SQL query:

```
SQL> set long 4000
SQL> select rule_name,
  2            rule_condition
  3     from dba_streams_rules
  4    where rule_name in ('SCOTT13','SCOTT14');

RULE_NAME   RULE_CONDITION
----------  ------------------------------------------------------------------
SCOTT14     ((:ddl.get_object_owner() = 'SCOTT' or :ddl.get_base_table_owner() =
            'SCOTT') and :ddl.is_null_tag() = 'Y' and :ddl.get_source_database_na
            me()  = 'DBXA.WORLD')
SCOTT13     ((:dml.get_object_owner() = 'SCOTT') and :dml.is_null_tag() = 'Y' and
            :dml.get_source_database_name() = 'DBXA.WORLD' )
```

Let's review how the rule conditions achieve the defined task. Be aware that these rules are in the positive rule set, meaning that when they evaluate to TRUE, the Streams client will perform its task.

The rule condition for the SCOTT14 rule uses several member functions from the SYS.LCR$_DDL_RECORD type. The function `get_object_owner()` returns the name of the owner of the object against which the DDL command was run, and the `get_base_table_owner()` function returns the name of the owner of the table involved in DDL statements such as ALTER TABLE, CREATE TABLE, or CREATE TRIGGER. It will contain NULL for other DDL commands, such as TRUNCATE TABLE. The `is_null_tag` function returns the value of the Streams tag. If this was not set when the DDL statement was run and was left to its default value of NULL, then this function will return a Y. The `get_source_database_name()` function returns the global name of the database. When all the returned values match the ones specified in the rule condition, the rule evaluates to TRUE and the Streams client will perform its task. In this example, the client is a capture process and it will capture this change.

Similarly, the SCOTT13 rule for DML changes uses a few member functions from the SYS.LCR$_ROW_RECORD type to evaluate the condition. When all returned values match the ones specified in the rule condition, the rule evaluates to TRUE and the Streams client will perform its task. In this case, it will capture the DML change.

NOTE
*The SYS.LCR$_ROW_RECORD and SYS.LCR$_
DDL_RECORD types are explained in Chapter 7.*

Adding a User-Defined Condition to a System-Created Rule

Procedures in the DBMS_STREAMS_ADM package that generate rules for Streams clients also allow you to append your own rule condition to the generated rule condition. This flexibility allows you to easily customize the rule condition for specific operations. For instance, you may decide to only replicate the INSERT and UPDATE commands and ignore the DELETE commands.

The following example shows how to do this. We are capturing only the DML changes made to objects in the SCOTT schema, but using the `and_condition` parameter for filtering out the LCRs for DELETE commands. The `include_ddl` parameter is set to FALSE so that it does not generate a rule for capturing DDL changes. Otherwise, the value for the `and_condition` parameter would get appended to the DDL rule also, which would not be correct and would cause DDL rule evaluation to fail. If the DDL changes are to be captured, we have to generate the DDL rule separately with `include_ddl` parameter set to TRUE and with the required value for the `and_condition` parameter. Using `and_condition` for the DDL rule, you can filter out certain DDL commands (for example, the TRUNCATE command).

```
SQL> declare
  2    l_dml_rule_name  varchar2(30);
  3    l_ddl_rule_name  varchar2(30);
  4  begin
  5    dbms_streams_adm.add_schema_rules (
  6        schema_name      => 'SCOTT',
  7        streams_type     => 'CAPTURE',
  8        streams_name     => 'DBXA_CAP',
  9        queue_name       => 'DBXA_CAP_Q',
 10        include_dml      => true,
 11        include_ddl      => false,
 12        inclusion_rule   => true,
 13        source_database  => 'DBXA.WORLD',
 14        and_condition    => '(:lcr.get_command_type() = ''INSERT'' OR
                                 :lcr.get_command_type() = ''UPDATE'')',
 15        dml_rule_name    => l_dml_rule_name,
 16        ddl_rule_name    => l_ddl_rule_name
 17        );
 18    dbms_output.put_line('DML Rule Name is: ' || l_dml_rule_name);
 19* end;
 20  /
DML Rule Name is: "STRMADMIN"."SCOTT40"
PL/SQL procedure successfully completed.
```

Here is the rule SCOTT40 with our modification highlighted:

```
RULE_NAME   RULE_CONDITION
----------  ----------------------------------------------------------------
SCOTT40     (((( :dml.get_object_owner() = 'SCOTT') and :dml.is_null_tag(
            ) = 'Y' and :dml.get_source_database_name() = 'DBXA.WORLD' ))
            and ((:dml.get_command_type() = 'INSERT' OR :dml.get_command_
            type = 'UPDATE')))
```

In several situations, you may find that using the and_condition parameter is much easier than setting up rules in negative rule sets, or writing your own rules.

NOTE
When specifying the condition for the and_ condition parameter, the variable :lcr is used. Oracle will convert it to :dml and :ddl when creating the DML or DDL rule, respectively.

Streams Rule Types

In Oracle Streams replication, the rules can be created at different levels of granularity to capture, propagate, and apply changes made to the database and objects. Using the procedures in the DBMS_STREAMS_ADM package, we can create global, schema, table, or subset rules. These are discussed in the following sections.

Global Rules   When you want to capture, propagate, and apply changes made to all objects in the database, you define global rules. You can define the global rules for all DML changes, for all DDL changes, or for both.

The global rules can be in a positive rule set or a negative rule set of a Streams client. However, it is very unlikely that you will define a global rule in a negative rule set.

The capture process will capture all DML and/or DDL changes when its global rule is in the positive rule set. The propagation process will propagate all changes from the source queue to the destination when its global rule is in the positive rule set. And, the apply process will apply all changes to the destination database when its global rule is in the positive rule set.

NOTE
Changes made to objects owned by SYS, SYSTEM, and CTXSYS are never captured for replication.

When global rules are defined in the positive rule set for the capture process, it will report errors if the change belonged to objects not supported by Oracle Streams.

You can query the DBA_STREAMS_UNSUPPORTED view to list the objects names and the reason as to why those objects are not supported. You can add either table- or schema-level (if all schema objects are unsupported) rules in the negative rule set for the capture process to ignore these unsupported objects.

Similarly, if the global rules are defined in the positive rule set for the apply process, it will report errors if the change belonged to unsupported columns. You can query the DBA_STREAMS_COLUMNS view to list the column name and the reason why the column is not supported in Oracle Streams. You can either add a table-level rule in the negative rule set of the apply process to discard changes at the table level, or remove the unsupported column from the LCR using the rule-based declarative transformation or a DML handler procedure.

You can also explore the use of `and_condition` to modify the system-created global rule that is in the positive rule set to exclude unsupported objects from the capture and apply processes.

To create global rules, you use procedures in the DBMS_STREAMS_ADM package. The ADD_GLOBAL_RULES procedure creates global rules for the capture and apply processes, and the ADD_GLOBAL_PROPAGATION_RULES procedure creates global rules for the propagation process.

The following example shows how to create global rules for the capture process. Here we set the `inclusion_rule` parameter to TRUE to add the rules to the positive rule set for the capture process.

```
SQL> declare
  2    l_dml_rule_name  varchar2(30);
  3    l_ddl_rule_name  varchar2(30);
  4  begin
  5    dbms_streams_adm.add_global_rules (
  6        streams_type     => 'CAPTURE',
  7        streams_name     => 'DBXA_CAP',
  8        queue_name       => 'DBXA_CAP_Q',
  9        include_dml      => true,
 10        include_ddl      => true,
 11        inclusion_rule   => true,
 12        source_database  => 'DBXA.WORLD',
 13        dml_rule_name    => l_dml_rule_name,
 14        ddl_rule_name    => l_ddl_rule_name
 15    );
 16    dbms_output.put_line('DML Rule Name is: ' || l_dml_rule_name);
 17    dbms_output.put_line('DDL Rule Name is: ' || l_ddl_rule_name);
 18* end;
 19  /
DML Rule Name is: "STRMADMIN"."DBXA29"
DDL Rule Name is: "STRMADMIN"."DBXA30"
PL/SQL procedure successfully completed.
```

This procedure creates the following two rule conditions in the positive rule set for the capture process:

```
RULE_NAME   RULE_CONDITION
----------  ------------------------------------------------------------
DBXA29      (:dml.is_null_tag() = 'Y' and :dml.get_source_database_name(
            ) = 'DBXA.WORLD' )
DBXA30      (:ddl.is_null_tag() = 'Y' and :ddl.get_source_database_name(
            ) = 'DBXA.WORLD' )
```

The rule conditions have a check for the global name of the database and the Streams tag value. The tag will be set to NULL by default in the redo entries for the database changes. The rules do not have a check to ignore captured changes that belonged to unsupported objects. To prevent errors in the capture process when such changes are encountered, you should add a negative rule set to the capture process at the table or schema level. Schema- and table-level rules are discussed in the subsequent sections.

Schema Rules   When you want to capture, propagate, and apply changes made to all objects in certain schemas in the database, you define schema rules. You can define the schema rules for all DML changes, for all DDL changes, or for both. The schema rules can be in a positive rule set or a negative rule set for a Streams client.

The capture process will capture all DML and/or DDL changes when its schema rule is in the positive rule set. The propagation process will propagate all changes from the source queue to the destination queue when its schema rule is in the positive rule set. And, the apply process will apply all changes to the destination database when its schema rule is in the positive rule set.

When schema rules are defined in the positive rule set for the capture process, it will report errors if the change belonged to objects not supported by Oracle Streams. You can query the DBA_STREAMS_UNSUPPORTED view to list the object names and the reason as to why those objects are not supported. You can add table-level rules in the negative rule set for the capture process to ignore changes to these unsupported objects.

Similarly, if the schema rules are defined in the positive rule set for the apply process, it will report errors if the change belonged to unsupported columns. You can query the DBA_STREAMS_COLUMNS view to list the column name and the reason as to why the column is not supported in Oracle Streams. You can either add a table-level rule in the negative rule set of the apply process to discard changes at the table level, or remove the unsupported column from the LCR using the rule-based declarative transformation or a DML handler procedure.

You can also explore the use of `and_condition` to modify the system-created schema rule that is in the positive rule set to exclude unsupported objects from the capture and apply processes.

To create schema rules, you use procedures in the DBMS_STREAMS_ADM package. The ADD_SCHEMA_RULES procedure creates schema rules for the capture and apply processes, and the ADD_SCHEMA_PROPAGATION_RULES procedure creates schema rules for the propagation process.

The following example shows how to create schema rules for the capture process. Here we have set the `inclusion_rule` parameter to TRUE to add the rules to the positive rule set for the capture process.

```
SQL> declare
  2    l_dml_rule_name  varchar2(30);
  3    l_ddl_rule_name  varchar2(30);
  4  begin
  5    dbms_streams_adm.add_schema_rules (
  6        schema_name      => 'SCOTT',
  7        streams_type     => 'CAPTURE',
  8        streams_name     => 'DBXA_CAP',
  9        queue_name       => 'DBXA_CAP_Q',
 10        include_dml     => true,
 11        include_ddl     => true,
 12        inclusion_rule  => true,
 13        source_database => 'DBXA.WORLD',
 14        dml_rule_name    => l_dml_rule_name,
 15        ddl_rule_name    => l_ddl_rule_name
 16        );
 17
 18    dbms_output.put_line('DML Rule Name is: ' || l_dml_rule_name);
 19    dbms_output.put_line('DDL Rule Name is: ' || l_ddl_rule_name);
 20
 21  end;
 22  /
DML Rule Name is: "STRMADMIN"."SCOTT13"
DDL Rule Name is: "STRMADMIN"."SCOTT14"
PL/SQL procedure successfully completed.
```

This procedure creates the following rules in the positive rule set for the capture process:

```
RULE_NAME   RULE_CONDITION
----------  -----------------------------------------------------------------
SCOTT14     ((:ddl.get_object_owner() = 'SCOTT' or :ddl.get_base_table_owner() =
            'SCOTT') and :ddl.is_null_tag() = 'Y' and :ddl.get_source_database_na
            me()  = 'DBXA.WORLD')
SCOTT13     ((:dml.get_object_owner() = 'SCOTT') and :dml.is_null_tag() = 'Y' and
            :dml.get_source_database_name() = 'DBXA.WORLD' )
```

These rules will capture DDL and DML changes to all objects in the SCOTT schema in the DBXA.WORLD database. The rules do not have a check to ignore captured changes that belonged to unsupported objects, if any, in the SCOTT schema.

To prevent errors in the capture process when such changes are encountered, you should add a negative rule set to the capture process at the table level. Table-level rules are discussed in the next section.

Suppose you had created global rules for the capture process in the positive rule set as discussed earlier, and all objects in the SCOTT schema were listed in the DBA_STREAMS_UNSUPPORTED view. You could then use the following procedure to add schema-level rules to the negative rule set of the capture process to discard changes made to these objects. Notice the setting of the `inclusion_rule` parameter. The capture process in this case will capture changes to all supported objects under other schemas.

```
SQL> declare
  2    l_dml_rule_name  varchar2(30);
  3    l_ddl_rule_name  varchar2(30);
  4  begin
  5    dbms_streams_adm.add_schema_rules (
  6        schema_name      => 'SCOTT',
  7        streams_type     => 'CAPTURE',
  8        streams_name     => 'DBXA_CAP',
  9        queue_name       => 'DBXA_CAP_Q',
 10        include_dml      => true,
 11        include_ddl      => true,
 12        inclusion_rule   => false,
 13        source_database  => 'DBXA.WORLD',
 14        dml_rule_name    => l_dml_rule_name,
 15        ddl_rule_name    => l_ddl_rule_name
 16      );
 17    dbms_output.put_line('DML Rule Name is: ' || l_dml_rule_name);
 18    dbms_output.put_line('DDL Rule Name is: ' || l_ddl_rule_name);
 19  end;
 20  /
DML Rule Name is: "STRMADMIN"."SCOTT43"
DDL Rule Name is: "STRMADMIN"."SCOTT44"
PL/SQL procedure successfully completed.
```

Table Rules   When you want to capture, propagate, and apply changes made to one or more tables in one or more schemas in the database, you define table rules. You can define the table rules for all DML changes, for all DDL changes, or for both.

The table rules can be in a positive rule set or a negative rule set for a Streams client.

The capture process will capture all DML and/or DDL changes when its table rule is in the positive rule set. The propagation process will propagate all changes from the source queue to the destination database when its table rule is in the positive rule set. And, the apply process will apply all changes to the destination database when its table rule is in the positive rule set.

You should query the DBA_STREAMS_UNSUPPORTED view to list the table names that may not be supported by Oracle Streams for replication. While adding table rules to the positive rule set for the capture process, you should not include these unsupported tables, to avoid errors in the capture process.

Similarly, you should query the DBA_STREAMS_COLUMNS view in the destination database to list the column names that are not supported by Oracle Streams. You can either add a table-level rule in the negative rule set of the apply process to discard changes at the table level, or remove the unsupported column from the LCR using the rule-based declarative transformation or a DML handler procedure (rule-based transformations are discussed in Chapter 9).

You can also explore the use of `and_condition` to modify the system-created schema rule that is in the positive rule set to exclude unsupported objects from the capture and apply processes.

To create table rules, you use procedures in the DBMS_STREAMS_ADM package. The ADD_TABLE_RULES procedure creates table rules for the capture and apply processes, and the ADD_TABLE_PROPAGATION_RULES procedure creates table rules for the propagation process.

The following example shows how to create table rules for the capture process. Here we have set the `inclusion_rule` parameter to TRUE to add the rules to the positive rule set for the capture process.

```
SQL> declare
  2      l_dml_rule_name   varchar2(30);
  3      l_ddl_rule_name   varchar2(30);
  4  begin
  5      dbms_streams_adm.add_table_rules (
  6          table_name       => 'SCOTT.DEPT',
  7          streams_type     => 'CAPTURE',
  8          streams_name     => 'DBXA_CAP',
  9          queue_name       => 'DBXA_CAP_Q',
 10          include_dml      => true,
 11          include_ddl      => true,
 12          inclusion_rule   => true,
 13          source_database  => 'DBXA.WORLD',
 14          dml_rule_name    => l_dml_rule_name,
 15          ddl_rule_name    => l_ddl_rule_name
 16          );
 17      dbms_output.put_line('DML Rule Name is: ' || l_dml_rule_name);
 18      dbms_output.put_line('DDL Rule Name is: ' || l_ddl_rule_name);
 19  end;
 20  /
DML Rule Name is: "STRMADMIN"."DEPT45"
DDL Rule Name is: "STRMADMIN"."DEPT46"
PL/SQL procedure successfully completed.
```

Suppose you had created global rules or schema rules for the capture process in the positive rule set as discussed earlier. And suppose a table titled EMP_ADDRESS from the SCOTT schema was listed in the DBA_STREAMS_UNSUPPORTED view due to an unsupported column. You could then use the following procedure to add table-level rules to the negative rule set of the capture process to discard changes made to this table. Notice the setting of the `inclusion_rule` parameter. The capture process will ignore all changes made to the SCOTT.EMP_ADDRESS table.

```
SQL> declare
  2    l_dml_rule_name  varchar2(30);
  3    l_ddl_rule_name  varchar2(30);
  4  begin
  5    dbms_streams_adm.add_table_rules (
  6         table_name      => 'SCOTT.EMP_ADDRESS',
  7         streams_type    => 'CAPTURE',
  8         streams_name    => 'DBXACAP',
  9         queue_name      => 'DBXA_CAP_Q',
 10         include_dml     => true,
 11         include_ddl     => true,
 12         inclusion_rule  => false,
 13         source_database => 'DBXA.WORLD',
 14         dml_rule_name   => l_dml_rule_name,
 15         ddl_rule_name   => l_ddl_rule_name
 16         );
 17    dbms_output.put_line('DML Rule Name is: ' || l_dml_rule_name);
 18    dbms_output.put_line('DDL Rule Name is: ' || l_ddl_rule_name);
 19  end;
 20  /
DML Rule Name is: "STRMADMIN"."EMP_ADDRESS47"
DDL Rule Name is: "STRMADMIN"."EMP_ADDRESS48"
PL/SQL procedure successfully completed.
```

Subset Rules   All the DML rules in the positive rule sets we've discussed thus far are applicable to changes made to any and all rows in the tables. What if you have a requirement to capture and replicate changes made to only a set of rows in a table, a kind of horizontal partitioning? That's when subset rules come into the picture. These are basically table rules, but applicable to only a subset of rows. Subset rules can be added to the positive rule set only and require a DML condition to be specified when adding those rules.

The subset rules for the capture process will capture DML changes made to the rows satisfying the specified DML condition. The subset rules for the propagation process will propagate LCRs that satisfy the specified DML condition. The apply process will select only those LCRs satisfying the DML condition to apply those to the destination table. You can also combine subset rules on different components, such as subset rules on capture, propagation, and apply.

The DBA_SUBSET_RULES procedure of the DBMS_STREAMS_ADM package adds subset rules to the positive rule set of the capture and apply processes. The DBA_SUBSET_PROPAGATION_RULES procedure adds those to the propagation process.

When you add subset rules, Oracle creates a separate rule for INSERT, UPDATE, and DELETE operations. The rule condition in these rules is different for each of the DML operations. Oracle also creates an appropriate action context for the INSERT and DELETE subset rules. In addition, Oracle defines rule transformation for these subset rules. The subset rule condition, the rule transformation, and the action context are used internally to modify the DML action to make sure that the replicated subset of the table is maintained properly without any data mismatching.

The following example creates subset rules for the capture process. Here we want to capture changes made to rows in the SCOTT.EMP table with DEPTNO equal to 20 and 30. Changes to all other rows are to be discarded. Notice the DML_CONDITION parameter. The SCOTT.EMP table at the destination database is a subset of the table at the source, and contains rows with DEPTNO equal to 20 and 30.

```
SQL> declare
  2    l_insert_rule_name  varchar2(30);
  3    l_update_rule_name  varchar2(30);
  4    l_delete_rule_name  varchar2(30);
  5  begin
  6    dbms_streams_adm.add_subset_rules (
  7        table_name       => 'SCOTT.EMP',
  8        dml_condition    => ' DEPTNO IN (20, 30) ',
  9        streams_type     => 'CAPTURE',
 10        streams_name     => 'DBXA_CAP',
 11        queue_name       => 'DBXA_CAP_Q',
 12        source_database  => 'DBXA.WORLD',
 13        insert_rule_name => l_insert_rule_name,
 14        update_rule_name => l_update_rule_name,
 15        delete_rule_name => l_delete_rule_name
 16      );
 17    dbms_output.put_line('Insert Rule Name is: ' || l_insert_rule_name);
 18    dbms_output.put_line('Update Rule Name is: ' || l_update_rule_name);
 19    dbms_output.put_line('Delete Rule Name is: ' || l_delete_rule_name);
 20 end;
 21 /

Insert Rule Name is: "STRMADMIN"."EMP53"
Update Rule Name is: "STRMADMIN"."EMP54"
Delete Rule Name is: "STRMADMIN"."EMP55"

PL/SQL procedure successfully completed.
```

In addition to the generated rules, Oracle also creates rule transformations and action contexts for subset rules. The view DBA_STREAMS_TRANSFORMATIONS lists the rule transformation definitions as shown here:

```
SQL> select rule_name,
  2          transform_type,
  3          subsetting_operation OPER,
  4          dml_condition
  5    from dba_streams_transformations
  6   where rule_name in ('EMP53','EMP54','EMP55');

RULE_NAME  TRANSFORM_TYPE                  OPER    DML_CONDITION
---------- ------------------------------- ------  --------------------
EMP53      SUBSET RULE                     INSERT  DEPTNO IN (20,30)
EMP54      SUBSET RULE                     UPDATE  DEPTNO IN (20,30)
EMP55      SUBSET RULE                     DELETE  DEPTNO IN (20,30)
```

The DBA_STREAMS_RULES view shows the action context created for these subset rules. The following query result shows that the action context is created for the INSERT and DELETE subset rule. There is no action context for the UPDATE subset rule with rule name EMP54.

```
SQL> select rule_name,
  2          rule_action_context
  3    from dba_rules
  4   where rule_name in ('EMP53','EMP54','EMP55');

RULE_NAME  RULE_ACTION_CONTEXT(ACTX_LIST(NVN_NAME, NVN_VALUE()))
---------- ----------------------------------------------------------------------------
EMP53      RE$NV_LIST(RE$NV_ARRAY(RE$NV_NODE('STREAMS$_ROW_SUBSET', ANYDATA())))
EMP54
EMP55      RE$NV_LIST(RE$NV_ARRAY(RE$NV_NODE('STREAMS$_ROW_SUBSET', ANYDATA())))
```

The generated rule condition for the INSERT rule EMP53 is listed next. The output is reformatted for readability.

```
RULE_NAME
----------
EMP53
RULE_CONDITION
--------------------------------------------------------------------------------
    :dml.get_object_owner()='SCOTT'
AND :dml.get_object_name()='EMP'
AND :dml.is_nul l_tag()='Y'
AND :dml.get_source_database_name()='DBXA.WORLD'
AND :dml.get_command_type() IN ('UPDATE','INSERT')
AND (:dml.get_value('NEW','"DEPTNO"') IS NOT NULL)
AND (:dml.get_value('NEW','"DEPTNO"').AccessNumber()=20 OR
    :dml.get_value('NEW','"DEPTNO"').AccessNumber()=30)
```

```
AND (:dml.get_command_type()='INSERT' OR
    (
       (:dml.get_value('OLD','"DEPTNO"') IS NOT NULL)
        AND (
             (
               (:dml.get_value('OLD','"DEPTNO"').AccessNumber() IS NOT NULL)
                AND NOT (:dml.get_value('OLD','"DEPTNO"').AccessNumber()=20 OR
                         :dml.get_value('OLD','"DEPTNO"').AccessNumber()=30)
             ) OR
             (
               (:dml.get_value('OLD','"DEPTNO"').AccessNumber() IS NULL)
                AND NOT EXISTS
                 (SELECT 1
                    FROM SYS.DUAL
                   WHERE (:dml.get_value('OLD','"DEPTNO"').AccessNumber()=20 OR
                          :dml.get_value('OLD','"DEPTNO"').AccessNumber()=30)
             )
           )
         )
     )
 )
```

Although this is named an INSERT rule, you can see that the rule applies to UPDATE and INSERT commands. If a row is inserted into the EMP table and belongs to DEPTNO 20 or 30, then there are no old values for DEPTNO, and the LCR for INSERT command satisfies the rule condition. If a row in the SCOTT.EMP table is updated and DEPTNO is changed to 20 or 30 from some other value, then the destination table should get this new row. Using the rule transformation and the action context, Oracle changes the UPDATE command in the LCR to an INSERT to add this row to the destination table. This satisfies the specified DML condition, and data in the table at the destination database matches the data in the source table for DEPTNO.

The generated rule condition for the UPDATE rule EMP54 is listed next. The output is reformatted for readability.

```
RULE_NAME
----------
EMP54
RULE_CONDITION
---------------------------------------------------------------------------
    :dml.get_object_owner()='SCOTT'
AND :dml.get_object_name()='EMP'
AND :dml.is_null_tag()='Y'
AND :dml.get_source_database_name()='DBXA.WORLD'
AND :dml.get_command_type()='UPDATE'
AND (:dml.get_value('NEW','"DEPTNO"') IS NOT NULL)
```

```
AND (:dml.get_value('OLD','"DEPTNO"') IS NOT NULL)
AND (:dml.get_value('OLD','"DEPTNO"').AccessNumber()=20   OR
     :dml.get_value('OLD','"DEPTNO"').AccessNumber()=30)
AND (:dml.get_value('NEW','"DEPTNO"').AccessNumber()=20   OR
     :dml.get_value('NEW','"DEPTNO"').AccessNumber()=30)
```

If rows in the SCOTT.EMP table with DEPTNO equal to 20 or 30 are updated without changing DEPTNO, then this rule evaluates to TRUE. There is no need to change the DML command in the LCR for this type of update. The updates are replicated to the destination table. There is no action context generated for this rule.

The generated rule condition for the DELETE rule EMP55 is listed next. The output is reformatted for readability.

```
RULE_NAME
----------
EMP55
RULE_CONDITION
--------------------------------------------------------------------------------
    :dml.get_object_owner()='SCOTT'
AND :dml.get_object_name()='EMP'
AND :dml.is_null_tag()='Y'
AND :dml.get_source_database_name()='DBXA.WORLD'
AND :dml.get_command_type() IN ('UPDATE','DELETE')
AND (:dml.get_value('OLD','"DEPTNO"') IS NOT NULL)
AND (:dml.get_value('OLD','"DEPTNO"').AccessNumber()=20   OR
     :dml.get_value('OLD','"DEPTNO"').AccessNumber()=30)
AND (:dml.get_command_type()='DELETE'   OR
   (
     (:dml.get_value('NEW','"DEPTNO"') IS NOT NULL)
     AND (
           (
             (:dml.get_value('NEW','"DEPTNO"').AccessNumber() IS NOT NULL)
             AND NOT (:dml.get_value('NEW','"DEPTNO"').AccessNumber()=20   OR
                      :dml.get_value('NEW','"DEPTNO"').AccessNumber()=30)
           ) OR
           (
             (:dml.get_value('NEW','"DEPTNO"').AccessNumber() IS NULL)
             AND NOT EXISTS
               (SELECT 1
                   FROM SYS.DUAL
                  WHERE (:dml.get_value('NEW','"DEPTNO"').AccessNumber()=20 OR
                         :dml.get_value('NEW','"DEPTNO"').AccessNumber()=30)
               )
           )
         )
   )
   )
```

Similar to the INSERT rule, you can see that this DELETE rule applies to UPDATE and DELETE commands. For DELETE commands affecting rows with DEPTNO equal to 20 and 30, the rule evaluates to TRUE, and the corresponding rows are deleted from the destination table. But if a row is updated in the EMP table, and DEPTNO is changed to a value other than 20 or 30, then this update should result in deleting rows in the destination table with DEPTNO equal to 20 or 30. Using the rule transformation and action context for this rule, Oracle changes the UPDATE command in the LCR to a DELETE to achieve this. This satisfies the specified DML condition, and data in the table at the destination database matches the data in the source table for DEPTNO.

The previous example explained how subset rules are created for the capture process and how they work. The subset rules behave the same way when created for the propagation and apply processes.

In Oracle Streams, the automatic conversion of an UPDATE operation to an INSERT or DELETE is called *row migration*. The rule condition, rule transformation, and action context are used to perform this conversion automatically. Do not confuse this conversion with the row migration that happens when the row does not fit in the data block.

Subset Rules and Supplemental Logging   As just discussed, the row migration process can change an UPDATE operation to an INSERT or DELETE operation. If only a few columns of the row were updated in the source table, then the captured LCR will not have the remaining columns of the row. This is because the redo logs will contain only the columns that were changed by this UDPATE. If this UDPATE operation gets converted to an INSERT, it may fail in the destination database for not having all the columns of the table in the LCR. So, how do we make sure that the LCR has all the required columns? This is where supplemental logging plays a crucial role.

Unconditional supplemental logging of columns of the table is required when adding subset rules. At the minimum, this should include all the key columns, all the columns in the subset rule condition, and all the columns in the destination table. This will ensure that the LCR will always contain all required columns for an INSERT and DELETE operation to succeed.

However, supplemental logging is not possible for columns with LONG or LOB data types. An LCR may not contain these columns for an INSERT or DELETE operation. This can result in an apply error and cause data mismatch. For this reason, you cannot add subset rules for tables that contain columns with these data types.

NOTE
An attempt to add a subset rule for a table with columns of the LONG or LOB data type will result in an ORA-23605 error.

User-Created Rules and Rule Sets

When the rule condition in the system-created rules does not meet your replication requirement, you may have to create your own rules and rule sets. For example, if you want to replicate only certain types of DML operations, use the IN or LIKE operator in the rule condition or create a customized filtering mechanism instead of using a negative rule set. These are called user-created rules and rule sets. You use procedures in the DBMS_RULE_ADM package to create these rules and rule sets. Following are the general steps you take when creating the rule and rule set to assign to a Streams client:

1. Create the rule set.

2. Create rules.

3. Add rules to the rule set.

4. Attach the rule set to the Streams client.

When you create your own rules, you need to create the evaluation context and the action context as needed. If you will be creating rules for analyzing LCRs for the DML or DDL conditions, then you must use the Oracle-provided evaluation context called SYS.STREAMS$_EVALUTION_CONTEXT.

Let's consider an example. We want to capture and replicate only the INSERT and UPDATE operations against all the tables in a given schema. We are not interested in replicating DELETE operations.

First, we need to create a rule set for the rule we will be creating to select only the interested LCRs for our requirement. The following listing creates the rule set called IGNORE_DELETE_RS. The rule owner will be STRMADMIN, the Streams Administrator. Since our rule condition will be selecting LCRs based on the DML commands, we use an Oracle-provided evaluation context. All rules assigned to this rule set will use this evaluation context if we do not specify it at the rule level.

```
SQL> begin
  2    dbms_rule_adm.create_rule_set(
  3      rule_set_name       => 'STRMADMIN.IGNORE_DELETE_RS',
  4      evaluation_context  => 'SYS.STREAMS$_EVALUATION_CONTEXT');
  5  end;
  6  /
PL/SQL procedure successfully completed.
```

Next, we create the rule called IGNORE_DELETE_R1 with our customized rule condition as follows. The rule owner will be STRMADMIN. Notice the syntax used for specifying the rule condition. Also, the evaluation context and action context are set to the default value of NULL. We can omit these parameters from the syntax. The rule will inherit those from the rule set when we add the rule to the rule set. When the evaluation context is not specified while creating the rule, Oracle cannot check the rule syntax and the variables used in the rule condition. If there were any syntax errors, you will not know about them until the rule is added to the rule set, when it inherits the evaluation context of the rule set. In the following example, the parameters `evaluation_context` and `action_context` are optional and could be omitted.

```
SQL> begin
  2    dbms_rule_adm.create_rule(
  3     rule_name   => 'STRMADMIN.IGNORE_DELETE_R1',
  4     condition   => ' :dml.get_object_owner() = ''SCOTT'' '
  5       || ' AND :dml.get_source_database_name() = ''DBXA.WORLD'' '
  6       || ' AND :dml.is_null_tag() = ''Y'' '
  7       || ' AND (:dml.get_command_type() = ''INSERT'' OR '
  8       || '      :dml.get_command_type() = ''UPDATE'' ) ' ,
  9     evaluation_context => NULL,
 10     action_context => NULL);
 11  end;
 12  /
PL/SQL procedure successfully completed.
```

The following procedure shows how to assign the rule IGNORE_DELETE_R1 to the rule set IGNORE_DELETE_RS we created earlier. RULE_COMMENT is optional. You can use it to describe the reason for adding the rule to the rule set.

```
SQL> begin
  2    dbms_rule_adm.add_rule(
  3       rule_name      => 'STRMADMIN.IGNORE_DELETE_R1',
  4       rule_set_name  => 'STRMADMIN.IGNORE_DELETE_RS',
  5       rule_comment   => 'To ignore DELETE commands');
  6  end;
  7  /
PL/SQL procedure successfully completed.
```

If the rule condition has an error in the syntax and you did not specify the evaluation context when creating the rule as shown in the previous example, you will receive an ORA-25448 error when executing the ADD_RULE procedure. This error will be followed by another ORA error telling you exactly what is wrong with your rule condition. You will need to correct the rule condition by using the ALTER_RULE procedure, or by dropping the rule with force using the DROP_RULE procedure and re-creating it.

The rule set IGNORE_DELETE_RS can now be assigned to the Streams client, such as the capture process. The capture process will then select only those LCRs that satisfy our rule condition. This is how we will only capture INSERT and UPDATE operations against the tables in the SCOTT schema. Since we did not create a rule to handle any DDL changes to the objects in the SCOTT schema, the capture process will ignore all DDL commands as well.

NOTE
You should not drop the rule and rule set assigned to a Streams client.

When creating rule conditions, the case of characters in the object names, such as the schema name, table name, and database name, must match the case of these characters in the data dictionary. Otherwise, the rule will not evaluate properly. If the object name was created with a mixed case, then use single quotes around the name when specifying it in the rule condition. Use of double quotes or two single quotes around such names is not allowed. So, for the table with a name Dept, use 'Dept' instead of "Dept" in the rule condition.

When creating your own rules, keep the rule condition simple. The example just discussed had a simple rule condition. If the condition contains user-defined functions to evaluate a variable or contains operators such as LIKE, NOT LIKE, IN, or NOT IN, then the condition is referred to as a complex rule condition. Complex rule conditions degrade the rule evaluation performance. But sometimes you may not be able avoid complex rule conditions.

Following is an example of a complex rule condition that uses a user-defined function. In this example we do not want to capture changes to a number of tables in the database. The function EXCLUDE_OBJ returns an N if the supplied table name is found in a list of tables available to the function, meaning we do not want to exclude the LCRs for this table. The function may read a table to get this list, or it may have it hard coded. If the function returns a Y, then the rule condition evaluates to FALSE, meaning the LCR should be discarded.

```
SQL> begin
  2    dbms_rule_adm.create_rule(
  3      rule_name  => 'STRMADMIN.EXCLUDE_RULE',
  4      condition  => ' :dml.get_source_database_name() = ''DBXA.WORLD'' '
  5      || ' AND :dml.is_null_tag() = ''Y'' '
  6      || ' AND STRMADMIN.EXCLUDE_OBJ(:dml.get_object_name()) = ''N'' ',
  7      evaluation_context => 'SYS.STREAMS$_EVALUATION_CONTEXT');
  8  end;
  9  /
PL/SQL procedure successfully completed.
```

In this example, the rule evaluation will invoke the function to be evaluated for each LCR. This overhead will adversely affect the rule evaluation process. You will notice an increase in the CPU utilization for the capture process, if this rule was associated with the capture process. Ultimately, the replication latency will be affected and, in some cases, will not be acceptable. Also, notice that we defined the proper evaluation context in this example when creating the rule. If the rule condition had any syntax errors, or if the EXCLUDE_OBJ function was not accessible, we would have received an error.

When possible, you should avoid creating your own rules and rule sets. In most cases the system-created rules are sufficient and address most replication requirements. In situations where the rule condition is not sufficient, consider using and_condition to modify it to suit your requirement.

In some situations you may have to replicate data from a higher release of the database to a lower release. Oracle Database 11g can replicate data to Oracle Database 10g and Oracle9i Database. However, in the higher releases, Oracle may support data types that were not supported in the earlier releases.

Also, if you configured Streams replication at the global (database) or schema level, you should ensure that changes made to any unsupported data types, if present, are ignored by Streams clients. Attempts at capturing or applying changes to objects with unsupported data types will result in errors, and in some situations the Streams processes may simply terminate.

So, how do you get around this problem? The solution, discussed next, involves using Oracle-supplied functions to check data type compatibility.

Rule Condition for Discarding Unsupported LCRs

To identify the unsupported data types in the LCRs, we need to know the compatibility level of the database itself, and the corresponding Streams compatibility of data types in the LCR. So, if the database compatibility is 10.2, then the Streams compatibility of the data types in the LCRs must be equal to or less than 10.2.

The SYS.LCR$_ROW_RECORD and SYS.LCR$_DDL_RECORD types contain a member function called GET_COMPATIBLE. This function returns the current compatibility of the database as defined by the COMPATIBLE initialization parameter of the database.

The DBMS_STREAMS package contains a number of functions that return a value corresponding to the release of Oracle software. These functions are

- **COMPATIBLE_9_2** Returns a value corresponding to Oracle 9.2.0 release

- **COMPATIBLE_10_1** Returns a value corresponding to Oracle 10.1.0 release

- **COMPATIBLE_10_2** Returns a value corresponding to Oracle 10.2.0 release

- **COMPATIBLE_11_1** Returns a value corresponding to Oracle 11*g* R1 release

- **MAX_COMPATIBLE** Returns a value which is always greater than any other values returned by other functions

If you create your own rules and would like to discard unsupported data types in, say, the Oracle 10.2.0 release, you will need a rule condition as shown next. The compatibility check is highlighted in bold.

```
SQL> begin
  2    dbms_rule_adm.create_rule(
  3      rule_name  => 'STRMADMIN.SCHEMA_RULE',
  4      condition  => ' :dml.get_object_owner() = ''SCOTT'' '
  5        || ' AND :dml.get_source_database_name() =  ''DBXA.WORLD'' '
  6        || ' AND :dml.is_null_tag() = ''Y'' '
  7        || ' AND :dml.get_compatible() >= dbms_streams.compatible_10_2 ',
  8      evaluation_context => NULL,
  9      action_context => NULL);
 10  end;
 11  /
PL/SQL procedure successfully completed.
```

So, if the SCOTT schema contained objects with Streams unsupported data types as of the Oracle 10.2 release, this rule will discard LCRs for all such objects.

Suppose you do not have user-created rules in your configuration and have only system-created rules; how would you discard LCRs for unsupported data types, if present? In this case, you would use the `and_condition` parameter to append the compatibility condition to the system-created rule in the positive rule set, as shown in the following example:

```
SQL> declare
  2    l_dml_rule_name  varchar2(30);
  3    l_ddl_rule_name  varchar2(30);
  4  begin
  5    dbms_streams_adm.add_schema_rules (
  6      schema_name      => 'SCOTT',
  7      streams_type     => 'CAPTURE',
  8      streams_name     => 'DBXA_CAP',
  9      queue_name       => 'DBXA_CAP_Q',
 10      include_dml      => true,
 11      include_ddl      => true,
 12      inclusion_rule   => true,
 13      source_database  => 'DBXA.WORLD',
```

```
14      and_condition => ' :lcr.get_compatible() >= dbms_streams.compatible_10_2 ',
15      dml_rule_name    => l_dml_rule_name,
16      ddl_rule_name    => l_ddl_rule_name
17      );
18      dbms_output.put_line('DML Rule Name is: ' || l_dml_rule_name);
19      dbms_output.put_line('DDL Rule Name is: ' || l_ddl_rule_name);
20    end;
21    /
DML Rule Name is: "STRMADMIN"."SCOTT89"
DDL Rule Name is: "STRMADMIN"."SCOTT90"
PL/SQL procedure successfully completed.
```

Starting in Oracle Database 11g R2, the DBMS_STREAMS.MAX_COMPATIBLE function can be used in the condition of the rule in the positive rule set to discard LCRs that are not supported by Streams in the current release of the database where the Streams client is configured. In this case, the condition will have the following syntax:

```
and_condition => ' :lcr.get_compatible() < dbms_streams.max_compatible()' ;
```

Note that if you created your own rules, then the :lcr variable in the example will change to :dml or :ddl for the DML or DDL rule type, respectively.

Use of DBMS_STREAMS.MAX_COMPATIBLE is recommended. This will avoid changing the rule condition after you upgrade the database to a new release and would like to include newly supported data types in Streams replication.

NOTE
The objects not supported by Streams are listed in the DBA_STREAMS_UNSUPPORTED and DBA_STREAMS_COLUMNS views.

Procedures to Manage Rules and Rule Sets

Table 3-2 lists some of the procedures available in the DBMS_RULE_ADM package to manage the rules and rule sets. You use these procedures primarily when creating your own rules and rule sets. You may have to use some of these procedures when modifying rule conditions and resolving problems with rules and rule sets. The *Oracle Database PL/SQL Packages and Types Reference* describes how to use these procedures.

Procedure Name	Description
ADD_RULE	Adds a rule to the rule set
ALTER_EVALUATION_CONTEXT	Alters the rule evaluation context
ALTER_RULE	Alters rule properties
CREATE_EVALUATION_CONTEXT	Creates an evaluation context
CREATE_RULE	Creates a new rule
CREATE_RULE_SET	Creates a new rule set
DROP_EVALUATION_CONTEXT	Removes the evaluation context
DROP_RULE	Drops the rule from the database
DROP_RULE_SET	Drops the rule set
REMOVE_RULE	Removes a rule from a rule set, but does not drop the rule from the database

TABLE 3-2. *DBMS_RULE_ADM Package Procedures to Manage Rule and Rule Sets*

Summary

Rules and rule sets control how Streams clients perform their actions. The rules can be defined at the database (global), schema, or table level for the Streams clients to perform their action. You can also create subset rules at the table level. The subset rule allows you to specify a DML condition to select the changes made to a subset of rows for replication. Use of subset rules requires additional supplemental logging.

The rule set can be defined as a positive rule set or a negative rule set for the Streams client. The built-in rules engine evaluates the rule set associated with the Streams client. The evaluation always results in TRUE or FALSE. If a rule set is a positive rule set and evaluates to TRUE, then the Streams client performs its action. If the positive rule set evaluates to FALSE, then the Streams client ignores the LCR. If the rule set is a negative rule set and evaluates to TRUE, then the Streams client does not perform its action and discards the LCR.

Oracle automatically creates rules and rule sets when you use procedures in the DBMS_STREAMS_ADM package to add rules. These are called system-created rules and rule sets. The system-created rules and rule sets use an Oracle-provided evaluation context called SYS.STREAMS$_EVALUATION_CONTEXT. Oracle creates the required application context for subset rules.

When system-created rule conditions are not sufficient for your requirements, you can define your own rules and rule sets. These are called user-created rules and rule set. The procedures in DBMS_RULE_ADM can be used to create, alter, drop, or remove these rules and rule sets. It is also possible to add a user-defined condition to a system-created rule condition.

You can also modify a system-created rule condition by appending your own condition. This can be particularly helpful when you must discard LCRs for objects with Streams unsupported data types.

When creating your own rules or modifying a system-created rule condition, be sure to check the syntax for the rule condition and the spelling of the hard-coded values for the variables to avoid unexpected ORA errors.

CHAPTER
4

Capture Process

racle Streams replication begins with capturing the changes made to the database objects. There are mainly two ways to capture this information: implicit and explicit.

In the implicit method, the DDL and DML changes are extracted from the redo log buffer, online redo logs, or archived logs. These changes can be captured for the whole database, the entire schema, or a number of tables. As discussed in Chapter 3, the rules determine how the changes are captured at these levels.

In the explicit method, the application creates the messages and enqueues them in the Streams queue. For example, in a heterogeneous environment, changes made to a non-Oracle database are formatted by the user application into LCRs and enqueued for consumption by other applications or the apply process.

This chapter discusses in detail how implicit capture works and describes the different types of implicit capture processes, including their configuration, requirements, and limitations.

Capture Process Types

There are two primary types of implicit capture process: local capture and downstream capture. You can choose the type of capture process based on your environment and replication requirements.

Local Capture Process

When the capture process runs in the source database, which generates the changes, the capture process is called a local capture process. The local capture process can mine the redo log buffer, redo log files, and archived log files of the database to extract changes to replicate. It is possible to configure multiple local capture processes in a single database. In a RAC environment, you can configure one or multiple capture processes to run in one or multiple instances of the database. The local capture process is by far the most commonly used capture process in Streams replication.

As of Oracle Database 11g, there are two types of local capture process: the asynchronous capture process and the synchronous capture process. The synchronous capture process does not use redo information to capture changes.

NOTE
Throughout this book, I refer to the asynchronous capture process simply as the capture process. I specifically mention "synchronous" when referring to the synchronous capture process.

Capture Process

Prior to Oracle Database 11*g*, there was only one type of implicit capture process, and it captured the database changes asynchronously by mining the redo information. The mining of the redo information is very similar to the way the LogMiner utility mines the redo logs. But, the capture process does not invoke the LogMiner utility. The log mining by capture process is highly optimized for Streams to mine the redo information in real time. In this book, the term *LogMiner* refers to the log mining by capture process, and not to the LogMiner utility as such.

This is by far the most commonly used capture process to replicate the changes. This type of capture process can be configured locally at the source database or remotely on another database. It uses a buffered queue (discussed in Chapter 5) to propagate messages created for the captured changes.

Synchronous Capture Process

Oracle Database 11*g* introduced a new type of implicit capture process called the synchronous capture process. The synchronous capture process does not mine the redo information to capture changes. Instead, the changes are captured using an internal mechanism that tracks the changes made to tables defined for the synchronous capture. For this reason, the synchronous capture must run on the source database. The captured changes are converted into the LCRs and queued to a persistent queue on the disk. Synchronous capture does not use a buffered queue. The synchronous capture process is the only method available to capture changes in Oracle Standard Edition.

The captured LCRs contain all the columns of the row even if some of the columns did not change. Therefore, synchronous capture does not need supplemental logging of additional column data. Synchronous capture does not capture any DDL changes.

If you decide to use synchronous capture, you must make sure that the application does not use the TRUNCATE command to remove all rows in tables. Otherwise, there will be data mismatch problems. Consider replacing TRUNCATE with the DELETE operation, if possible.

The synchronous capture process is especially useful when replicating a small number of tables that have low DML activity.

NOTE
The synchronous capture process can be used when the source database is running in NOARCHIVELOG mode, as it does not use redo information to capture changes.

Use of synchronous capture for replicating changes for a large number of tables, or tables with high DML activity, may result in poor replication latency.

Downstream Capture Process

Unlike the capture and synchronous capture processes, the downstream capture process runs on a database other than the source database. The database running the downstream capture process is called the *downstream database*. The downstream capture process can mine the redo information generated by the source database to capture changes. The logs containing the redo information must be transported to the downstream database to mine. Oracle Streams uses the Oracle Data Guard technology of *redo transport* to copy the redo information from the source database to the downstream database.

There are two types of downstream capture process: real-time downstream and archived-log downstream. Capture process parameter `downstream_real_time_mine` determines if the downstream capture process is operating in real-time downstream or archived-log downstream mode.

Real-Time Downstream Capture

In the real-time downstream capture process, the LogWriter Network Service (LNS) in the source database sends the redo information to the Remote File Service (RFS) in the downstream database. The RFS writes this redo information to the standby redo log files. The capture process running in the downstream database mines these standby logs to capture changes. When the redo log of the source database switches, the standby redo log at the downstream database also switches, creating its own archived log file (standby archived log) that the downstream capture process continues to mine when necessary. Figure 4-1 shows the real-time downstream capture process configuration.

Compared to the archived-log downstream capture process, the real-time downstream capture process performs better because the changes are captured quickly from the standby redo logs instead of waiting for the log switch and copying the archived log file to the downstream database. However, you must make sure that the required standby archived log files are available to the downstream capture process in case the process is stopped and restarted afterward. You will also need to manage the backup and removal of these archived log files at the downstream database. RMAN cannot be used to manage these files.

You can create more than one real-time downstream capture process in a single downstream database for the same source database. One downstream database can have only one source database for a real-time downstream capture process.

Archived-Log Downstream Capture

In the archived-log downstream capture process, the archived log files at the source database are copied to the downstream database for the capture process to mine. The files can be copied automatically using the redo transport services, FTP, the

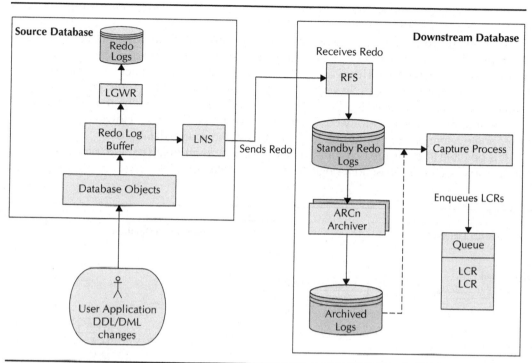

FIGURE 4-1. *Real-time downstream capture*

DBMS_FILE_TRANSFER package, or any other means. If you're using the redo transport services, the archiver process in the source database will send the archived log file to the RFS at the downstream database. The RFS will write the archived log file to a local archived file destination and register it at the downstream database for the capture process to mine. In other file-copying procedures, you will need to automate the registration procedure using the ALTER DATABASE REGISTER LOGICAL LOGFILE command. It is recommended to use the redo transport service mechanism to transfer the archived log file to the downstream database.

NOTE
When using archived-log downstream capture, you can use the database parameter `archive_lag_target` *to automatically switch the redo log file at the source database at fixed intervals to initiate copying of the archived log file to downstream database.*

Figure 4-2 shows the archived-log downstream capture process configuration using the redo transport service.

The advantage of archived-log downstream capture is that the downstream database allows multiple downstream capture processes to capture changes from multiple source databases. This way, the downstream database can act as a central location for capturing changes. In addition, RMAN can be used at the source database to manage the local archived log files. These archived log files will not be removed by RMAN until they are successfully copied to the downstream database. However, an appropriate retention policy must be set for RMAN at the source database.

It is possible to configure real-time and archived-log downstream capture processes for the same source database in a single downstream database.

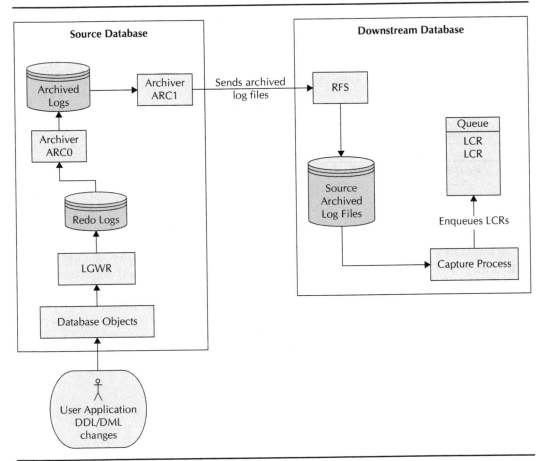

FIGURE 4-2. *Archived-log downstream capture*

Capture Process Checkpoints and System Change Numbers

While mining the redo information to capture changes to replicate, the capture process also performs some housekeeping activity. This housekeeping activity is crucial to make sure that the capture process does not miss any changes that took place when the capture process was not active for whatever reason.

To guarantee that the changes are not missed, particularly during the recovery of the source database, the capture process tracks system change numbers (SCNs) and records those in the internal tables along with information about its current state. The capture process tracks a number of SCNs. Recording of such information is called *checkpointing*, and associated SCNs are called checkpoint SCNs. There are required checkpoint SCNs and maximum checkpoint SCNs. In addition, there are several other SCNs that the capture process records. The DBA_CAPTURE view shows information about the capture process and lists various different SCNs associated with it.

NOTE
The capture process checkpoint is not the same as the database checkpoint.

The capture process performs a checkpoint at routine intervals, called the *checkpoint interval*. By default, the capture process performs a checkpoint when it has mined 1GB of redo information or when 30 minutes has passed since the last checkpoint, whichever occurs first. The checkpoint information is stored in the SYSTEM-owned table called LOGMNR_RESTART_CKPT$. The default checkpoint interval is adequate in most situations; however, you can change the checkpoint interval, or force a checkpoint on demand, using an internal parameter (_CHECKPOINT_FORCE) for the capture process.

NOTE
Performing checkpoints too frequently will increase the amount of checkpoint data stored internally and can slow down startup of the capture process.

Required Checkpoint SCN

The required checkpoint SCN corresponds to the lowest checkpoint for which the redo information is required by the capture process. The redo log or archived log file that contains information as of this SCN, and all subsequent archived log files, must be made available to the capture process to scan for changes to capture or to make sure those changes were already captured and not missed.

When you stop and restart the capture process, it starts reading the log file from the required checkpoint SCN. The capture process updates the required checkpoint SCN whenever it purges old checkpoint information. The required checkpoint SCN is recorded in the REQUIRED_CHECKPOINT_SCN column of the DBA_CAPTURE view.

Maximum Checkpoint SCN

The maximum checkpoint SCN corresponds to the latest checkpoint recorded by the capture process. This SCN plays a role in deciding if a new LogMiner data dictionary should be created when an additional capture process is created to capture changes from the same source database. The maximum checkpoint SCN is recorded in the MAX_CHECKPOINT_SCN column of the DBA_CAPTURE view.

First SCN

This is the lowest SCN in the redo or archived log file from which the capture process can capture changes. The first SCN gets established for the capture process upon its creation. Once established, the capture process maintains it by routinely updating it when purging obsolete checkpoint information. The capture process will write the following message in the alert log file of its database when the first SCN is changed upon purging the checkpoint information:

```
STREAMS Capture C  1: first scn changed.
scn: 0x0000.0041964e
```

You can specify the first SCN when creating the capture process explicitly using the DBMS_CAPTURE_ADM.CREATE_CAPTURE procedure. You have to make sure that the archived log file with this SCN is available and that it contains the source data dictionary information. All subsequent archived log files should also be available to the capture process. The following query will list the names of the archived log files with data dictionary information:

```
set numwidth 18
set lines 132
select first_change#,
       name
  from v$archived_log
 where dictionary_begin = 'YES';
```

If this query returns multiple rows, you can choose the first SCN from which you want the capture process to begin capturing changes. Just make sure that the archived log files from this SCN onward are available.

If the query does not return any rows, then you do not have an archived log file with source database data dictionary information. You can extract the data dictionary information and obtain the corresponding SCN to use as the first SCN. The source database data dictionary information can be extracted to the redo log using the DBMS_CAPTURE_ADM.BUILD procedure as shown here:

```
set serveroutput on
declare
    scn number;
begin
    dbms_capture_adm.build(first_scn => scn);
    dbms_output.put_line('First SCN = ' || scn);
end;
/
```

If you use the procedures in the DBMS_STREAMS_ADM package to implicitly create the capture process, the source database dictionary will be automatically extracted and the first SCN will be established for the capture process. The procedures ADD_GLOBAL_RULES, ADD_SCHEMA_RULES, ADD_TABLE_RULES, and ADD_SUBSET_RULES will trigger these additional steps if the specified capture process did not exist when you were creating rules for the capture process.

Start SCN

This is the SCN from which the capture process will begin capturing the changes. The first SCN and start SCN can be specified when you create the capture process explicitly. If the capture process is created implicitly, then the start SCN and first SCN are identical. The capture process maintains the start SCN during its normal operation. However, you may have to change it after performing a point-in-time recovery of the destination database to capture changes that were made to the source database after the recovery. The capture process must be stopped to change the start SCN. Again, the archived log files from this new start SCN must be available.

If specified when creating the capture process manually, the start SCN must be equal to or greater than the first SCN. The capture process always reads all the unread archived logs with SCNs that are greater than the first SCN. But it will not capture changes with SCNs lower than the start SCN. Such scanning is required to guarantee that all qualified changes are captured. However, if there is a wide gap between the first SCN and the start SCN, then the capture process will spend a considerable amount of time scanning the logs prior to the start SCN. So, when you create the capture process explicitly, keeping the start SCN and the first SCN close to each other will speed up the initial startup of the capture process.

Captured SCN

This is the SCN corresponding to the most recent change that was read from the redo log information by the capture process. The name may be misleading—the change at this SCN is not necessarily replicated, but simply read from the redo log.

The column CAPTURED_SCN in the DBA_CAPTURE view reports this SCN, and it will constantly change as the capture process reads the redo information.

Last Enqueued SCN

This is the SCN corresponding to the most recent change that was captured and enqueued for replication. The capture process updates this information as it creates the LCRs and enqueues those to the Streams queue. The column LAST_ENQUEUED_ SCN in the DBA_CAPTURE view lists this SCN.

Applied SCN

In Oracle Streams, the captured messages (LCRs) are kept in the buffered or persistent queue for the capture process until they are dequeued by the apply process. When the apply process dequeues the LCRs, an acknowledgement is sent back to the capture process. This acknowledgement contains the SCN corresponding to the most recent change that was dequeued by the apply process. This SCN indicates that changes below this SCN have been successfully dequeued by the apply process. The capture process updates this information in internal tables. The APPLIED_SCN column in the DBA_CAPTURE view lists this SCN. As far as the capture process is concerned, the change was dequeued and applied even if it resulted in an apply error and was written to the apply error queue.

Source Reset Logs SCN

This SCN is associated with the incarnation of the source database. The capture process stores this SCN in the SOURCE_RESETLOGS_SCN column of the DBA_ CAPTURE view. This information comes from the RESETLOGS_CHANGE# column in the V$DATABASE_INCARNATION view. This SCN is used by RMAN internally to manage archived log file retention. The capture process does not use this information for its functionality.

Checkpoint Retention Time

As time goes by, the capture process accumulates sizable amounts of information from checkpointing. What happens to this information? Does the capture process need all this historical information? Well, information stays in the internal tables for 60 days by default and gets purged automatically. The capture process parameter called `checkpoint_retention_time` controls the life of such checkpoint information. Its default value is 60 days, but, this value can be changed. Typically it is changed to a lower number. The value you choose for this parameter should match your policies for archived log file retention. Otherwise, the capture process may get stuck, when restarted, looking for the archived log file that has been purged.

The capture process periodically computes the age of the checkpoint information and purges the information that is older than the checkpoint_retention_time value. The capture process uses the FIRST_TIME value of the archived redo log that contains the REQUIRED_CHECKPOINT_SCN value, and subtracts the NEXT_TIME value of the archived log file that contains older checkpoint SCNs. When the difference between the FIRST_TIME and NEXT_TIME values is more than the value of the CHECKPOINT_RETENTION_TIME column, it purges all checkpoints prior to and including this older checkpoint SCN. For this computation, the capture process refers to the REQUIRED_CHECKPOINT_SCN and CHECKPOINT_RETENTION_TIME columns in the DBA_CAPTURE data dictionary view. The FIRST_TIME and NEXT_TIME values are taken from the DBA_REGISTERED_ARCHIVED_LOG data dictionary view for the archived logs.

However, if you choose to retain the checkpoint information for a longer duration and also retain all corresponding archived log files, then it is possible to recapture past changes to recover destination database objects.

Creating the Capture Process

Although the capture process is a background database process, it must be created for capturing changes. Without the capture process, there won't be any data replication. There is more than one way to create the capture process. The next few sections explore how to create the capture process to suit your replication requirements.

But, before you create the capture process, you must create the Streams queue that will stage the created LCRs. Creating the queue is a prerequisite to creating the capture process.

The Streams queue is created using the SET_UP_QUEUE procedure of the DBMS_STREAMS_ADM package. Generally, the procedure is executed as the Streams Administrator. The procedure performs several tasks internally to create the queue with the proper queue type, create several internal supporting queue tables, grant proper privileges to the queue user, and so forth. Chapter 5 describes in detail the Streams queue and how to create it.

Create the Local Capture Process

If you decided to create the capture process locally on the source database, you have more than one way to create the capture process.

Automatic Capture Process Creation

The following procedures in the DBMS_STREAMS_ADM package can create a capture process automatically. Using one of these procedures to create the capture process is relatively very simple, and Oracle performs several tasks behind the scenes that are necessary for Streams replication.

- ADD_GLOBAL_RULES

- ADD_SCHEMA_RULES

- ADD_TABLE_RULES

- ADD_SUBSET_RULES

- MAINTAIN_* procedures

NOTE
The MAINTAIN_* procedures are discussed in detail in Chapter 8.

Each of these procedures performs the following tasks:

1. Creates the specified capture process, if it does not exist. If this is the first capture process in the database, then the data dictionary will be extracted into the redo log, which will be later used to construct the LogMiner data dictionary.

2. Creates a rule set with a system-created name, for the capture process, if one does not exist. The rule set can be positive or negative depending on the option selected.

3. Depending on the procedure used, adds a table, schema, global, or subset rule to the rule set for the capture. The rule name is system-created.

4. Prepares the table, schema, or database for instantiation.

5. Creates supplemental log groups for the key columns of the tables. Supplemental logging will be unconditional for primary key columns and conditional for the unique index and foreign key columns.

All these procedures have almost identical input and output parameters. We will discuss the ADD_SCHEMA_RULES procedure in detail to see how it creates the capture process, rule set, and schema rules. Table 4-1 shows the parameters of the ADD_SCHEMA_RULES procedure. Please note the two out parameters are optional. These parameters are described here:

- **schema_name**   Name of the schema.

- **streams_type**   Type of Streams client or process. For the capture process, specify CAPTURE.

Parameter Name	In/Out	Data Type
schema_name	IN	VARCHAR2
streams_type	IN	VARCHAR2
streams_name	IN	VARCHAR2 default NULL
queue_name	IN	VARCHAR2 default 'streams_queue'
include_dml	IN	BOOLEAN default TRUE
include_ddl	IN	BOOLEAN default FALSE
include_tagged_lcr	IN	BOOLEAN default FALSE
source_database	IN	VARCHAR2 default NULL
dml_rule_name	OUT	VARCHAR2
ddl_rule_name	OUT	VARCHAR2
inclusion_rule	IN	BOOLEAN default TRUE
and_condition	IN	VARCHAR2 default NULL

TABLE 4-1. *Parameters of ADD_SCHEMA_RULES Procedure*

- **streams_name**   Name of Streams client or process, for CAPTURE, the name of the capture process.

- **queue_name**   Name of the queue into which the capture process enqueues LCRs.

- **include_dml**   TRUE, if you want to replicate DML changes. Defaults to TRUE.

- **include_ddl**   TRUE, if you want to replicate DDL changes. Defaults to FALSE.

- **include_tagged_lcr**   Defaults to FALSE, meaning the procedure adds a condition to each rule to evaluate to TRUE only if the Streams tag in the redo log is NULL, and the LCR will be captured. If set to TRUE, then the procedure does not generate this condition, and the Streams tag is not checked in the rule. All LCRs, irrespective of the Streams tag value, will be captured.

- **source_database**   Global name of the source database where the change originated.

■ **dml_rule_name** If `include_dml` is TRUE, then this out parameter will contain the name of the DML rule created.

■ **ddl_rule_name** If `include_ddl` is TRUE, then this out parameter will contain the name of the DDL rule created.

■ **inclusion_rule** If TRUE, then the procedure adds the generated rule to the positive rule set. If FALSE, then the rule is added to the negative rule set. If the rule set does not exist, the procedure creates one. Defaults to TRUE.

■ **and_condition** If specified, the procedure adds the condition to the system-created rule using an AND clause. The LCR variables used in the condition must be specified using the `:lcr` format. The procedure will convert it to the appropriate DML or DDL variable in the generated rule.

The following example creates a capture process called DBXA_CAP that captures DDL and DML changes made to tables in the SCOTT schema in the DBXA database. Notice the `and_condition` parameter specified in the example. This condition ensures that changes made to tables that have unsupported columns will not be captured.

```
SQL> declare
  2   l_dml_rule_name  varchar2(30);
  3   l_ddl_rule_name  varchar2(30);
  4  begin
  5   dbms_streams_adm.add_schema_rules (
  6       schema_name       => 'SCOTT',
  7       streams_type      => 'CAPTURE',
  8       streams_name      => 'DBXA_CAP',
  9       queue_name        => 'DBXA_CAP_Q',
 10       include_dml       => true,
 11       include_ddl       => true,
 12       include_tagged_lcr => false,
 13       source_database   => 'DBXA.WORLD',
 14       dml_rule_name     => l_dml_rule_name,
 15       ddl_rule_name     => l_ddl_rule_name,
 16       inclusion_rule    => true,
 17       and_condition => ' :lcr.get_compatible() < dbms_streams.max_compatible()'
 18   );
 19
 20   dbms_output.put_line('DML Rule Name is: ' || l_dml_rule_name);
 21   dbms_output.put_line('DDL Rule Name is: ' || l_ddl_rule_name);
 22
 23  end;
 24  /
DML Rule Name is: "STRMADMIN"."SCOTT131"
DDL Rule Name is: "STRMADMIN"."SCOTT132"
PL/SQL procedure successfully completed.
```

The view DBA_CAPTURE shows information about the capture process DBXA_CAP. Some of the columns of this view are listed here:

```
SQL> select queue_name,
  2            rule_set_name,
  3            first_scn,
  4            start_scn,
  5            status,
  6            capture_type type
  7    from dba_capture
  8   where capture_name = 'DBXA_CAP';
QUEUE_NAME      RULE_SET_NAME   FIRST_SCN   START_SCN  STATUS     TYPE
-------------   -------------   ---------   ---------- --------   ------
DBXA_CAP_Q      RULESET$_133    2323481     2323481    DISABLED   LOCAL
```

Automatically created rule set RULESET$_133 is associated with the capture process DBXA_CAP. The DML and DDL schema rules, SCOTT131 and SCOTT132, are defined within this rule set. The following query shows the system-created rules (the output is reformatted to fit the page):

```
SQL> select rule_name,
  2            rule_condition
  3    from dba_streams_rules
  4   where rule_set_name = 'RULESET$_133';
RULE_NAME
-----------------------------

RULE_CONDITION
--------------------------------------------------------------------------

SCOTT132
(((( (:ddl.get_object_owner() = 'SCOTT'
     or :ddl.get_base_table_owner() = 'SCOTT')
    and :ddl.is_null_tag() = 'Y'
    and :ddl.get_source_database_name() = 'DBXA.WORLD' ))
    and ( :ddl.get_compatible() < dbms_streams.max_compatible()))
SCOTT131
(((( (:dml.get_object_owner() = 'SCOTT')
    and :dml.is_null_tag() = 'Y'
    and :dml.get_source_database_name() = 'DBXA.WORLD' ))
    and ( :dml.get_compatible() < dbms_streams.max_compatible()))
```

During the creation of the capture process, the database alert log file of the source database will report messages similar to the following. The text of these messages could be different in earlier Oracle releases. These messages indicate that the LogMiner data dictionary has been extracted in the redo log for Streams. Subsequently, when the capture process is started, it will use this information to build the Streams data dictionary in the internal tables in the local database where it runs.

```
Logminer Bld: Build started
.....
Logminer Bld: Lockdown Complete.  DB_TXN_SCN is 0 6096099 LockdownSCN is 6096099
.....
Logminer Bld: Done
```

Also, the tables in the SCOTT schema will be prepared for instantiation, and supplemental logging of the key columns of these tables will also be configured.

Manual Capture Process Creation

You can manually create the capture process using the CREATE_CAPTURE procedure in the DBMS_CAPTURE_ADM package. The procedure simply creates the capture process as specified without performing any additional tasks for replication. This procedure is more flexible and allows you to create the capture process using existing rule sets and your choice of start SCN. On occasions when you must drop and re-create the capture process to capture changes from a particular SCN, you will need to use this procedure.

Table 4-2 shows the parameters of the CREATE_CAPTURE procedure.

Parameter Name	In/Out	Data Type
queue_name	IN	VARCHAR2
capture_name	IN	VARCHAR2
rule_set_name	IN	VARCHAR2 default NULL
start_scn	IN	NUMBER default NULL
source_database	IN	VARCHAR2 default NULL
use_database_link	IN	BOOLEAN default FALSE
first_scn	IN	NUMBER default NULL
logfile_assignment	IN	VARCHAR2 default 'implicit'
negative_rule_set_name	IN	VARCHAR2 default NULL
capture_user	IN	VARCHAR2 default NULL
checkpoint_retention_time	IN	NUMBER default 60

TABLE 4-2. *Parameters of CREATE_CAPTURE Procedure*

These parameters are described here:

- **queue_name**   Name of the queue into which the capture process enqueues LCRs. The queue name is required and the queue must already exist.

- **capture_name**   Name of the capture process without the owner name.

- **rule_set_name**   Name of the existing positive rule set name. If set to NULL and you do not specify `negative_rule_set_name`, the capture process will capture all supported changes for all objects in the database. If set to NULL and you specify `negative_rule_set_name`, then the capture process will capture changes not discarded by the negative rule set.

- **start_scn**   The SCN from which the capture process should start capturing changes.

- **source_database**   Global name of the source database from which the change to be captured originated.

- **use_database_link**   If FALSE, then either the capture process is a local capture or the downstream capture does not connect to the source database to perform internal tasks. If TRUE, then the downstream capture process connects to the source database to perform internal tasks.

- **first_scn**   The lowest SCN from which the capture process can read archived log files to capture changes. You specify a value for `first_scn` only if the source database data dictionary has been extracted in the redo log using the DBMS_STREAMS_ADM.BUILD procedure.

- **logfile_assignment**   Defaults to IMPLICIT, meaning the downstream capture process reads all redo log files copied manually or by the RFS from the source database to the downstream database. When set to EXPLICIT for the downstream capture process, you have to manually register the log files for the capture process. When set to EXPLICIT for a local capture, the capture process will not scan online redo log files to extract changes; it will only scan the archived log files.

- **negative_rule_set_name**   Name of the existing negative rule set. If set to NULL, then no negative rule set will be associated with the capture process. If a name is specified, then changes that satisfy the rule set will be discarded.

- **capture_user**   If left to NULL, the user running the procedure will be set as the capture user. Otherwise, the capture process will execute its tasks under the security domain of this user. The user must have proper privileges. Typically, this is the Streams Administrator user.

■ **checkpoint_retention_time** Specifies a number of days for which the capture process must keep the LogMiner checkpoint information before purging. Default is 60 days. Partial days can be specified to set such retention to hours, if needed. For example, specify .50 for a 12-hour retention. You can also specify DBMS_CAPTURE_ADM.INFINITE to suppress automatic purging of the checkpoint information.

The following example creates a local capture process called DBXA_CAP using the existing positive rule set RULESET$_250. The `first_scn` and `start_scn` parameters are assigned explicitly after confirming that there is data dictionary information available in the archived log file with FIRST_CHANGE# matching the `first_scn` value specified.

```
SQL> begin
  2    dbms_capture_adm.create_capture(
  3        queue_name        => 'DBXA_CAP_Q',
  4        capture_name      => 'DBXA_CAP',
  5        rule_set_name     => 'RULESET$_250',
  6        start_scn         => 2333429,
  7        source_database   => 'DBXA.WORLD',
  8        first_scn         => 2333429,
  9        checkpoint_retention_time => .50
 10    );
 11  end;
SQL> /
PL/SQL procedure successfully completed.
```

If we were to set `first_scn` and `start_scn` to NULL, then Oracle would extract the data dictionary in the redo log file prior to creating the capture process.

NOTE
The DBMS_CAPTURE_ADM package provides a number of other procedures to manage the capture process. They are discussed in Chapter 11.

Create the Downstream Capture Process

The downstream capture process must be created using the CREATE_CAPTURE procedure of the DBMS_CAPTURE_ADM package. You must also configure the source and the downstream database initialization parameters for the redo transport.

This section focuses only on the actual creation of the downstream capture process. Chapter 8 will discuss the configuration of redo transport for a fully functional replication environment using the downstream capture process.

The following example shows how to create the downstream capture process in the DBXB.WORLD database. It is assumed that the Streams queue is already created at the downstream database, and the database link from/to source/downstream database exists under the STRMADMIN schema.

```
SQL> connect strmadmin/strmadmin@DBXB.WORLD
Connected.
SQL> -- Create downstream capture process
SQL> begin
  2    dbms_capture_adm.create_capture (
  3      capture_name         => 'DBXA_CAP',
  4      queue_name           => 'DBXA_APP_Q',
  5      use_database_link => true,
  6      source_database      => 'DBXA.WORLD',
  7      checkpoint_retention_time => 2);
  8  end;
  9  /
PL/SQL procedure successfully completed.
```

In this example, we did not use `first_scn` and `start_scn` and specified the `use_database_link` parameter. This will trigger the extraction of the data dictionary into the redo log at the source database, and the corresponding SCN will be used for the `first_scn` and `start_scn` values for the capture process.

If the `use_database_link` parameter were set to NULL, then the data dictionary build would not have taken place automatically. In this case, before creating the capture process, we would need to build the data dictionary manually in the source database and acquire the corresponding SCN to set the `first_scn`, as shown here:

```
SQL> -- Acquire Data Dictionary build SCN from source database
SQL> connect strmadmin/strmadmin@DBXA.WORLD
Connected.
SQL> set serveroutput on
SQL> declare
  2      scn number;
  3  begin
  4      dbms_capture_adm.build(first_scn => scn);
  5      dbms_output.put_line('First SCN Value = ' || scn);
  6  end;
  7  /
First SCN Value = 13722837

PL/SQL procedure successfully completed.

SQL> -- Connect to Downstream Database
SQL> connect strmadmin/strmadmin@DBXB.WORLD
Connected.
SQL> -- Create downstream capture process.
SQL> -- Enter the First SCN obtained in the previous step.
```

```
SQL> begin
  2  dbms_capture_adm.create_capture (
  3      capture_name       => 'DBXA_CAP',
  4      queue_name         => 'DBXA_CAP_Q',
  5      use_database_link  => NULL,
  6      source_database    => 'DBXA.WORLD',
  7      first_scn          => &First_SCN_Value,
  8      checkpoint_retention_time => 2);
  9  end;
 10  /
Enter value for first_scn_value: 13722837
old    7:      first_scn          => &First_SCN_Value,
new    7:      first_scn          => 13722837,

PL/SQL procedure successfully completed.
```

We can now create capture rules for the downstream capture process using the appropriate ADD_SCHEMA_RULES or ADD_TABLE_RULES procedure of the DBMS_STREAMS_ADM package. If we do not create any capture rules, the capture process will capture all supported changes at the database level for all tables.

The DBA_CAPTURE view shows information about the capture process we just created. The CAPTURE_TYPE column will report DOWNSTREAM.

It is also possible to create the downstream capture process and Streams rules automatically using the MAINTAIN_GLOBAL, MAINTAIN_SCHEMAS, or MAINTAIN_TABLES procedure of the DBMS_STREAMS_ADM package. These procedures are discussed in Chapter 8.

Create the Synchronous Capture Process

The synchronous capture process can be created automatically in the source database using the ADD_TABLE_RULES or ADD_SUBSET_RULES procedure of the DBA_STREAMS_ADM package. When executing one of these procedures, Oracle creates the synchronous capture process, and creates required rules set and rules if they did not already exist. If it already existed, then Oracle adds rules to the existing rule set for the synchronous capture process.

The following example shows how to create the synchronous capture process using ADD_TABLE_RULES procedure. It is assumed that the Streams queue DBXA_S_CAP for the capture process has already been created. Notice the value SYNC_CAPTURE for the streams_type parameter.

```
SQL> conn strmadmin/strmadmin@DBXA.WORLD
Connected.
SQL> begin
  2  dbms_streams_adm.add_table_rules (
  3      table_name      => 'SCOTT.DEPT',
  4      streams_type    => 'SYNC_CAPTURE',
```

```
 5            streams_name    => 'DBXA_S_CAP',
 6            queue_name      => 'DBXA_S_CAP_Q',
 7            include_dml     => true,
 8            inclusion_rule  => true,
 9            source_database => 'DBXA.WORLD'
10          );
11   end;
12   /
PL/SQL procedure successfully completed.
```

The DBA_CAPTURE view will not display any information about the synchronous capture process. Instead, the view DBA_SYNC_CAPTURE shows information about the synchronous capture process.

```
SQL> select capture_name,
  2             queue_name,
  3             queue_owner,
  4             rule_set_name,
  5             rule_set_owner,
  6             capture_user
  7    from dba_sync_capture;
```

CAPTURE_NAME	QUEUE_NAME	QUEUE_OWNER	RULE_SET_NAME	RULE_SET_OWNER	CAPTURE_USER
DBXA_S_CAP	DBXA_S_CAP_Q	STRMADMIN	RULESET$_135	STRMADMIN	STRMADMIN

The synchronous capture process uses the persistent queue DBXA_S_CAP_Q to store captured LCRs on disk. It does not use the in-memory buffered queue.

The rule set, RULESET$_135, created in the previous example is the positive rule set for the synchronous capture. It will contain the DML rules for the SCOTT.DEPT table.

NOTE
The synchronous capture process can only capture DML changes, and can have only a positive rule set.

After its creation, the synchronous capture process is active automatically to begin capturing changes for the defined tables. We don't have to start it. We can query the DBA_SYNC_CAPTURE_TABLES view to see a list of tables for which synchronous capture has been enabled:

```
SQL> select table_owner,
  2             table_name,
  3             enabled
  4    from dba_sync_capture_tables;
```

TABLE_OWNER	TABLE_NAME	ENABLED
SCOTT	DEPT	YES

The synchronous capture process can be created explicitly using the CREATE_ SYNC_CAPTURE procedure of the DBMS_CAPTURE_ADM package:

```
SQL> begin
  2    dbms_capture_adm.create_sync_capture(
  3      capture_name    => 'DBXA_S_CAP',
  4      queue_name      => 'DBXA_S_CAP_Q',
  5      rule_set_name   => 'RULESET$_146'
  6    );
  7 end;
  8 /
PL/SQL procedure successfully completed.
```

The rule set must be present when creating the synchronous capture process. After creating the process, you can add rules to the rule set using the ADD_TABLE_ RULES or ADD_SUBSET_RULES procedure of the DBMS_STREAMS_ADM package.

NOTE
The synchronous capture process does not need LogMiner data dictionary and supplemental logging of key columns.

The Capture User

A capture user is a user under whose security domain the DML and DDL changes are captured by the capture process. The capture user also executes custom rule-based transformation, if defined. It must have proper privileges to perform these actions.

If you create the capture process explicitly using the CREATE_CAPTURE procedures in the DBMS_CAPTURE_ADM package, you can specify the capture user. But, if the capture process was created implicitly using the ADD_*_RULES or the MAINTAIN_* procedures of the DBMS_STREAMS_ADM package, then Oracle assigns the capture user as the user who executed the procedure, typically the Streams Administrator.

If you granted DBA privilege to the Streams Administrator user while creating it, and it is also your capture user, then it has all the required privileges. You do not have to grant any additional privileges.

It is very common practice to keep the Streams Administrator as the capture user. Although it is not a requirement, it does help keep Streams setup a bit simpler because you don't have to worry about yet another Oracle account with powerful privileges.

The current capture user name is listed in the CAPTURE_USER column of the DBA_CAPTURE view. Chapter 11 discusses how to change the capture user and grant required privileges.

Capture Process Components

Although you name the capture process when creating it, Oracle refers to it internally using an operating system process name of the form CP*xx*, where CP stands for capture and *xx* can contain numbers and letters. For our discussion in this section, let us assume that we have one capture process called CP01. By default, the CP01 process has three other slave processes, or components, operating in parallel, called the reader, preparer, and builder process, as shown in the Figure 4-3. The operating system names for these processes are MS00, MS02, and MS01, respectively. Together these processes perform the log-mining task and capture changes to replicate.

- **Reader process**   The capture process has one reader process. Its operating system name is MS00. The reader process reads the redo log and divides it into regions. The regions information is sent to the next process—the preparer.

- **Preparer process**   By default, each capture process has one preparer process with an operating system name MS02. The number of preparer processes is controlled by the capture process parameter, `parallelism`. If `parallelism` is set to more than 1, then additional preparer processes are created (MS03 and onward). The preparer process reads the redo information in parallel from regions defined by the reader. It sends some of the information from the changes to the rules engine for prefiltering and receives the result of prefiltering. Typically, prefiltering uses the schema and object name for the captured change. It sends the redo information and the result of the prefiltering to the builder process.

- **Builder process**   Each capture process has one builder process with an operating system name MS01. It receives the redo information from the preparer servers and merges it together, preserving the SCN order of the changes, and passes this information to the capture coordinator process CP01.

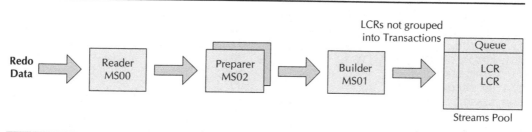

FIGURE 4-3.   *Capture process components*

The CP01 process then formats each change it received from the builder process into an LCR. If the prefiltering performed by the preparer process was conclusive, then the CP01 process discards the LCR. If the prefiltering was not conclusive, then the CP01 process sends the LCR to the rules engine for a full rule evaluation. The LCR gets discarded if the result of the full evaluation satisfies the available negative rule set or it does not satisfy the available positive rule set. If the result satisfies the available positive rule set, then the capture process enqueues the LCR into the capture queue. However, the capture process does not group these LCRs into transactions. The apply process does the grouping.

Capture Process Parameters

There are a number of parameters associated with the capture and synchronous capture processes. These parameters define and control their functionality. The parameters have default values. Generally you do not need to change these values. However, depending on your requirements and replication environment, you might be required to change the values of some of these parameters. The data dictionary view DBA_CAPTURE_PARAMETERS lists these parameters, as shown next for a local capture process. All values shown are default values. If you modify any of these parameters, then the SET_BY_USER column will contain YES, indicating that the default value was changed at least once.

```
SQL> select parameter,
  2          value,
  3          set_by_user
  4    from dba_capture_parameters
  5   where capture_name = 'DBXA_CAP'
  6   order by parameter;
```

PARAMETER	VALUE	SET_BY_USER
DISABLE_ON_LIMIT	N	NO
DOWNSTREAM_REAL_TIME_MINE	Y	NO
MAXIMUM_SCN	INFINITE	NO
MERGE_THRESHOLD	60	NO
MESSAGE_LIMIT	INFINITE	NO
MESSAGE_TRACKING_FREQUENCY	2000000	NO
PARALLELISM	1	NO
SKIP_AUTOFILTERED_TABLE_DDL	Y	NO
SPLIT_THRESHOLD	1800	NO
STARTUP_SECONDS	0	NO
TIME_LIMIT	INFINITE	NO
TRACE_LEVEL	0	NO
WRITE_ALERT_LOG	Y	NO

```
13 rows selected.
```

These parameters are described here:

- **DISABLE_ON_LIMIT**   This parameter works in conjunction with `time_limit` and `message_limit` parameters described later in this list. By default, it is set to N, meaning that the capture process is not disabled upon reaching the limit set by the `time_limit` or `message_limit` parameter. However, it will be stopped momentarily and restarted automatically. If the value of this parameter is set to Y, then the capture process will be disabled upon reaching the limit set by `time_limit` or `message_limit`, and will stay shut down until restarted manually.

- **DOWNSTREAM_REAL_TIME_MINE**   Used only in downstream capture process configuration. If set to Y, then the downstream capture process is real-time downstream capture and will mine the standby redo logs that receive redo log information from the source database. If set to N, then the capture process is an archived-log downstream capture process. The value defaults to Y for a local capture process and N for a downstream capture process. This parameter is ignored for a local capture process. It does not exist for a synchronous capture process and hence is not listed in the DBA_CAPTURE_PARAMETERS view for the synchronous capture process.

- **MAXIMUM_SCN**   The default value is INFINITE. If an SCN is specified instead, then the capture process is disabled right before capturing a change with an SCN greater than or equal to the specified SCN for this parameter. If set to INFINITE, the capture process will run irrespective of the SCN in the change record. Use of this parameter may be required when recapturing changes after performing data recovery operations at the source or destination database. Typically the default value is in effect.

- **MESSAGE_LIMIT**   When a number is specified for this parameter, then the capture process disables after capturing that many messages. However, it may restart automatically depending on the value set for the `disable_on_limit` parameter. The default is set to INFINITE, meaning the capture process will not be disabled based on the number of messages captured.

- **MERGE_THRESHOLD** and **SPLIT_THRESHOLD**   These parameters are effective only for the Split and Merge of the capture process when the capture process sends changes to multiple destinations and one or more of those destinations become unavailable. These parameters will be discussed in Chapter 11 along with the Split and Merge functionality.

- **MESSAGE_TRACKING_FREQUENCY**   By default, every 2,000,000th LCR is automatically tracked within the replication by the automatic message tracking mechanism. No messages will be tracked automatically if the value is set to 0. The automatically tracked information can be useful in troubleshooting of the capture process.

■ **PARALLELISM** This parameter controls the number of preparer servers that can concurrently mine the redo log for the capture process. By default, each capture process has one reader, one preparer, and one builder process. Together there are four such processes. Setting this parameter to, say, 4 will cause three additional parallel slave processes to start. When increasing the number of preparer servers by changing the value of this parameter, be sure to confirm that the PROCESSES and PARALLEL_MAX_SERVERS parameters are set sufficiently higher to allow for additional preparer servers for the capture process.

■ **SKIP_AUTOFILTERED_TABLE_DDL** Defaults to Y, and the process does not capture DDL changes to tables that are automatically filtered by the capture process. If set to N, then the capture process can capture DDL changes against such tables only if the DDL changes satisfy the capture process rule sets. The AUTO_FILTERED column in the DBA_STREAMS_UNSUPPORTED view shows which tables the capture process automatically filters out.

■ **STARTUP_SECONDS** Defaults to 0. This parameter works in conjunction with the `time_limit`, `message_limit`, and `disable_on_limit` parameters. It is specified in number of seconds. If `disable_on_limit` is set to N, then the capture process is restarted after it was shut down upon reaching the limits set by the `time_limit` or `message_limit` parameter. However, the capture process may take some time to shut down due its state when the shutdown was issued. This parameter is used to induce a delay in restarting it, if `disable_on_limit` was set to N. The default value of 0 indicates that the startup of the capture process will be issued immediately. If the value is set to INFINITE, then the capture process will not be automatically started.

■ **TIME_LIMIT** The capture process stops as soon as possible after the specified number of seconds since it started. If INFINITE, then the capture process continues to run until it is stopped explicitly. Depending on the value set for the `disable_on_limit` parameter, the capture process may start automatically.

■ **TRACE_LEVEL** Defaults to 0. Do not change the value of this parameter unless directed by Oracle Support. The parameter is used to generate trace information during troubleshooting of the capture process. The generated trace file will be in the trace directory along with the alert log file for the database.

■ **WRITE_ALERT_LOG** Defaults to Y, indicating that the capture process will write a message to the alert log file when it exits, including the reason why the process stopped. If set to N, then the writing to the alert log file is disabled.

NOTE
The DBA_CAPTURE_PARAMETERS view will list similar parameters with their default values for the synchronous capture process. However, the synchronous capture process does not use these.

In addition to these parameters, there are also a number of hidden parameters. The following query can be used to view these hidden parameters and their values. A value of 0 for USER_CHANGED_FLAG indicates that the default value is in effect. A value of 1 indicates that the default value for the parameter was changed at least once.

```
SQL> select p.name parameter,
  2          p.value,
  3          p.user_changed_flag,
  4          p.internal_flag
  5     from sys.streams$_process_params  p,
  6          sys.streams$_capture_process c
  7    where p.process# = c.capture#
  8      and c.capture_name  = 'DBXA_CAP'
  9      and p.name like '\_%' escape '\'
 10    order by parameter;
```

PARAMETER	VALUE	USER_CHANGED_FLAG	INTERNAL_FLAG
_ACK_INTERVAL	5	0	1
_APPLY_BUFFER_ENTRIES	10000	0	1
_APPLY_UNRESPONSIVE_SECS	300	0	1
_CHECKPOINTS_PER_DAY	4	0	1
_CHECKPOINT_FORCE	N	0	1
_CHECKPOINT_FREQUENCY	1000	0	1
_CKPT_FORCE_FREQ	1800	0	1
_CKPT_RETENTION_CHECK_FREQ	21600	0	1
_DIRECT_APPLY	AUTO	0	1
_DISABLE_PGAHC	N	0	1
_EXPOSE_UNSUPPORTED	NO	0	1
_FILTER_PARTIAL_ROLLBACK	AUTO	0	1
_FLUSH_TIMEOUT	2	0	1
_IGNORE_TRANSACTION		0	1
_IGNORE_UNSUPERR_TABLE		0	1
_LCR_CACHE_PURGE_PERIOD	604800	0	1
_LCR_CACHE_PURGE_RATIO	0	0	1
_LOGMINER_IDLE_READ_POLL_FREQ	0	0	1
_MIN_APPLY_BUFFER_ENTRIES	1000	0	1
_MIN_DAYS_KEEP_ALL_CKPTS	1	0	1
_SEND_STREAMS_DICTIONARY	0	0	1
_SGA_SIZE	10	0	1
_SKIP_LCR_FOR_ASSERT		0	1
_TURN_OFF_LIMIT_READ	N	0	1

```
24 rows selected.
```

You are not supposed to change these hidden parameters without the approval from Oracle Support. However, the _SGA_SIZE parameter can be changed under certain circumstances. It controls the amount of memory, from the Streams Pool size, that the LogMiner process can use. It is specified in megabytes and by default uses 10MB. You may have to increase this memory allocation if you receive an ORA-1341 or ORA-1280 error. Also note that Oracle allocates memory specified by this parameter to each of the preparer processes. So, the total memory allocated to LogMiner will be _SGA_SIZE times the `parallelism` set for the capture process.

Changing Capture Process Parameters

The procedure SET_PARAMETER in the DBMS_CAPTURE_ADM package allows you to change the value of the capture parameter. The SET_BY_USER column will indicate that the parameter was modified. In the following example, the `parallelism` of the capture process is changed to 2. Setting the value to NULL will restore the default value of the parameter.

```
SQL> begin
  2     dbms_capture_adm.set_parameter(
  3          capture_name => 'DBXA_CAP',
  4          parameter    => 'PARALLELISM',
  5          value        => '2'
  6     );
  7  end;
  8  /
PL/SQL procedure successfully completed.
-- Querying the DBA_CAPTURE_PARAMETERS view will show:
PARAMETER                        VALUE      SET_BY_USER
------------------------------   ---------  --------------

PARALLELISM                      2          YES
```

The SET_PARAMETER procedure is not allowed for the synchronous capture process. If you attempt to use it, you will receive an ORA-25338 error.

What Changes Are Not Captured?

Before you decide to use Streams replication, you must confirm that required changes could be captured by the capture process or synchronous capture process. You may have to deploy a workaround or other means to replicate data if you find that the objects contain unsupported data types or are subjected to unsupported replication operations, such as the TRUNCATE table command for synchronous capture process.

Neither the capture process nor the synchronous capture process captures any changes made to objects in SYS or SYSTEM or changes made to schemas for Oracle ConText Cartridge, Oracle Intelligent Agent, Oracle Data Miner, Oracle Database Vault, Oracle Rules Manager and Expression Filter, Oracle Label Security, Oracle

Spatial, OracleMultimedia, Oracle OLAP, Oracle interMedia, Oracle Time Series, Oracle Enterprise Manager, Oracle Workspace Manager, and SQL XML Manager. These schemas are listed here:

CTXSYS	DBSNMP	DMSYS
DVSYS	EXFSYS	LBACSYS
MDDATA	MDSYS	SI_INFORMTN_SCHEMA
OLAPSYS	ORDPLUGINS	ORDSYS
OUTLN	SYS	SYSMAN
SYSTEM	WMSYS	XDB

NOTE
Changes made to the SYS-owned table used for sequence number generation are not replicated.

The capture and synchronous capture processes will not capture changes made to temporary tables, object tables, or tables compressed with hybrid columnar compression. However, changes made to tables compressed with basic compression and OLTP table compression will be captured, if the compatibility level for the source and destination database is set to at least 11.2.0. In addition, they will not capture changes made to tables that use Oracle Label Security (OLS).

Changes Not Captured by the Capture Process

The capture process does not capture changes involving the following data types:

- ROWID
- BFILE
- User-defined types
- Varrays
- Nested tables
- XMLType (stored as other than CLOB)
- Oracle-supplied types: ANYTYPE, spatial types, media types

The capture process raises an ORA-26744 error and aborts when creating an LCR for a row with one of these unsupported data types. The contents for the attempted LCR creation will be written to the trace file of the process. You can modify the rule to ignore this change and restart the capture process.

However, you can still configure a capture process to address such issues by reviewing article 556742.1 available at the My Oracle Support (formerly MetaLink) website. It describes how to install the Extended Data Support (EDS) package procedure that will provide a workaround to enable support for the following data types:

■ Object column with simple object types

■ Object column with nested object types

■ Varrays

■ Spatial type SDO_GEOMETRY (requires Oracle Database patch 6868751)

■ XMLTypes

The capture process does not capture the following DDL changes:

■ ALTER DATABASE

■ CREATE CONTROLFILE

■ CREATE DATABASE

■ CREATE PFILE

■ CREATE SPFILE

The capture process captures and replicates the actual DDL statement and not the result of the DDL statement, except for the CREATE TABLE AS SELECT statement. In this case, the CREATE TABLE and the recursive INSERT statements will be replicated. In addition, the capture process ignores the following:

■ Changes to sequence values.

■ ALTER SESSION command.

■ SET ROLE command.

■ ALTER SYSTEM command.

■ Changes resulting from using online redefinition package DBMS_REDEFINITION for table or schema redefinition. If the logical structure of the table is not changed, then the capture process will capture changes for the table.

■ CALL, EXPLAIN PLAN, and LOCK TABLE statements.

Changes Not Captured by the Synchronous Capture Process

Unfortunately, the synchronous capture process has more restrictions than the capture process. First of all, synchronous capture can only use table rules. You cannot configure synchronous capture for the entire schema or the database. Synchronous capture ignores all DDL statements. Replication of only DML statement is possible.

The synchronous capture process can capture the following DML changes:

- INSERT

- UPDATE

- DELETE

- MERGE (each MERGE is changed into an INSERT or UPDATE change)

The synchronous capture process does not capture changes involving the following data types:

- ROWID

- BFILE

- User-defined types

- Varrays

- Nested tables

- XMLType

- Oracle-supplied types: ANYTYPE, spatial types, media types

Similar to the capture process, the synchronous capture process raises an ORA-26744 error and aborts when creating an LCR for a row with one of the unsupported data types. The contents for the attempted LCR creation will be written to the trace file of the process. You can modify the capture rule to ignore such a change. There is no Extended Datatype Support (EDS) for the synchronous capture process.

How to Check for Unsupported Objects

Oracle provides two data dictionary views to help you quickly find unsupported objects and the reason why they are unsupported. In fact, you should consult these views before you decide to replicate any objects.

The DBA_STREAMS_UNSUPPORTED and DBA_STREAMS_COLUMNS views provide sufficient information about unsupported objects. The following example shows sample output from the DBA_STREAMS_UNSUPPORTED view. In this example, the REASON shows why the table SCOTT.EMP_ROWID is not supported.

```
SQL> select owner, table_name, reason, auto_filtered
  2    from dba_streams_unsupported
  3   where owner = 'SCOTT';
OWNER    TABLE_NAME          REASON                         AUT
-------  ------------------  -----------------------------  ---
SCOTT    EMP_ROWID           unsupported column exists      NO
```

Note that the column TABLE_NAME in this view really means the object name. The view will list unsupported tables and indexes. In the previous example, the AUTO_FILTERED column (AUT) shows NO. This means that the capture process does not filter out (ignore) changes made to the table EMP_ROWID. To ignore changes made to such unsupported objects, and avoid errors in the capture process, you have to use a negative rule set, or modify the rule in the positive rule set. A value of YES in the AUTO_FILTERED column means that the capture process automatically ignores changes made to the unsupported objects, so there will be no need to use rules. Examples of automatically filtered objects are domain indexes, internal tables created by data pump, and so forth.

The view DBA_STREAMS_COLUMNS lists all columns of the tables from all the schemas, excluding the ones that are not supported by Streams. The view lists the Oracle version that supports the use of the columns for the synchronous capture process and the apply process. If the synchronous capture process supports a particular column, then the capture process also supports it.

```
SQL> select table_name,
  2          column_name "COL_NAME",
  3          sync_capture_version "S_CAP_VER",
  4          sync_capture_reason "S_CAP_REASON",
  5          apply_version "APP_VER",
  6          apply_reason "APP_REASON"
  7    from dba_streams_columns
  8   where owner = 'SCOTT'
  9     and table_name in ('DEPT','EMP_ROWID')
 10   order by table_name, column_name;
```

TABLE_NAME	COL_NAME	S_CAP_VER	S_CAP_REASON	APP_VER	APP_REASON
DEPT	DEPTNO	11.1		9.2	
DEPT	DNAME	11.1		9.2	
DEPT	LOC	11.1		9.2	
EMP_ROWID	EMPNO	11.1		9.2	
EMP_ROWID	ROW_ID		rowid column		rowid column

This example lists only the DEPT and EMP_ROWID tables from the DBA_STREAMS_COLUMNS view. All the columns of the DEPT table are listed. The columns for the reasons, S_CAP_REASON and APPLY_REASON, are blank for all these columns. This means that all these columns are supported columns in Streams. The S_CAP_VER and APP_VER columns show the Oracle version from which the support for the column starts. As you can see, the column ROW_ID in the EMP_ROWID table is defined with ROWID data type, which is not supported in Streams. If we defined the SCOTT.EMP_ROWID table in the capture process, the capture process would abort when trying to construct the LCR for a change against this table.

Reviewing the contents of the DBA_STREAMS_COLUMNS for not null SYNC_CAPTURE_REASON and not null APPLY_REASON will provide you with a list of columns that you cannot replicate.

NOLOGGING Operations

The discussion in this section pertains to the capture process and does not pertain to the synchronous capture process. The synchronous capture process does not use redo log information to capture changes to replicate.

Oracle Streams uses the LogMiner functionality to mine the redo information. This functionality is optimized to mine this information seamlessly from the redo log buffer, the redo logs, or the archived logs as required. Oracle must mine all the redo information to look for changes that must be captured for replication, and expects these changes to be present in the redo information.

The database must also be running in ARCHIVELOG mode so that the redo log switching will not overwrite redo information that may contain changes to be replicated. In fact, you cannot create a capture process in a database that is not running in ARCHIVELOG mode. You will get an ORA-258 error if you to try to do so.

Also, database changes that use the NOLOGGING or UNRECOVERABLE option to suppress generation of the redo information will not be replicated. If the change is not in the redo log (or archived log), the LogMiner process won't be able to find it. When replicating DML and DDL changes at the global (database) or schema level, you have to ensure that there are no NOLOGGING operations taking place. What if you have no control over what the application does with respect to LOGGING and NOLOGGING options? Can you still replicate the changes? Not unless you suppress the use of the NOLOGGING option in the SQL operation. In some situations, this may cause a performance issue because it defeats the purpose of not generating the redo information to complete the operation faster. In such cases, you will have to perform the SQL operation in the destination database to keep data in synchronization.

You can suppress the NOLOGGING operation by setting what is called the FORCE LOGGING mode for the database or for the tablespaces where the replicated objects reside. By default, the FORCE LOGGING mode for the database and tablespace is not set, meaning forced logging of changes is not in effect.

Depending on your requirements, you can choose to set FORCE LOGGING at the database level or the tablespace level. If all the tables you want to replicate reside only in a certain number of tablespaces, you may decide to set FORCE LOGGING at the tablespace level.

The following examples show how to set FORCE LOGGING mode for the database and tablespace, respectively:

```
SQL> alter database force logging;
Database altered.
SQL> alter tablespace data_1 force logging;
Tablespace altered.
```

The column FORCE_LOGGING in the V$DATABASE and DBA_TABLESPACES views will show the current logging mode for the database and tablespace, respectively.

By default, the DML operations against tables are logged, and the LOGGING mode at the table level is set to YES. If the FORCE LOGGING mode is not set at the database or tablespace level, it is a good idea to confirm that the LOGGING mode at the table is set to YES. You can check the column LOGGING in the DBA_TABLES view for the table. If it is set to NO, then DML operations in NOLOGGING mode can be performed against the table. You can set the LOGGING column to YES using the following SQL command:

```
SQL> col logging for a10
SQL> alter table scott.dept logging;
Table altered.
SQL> select logging
  2     from dba_tables
  3   where owner = 'SCOTT'
  4     and table_name = 'DEPT';
LOGGING
----------
YES
```

However, if the application uses the SQL*Loader utility to load data in the replicated tables using the DIRECT path option with the UNRECOVERABLE clause in its control file, Oracle will not generate redo information. The FORCE LOGGING mode at the database or tablespace level will not be of help in this case. So, to capture all the inserts performed by the SQL*Loader utility, you must not use the UNRECOVERABLE clause. If you must use it, then it is suggested that you run the SQL*Loader job in the destination database as well to avoid data mismatch and prevent apply errors.

In essence, proper logging of the database changes is a primary requirement for the implicit capture to replicate the changes.

Supplemental Logging

The discussion in this section pertains to the capture process and does not pertain to the synchronous capture process. The synchronous capture process does not need supplemental logging information.

In addition to proper logging of the database changes in the redo log, supplemental logging of the column data is also very important. The redo information contains the values for the columns that changed at the source database. This information may not always be sufficient to identify correctly the row in the destination table to apply the change. Supplemental logging is a process of recording additional column data into the redo log. It records the old values of these columns in the redo log in addition to the other changed information.

The capture process extracts this additional column data from the redo log into the LCRs. The apply process uses this additional information to properly apply the change to the destination database. Of course, supplemental logging will increase the amount of redo information generated for the same change. For this reason, supplemental logging needs to be carefully reviewed and configured.

What Needs Supplemental Logging

Typically, supplemental logging of the primary key columns for the table is required. If the table only has a unique index and no primary key, then supplemental logging of the unique index columns will be required. If the table does not have a primary key or unique index, then supplemental logging of all its columns, with the exception of columns of LOB and LONG data type, may be required. When replicating only a subset of table data using a DML condition, supplemental logging of the columns in the DML predicate will be required.

If you define conflict-handling procedures in your Streams environment, then supplemental logging of columns used in conflict detection will be required. This will guarantee their presence in the LCR to detect and resolve a conflict. Chapter 10 discusses conflict handling.

NOTE
Supplemental logging is always configured at the source database.

Types of Supplemental Logging

There are two types of supplemental logging: database-level supplemental logging, which is configured at the database level, and table-level supplemental logging, which is configured at the individual table level.

If you are replicating changes made to all qualified tables in the database, it is easier to configure database-level supplemental logging. If you are replicating changes made to selected tables, then using table-level supplemental logging is recommended.

Database-Level Supplemental Logging

Database-level supplemental logging can be configured for the primary key, unique index, bitmap index, or foreign key columns, or for all the columns of the tables except the ones with LOB, LONG, and LONG RAW data types. By default, supplemental logging of key columns is not configured at the database level. Only the minimal supplemental logging is configured. The LogMiner requires minimal supplemental logging at the database level to mine logging information for chained rows and index-organized tables.

The minimal supplemental logging is set to YES or IMPLICIT. By default, it is set to YES, but if you disable it and later add supplemental logging for primary key columns, unique index columns, foreign key columns, or all columns of the table, then it will be set to IMPLICIT. To disable minimal supplemental logging, you first need to disable all other supplemental logging at the database level.

The following example shows how to check for database supplemental logging:

```
SQL> select supplemental_log_data_min "MIN",
  2            supplemental_log_data_pk "PK",
  3            supplemental_log_data_ui "UI",
  4            supplemental_log_data_fk "FK",
  5            supplemental_log_data_all "ALL"
  6     from v$database;
MIN       PK  UI  FK  ALL
--------- --- --- --- ---
YES       NO  NO  NO  NO
```

The following examples show how to enable supplemental logging at the database level for various key columns. You may be required to enable supplemental logging of key columns at the database level when configuring Streams replication at the global (database) level.

```
SQL> alter database add supplemental log data (primary key) columns;
Database altered.
SQL> alter database add supplemental log data (foreign key) columns;
Database altered.
SQL> alter database add supplemental log data (unique index) columns;
Database altered.
SQL> alter database add supplemental log data (all) columns;
Database altered.
SQL> select supplemental_log_data_min "MIN",
  2            supplemental_log_data_pk "PK",
  3            supplemental_log_data_ui "UI",
  4            supplemental_log_data_fk "FK",
  5            supplemental_log_data_all "ALL"
  6     from v$database;
MIN       PK  UI  FK  ALL
--------- --- --- --- ---
YES       YES YES YES YES
```

You can also specify various key columns together in a single command to enable supplemental logging at the database level:

```
SQL> alter database add supplemental log data
  2        (primary key, unique index, foreign key) columns;
Database altered.
```

Table-Level Supplemental Logging

Using database-level supplemental logging when replicating only a select number of tables will cause the database to generate unnecessary redo information and waste resources. For this reason, it is recommended to configure supplemental logging at the table level in such cases.

There are two types of table-level supplemental logging. Each type creates a supplemental log group for the table. These supplemental log groups are: conditional and unconditional.

Conditional supplemental logging records the before image of all specified columns, or all the columns of the specified key, only when at least one of those columns is updated. This may potentially create a problem for the apply process when selecting the correct row to apply the change to because the LCR may not contain old values for all key columns.

Unconditional supplemental logging, on the other hand, will record the before image of all the specified columns, or all the columns of the specified key in the redo log, whether or not any of those columns changed. Even if some other columns of the row are changed, the defined columns for supplemental logging will be recorded in the redo log. This ensures that the LCR always contains old values for all key columns. Sometimes, this is called "always logging."

Conditional Supplemental Logging   The following examples show how to create a conditional supplemental log group. In this example, the EMP table in the SCOTT schema has a unique index and a foreign key constraint.

```
SQL> alter table scott.emp add supplemental log data
  2        (unique, foreign key) columns;
Table altered.
```

To list the defined supplemental log groups, we query the DBA_LOG_GROUPS table:

```
SQL> select table_name,
  2           log_group_name,
  3           log_group_type,
  4           always,
  5           generated
  6     from dba_log_groups
  7    where owner='SCOTT';
```

```
TABLE_NAME   LOG_GROUP_NAME   LOG_GROUP_TYPE        ALWAYS       GENERATED
-----------  ---------------  --------------------  -----------  --------------
EMP          SYS_C006447      UNIQUE KEY LOGGING    CONDITIONAL  GENERATED NAME
EMP          SYS_C006448      FOREIGN KEY LOGGING   CONDITIONAL  GENERATED NAME
```

There are two supplemental groups created: one for the unique key columns logging and other for the foreign key columns logging. As indicated by the ALWAYS column, these are conditional supplemental log groups.

NOTE
The ADD SUPPLEMENTAL LOG DATA option of the ALTER TABLE command will always create an unconditional log group when used for primary key columns.

The following example shows how to create a conditional supplemental log group for a specific set of columns. Notice the change in the syntax for the ALTER TABLE command. The log group name must be specified.

```
SQL> alter table scott.emp
  2    add supplemental log group slg_emp (empno, sal);
Table altered.
```

Querying the DBA_LOG_GROUPS view shows the following. The log group type is user defined and the log group name is what was used in the previous command.

```
TABLE_NAME   LOG_GROUP_NAME   LOG_GROUP_TYPE        ALWAYS       GENERATED
-----------  ---------------  --------------------  -----------  --------------
EMP          SLG_EMP          USER LOG GROUP        CONDITIONAL  USER NAME
```

Unconditional Supplemental Logging   By default, the supplemental logging for the primary key columns is unconditional. The following example shows how to configure the supplemental logging for the primary key columns:

```
SQL> alter table scott.emp
  2    add supplemental log data (primary key) columns;
Table altered.
```

The DBA_LOG_GROUPS view will show the following. The contents of the ALWAYS column shows that it is an unconditional log group.

```
TABLE_NAME   LOG_GROUP_NAME   LOG_GROUP_TYPE        ALWAYS       GENERATED
-----------  ---------------  --------------------  -----------  --------------
EMP          SYS_C006451      PRIMARY KEY LOGGING   ALWAYS       GENERATED NAME
```

When the table does not have a primary key, then you can create an unconditional supplemental log group for the unique index columns, as shown next. Assume that the

EMPNO column is the only column in the unique index. Notice the use of the ALWAYS keyword in the command to create an unconditional supplemental log group.

```
SQL> alter table scott.emp
  2    add supplemental log group slg_emp (empno) always;
Table altered.
```

The DBA_LOG_GROUPS view shows the following. Notice the contents of the ALWAYS column.

TABLE_NAME	LOG_GROUP_NAME	LOG_GROUP_TYPE	ALWAYS	GENERATED
EMP	SLG_EMP	USER LOG GROUP	ALWAYS	USER NAME

If the table does not have any primary key or unique index columns, then you can create an unconditional supplemental log group for all its columns except the columns with LOB, LONG, and LONG RAW data types:

```
SQL> alter table scott.emp
  2    add supplemental log data (all) columns;
Table altered.
```

System-Created Supplemental Log Groups

The procedures ADD_GLOBAL_RULES, ADD_TABLE_RULES, ADD_SCHEMA_RULES, ADD_SUBSET_RULES, and MAINTAIN_* in the DBMS_STREAMS_ADM package create supplemental log groups for the primary key, unique index, bitmap index, and foreign key columns by default when adding rules to the capture process. The supplemental logging for the primary key columns is unconditional, while it is conditional for the unique index, bitmap index, and foreign key columns. When a table has a primary key, then the automatically created supplemental log group is adequate and sufficient. However, if the table does not have a primary key, then you must review and re-create the unconditional supplemental logging for all the required columns to avoid potential apply errors.

NOTE
Improper supplemental logging can cause the apply process to report ORA-26787 and ORA-1403 errors.

Disabling Supplemental Logging

The following example shows how to disable supplemental logging at the database level for the primary key columns:

```
SQL> alter database
  2    drop supplemental log data (primary key) columns;
Database altered.
```

Change `primary key` to `unique index`, `foreign key`, or `all` to disable logging of the relevant columns. The following command will drop the minimum supplemental logging at the database level:

```
SQL> alter database
  2    drop supplemental log data;
Database altered.
```

The following query shows that there is no supplemental logging configured at the database level:

```
SQL> select supplemental_log_data_min "MIN",
  2             supplemental_log_data_pk "PK",
  3             supplemental_log_data_ui "UI",
  4             supplemental_log_data_fk "FK",
  5             supplemental_log_data_all "ALL"
  6  from v$database;

MIN        PK  UI  FK  ALL
--------   --- --- --- ---
NO         NO  NO  NO  NO
```

The following example shows how to disable the table-level supplemental log group called SLG_EMP created earlier. The command will drop the user-created supplemental log group.

```
SQL>  alter table scott.emp
  2     drop supplemental log group slg_emp;
Table altered.
```

To disable table-level supplemental logging for the primary key, unique index, and foreign key columns and all columns of the table, you can use the following commands. The commands will drop the system-created supplemental log groups. Change `primary key` to `unique index`, `foreign key`, or `all` to disable logging of the relevant columns.

```
alter table scott.emp
   drop supplemental log data (primary key) columns;
```

Summary

This chapter introduced you to the types of capture processes and how to create these processes. Depending on your requirements, you can create the capture process automatically along with the capture rules and rule set, or you can use an existing rule set when creating the capture process manually. The downstream capture process needs to be created before you can add rules to it. The downstream capture process can mine archived log files copied from the source database, or it can read a copy of the online redo logs, or standby redo logs, from the source database in real time.

When active, the capture process performs internal housekeeping activity to record various SCNs. When the capture process is stopped and restarted, it uses these SCNs to resume log mining for capturing changes from the correct position in the log file to guarantee no data loss.

Oracle-supplied packages DBMS_STREAMS_ADM and DBMS_CAPTURE_ADM contain procedures that can automatically and manually, respectively, create the capture process or the synchronous capture process. The Streams queue must be created before you can create a capture or synchronous capture process. The views DBA_CAPTURE and DBA_SYNC_CAPTURE provide information about and the status of the capture process and the synchronous capture process, respectively.

The synchronous capture process is always created on the source database, and is enabled and active as soon as it is created. It uses a persistent disk queue to enqueue LCRs. You should use the synchronous capture process only for tables with low DML activity, or when changes can't be captured from the redo logs. It cannot be used to capture DDL changes. It is possible to create the synchronous capture process when the database is operating in NOARCHIVELOG mode or when Oracle Standard Edition is used for the source database.

The capture process has at least three slave processes that scan and capture changes from the redo log. The reader process reads the redo logs and divides those into regions for the preparer process to scan and prefilter the changes based on capture rules. The builder process merges the information from the preparer process and passes it to the capture process for reformatting into LCRS and full rule evaluation. Based on the rule evaluation result, the capture process will either discard the LCR or enqueue it into the capture queue.

To be able to capture the change from the redo log, the change must be recorded in the redo log. For the replicated tables, you must not allow NOLOGGING operations. In addition, the redo information must contain all identifying columns for the rows. Otherwise, the apply process may not correctly identify the row to which to apply changes. Proper supplemental logging of the key columns at the source database is crucial. When adding rules to the capture process, Oracle automatically configures unconditional supplemental logging for primary key columns of the table. You may have to manually configure supplemental logging when tables do not have a primary key. Synchronous capture does not need supplemental logging of key columns.

There are certain data types and certain DML/DDL operations that can't be captured for replication. The view DBA_STREAMS_UNSUPPORTED lists the tables that cannot be replicated and provides the reason why they can't be replicated. You should consult this view to confirm that the table you want to replicate is not listed in this view.

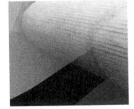

CHAPTER
5

Staging and
Propagation Process

s described in Chapter 4, once the capture or synchronous capture process captures the changes that satisfy the capture rules, those changes are converted into LCRs and stored in queues. The queue is an abstract storage unit used by the Oracle messaging system. These changes are also referred to as messages. Storing these messages in the queue is called staging.

Propagation is the process of copying the contents of the source queue to the destination queue. The messages staged in the queue can be propagated to another queue in the same database, to another queue in a different database running on the same server, or to another queue in a different database running on a remote server, where it will be consumed, or read, by the client process. The propagation process uses a database link over Oracle Net to propagate messages to remote queues. The Oracle client process running in the same database as the queue itself can also consume the messages. In this case, there is no need to propagate the messages to another queue.

Although there are various types of queues available in Oracle Database 11g, only certain types of queues are supported by Oracle Streams.

This chapter discusses how Oracle Streams uses queues to stage messages and how the messages are propagated from the source queue to destination queues.

Queue Models

Oracle Streams Advance Queuing (AQ) supports two queue models—point-to-point and publish/subscribe. A point-to-point queue is also known as a single-consumer queue. The message producer and consumer use a common queue to exchange messages. The producer enqueues a message to the queue and the consumer dequeues it. The message in a point-to-point or single-consumer queue can be dequeued only once from the queue.

Publish/subscribe queues are also known as multiconsumer queues because the message is intended to reach multiple targets. In other words, this type of queue is used to broadcast a message to multiple clients. The message producer enqueues the message to the queue. The message stays in the queue until it is dequeued by each message consumer. The applications or consumers that want to receive the message have to subscribe to the queue to receive the message. Oracle Streams AQ keeps track of the subscribers and notifies each one when the message is ready in the queue to be dequeued. These queues support rules for delivery to consumers.

Queue Types

Oracle Database 11*g* Streams supports the following types of queues:

- Typed queue of ANYDATA type
- Buffered queue
- Persistent queue
- Secure queue
- Transactional queue
- Nontransactional queue
- Commit-time queue

Typed Queue of ANYDATA Type

A typed queue is a queue in which only the messages of a certain data type can be staged. The Streams queue is a typed queue that accepts messages of type ANYDATA. Oracle Streams clients always use ANYDATA queues. The LCRs are wrapped into an ANYDATA object and staged into the queue. It is easy to wrap data of other types into ANYDATA object and, as such, stage them in ANYDATA queue. Internally, Oracle Streams uses the `ANYDATA.convert<data_type>` static functions to convert the LCRs into ANYDATA type.

Buffered Queue

This type of queue is created in the Oracle system global area (SGA). The Streams pool in the SGA contains buffered queues. The capture process enqueues, or stages, the LCRs in the buffered queue. These are referred to as captured LCRs. The buffered queue offers better performance, as messages are readily available in the memory for consumption. However, it does not support some of the messaging features, such as message retention after consumption. Once the message is dequeued from the queue, it is not available. Since the buffered queue is a memory-resident queue, the information in the queue can be lost if the instance containing this queue shuts down normally or abnormally. The number of messages that can be queued in the buffered queue depends on the size of the buffered queue. By default, the queue requires a minimum of 10MB of memory. Generally the memory allocated to the Streams pool is much larger than this default. But, if there is not enough memory to hold all the messages, then the messages are spilled from memory into the queue table on the disk. The queue table on the disk acts as an overflow container for the buffered queues.

Persistent Queue

This type of queue is created using a queue table. Messages are always stored on the disk in the queue table. The messages persist in the queue table on disk until the Streams client consumes them. Once consumed, the message is removed from the queue table. The LCRs in this queue are referred to as persistent LCRs.

The synchronous capture process always enqueues LCRs in a persistent queue; it does not use a buffered queue.

Secure Queue

This type of queue allows dequeue and enqueue operations to only registered users of the queue. By default, only the owner of the queue can perform such operations. In Oracle Streams, secure queues ensure that only authorized users and Streams clients can enqueue and dequeue messages. When you create a Streams client (capture, synchronous capture, or apply process), an Oracle Streams AQ agent of the queue associated with the Streams client is created automatically, and the user, typically the Streams Administrator, who runs the process, is specified as the secure queue user. In this way, the capture process is automatically configured to enqueue LCRs into its secure queue, and the apply process is automatically configured to dequeue LCRs from its own secure queue. The secure queue can be a buffered queue or a persistent queue.

Transactional Queue

The transactional queue is a queue where messages can be grouped together as a set that is applied by the apply process as a single transaction. For captured LCRs, the apply process applies the set of these messages to the destination objects while preserving the original source transaction. For persistent LCRs, the apply process can apply a user-defined group of messages as a single transaction. The messages can be grouped together in a user-defined sequence.

Nontransactional Queue

Unlike the transactional queue, the messages in the nontransactional queue are not grouped together as a set. Instead, each individual message is considered a separate transaction. For captured LCRs, the apply process preserves the original source transaction. For persistent LCRs, the apply process issues a COMMIT after applying each message.

Commit-Time Queue

The messages in the persistent queue are grouped in a particular order. The order is determined by the queue table property when creating the queue table. The messages can be ordered by their priority, enqueue time, approximate commit time, or a combination of these. The queues that order the messages by the approximate commit-time SCN are called commit-time queues. This SCN is acquired when the transaction commits.

How Streams Clients Use Queues

Here is how various Oracle Streams clients use the queues:

- **Capture process**   Creates LCRs and enqueues them into the buffered queues. These captured LCRs can only be dequeued by another Streams client, such as propagation and apply processes. Any other external application process or a user cannot dequeue these captured LCRs from the queue.

- **Synchronous capture process**   Creates LCRs and enqueues them only in the persistent queues. These LCRs can be dequeued by other Streams clients, messaging clients, applications, and other user applications.

- **Propagation process**   Propagates any message from the buffered queue as well as the persistent queue. The message is propagated from the source queue in the source database to one or more destination queues in the same or different databases.

- **Apply process**   Can dequeue messages from the buffered queue as well as the persistent queue. A single apply process can dequeue messages from either a buffered queue or a persistent queue, but not from both queues. To dequeue LCRs queued by the capture process, the apply process must be configured with the `apply_captured` parameter set to TRUE. To dequeue LCRs from a persistent queue, the apply process must be configured with the `apply_captured` parameter set to FALSE. The latter setting is required when using the synchronous capture process.

Creating a Streams Queue

The supplied DBMS_STREAMS_ADM package provides a procedure called SET_UP_QUEUE. This procedure, generally executed as the Streams Administrator, performs several tasks internally to create the queue with the proper queue type, create several internal supporting queue tables, and grant proper privileges to the queue user etc. Using this procedure to create the queue for Streams clients is recommended. It is possible to create queues, queue tables and grant privileges to queue users using several procedures available in the DBMS_AQADM package. However, the SET_UP_QUEUE procedure makes this job much easier, so this chapter only discusses this procedure.

Parameter	Description	Default
queue_table	Name of queue table; can be specified as `schema.queue_table`	STREAMS_QUEUE_TABLE
storage_clause	Any valid storage clause for the queue table	Executing user's default tablespace
queue_name	Name of queue; can be specified as `schema.queue_name`	STREAMS_QUEUE
queue_user	Name of user who can enqueue and dequeue messages from the queue	Executing user
comment	Comment for the queue	NULL

TABLE 5-1. *Parameters of the SET_UP_QUEUE Procedure*

Table 5-1 lists the parameters of the SET_UP_QUEUE procedure and their default values. All are of VARCHAR2 data type and are input parameters.

The following example demonstrates the use of the SET_UP_QUEUE procedure to create a queue called DBXA_CAP_Q to enqueue changes captured in the DBXA database:

```
SQL> conn strmadmin/strmadmin@DBXA.WORLD
Connected.
SQL> begin
  2    dbms_streams_adm.set_up_queue(
  3        queue_table     => 'DBXA_CAP_Q_T',
  4        storage_clause  => 'TABLESPACE STREAMS_TBS',
  5        queue_name      => 'DBXA_CAP_Q',
  6        queue_user      => 'STRMADMIN',
  7        comment         => 'Queue for Capture Process'
  8     );
  9  end;
 10  /

PL/SQL procedure successfully completed.
```

NOTE
The queue name and queue table name must have fewer than 25 characters.

The previous example created a queue called DBXA_CAP_Q that uses the queue table called DBXA_CAP_Q_T that resides in the STREAMS_TBS tablespace. The queue owner is STRMADMIN. The comment states that it is a queue for the capture process. The procedure was executed as the Streams Administrator called STRMADMIN.

Let's see which objects this procedure created under the STRMADMIN schema:

```
SQL> select table_name,
  2         tablespace_name,
  3         iot_type
  4    from tabs
  5   where table_name like '%DBXA%';


TABLE_NAME               TABLESPACE_NAME IOT_TYPE
------------------------ --------------- ------------
DBXA_CAP_Q_T             STREAMS_TBS
AQ$_DBXA_CAP_Q_T_S       STREAMS_TBS
AQ$_DBXA_CAP_Q_T_L       STREAMS_TBS
AQ$_DBXA_CAP_Q_T_P       STREAMS_TBS
AQ$_DBXA_CAP_Q_T_C                       IOT
AQ$_DBXA_CAP_Q_T_D                       IOT
AQ$_DBXA_CAP_Q_T_G                       IOT
AQ$_DBXA_CAP_Q_T_H                       IOT
AQ$_DBXA_CAP_Q_T_I                       IOT
AQ$_DBXA_CAP_Q_T_T                       IOT

10 rows selected.
```

Only the queue table DBXA_CAP_Q_T to be created in the STREAMS_TBS tablespace was provided, but the procedures created a number of internal tables, most with index organization. These are required for managing the queue and its contents in the event the queue overflows—recall that the queue is a buffered queue in the Streams pool in the SGA. Notice that these internal tables contain six new characters in the name that was provided. Because the overall length should not exceed 30 characters, you must name your queue and queue table with fewer than 25 characters. If not, you will get the following ORA errors:

```
-- If the name you provided has more than 30 characters:
ORA-04043: object QUEUE_TABLE_NAME_MORE_THAN_30_CHARACTERS does not exist
ORA-00972: identifier is too long
-- If the name you provided has > 24 but < 31 characters
ORA-24019: identifier for QUEUE_TABLE too long, should not be greater than 24 characters
```

In addition to these tables, the procedure also created a buffered queue, and an exception queue to store messages that caused any errors. Both queues are associated with the single queue table. The DBA_QUEUES view shows information about the queues. The following example lists a few columns from this view:

```
SQL> select name,
  2          queue_table,
  3          queue_type,
  4          user_comment
  5    from dba_queues
  6   where name like '%DBXA_CAP_Q%';
NAME                   QUEUE_TABLE    QUEUE_TYPE        USER_COMMENT
-------------------    -------------  ----------------  ------------------------
DBXA_CAP_Q             DBXA_CAP_Q_T   NORMAL_QUEUE      Queue for Capture Process
AQ$_DBXA_CAP_Q_T_E     DBXA_CAP_Q_T   EXCEPTION_QUEUE   exception queue
```

The data dictionary view DBA_QUEUE_TABLES describes the queues associated with the queue table, as shown here:

```
SQL> select queue_table,
  2          object_type,
  3          sort_order,
  4          message_grouping,
  5          secure
  6    from dba_queue_tables
  7   where owner = 'STRMADMIN';
QUEUE_TABLE    OBJECT_TYPE    SORT_ORDER    MESSAGE_GROUP SEC
-------------  -------------  ------------  ------------- ---
DBXA_CAP_Q_T   SYS.ANYDATA    COMMIT_TIME   TRANSACTIONAL YES
```

This output shows that the queue table contains queues of type SYS.ANYDATA, the SORT_ORDER of messages stored in the queue is COMMIT_TIME, and the MESSAGE_GROUPING is TRANSACTIONAL. This means that messages (LCRs) in the queue are grouped in a set to be applied by the apply process as one transaction when it receives that commit SCN. The NONTRANSACTIONAL grouping causes the apply process to apply a single message (LCR) as a single transaction. Also, the queue associated with the queue table is a secure queue as indicated by YES in the SEC column. This means that the owner of the queue can perform the enqueue and dequeue operations on the queue. Other users must have proper privileges to perform these operations.

Queues and Real Application Clusters

When you create the queue in an instance of the database, the instance assumes the ownership of the associated queue table. The capture and apply processes run in the instance that owns the queue table associated with their respective queues. This is not of any concern in single-instance databases. However, in RAC environments, it is possible to specify the ownership of the queue table. You can specify the primary instance and secondary instance for a given queue table. The primary instance becomes the default owner of the queue table and runs the Streams processes that use this queue table. When the primary instance becomes unavailable, the secondary instance assumes the ownership of the queue, and the Streams processes are restarted on the secondary instance automatically. When the primary instance becomes available, the queue ownership and the Streams processes switch back to the primary instance.

In a RAC environment with more than two nodes, if both the primary and secondary instances become unavailable at the same time, Oracle automatically switches the queue ownership and the Streams processes to the next available instance that responds first.

You can use the ALTER_QUEUE_TABLE procedure in the DBMS_AQADM package to define the primary and secondary instances for the queue table. In the following example, the queue table is owned by instance 2 as its primary instance and instance 3 as its secondary instance:

```
SQL> begin
  2    dbms_aqadm.alter_queue_table (
  3      queue_table        => 'DBXA_CAP_Q_T',
  4      primary_instance   => 2,
  5      secondary_instance => 3);
  6  end;
  7  /
PL/SQL procedure successfully completed.
```

The view DBA_QUEUE_TABLES shows information about the queue table ownership and its current owner instance:

```
SQL> select queue_table,
  2         owner_instance,
  3         primary_instance,
  4         secondary_instance
  5    from dba_queue_tables
  6   where owner = 'STRMADMIN';
```

QUEUE_TABLE	OWNER_INSTANCE	PRIMARY_INSTANCE	SECONDARY_INSTANCE
DBXA_CAP_Q_T	2	2	3

Propagation

In Oracle Streams, the changes, or messages, are pushed from the source queue to the destination queue. Streams clients do not pull these messages. When the messages are staged in the source queue, a process called the propagation process sends, or pushes, these changes to the destination queue. For a given source queue, there could be multiple destination queues, and for a single destination queue, there could be multiple source queues. A single queue can be a destination queue for one or more propagations and a source queue for other propagations.

Rules can be defined for the propagation process to propagate or discard messages. The rules can be in a positive rule set or a negative rule set. If the propagation process must propagate all messages from the source queue to the destination queue, you do not need any rule set attached to the propagation. Rules can be defined at the global (database) level, schema level, or table level. At the table level, subset rules can be defined that satisfy a certain DML condition to replicate only a portion of a given table.

The propagation is performed by a *propagation job*, which uses the Oracle Scheduler interface. The propagation job is automatically created when you configure the propagation process during Streams replication setup. The job will be owned by SYS irrespective of who created that job.

The propagation component consists of two internal processes: the propagation sender process at the source database, and the propagation receiver process at the destination database. The propagation sender process dequeues the LCRs that satisfy the rules defined for the propagation, and sends these LCRs over Oracle Net to the propagation receiver process. Upon receiving these LCRs over the network, the propagation receiver process enqueues them to the destination queue. From there the LCRs are dequeued by the apply process. The dynamic performance views V$PROPAGATION_SENDER and V$PROPAGATION_RECEIVER display information about the source and destination queues, including the statistics about the message propagation between them.

When creating the propagation process, you can define either of two ways in which the propagation takes place from the source queue to the destination queue: queue-to-database link propagation or queue-to-queue propagation.

Queue-to-Database Link Propagation

When creating the propagation, if you set the `queue_to_queue` parameter to FALSE, Oracle creates the propagation process using the source queue name and the destination database link name. The created propagation job and job schedule can be shared by multiple propagations that use the same database link and same source queue. Since all such propagations share the same schedule, any change in the schedule for one of the propagations affects all other propagations.

Queue-to-database link propagation does not support automatic failover in a RAC environment. If the destination instance with the queue becomes unavailable, the propagation fails. It is recommended that you do not use queue-to-database link propagation in a RAC environment.

Queue-to-Queue Propagation

When creating the propagation, if you set the `queue_to_queue` parameter to TRUE or leave it at its default value of NULL, Oracle defines the propagation process using the source queue name and the destination queue name. The created propagation job will be exclusively used by this propagation process to propagate messages from the source queue to the destination queue. Even if there are multiple queue-to-queue propagations, their propagation jobs and schedules can be managed separately. These propagations can still share the same database link name. However, the database link must be created using the service name specified as the global name of the destination database.

Queue-to-queue propagation supports automatic failover in a RAC environment. When the destination instance with the queue becomes unavailable, the propagation continues with another running instance.

Directed Networks

In a typical Streams replication environment, the propagation takes place directly between the source queue on the source database and the destination queue on the destination database. What if the destination database is not on the same network as the source database? What if the same change must be sent to multiple destinations? In such situations, the message can be routed through a number of queues, or staging areas in the intermediate databases, before reaching the destination database. In Oracle Streams environment, such routing is referred to as directed networks.

Directed networks are useful when there is no direct network connection between the source database and destination database, but an intermediate database can connect to both these databases. In this way, you can configure Streams replication without modifying your existing network. When sending the same change to multiple destinations, you can direct the change through one or more intermediate staging areas to reduce the network traffic between the source and all these destinations.

Depending on what the intermediate database does with messages, there are two types of directed networks: queue forwarding and apply forwarding.

Queue Forwarding

The directed network is of queue forwarding type when the intermediate database simply forwards the messages from its source queue to the next staging area. The next staging area can be another intermediate database or the final destination database. The source database for this message is still the database where the message originated, or where the database change took place. The intermediate databases never become the source for the message. This is important when configuring propagation process at these intermediate databases and the apply process at the final destination. Figure 5-1 shows queue forwarding. The database DBXA sends changes to the intermediate database DBXC, which simply forwards those to the DBXB database where the changes will be applied.

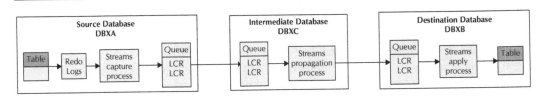

FIGURE 5-1. *Directed networks: queue forwarding*

Apply Forwarding

In this type of directed network, the message is applied at the intermediate database by an apply process. It is then recaptured by the local capture process and forwarded to the next intermediate database, or the destination database. The intermediate database becomes the source database of the message for the next staging area. Since the messages are applied and recaptured by the intermediate database, the local conflict handlers, apply handlers, or apply rule transformations can change the message depending on your requirements. Also, configuring apply forwarding requires proper setting of the Streams tag field. When messages or LCRs are applied, the apply process sets a default tag field in the redo records. The rules for the capture process must allow for such tagged changes to be captured. Figure 5-2 shows apply forwarding where the changes from DBXA are applied and recaptured at DBXC and forwarded to DBXB.

Creating the Propagation Process

The propagation process can be created automatically using procedures in the DBMS_STREAMS_ADM package, or it can be created manually using a procedure in the DBMS_PROPAGATION_ADM package.

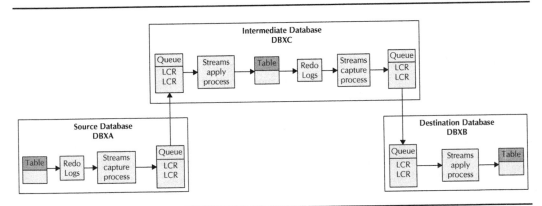

FIGURE 5-2. *Directed networks: apply forwarding*

Automatic Propagation Process Creation

The following procedures in the DBMS_STREAMS_ADM package can create the propagation process automatically if the specified propagation does not exist. Using one of these procedures to create propagation process is relatively very simple. These procedures perform additional tasks behind the scenes that are necessary for Streams replication.

- ADD_TABLE_PROPAGATION_RULES

- ADD_SCHEMA_PROPAGATION_RULES

- ADD_GLOBAL_PROPAGATION_RULES

- ADD_SUBSET_PROPAGATION_RULES

- MAINTAIN_* procedures

NOTE
The MAINTAIN_* procedures are discussed in detail in Chapter 8.

When you create the propagation process using any of these procedures other than the MAINTAIN_* procedures, you must create the Streams queue if it does not exist. In addition, you must create a database link between the database that contains the source queue and the database that contains the destination queue. If the destination queue is in the same database, then the database link is not required.

These procedures have slight variations in their input parameters to generate global, schema, table, or subset rules for the propagation process. The procedures are overloaded, and one version offers output parameters that contain the names of the generated rules. These procedures perform the following tasks:

1. Create the specified propagation process, if it does not exist, and create a propagation job.

2. Create a rule set with a system-created name. The rule set can be positive or negative depending on the option selected.

3. Depending on the procedure used, add table, schema, or global rules or the subset rule for the table to the rule set for the propagation. The rule names are system created.

This section next discusses the ADD_SCHEMA_PROPAGATION_RULES procedure in detail to show how it creates the propagation process, rule set, rules, and propagation job.

Parameter	In/Out	Data Type
schema_name	IN	VARCHAR2
streams_name	IN	VARCHAR2 default NULL
source_queue_name	IN	VARCHAR2
destination_queue_name	IN	VARCHAR2
include_dml	IN	BOOLEAN default TRUE
include_ddl	IN	BOOLEAN default FALSE
include_tagged_lcr	IN	BOOLEAN default FALSE
source_database	IN	VARCHAR2 default NULL
dml_rule_name	OUT	VARCHAR2
ddl_rule_name	OUT	VARCHAR2
inclusion_rule	IN	BOOLEAN default TRUE
and_condition	IN	VARCHAR2 default NULL
queue_to_queue	IN	BOOLEAN default NULL

TABLE 5-2. *Parameters of ADD_SCHEMA_PROPAGATION_RULES Procedure*

The parameters of the overloaded ADD_SCHEMA_PROPAGATION_RULES procedure are listed in Table 5-2. Note the two OUT parameters for this procedure. If you are not interested in knowing the schema rules created by this procedure, you can omit these parameters when running the procedure.

These parameters are described here:

■ **schema_name**   Name of the schema.

■ **streams_name**   Name of the propagation process. If the specified process does not exist, Oracle creates it. If the name is not specified or is set to NULL, then the procedure uses the name of the propagation process associated with the source queue, if available; otherwise, Oracle assigns a system-created name for the propagation.

■ **source_queue_name**   Name of the source queue in the current database from which messages will be propagated to another queue. The name can be specified as schema.queue_name. If the schema name is not specified, then the executing user is the default. The queue must be of ANYDATA type.

- **destination_queue_name**   Name of the destination queue in the destination database. The name is specified as `schema.destination_queue_name@db_link` if the destination queue is on another database. The `db_link` portion is the database link name for the destination database. If the schema name is not specified, then the executing user is the default. If the database link is not specified, then the global name of the current database is used and the source queue and destination queues must exist in the same database.

- **include_dml**   TRUE, if you want to replicate DML changes. Defaults to TRUE.

- **include_ddl**   TRUE, if you want to replicate DDL changes. Defaults to FALSE.

- **include_tagged_lcr**   Defaults to FALSE, meaning the procedure adds a condition to each rule to evaluate to TRUE only if the Streams tag in the redo information is NULL for the LCRs to be captured. If set to TRUE, then the procedure does not generate this condition, and the Streams tag is not checked in the rule. All LCRs, irrespective of the Streams tag value, will be captured.

- **source_database**   Global name of the source database where the change originated. If left to NULL, then the procedure does not add a condition to the rule that checks for the source database name.

- **dml_rule_name**   If `include_dml` is TRUE, then this out parameter will contain the name of the DML rule created.

- **ddl_rule_name**   If `include_ddl` is TRUE, then this out parameter will contain the name of the DDL rule created.

- **inclusion_rule**   If TRUE, then the procedure adds the generated rule to the positive rule set. If FALSE, then the rule is added to the negative rule set. The procedure first creates the rule set if it does not exist.

- **and_condition**   If specified, the procedure adds this condition to the system-created rule using an AND clause. The variables used in the condition must reference the LCR using `:lcr`. The procedure will convert it to the appropriate DML or DDL variable in the generated rule.

- **queue_to_queue**   If left to NULL or set to TRUE, then the procedure creates a queue-to-queue propagation. If set to FALSE, then the procedure creates a queue-to-database link propagation.

The following example creates a propagation process called DBXA_TO_DBXB_ PROP. This process propagates DDL and DML changes made to tables in the SCOTT schema in the DBXA database to the DBXB database.

```
SQL> declare
  2    l_dml_rule_name varchar2(30);
  3    l_ddl_rule_name varchar2(30);
  4  begin
  5   dbms_streams_adm.add_schema_propagation_rules (
  6     schema_name           => 'SCOTT',
  7     streams_name          => 'DBXA_TO_DBXB_PROP',
  8     source_queue_name     => 'DBXA_CAP_Q',
  9     destination_queue_name => 'DBXA_APP_Q@DBXB.WORLD',
 10     include_dml           => true,
 11     include_ddl           => true,
 12     source_database       => 'DBXA.WORLD',
 13     dml_rule_name         => l_dml_rule_name,
 14     ddl_rule_name         => l_ddl_rule_name,
 15     inclusion_rule        => true,
 16     queue_to_queue        => true,
 17     and_condition => ' :lcr.get_compatible() < dbms_streams.max_compatible()'
 18   );
 19   dbms_output.put_line('DML Rule Name is : ' || l_dml_rule_name);
 20   dbms_output.put_line('DDL Rule Name is : ' || l_ddl_rule_name);
 21  end;
 22  /
DML Rule Name is : "STRMADMIN"."SCOTT153"
DDL Rule Name is : "STRMADMIN"."SCOTT154"

PL/SQL procedure successfully completed.
```

The procedure created the specified propagation process, a positive rule set with one DML rule and one DDL rule with the rule names shown in the preceding code.

The DBA_PROPAGATION view shows information about the propagation process. The following query lists the rule set name, the source and destination queue names, and the database link name the propagation will use:

```
SQL> select rule_set_name,
  2          source_queue_name,
  3          destination_queue_name  dest_queue_name,
  4          destination_dblink  dest_dblink
  5    from dba_propagation
  6   where propagation_name = 'DBXA_TO_DBXB_PROP';
```

RULE_SET_NAME	SOURCE_QUEUE_NAME	DEST_QUEUE_NAME	DEST_DBLINK
RULESET$_155	DBXA_CAP_Q	DBXA_APP_Q	DBXB.WORLD

RULESET$_155 will contain the DML and DDL rules the procedure created for this propagation process.

The following query against the DBA_PROPAGATION view shows additional information about the propagation process:

```
SQL> select status,
  2          source_queue_owner src_owner,
  3          source_queue_name  src_q_name,
  4          destination_queue_owner dest_owner,
  5          destination_queue_name  dest_q_name,
  6          destination_dblink dest_dblink,
  7          queue_to_queue q_to_q
  8     from dba_propagation
  9    where propagation_name = 'DBXA_TO_DBXB_PROP';


STATUS    SRC_OWNER   SRC_Q_NAME   DEST_OWNER DEST_Q_NAME  DEST_DBLINK Q_TO_Q
--------  ----------  -----------  ---------- ------------ ----------- ------
ENABLED   STRMADMIN   DBXA_CAP_Q   STRMADMIN  DBXA_APP_Q   DBXB.WORLD  TRUE
```

The newly created propagation process is already in an ENABLED state, and is ready for propagating contents from the source queue DBXA_CAP_Q to the destination queue DBXA_APP_Q using the DBXB.WORLD link defined in the source database.

Manual Propagation Process Creation

You can manually create the propagation process using the CREATE_PROPAGATION procedure in the DBMS_PROPAGATION_ADM package. The procedure creates the propagation process as specified but does not create any rule set and rules.

You can specify an existing rule set, but doing so is not mandatory. If you do not specify any rule set, the propagation process propagates all messages from the source queue to the destination queue.

The CREATE_PROPAGATION procedure must be used in situations where you have to drop the existing propagation process and re-create it using the same rule set. This procedure makes it easy to create a propagation process without any rule set when you want to simply propagate all changes to the destination queue without performing any changes to data in the LCR—that is, no rule transformations are required.

Table 5-3 shows the parameters of the CREATE_PROPAGATION procedure. These parameters are discussed here:

- **propagation_name**   Name of the propagation process. It must be specified.

- **source_queue**   Name of the source queue. It can be specified in `schema.queue_name` format. If the schema is not specified, then it defaults to the user running the procedure. The source queue must be defined in the database where the procedure is run.

Parameter Name	In/Out	Data Type
propagation_name	IN	VARCHAR2
source_queue	IN	VARCHAR2
destination_queue	IN	VARCHAR2
destination_dblink	IN	VARCHAR2 default NULL
rule_set_name	IN	VARCHAR2 default NULL
negative_rule_set_name	IN	VARCHAR2 default NULL
queue_to_queue	IN	BOOLEAN default NULL
original_propagation_name	IN	VARCHAR2 default NULL
auto_merge_threshold	IN	NUMBER default NULL

TABLE 5-3. *Parameters of CREATE_PROPAGATION Procedure*

- **destination_queue** Name of the destination queue. It can be specified in schema.queue_name format. If the schema is not specified, then it defaults to the user running the procedure.

- **destination_dblink** Name of the database link used by the propagation process to propagate messages. The database link must be from the source database to the destination database. If left to NULL, Oracle assumes that the current database contains the source queue and destination queue.

- **rule_set_name** Name of the positive rule set. If specified, the rule set must exist; otherwise, an error is returned. It can be specified in the schema.rule_set_name format. If the schema is not specified, then it defaults to the user running the procedure. If you specified NULL and did not specify negative_rule_set_name, then the propagation process will propagate all messages in the queue. If negative_rule_set_name is specified, then the propagation process will only propagate messages there were not discarded by the negative rule set.

- **negative_rule_set_name** Name of the negative rule set. If specified, the rule set must exist or an error will be returned. It can be specified in the schema.rule_set_name format. If schema is not specified, then it defaults to the user running the procedure. If you specified a negative rule set, and did not specify a positive rule set, then the propagation process will only propagate messages that did not satisfy the negative rule set.

- **queue_to_queue**   If left to NULL or set to TRUE, then the procedure creates a queue-to-queue propagation. If set to FALSE, then the procedure creates a queue-to-database link propagation.

- **original_propagation_name**   Used in split and merge operation only. This is the name of the original propagation process if you are creating the propagation as a part of a split and merge operation. The split operation clones the original propagation using a new name. Leave it to NULL if the propagation you are creating is not part of the split and merge operation.

- **auto_merge_threshold**   Used in split and merge operations only. This is specified as the number of seconds. It is used to determine how the Streams path will be merged back automatically after it was split from the original configuration. Specify NULL, or leave it to its default (NULL), if the propagation is not part of the split and merge, or the propagation will never be merged with the original propagation automatically.

The following example creates the DBXA_TO_DBXB_PROP propagation process using the CREATE_PROPAGATION procedure that uses the positive rule set RULESET$_155. The procedure is run as the Streams Administrator in the source database.

```
SQL> begin
  2   dbms_propagation_adm.create_propagation (
  3      propagation_name      => 'DBXA_TO_DBXB_PROP',
  4      source_queue          => 'DBXA_CAP_Q',
  5      destination_queue     => 'DBXA_APP_Q',
  6      destination_dblink    => 'DBXB',
  7      rule_set_name         => 'RULESET$_155',
  8      queue_to_queue        => TRUE
  9      );
 10   end;
 11  /
PL/SQL procedure successfully completed.
```

Querying the DBA_PROPAGATION view as done previously provides the following information:

```
STATUS    SRC_OWNER   SRC_Q_NAME   DEST_OWNER  DEST_Q_NAME   DEST_DBLINK  Q_TO_Q
--------  ----------  -----------  ----------  ------------  -----------  ------
ENABLED   STRMADMIN   DBXA_CAP_Q   STRMADMIN   DBXA_APP_Q    DBXB.WORLD   TRUE
```

The procedures to manage propagation process are discussed in Chapter 11.

Propagation Rule Set and Rules

As in the case of the capture process, the propagation process can have a positive rule set and a negative rule set. If the negative rule set is present, it is evaluated first. If the result of this evaluation is TRUE, then the change is discarded without evaluating the positive rule set. If there is no negative rule set, or it evaluates to FALSE, then the positive rule set is evaluated. If the positive rule set evaluates to TRUE, then the change is propagated to the destination queue.

If there is no need to modify the captured change using rule-based transformation, where the contents of the LCR are changed, you can improve propagation performance by eliminating the rule set. Rule set evaluation requires CPU resources. By not performing any rule set evaluation in propagation, you can conserve CPU resources.

If the propagation process is created using the CREATE_PROPAGATION procedure in the DBMS_PROPAGATION_ADM package, you can create propagation that does not have any rule set associated with it.

If the propagation process is created using one of the ADD_*_RULES procedures in the DBMS_STREAMS_ADM package, you can remove the rule set from the propagation process as shown next. The following example removes the positive rule set from the propagation process:

```
SQL> begin
  2    dbms_propagation_adm.alter_propagation(
  3        propagation_name => 'DBXA_TO_DBXB_PROP',
  4        remove_rule_set  => TRUE);
  5  end;
  6  /
PL/SQL procedure successfully completed.
```

Similarly, if you want to remove the negative rule set, if present, you use the remove_negative_rule_set parameter in this procedure.

The rule set is not removed from the database. It remains defined in the database. You have to drop it explicitly if it is not needed. The previous procedure merely detaches the rule set from the propagation process.

Propagation Job and Schedule

Both procedures to create the propagation process, as discussed in the previous sections, also create a propagation job. The propagation job uses the Oracle Scheduler interface and the Oracle background job queue process to run the propagation job. In Oracle Database 11g there is no need to set any parameter for the job queue process. Oracle Scheduler automatically starts and manages the required slave processes for the propagation job schedule. The created propagation job is owned by SYS, although it was created by the Streams Administrator account, STRMADMIN, who executed the procedures to create the propagation. Upon creation, the propagation job is automatically enabled, making it visible through the DBA_SCHEDULER_JOBS view.

The propagation schedule for the job specifies how often the LCRs are propagated from the source queue to the destination queue. If the propagation is defined as queue-to-queue, then it has its own propagation job and schedule. If the propagation is defined as queue-to-database link, then the propagation process shares the job and schedule associated with the queue. The same job and schedule will be used by other propagations, if defined, that use the same queue.

The default propagation schedule has the following properties to control the propagation:

- **start_time**   The initial start time for the propagation window to send the LCRs from the source queue to the destination queue. A NULL value means the propagation window is open as soon as the propagation process is enabled. The default value is NULL.

- **duration**   Indicates the length of the propagation window, defined in seconds. A NULL value means the propagation window remains open forever or until the propagation process is disabled. The default value is NULL.

- **next_time**   A date function that specifies the start time of the next propagation window from the end of the current open window. If set to NULL, then the propagation restarts as soon as its current window expires. The default value is NULL.

- **latency**   Indicates the wait time, defined in seconds, during which the schedule coordinator process checks if there are messages (LCRs) available to propagate. The default value is three seconds.

Based on these values, the default propagation schedule is always enabled, with a propagation window that is open forever, and the queue is polled every three seconds to check if there are any messages to be propagated.

The view DBA_QUEUE_SCHEDULES describes all propagation schedules in the database. For each queue, there will be two entries in this view, one for the buffered queue and the other for the persistent queue. Each buffered queue has its own persistent queue. The following example shows the default schedule for the queue DBXA_CAP_Q:

```
SQL> select job_name,
  2         message_delivery_mode delivery_mode,
  3         start_date,
  4         start_time,
  5         next_time,
  6         propagation_window window,
  7         latency
  8    from dba_queue_schedules
  9   where qname = 'DBXA_CAP_Q'
 10  /
```

```
JOB_NAME       DELIVERY_M START_DATE START_TIME NEXT_TIME  WINDOW LATENCY
-------------  ---------- ---------- ---------- ---------- ------ -------
AQ_JOB$_228    PERSISTENT                                              3
AQ_JOB$_228    BUFFERED                                                3
```

Notice that `start_date`, `start_time`, `next_time`, and `propagation_window` are all set to NULL. The propagation job has a system-generated name of AQ_JOB$_228.

The view DBA_SCHEDULER_JOBS displays information about all scheduler jobs in the database. The following query shows the information about the propagation job. Oracle created the propagation job automatically when the propagation process was created using one of the procedures discussed earlier.

```
SQL> select schedule_type sched_type,
  2         state,
  3         event_queue_name event_qname,
  4         event_queue_agent event_qagent,
  5         event_condition e_C
  6    from dba_scheduler_jobs
  7   where job_creator = 'STRMADMIN'
  8     and job_name = 'AQ_JOB$_228';

SCHED_TYPE   STATE      EVENT_QNAME   EVENT_QAGENT                             E_C
----------   ---------- ------------- ------------------------------------ ... -----
EVENT        SCHEDULED  DBXA_CAP_Q    AQ$_P@"STRMADMIN"."DBXA_APP_Q"@DBXB  (1=1)
```

In this output we see that the automatically created job is an event-based job, as indicated by the schedule type. Event-based jobs are started automatically when an event takes place, if the job is not running already. This job does not run on any particular schedule. The default schedule we saw earlier has no `start_time`, `next_time`, or `propagation_window` defined. The event queue is the source queue that we provided when creating the propagation process. Oracle also created an agent for this queue with a system-created name. This agent dequeues messages from the event queue and enqueues those into the destination queue DBXA_APP_Q at the destination database. When an event takes place in the source queue, such as messages (LCRs) enqueued by the capture process, the propagation job starts, if it was not running already, and the agent dequeues messages from the source queue and enqueues those into the destination queue.

It is possible to change the default job schedule if needed. However, in most cases, there is no need to change the default schedule other than to change `latency` to one second so that the schedule coordinator will check the queue more often. Reducing the length of the propagation window by changing `duration` will cause the messages either to stay in the queue for a long time, consuming memory, or to be spilled to the disk queue, thus slowing down replication.

The following example shows how to change the propagation job schedule. It changes the propagation window to remain open for a duration of one hour (3600 seconds). The window will open again after 30 minutes (1800 seconds), and the schedule coordinator will poll the queue every 60 seconds when the propagation window is open. Notice the destination queue name specification.

```
SQL> begin
  2      dbms_aqadm.alter_propagation_schedule(
  3          queue_name  => 'STRMADMIN.DBXA_CAP_Q',
  4          destination => '"STRMADMIN"."DBXA_APP_Q"@DBXC.WORLD',
  5          duration    => 3600,
  6          next_time   => 'SYSDATE + 1800/86400',
  7          latency     => '60'
  8      );
  9  end;
 10  /

PL/SQL procedure successfully completed
```

Querying the view DBA_QUEUE_SCHEDULE as done previously shows the following change:

```
JOB_NAME       DELIVERY_M START_DATE  START_TIME  NEXT_TIME              WINDOW LATENCY
-----------    ---------- ----------  ----------  --------------------   ------ -------
AQ_JOB$_228    PERSISTENT                         SYSDATE + 1800/86400    3600      60
AQ_JOB$_228    BUFFERED                           SYSDATE + 1800/86400    3600      60
```

With this change, the propagation job schedule is no longer based on the event, but rather on a fixed schedule that we defined. The view DBA_JOB_SCHEDULES shows the following information for the job:

```
SCHED_TYPE   STATE      EVENT_QNAME  EVENT_QAGENT                            E_C
-----------  ---------- ------------ ------------------------------------    -----
PLSQL        SCHEDULED
```

The `scheduled_type` column shows PLSQL and not EVENT. Since this is not an event-based schedule, `event_queue_name`, `event_queue_agent`, and `event_condition` are set to NULL. However, the schedule type remains EVENT if only the duration of the `propagation_window` is changed. Event-based schedules offer better efficiency in propagating queue contents.

In Oracle Database 11*g*, there is an automatic optimization of the propagation process. Under certain conditions, the capture process sends the LCRs directly to the destination queue for the apply process to dequeue. This optimized configuration is called combined capture and apply.

Combined Capture and Apply

Combined capture and apply (CCA), introduced in Oracle Database 11*g*, improves performance in sending LCRs from the capture process to the apply process. The capture process does not stage the LCRs in its queue and does not use the propagation process to deliver the LCRs to the destination queue. In other words, the capture and apply processes take on the role of propagation sender and propagation receiver, respectively. CCA is possible when the capture and apply processes reside in the same database or in different databases.

Oracle selects CCA automatically when certain requirements are satisfied. It does not need any specific configuration in such scenarios. When the capture process starts, it automatically detects if these requirements are met. If they are met, the capture process establishes a connection with the queue at the destination database where the apply process is running. The captured LCRs are then directly sent to the apply process, bypassing the propagation process.

When the capture and apply processes run in the same database, CCA will be configured automatically if all the following conditions are met:

- The database running the capture and apply processes is an Oracle Database 11*g* or later database.

- The capture and apply processes use the same queue.

- The queue has only one publisher; that is, only the capture process enqueues messages to the queue.

- The queue has only one consumer; that is, only the apply process dequeues messages from the queue.

When the capture and apply processes run in different databases, CCA will be configured automatically if all the conditions listed here are met:

- The database running the capture process and the database running the apply process both must be Oracle Database 11*g* or later databases.

- The capture process queue has only one publisher; that is, only the capture process enqueues the message to the queue.

- Propagation process must be configured between queues for the capture and apply processes, and propagation cannot be part of the directed networks (no queue forwarding or apply forwarding).

- The capture process queue has only one consumer and it is the propagation process between the capture process queue and the apply process queue.

- The apply process queue has only one publisher and it is the propagation process between the capture process queue and the apply process queue.

In summary, if you have a very straightforward replication environment that contains a capture process, a propagation process, and an apply process, without any intermediate queues, CCA will be configured automatically.

How to Check if CCA Is in Effect

Since CCA is automatically configured, how do you know if your Streams environment is using it? There are a couple of ways to check if CCA is in effect.

When the capture process is running, Oracle populates the V$STREAMS_CAPTURE view. This view provides information about the performance and state of the capture process.

The columns OPTIMIZATION, APPLY_NAME, and APPLY_DBLINK of the V$STREAMS_CAPTURE view indicate if CCA is in effect. If CCA is in effect, the OPTIMIZATION column contains a number greater than zero and the APPLY_NAME column contains the name of the apply process that will receive the LCRs directly from the capture process.

If the apply process is running in a remote database, then the APPLY_DBLINK column contains the name of the database link to the remote database. When CCA is not in use, the OPTIMIZATION column is set to zero, and the APPLY_NAME and APPLY_DBLINK columns are null.

The following example shows that CCA is in use between the capture process DBXA_CAP and the apply process DBXA_APP. The apply process is running in the DBXB.WORLD database.

```
SQL> select capture_name,
  2          optimization,
  3          apply_name,
  4          apply_dblink
  5    from v$streams_capture
  6   where capture_name = 'DBXA_CAP';

CAPTURE_NAME    OPTIMIZATION APPLY_NAME   APPLY_DBLINK
--------------- ------------ ------------ --------------------
DBXA_CAP                   2 DBXA_APP     DBXB.WORLD
```

In addition, when the capture process starts and CCA is selected, Oracle writes a message to that effect in the database instance alert log file. An example of this message is shown here:

```
Streams CAPTURE CP01 for DBXA_CAP with pid=35, OS id=4020 is in combined capture and apply mode.
```

Summary

Oracle Streams replication works with buffered and persistent queues of type ANYDATA. The queues are secured and transactional in nature. By default, these are commit-time queues. The queue must be created for Streams clients such as capture, apply, and propagation processes. The associated queue table is owned by the instance where the queue is created. The Streams client process runs on the instance that owns the queue table. It is possible to specify the primary and secondary instances for the queue table in a RAC environment. This facilitates the failover of the Streams client process when the instance that owns the queue table becomes unavailable.

Messages enqueued to the source queue are propagated, or copied, to the destination queue by the propagation process. The propagation process can be created implicitly or explicitly. The procedure that adds rules to the propagation process also creates propagation if it did not exist. An explicitly created propagation process can use an existing rule set. Oracle also creates a propagation job and a schedule to run the propagation job. By default, the job is of type EVENT with a propagation window that is open forever or until the propagation is disabled. This enables speedier delivery of the messages to the destination queue.

Starting in Oracle Database 11g, the propagation process is optimized with the use of what is called combined capture and apply (CCA). When certain requirements are met in your replication environment, Oracle automatically configures CCA, and LCRs are transmitted directly from the capture process to the apply process, bypassing the propagation steps. However, the propagation process must be defined. Such optimization speeds up the delivery of the captured message to the apply process, thereby improving the replication latency.

CHAPTER
6

Apply Process

hen the captured messages reach the intended destination, an Oracle background process called the apply process implicitly consumes—or, generally speaking, dequeues—those messages from the Streams queue.

Typically, the dequeued message is directly applied to the database object where the apply process runs. However, it is possible to configure the apply process to pass the dequeued message as a parameter to a user-defined procedure called the apply handler, which can perform customized actions based on the information in the message. The apply process can also send the message to a remote, non-Oracle database in a heterogeneous replication environment.

The apply process is a very crucial part of the Streams environment. It is the most sophisticated and complex process because it provides various means to control how the messages will be processed. It is also quite often the bottleneck in the replication process. The efficiency of the apply process in applying the messages is critical to have an efficient Streams replication environment.

This chapter discusses in detail how the apply process works, including its configuration, requirements, and limitations.

Overview of the Apply Process

The apply process is a configurable Oracle database background process. It consists of a set of three components: the reader server, the coordinator process, and the apply server. The apply server can have multiple slaves running in parallel. Together, this set of components forms what is called the Streams apply engine. The terms *apply engine* and *apply process* are used interchangeably in this chapter.

There can be multiple apply engines in the destination database, but one apply engine can dequeue messages (LCRs) from only one and the same queue. In addition, one apply engine can apply captured LCRs from only one source database, irrespective of the type of the capture process (asynchronous capture or synchronous capture). It is possible to propagate captured LCRs from multiple source databases to a single destination queue in the destination database, but you must configure multiple apply processes, each dequeuing LCRs from only a single source database using appropriate apply rules. However, Oracle recommends that you configure multiple destination queues for applying changes from multiple source databases to the single destination database.

After dequeuing the LCR, the apply engine typically applies it to the destination table directly. However, the LCR can be passed to a user-defined apply handler procedure that can modify the LCR before applying it to the destination table. Such handler procedures are useful when you want to ignore replication of certain DDL or DML commands, modify data values, track the DDL or DML changes for audit purposes, or fulfill any other business requirement that calls for modifying the replicated change in the destination database.

Apply Process States

The apply process maintains a persistent state across database instance restarts. This means that if the apply process is running when the database instance is shut down, it automatically restarts when the database instance starts again. If the apply process was stopped, or was aborted, prior to the database shutdown, then it will not be automatically restarted when the database instance starts. You will have to manually start the apply process.

However, if the database instance is started in the restricted session using the STARTUP RESTRICT command, the apply process will not start, irrespective of its state when the instance was shut down. If the apply process is running when the restricted session is enabled using the ALTER SYSTEM command, then the apply process continues to operate normally. If an already stopped apply process is started in a restricted session, you won't get an error, but the process won't really start until the restricted session is disabled.

Apply Process Components

Although you name the apply process when creating it, Oracle refers to it internally using an operating system process name of the form AP*xx*, where AP stands for apply and *xx* contains numbers and letters. As mentioned earlier, the apply process has three components, operating in parallel, called the reader server, the coordinator, and the apply server, as shown in the Figure 6-1.

The apply process and the coordinator process share the operating system name AP*xx*. The reader server and the apply servers have an operating system name of the form AS*xx*, where AS stands for apply server and *xx* contains numbers and letters. The following sections describe these components in more detail.

Reader Server

The reader server component of the apply process is responsible for dequeuing the message from the apply queue. During the dequeuing of the message, the reader

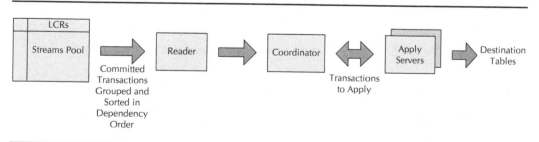

FIGURE 6-1.   *Apply process components*

server invokes the rules engine to evaluate apply rules, if any, and discards the message based on the result of the rule set evaluation. The reader server also computes the dependencies between LCRs and arranges them in proper sequence before assembling them into transactions. The dependencies are computed using the user-defined virtual dependencies (discussed later in this chapter) and the referential integrity constraints in the destination database. The assembled transaction looks different from the original transaction in the source database. For example, suppose that in the source database, one single DELETE statement deleted, say, 1000 rows. At the destination database, the assembled transaction will contain 1000 different DELETE statements. The assembled transactions are then passed to the next component—the apply coordinator process.

The view V$STREAMS_APPLY_READER shows information about the reader process and its progress for the defined apply process. You can query this view as shown next to see what the process is doing at the current time and its progress thus far:

```
SQL> select sid,
  2         serial#,
  3         state,
  4         total_messages_dequeued msgs_dequeued,
  5         elapsed_dequeue_time dequeue_time,
  6         dequeued_message_number dequeued_scn
  7    from v$streams_apply_reader
  8   where apply_name = 'DBXA_APP';

 SID SERIAL# STATE              MSGS_DEQUEUED DEQUEUE_TIME    DEQUEUED_SCN
---- ------- ------------------ ------------- ------------    -----------------
 331   61373 DEQUEUE MESSAGE           41741         21629    5662035596739
```

As shown in the example, the reader process has dequeued 41,741 messages since the apply process started. The information from this view can be helpful when you are diagnosing problems and think the change made at the source has not been replicated at the destination, or has not yet been dequeued by the apply process.

The STATE column of the V$STREAMS_APPLY_READER view can have the following values:

- **DEQUEUE MESSAGE**   The messages from the apply queue are being dequeued.

- **IDLE**   The reader process has no work to do. There are no messages to dequeue.

- **INITIALIZING**   The process is starting up.

- **PAUSED - WAITING FOR THE DDL TO COMPLETE**   The reader process is waiting for the DDL LCRs to be applied.

- **SCHEDULE MESSAGES**   The process is computing dependencies between messages while assembling them into transactions.

- **SPILLING**   The process is spilling unapplied messages from the memory queue to the disk queue. This happens when the transaction is too large to be kept in the Streams in-memory buffer.

Coordinator Process

The coordinator process receives the assembled transactions from the reader server. The assembled transactions are then passed to the apply server process. The coordinator is responsible for keeping track of transactions and monitoring the server process to ensure that the transactions are applied in proper order. It can also direct the server to roll back a transaction in situations in which the transaction currently processed by the apply server has a dependency on another transaction that has not yet been applied.

The view V$STREAMS_APPLY_COORDINATOR shows information about the current state of the coordinator process and its current progress. You can query this view as shown here to see what the coordinator is doing at the current time:

```
SQL> select sid,
  2          serial#,
  3          state,
  4          total_applied applied,
  5          total_errors errors
  6    from v$streams_apply_coordinator
  7   where apply_name = 'DBXA_APP';

 SID  SERIAL# STATE               APPLIED     ERRORS
 ---- -------- ---------------- ---------- ----------
  221    1825 APPLYING               4857          2
```

The information in this view can be used for monitoring the progress of the apply process. The example shows the number of transactions applied since the apply process was started and the number of transactions in error.

The STATE column of the V$STREAMS_APPLY_COORDINATOR view can have the following values:

- **ABORTING**   The coordinator is stopping due to an apply error.

- **APPLYING**   The assembled transactions are being passed to the apply server.

- **IDLE**   The coordinator process has no work to do at this time.

- **INITIALIZING**   The process is starting up.

- **SHUTTING DOWN CLEANLY**   A normal shutdown of the process.

Server Process

The server process receives the assembled transactions from the coordinator process. There can be more than one server process. Each server process is a background Oracle process. Generally, the server process applies those transactions as DML or DDL statements to the database tables. However, if the apply process has any handler procedures defined, then the LCR is passed to the appropriate handler process. The handler process then decides how to process the LCR. It is also possible to enqueue the LCR into a persistent queue for a user application to process the LCR. If the changes are to be replicated to a non-Oracle database, such enqueuing to a persistent queue is required.

The apply server detects conflicts in data when applying the changes to the destination table row. If a user-defined conflict handler procedure is specified, then the server executes the procedure to resolve the conflict. If there is no such conflict handler procedure, then the apply server rolls back the changes it has applied thus far and marks the entire transaction as an error transaction. All LCRs belonging to this transaction are written to a persistent error queue on disk.

NOTE
The entire transaction is written to the error queue when the first irresolvable error is encountered, and any LCRs remaining in the transaction are not processed.

At the end of the transaction, the server process executes the COMMIT, when the commit directive is received by the apply process, and the transaction is considered applied to the destination database. Even if the transaction is errored out and written to the error queue, it is considered applied to the database.

The view V$STREAMS_APPLY_SERVER shows information about the server processes for the defined apply process. You can query this view as shown here to see what the apply server is doing at the current time:

```
SQL> select sid,
  2         serial#,
  3         server_id snbr,
  4         state,
  5         total_assigned txn_assigned,
  6         total_messages_applied msgs_applied,
  7         applied_message_number app_scn
  8    from v$streams_apply_server
  9   where apply_name = 'DBXA_APP';

 SID SERIAL# SNBR STATE               TXN_ASSIGNED  MSGS_APPLIED      APP_SCN
---- ------- ---- ------------------- ------------ ------------- -------------
 330   43749    1 EXECUTE TRANSACTION        93524        238165 5662037203509
```

In this example, there is only one apply server, with a `server_id` of 1. If you configured parallelism for the apply process, you will see as many lines showing the state and other statistics for each of these server processes.

The STATE column of the V$STREAMS_APPLY_SERVER view can have the following values:

- **ADD PARTITION**   The server is performing an internal administration task that adds a partition to an Oracle's internal table that is used for recording information of the in-progress transaction.

- **DROP PARTITION**   The server is dropping a partition of an internal table that was used to record information about the transaction that just completed.

- **EXECUTE TRANSACTION**   The server is currently executing a DDL or DML transaction and applying the changes to the destination table.

- **INITIALIZING**   The server is starting up.

- **IDLE**   The server is idle and waiting for work.

- **TRANSACTION CLEANUP**   The server is performing internal tasks that include removing the LCRs of the recently completed transaction from the apply queue. The transactions could have been applied successfully or written to the error queue.

- **WAIT COMMIT**   The server is waiting to commit a transaction until all other transactions with a lower commit SCN are completed. This state is only possible when there are more than one apply server processes configured using the apply process parameter `parallelism`, and the `commit_serialization` parameter is set to FULL (changed from its default value DEPENDENT_TRANSACTIONS).

- **WAIT DEPENDENCY**   The server process is waiting to apply an LCR in the current transaction until another transaction, on which the LCR has a dependency, is applied and committed. This state is possible only when the `parallelism` parameter for the apply process is set to a value greater than 1.

Apply User

An apply user is a user under whose security domain the DML and DDL changes are applied to the destination tables. Each apply process has it own apply user. The apply user must have appropriate privileges to apply these changes. If there are apply handler procedures in use, then the apply user must also have the execute privilege on these procedures.

If the apply process is created explicitly using the CREATE_APPLY procedure of the DBMS_APPLY_ADM package, you can specify the apply user. If the apply process is created implicitly using the ADD_*_RULES or the MAINTAIN_* procedures of the DBMS_STREAMS_ADM package, then Oracle creates the apply user as the user who executed the procedure.

If you granted DBA privilege to the Streams Administrator user while creating it, and it is also your apply user, then it has all the required privileges. You do not have to grant any additional privileges.

It is very common practice to keep the Streams Administrator as the apply user. Although it is not a requirement, it does help keep Streams setup a bit simpler because you don't have to worry about yet another Oracle account with powerful privileges.

The current apply user name is listed in the APPLY_USER column of the DBA_APPLY view. Chapter 11 discusses how to change the apply user and grant required privileges.

Creating the Apply Process

Although the apply process is a background database process, it must be created for processing the LCRs. Similar to the creation of the capture and propagation processes, there is more than one way to create the apply process. This section explores how to create the apply process to suit your replication requirements.

Before you create the apply process, you must create the Streams queue that will receive the changes from either the capture process or the propagation process. The apply process dequeues these changes from this queue. In a replication environment where the capture and apply processes may run on the same database (for example, in a downstream capture environment), the capture and apply processes can share the same Streams queue.

The Streams queue is created using the SET_UP_QUEUE procedure of the DBMS_STREAMS_ADM package. Chapter 5 describes the Streams queue and how to create it in detail.

Once the apply queue is created, you can create the apply process automatically or manually. Which one of these two methods you use depends on your replication requirements and also the type of capture process you will create, or have already created, to capture the changes. If you use the synchronous capture process, then you must manually create the apply process, because the automatically created apply process does not apply the LCRs staged in the persistent queue used by the synchronous capture process.

Automatic Apply Process Creation

The following procedures in the DBMS_STREAMS_ADM package can create an apply process automatically. Using one of these procedures to create the apply process is relatively simple, and Oracle performs a number of tasks behind the scene that are necessary for Streams replication.

- ADD_GLOBAL_RULES

- ADD_SCHEMA_RULES

- ADD_TABLE_RULES

- ADD_SUBSET_RULES

- MAINTAIN_* procedures

NOTE
The MAINTAIN_* procedures are discussed in detail in Chapter 8.

Each of the previous procedures (other than MAINTAIN_*) performs the following tasks:

1. Creates the specified apply process, if it does not exist.

2. Creates a rule set with a system-created name for the apply process, if one does not exist. The rule set can be positive or negative depending on the option selected.

3. Depending on the procedure used, adds table rules, schema rules, global rules or the subset rule for the table to the rule set for the apply process. The rule names are system created.

4. Creates the apply user as the user who executed the procedure, and grants the apply user the privilege to dequeue messages from the apply queue.

All these procedures have almost identical input and output parameters. This section next discusses the ADD_SCHEMA_RULES procedure in detail to show how it creates the apply process, rule set, and schema rules.

Table 6-1 shows the parameters of the ADD_SCHEMA_RULES procedure. Note that there are two optional OUT parameters for this procedure. These parameters are described here:

- **schema_name**   Name of the schema.

- **streams_type**   Type of Streams client or process; for the apply process, specify APPLY.

Parameter Name	In/Out	Data Type
schema_name	IN	VARCHAR2
streams_type	IN	VARCHAR2
streams_name	IN	VARCHAR2 default NULL
queue_name	IN	VARCHAR2 default 'streams_queue'
include_dml	IN	BOOLEAN default TRUE
include_ddl	IN	BOOLEAN default FALSE
include_tagged_lcr	IN	BOOLEAN default FALSE
source_database	IN	VARCHAR2 default NULL
dml_rule_name	OUT	VARCHAR2
ddl_rule_name	OUT	VARCHAR2
inclusion_rule	IN	BOOLEAN default TRUE
and_condition	IN	VARCHAR2 default NULL

TABLE 6-1. *Parameters of ADD_SCHEMA_RULES Procedure*

- **streams_name**   Name of Streams client or process; for APPLY, specify the name of the apply process.

- **queue_name**   Name of the queue from which the apply process dequeues messages.

- **include_dml**   TRUE, if you want to replicate DML changes. Default value is TRUE.

- **include_ddl**   TRUE, if you want to replicate DDL changes. Default value is FALSE.

- **include_tagged_lcr**   Defaults to FALSE, meaning the procedure adds a condition to each rule to evaluate to TRUE only if the Streams tag field in the LCR is NULL. If set to TRUE, then the procedure does not generate this condition, and the Streams tag is not checked in the rule. All LCRs, irrespective of the Streams tag value, will be applied.

- **source_database**   Global name of the source database where the change originated.

■ **dml_rule_name**   If `include_dml` is TRUE, then this `out` parameter will contain the name of the DML rule created.

■ **ddl_rule_name**   If `include_ddl` is TRUE, then this `out` parameter will contain the name of the DDL rule created.

■ **inclusion_rule**   If TRUE, then the procedure adds the generated rule to the positive rule set. If FALSE, then the rule is added to the negative rule set. If the rule set does not exist, the procedure creates one. Default value is TRUE.

■ **and_condition**   If specified, the procedure adds the condition to the system-created rule using an AND clause. The LCR variables used in the condition must be specified using the `:lcr` format. The procedure will convert it to the appropriate DML or DDL variable in the generated rule.

The following example creates an apply process called DBXA_APP that applies DDL and DML changes made to tables in the SCOTT schema in the source database DBXA. The Streams Administrator user called STRMADMIN in the destination database DBXB executed the procedure. Notice the `and_condition` value specified in the example. This condition ensures that changes made to tables that have unsupported columns will not be applied.

```
SQL> declare
  2    l_dml_rule_name  varchar2(30);
  3    l_ddl_rule_name  varchar2(30);
  4  begin
  5    dbms_streams_adm.add_schema_rules (
  6        schema_name       => 'SCOTT',
  7        streams_type      => 'APPLY',
  8        streams_name      => 'DBXA_APP',
  9        queue_name        => 'DBXA_APP_Q',
 10        include_dml       => true,
 11        include_ddl       => true,
 12        include_tagged_lcr => false,
 13        source_database   => 'DBXA.WORLD',
 14        dml_rule_name     => l_dml_rule_name,
 15        ddl_rule_name     => l_ddl_rule_name,
 16        inclusion_rule    => true,
 17        and_condition => ' :lcr.get_compatible() < dbms_streams.max_compatible()'
 18    );
 19
 20    dbms_output.put_line('DML Rule Name is: ' || l_dml_rule_name);
 21    dbms_output.put_line('DDL Rule Name is: ' || l_ddl_rule_name);
 22
 23  end;
 24  /
DML Rule Name is: "STRMADMIN"."SCOTT66"
DDL Rule Name is: "STRMADMIN"."SCOTT67"
PL/SQL procedure successfully completed.
```

The view DBA_APPLY shows information about the apply process. Some of the columns of this view are shown here:

```
SQL> select queue_name,
  2          rule_set_name,
  3          apply_user,
  4          status,
  5          apply_captured
  6    from dba_apply
  7* where apply_name = 'DBXA_APP'
SQL> /

QUEUE_NAME    RULE_SET_NAME    APPLY_USER       STATUS    APPLY_CAPTURED
------------  ---------------  ---------------  --------  --------------
DBXA_APP_Q    RULESET$_68      STRMADMIN        DISABLED  YES
```

Note that the APPLY_CAPTURED column shows YES. This means that the apply process will apply captured LCRs that are dequeued from its buffered queue. The apply process will not apply LCRs from a persistent queue used by the synchronous capture (or messages enqueued by the user application). You must create two separate apply processes to process messages from these two different queue types.

Automatically created positive rule set RULESET$_68 is associated with the apply process DBXA_APP. The DML and DDL schema rules, SCOTT66 and SCOTT67, are defined within this rule set. The following query shows the system-created rules (the output is reformatted to fit the page):

```
SQL> select rule_name,
  2          rule_condition
  3    from dba_streams_rules
  4    where rule_set_name = 'RULESET$_68';
RULE_NAME
------------------------------
RULE_CONDITION
----------------------------------------------------------------------
SCOTT67
(((((:ddl.get_object_owner() = 'SCOTT'
    or :ddl.get_base_table_owner() = 'SCOTT')
    and :ddl.is_null_tag() = 'Y'
    and :ddl.get_source_database_name() = 'DBXA.WORLD' ))
    and ( :ddl.get_compatible() < dbms_streams.max_compatible()))
SCOTT66
(((((:dml.get_object_owner() = 'SCOTT')
    and :dml.is_null_tag() = 'Y'
    and :dml.get_source_database_name() = 'DBXA.WORLD' ))
    and ( :dml.get_compatible() < dbms_streams.max_compatible()))
```

If you recall the rule conditions from the capture process creation procedure in Chapter 4, you will notice that, in our example for creating Streams replication for the SCOTT schema, the rule conditions are identical to those for the apply process. If we are capturing the changes for the SCOTT schema using appropriate rules, and we are not using any rule-based transformation to manipulate the captured data prior to applying it, then these apply rules are redundant. We can detach the generated rule set from the apply process. In this case, the apply process will apply all dequeued messages to the destination objects. This will save some CPU cycles since no rule evaluation is required. The following example shows how to remove the positive rule set from the apply process:

```
SQL> begin
  2    dbms_apply_adm.alter_apply(
  3      apply_name => 'DBXA_APP',
  4      remove_rule_set => true);
  5  end;
  6  /
PL/SQL procedure successfully completed.
```

The detached rule set remains defined in the database. We can optionally drop it using the DROP_RULE_SET procedure in the DBMS_RULE_ADM package, but then we will need to re-create the rule set if we want to perform any rule-based transformations in the apply process. The following example shows how to attach an existing positive rule set to an existing apply process:

```
SQL> begin
  2    dbms_apply_adm.alter_apply(
  3      apply_name => 'DBXA_APP',
  4      rule_set_name => 'STRMADMIN.RULESET$_68');
  5  end;
  6  /
PL/SQL procedure successfully completed.
```

Although the ADD_*_RULES procedures create the apply process, and a rule set if these did not exist, their primary function is to add rules to the rule set for the Streams process and, in this case, the apply process. These procedures are limited to these tasks and do not provide a mechanism to define apply handler procedures. Such handler procedures must be specified afterward using the ALTER_APPLY procedure of the DBMS_APPLY_ADM package. If you created the apply process manually, then such handlers can be defined for the apply process during its creation.

Similar to the capture process, the apply process does not start automatically after its creation. The STATUS column in the DBA_APPLY view shows DISABLED. It must be started using the START_APPLY procedure in the DBMS_CAPTURE_ADM package.

Manual Apply Process Creation

You can manually create the apply process using the CREATE_APPLY procedure in the DBMS_APPLY_ADM package. The procedure simply creates the apply process using the specified queue name. This procedure is more flexible and allows you to create the apply process using an existing rule set, if available, or by assigning no rule set to the apply process. The procedure also provides options to define appropriate handler procedures if required.

You must manually create the apply process when the LCRs are either enqueued by user applications or were created in a persistent queue by the synchronous capture process. Also, in some rare situations in which you must drop and re-create the apply process without re-creating rule sets and rules, if required, you will need to use this method.

Table 6-2 lists the parameters of the CREATE_APPLY procedure and they are described here:

- **queue_name**   Name of the queue from which the apply process dequeues LCRs. The queue must already exist. The name can be specified in the form of schema.queue_name. The queue name is a required parameter.

- **apply_name**   Name of the apply process without its owner name.

Parameter Name	In/Out	Data Type
queue_name	IN	VARCHAR2
apply_name	IN	VARCHAR2
rule_set_name	IN	VARCHAR2 default NULL
message_handler	IN	VARCHAR2 default NULL
ddl_handler	IN	VARCHAR2 default NULL
apply_user	IN	VARCHAR2 default NULL
apply_database_link	IN	VARCHAR2 default NULL
apply_tag	IN	RAW default 0x00
apply_captured	IN	BOOLEAN default FALSE
precommit_handler	IN	VARCHAR2 default NULL
negative_rule_set_name	IN	VARCHAR2 default NULL
source_database	IN	VARCHAR2 default NULL

TABLE 6-2.   *Parameters of CREATE_APPLY Procedure*

- **rule_set_name**   Name of the existing positive rule set. If set to NULL and you do not specify `negative_rule_set_name`, the apply process will apply all supported and applicable changes to the destination objects. If set to NULL and you specify `negative_rule_set_name`, then the apply process will apply changes not discarded by the negative rule set.

- **message_handler**   Specifies a user procedure to process non-LCR-type (user created) messages. Leave it to its default value of NULL when processing LCRs captured by the capture process or synchronous capture process.

- **ddl_handler**   Specifies a user-defined procedure (PL/SQL) that is invoked when the apply process encounters LCRs for DDL changes. The LCR will be passed to the DDL handler procedure. Default value is NULL.

- **apply_user**   The user who applies the DDL and DML changes and executes any apply handler procedures. The user must exist in the database.

- **apply_database_link**   If the apply process is to apply changes to the database it is running in, leave this parameter to NULL. The parameter specifies the database link name to which the apply process applies changes. The parameter is used when applying changes to a remote, non-Oracle database.

- **apply_tag**   A binary tag that is added to the redo entries for the changes generated by the apply process in the local database. By default, it is set to 0x00 (that is, hexadecimal double zero). The parameter is relevant in situations in which there is a capture process running in the destination database that needs to capture local changes as well as changes applied by the apply process. It can also be used in bidirectional and N-way replication to identify the source of the change.

- **apply_captured**   Specifies if the apply process processes the LCRs that were staged in a buffered queue or a persistent queue. The value of this parameter can be set to TRUE or FALSE. Default value is FALSE. The parameter must be set to TRUE if the capture process enqueued the LCRs and the apply process dequeued those from the buffered queue. If the synchronous capture process captured the LCRs, then this parameter must be set to FALSE. The value of this parameter cannot be altered once set. You will need to define separate apply processes to apply LCRs captured by the capture process and synchronous capture process.

- **precommit_handler**   Specifies a user-defined procedure that is invoked when the apply process receives the commit directive to commit the transaction. Default value is NULL.

- **negative_rule_set_name**   Name of the existing negative rule set. If set to NULL, then no negative rule set will be associated with the apply process. If a name is specified, then changes that satisfy the rule set will be discarded. Default value is NULL.

- **source_database**   Specifies the global name of the database where the change originated. Default value is NULL.

The following example creates an apply process called DBXA_APP using the existing positive rule set RULESET$_68. This example does not specify any handler procedures for the apply process. Note that the `apply_captured` parameter is set to TRUE, indicating that this apply process will only apply LCRs captured by the capture process. This apply process cannot apply LCRs captured by the synchronous capture process or LCRs enqueued by user applications. Also, the `apply_tag` parameter is set to a value of 0x11 (hex 11) instead of its default value of 0x00. This means the redo entries are tagged with this value when changes are applied to the destination tables. These tag values are important when changes made by the apply process are to be recaptured for replication to other destinations.

```
SQL> connect strmadmin/strmadmin@DBXB.WORLD
Connected.
SQL> begin
  2    dbms_apply_adm.create_apply(
  3      queue_name       => 'STRMADMIN.DBXA_APP_Q',
  4      apply_name       => 'DBXA_APP',
  5      rule_set_name    => 'STRMADMIN.RULESET$_68',
  6      apply_captured   => TRUE,
  7      apply_tag        => HEXTORAW('11'),
  8      source_database  => 'DBXA.WORLD');
  9    end;
 10  /

PL/SQL procedure successfully completed.
```

The apply process is in a disabled state upon creation, so you have to start it manually using the START_APPLY procedure in the DBMS_APPLY_ADM package. Chapter 11 discusses apply process management, which includes starting and stopping an apply process.

Apply Process Parameters

There are a number of parameters associated with the apply process. These define and control its functionality, and have default values. You may need to change a few of these parameters depending on your requirements. The data dictionary view DBA_APPLY_PARAMETERS lists these parameters as shown next. All values shown

are default values, indicated by the NO under the column SET (for SET_BY_USER).
If the value of the apply parameter is changed, then the column SET_BY_USER will
report YES.

```
SQL> select parameter,
  2          value,
  3          set_by_user
  4     from dba_apply_parameters
  5    where apply_name = 'DBXA_APP'
  6    order by parameter;


PARAMETER                          VALUE                    SET
-------------------------------    ----------------------   ---
ALLOW_DUPLICATE_ROWS               N                        NO
COMMIT_SERIALIZATION               DEPENDENT_TRANSACTIONS   NO
DISABLE_ON_ERROR                   Y                        NO
DISABLE_ON_LIMIT                   N                        NO
MAXIMUM_SCN                        INFINITE                 NO
PARALLELISM                        4                        NO
PRESERVE_ENCRYPTION                Y                        NO
RTRIM_ON_IMPLICIT_CONVERSION       Y                        NO
STARTUP_SECONDS                    0                        NO
TIME_LIMIT                         INFINITE                 NO
TRACE_LEVEL                        0                        NO
TRANSACTION_LIMIT                  INFINITE                 NO
TXN_AGE_SPILL_THRESHOLD            900                      NO
TXN_LCR_SPILL_THRESHOLD            10000                    NO
WRITE_ALERT_LOG                    Y                        NO
15 rows selected.
```

These parameters are described here:

■ **allow_duplicate_rows**   Default value is N. If set to Y, and if the apply
process finds two rows in the destination table for the single-row LCR, then
the UPDATE or DELETE operation will be performed on only one of those
rows. If set to N, then the apply process will raise an error (ORA-1422) if the
single-row LCR affects multiple table rows. The apply process will always
report an error for changes to tables with LOB, LONG, and LONG RAW
data types when duplicate rows are encountered, ignoring the value set for
this parameter.

■ **commit_serialization**   Default value is DEPENDENT_TRANSACTIONS in
Oracle 11*g* R2. This default is equivalent to the value NONE in the previous
Oracle releases, including Oracle 11*g* R1. The value can be changed to FULL.
When left to the default value, the apply server will commit independent
transactions in any order. Dependent transactions will always commit in the

same order as in the source database. Apply process performance is best with the default value. When set to FULL, the apply process commits transactions in the same order as they were committed in the source database. If the destination database does not enforce constraints, but the application enforces those outside the database, then it is suggested that you change the value of this parameter to FULL until you review the constraints and data dependency requirements in the destination database. The default value of this parameter may cause momentary data integrity problems in logically related information between tables when such relationships are not enforced using database referential integrity constraints.

- **disable_on_error** Default value is Y. This means that the apply process is automatically disabled upon encountering an error while processing the LCR and after it writes the transaction to the error queue. If you change the value to N, then the apply process stays operational after writing the transaction to the error queue. It is suggested to keep the default value to disable the apply process, so that you can concentrate on debugging the cause of the error and implement a proper solution to avoid it, particularly if you are new to Streams replication. Also, processing a large number of errors from the error queue is a slow process and can adversely affect apply process performance.

- **disable_on_limit** Default value is N. Works in conjunction with the `time_limit` or `transaction_limit` parameter. If changed to Y, then the apply process is stopped upon reaching the values set for one of these parameters. If left to its default (N), then the apply process is restarted after stopping upon reaching the values set for these parameters.

- **maximum_scn** Default value is INFINITE. If a particular SCN is specified, then the apply process stops before applying the LCR with a commit SCN that is higher than the specified SCN. When left to its default, the apply process does not stop, irrespective of the commit SCN in the LCR. This parameter is helpful when you want to stop the apply process once it has applied all transactions from the source up to a known SCN value. This is something you might have to do during database recovery operations.

- **parallelism** Default value is 4. It is an integer value that specifies the number of apply server processes to run when the apply process is started. All server processes can concurrently apply transactions. There is no defined upper limit for the value of this parameter. It will be constrained by the value set for the operating system processes and the `processes` parameter of the database. If you need to increase the value of this parameter, Oracle recommends it be set to a multiple of 4.

- **preserve_encryption** Default value is Y. This parameter specifies whether encrypted columns (which are encrypted using Transparent Data Encryption, or TDE) at the source database should be kept encrypted at the destination database after applying the changes. By default, the encryption will be preserved and you will be required to have a wallet installed for the destination database. If the parameter is set to Y and the columns are encrypted at the source but not encrypted at the destination, the apply process will raise an error. If the parameter is set to N, then the apply process does not raise an error even if the columns are encrypted at the source, and applies the changes to the destination table. If the value of this parameter is changed while the apply process is running, then the apply process will be restarted upon committing currently active transactions.

- **rtrim_on_implicit_conversion** Default value is Y. The parameter specifies whether the trailing blank padding should be removed from the column values when performing automatic data conversion while applying changes. If set to Y, then trailing blank padding will be removed when converting CHAR or NCHAR columns in the LCR to VARCHAR2, NVARCHAR2, or CLOB. If set to N, blank padding will not be removed.

- **startup_seconds** Default value is 0. This parameter works in conjunction with the `time_limit`, `transaction_limit`, and `disable_on_limit` parameters. It is specified in number of seconds. If `disable_on_limit` is set to N, then the apply process is restarted after it was shut down upon reaching the limits set by the `time_limit` or `transaction_limit` parameter. However, the apply process may take some time to shut down due to in-flight transactions. This parameter is used to induce a delay in restarting it if `disable_on_limit` was set to N. The default value of 0 indicates that the startup of the apply process will be issued immediately. If the value is set to INFINITE, then the apply process will not be automatically started.

- **time_limit** Default value is INFINITE. This parameter specifies the amount of time in seconds that the apply process should continue to run. After reaching this limit, the apply process is stopped automatically as soon it completes the current transaction. Depending on the value set for the `disable_on_limit` parameter, the apply process may restart or stay disabled. The default value specifies that the apply process will keep running until it is manually stopped.

- **trace_level** Default value is 0. The parameter is used to trace the behavior of the apply process. By default, there is no tracing enabled. Do not change the default value unless asked to do so by Oracle Support.

- **transaction_limit** Default value is INFINITE. This parameter specifies the number of transactions the apply process should apply. The apply process stops after applying the specified number of transactions. It may restart automatically depending on the value set for the `disable_on_limit` parameter. By default, the apply process keeps running and does not stop after applying a certain number of transactions.

■ **txn_age_spill_threshold**   Default value is 900 seconds. The apply process may spill the transaction from the memory queue to a table stored on the disk when any LCR in a transaction stays in the memory without getting dequeued for longer than the duration set by this parameter. By default, LCRs that are present in memory for longer than 900 seconds can cause the transaction to spill to the disk table. If the value is set to INFINITE, then the apply process does not spill any transactions to the disk table based on its age in the memory.

■ **txn_lcr_spill_threshold**   Default value is 10,000. When the number of messages (LCRs) in a particular transaction in the memory exceeds the value set for this parameter, the apply process will begin to spill those messages to a disk table. This is called *apply spill*. The transaction spills to the disk in batches. The number of messages in the first batch equals the value of this parameter. If the reader process detects more messages for the same transaction, then each subsequent batch will have up to either 100 messages or the number specified for this parameter, whichever is less. To illustrate this spilling process, consider an example in which the value of this parameter is left to the default 10,000, and a transaction has 10,150 messages. When the reader process detects more messages after reading the first 10,000 in memory, it spills the first batch of 10,000 messages to the disk table. The reader process continues reading more messages, and when it detects there are more than 100, it spills this batch of 100 messages to the disk table. In the next go, there are only 50 LCRs read. These will stay in the memory since the number is less than 100. The apply process will then begin to read the messages from the disk table to apply to the destination database. After applying 10,100 messages that were fetched from the disk table, the apply process will apply the last 50 messages from the memory. Once the transaction is complete, the apply process purges the messages from the disk table. If the value for this parameter is set to INFINITE, then the reader process will not spill the transaction to the disk table. If there is lack of memory to hold transactions, then Oracle triggers an automatic flow control that prevents transmission of messages to the apply queue by the propagation process or capture process.

■ **write_alert_log**   Default value is Y. This parameter specifies whether the apply process should write a message in the alert log file when it stops. If set to Y, the apply process will write a message when it stops. If set to N, then it will not. However, if the apply process is aborted for some reason, a message will be written to the alert log regardless of the value of this parameter.

In addition to these parameters, there are also a number of hidden parameters. You are not supposed to change these hidden parameters without approval from Oracle Support. However, the following query can be used to view these hidden parameters and their values:

```
SQL> select p.name parameter,
  2            p.value,
  3            p.user_changed_flag,
  4            p.internal_flag
  5    from sys.streams$_process_params p,
  6            sys.streams$_apply_process a
  7    where p.process#    = a.apply#
  8      and a.apply_name = 'DBXA_APP'
  9      and p.name like '\_%' escape '\'
 10    order by parameter;
```

PARAMETER	VALUE	USER_CHANGED_FLAG	INTERNAL_FLAG
_APPLY_SAFETY_LEVEL	1	0	1
_CMPKEY_ONLY	N	0	1
_COMMIT_SERIALIZATION_PERIOD	0	0	1
_DATA_LAYER	Y	0	1
_DYNAMIC_STMTS	Y	0	1
_HASH_TABLE_SIZE	1000000	0	1
_IGNORE_CONSTRAINTS	NO	0	1
_IGNORE_TRANSACTION		0	1
_KGL_CACHE_SIZE	100	0	1
_LCR_CACHE_PURGE_PERIOD	604800	0	1
_LCR_CACHE_PURGE_RATIO	0	0	1
_MIN_USER_AGENTS	0	0	1
_PARTITION_SIZE	10000	0	1
_RECORD_LWM_INTERVAL	1	0	1
_RESTRICT_ALL_REF_CONS	Y	0	1
_SGA_SIZE	1	0	1
_TXN_BUFFER_SIZE	320	0	1
_XML_SCHEMA_USE_TABLE_OWNER	Y	0	1

```
18 rows selected.
```

Handling Triggers

When implementing Streams replication for tables that have triggers defined in both the source and destination databases, a common question is how Oracle Streams handles triggers in the destination database. Will the trigger fire and attempt to perform the same action that was performed at the source, or will it not fire and possibly create a data mismatch at the destination database? The answer depends on how the replication is configured, and how the trigger firing property is set at the destination database.

By default, the triggers at the destination database are not fired if the apply process, or the procedures that reapply transactions from the error queue, made the changes to the tables. The triggers are fired if a user process (or a SQL session) made the changes directly to the tables in the destination database.

So, for example, consider that the table EMP in the SCOTT schema in the source and destination databases has a trigger called EMP_TRIG that inserts a row in the EMP_HIST table whenever the EMP row is modified. Both EMP and EMP_HIST tables are defined in Streams replication. In this case, by default the trigger EMP_TRIG in the destination database will not fire. The capture process will capture changes made to the EMP table by the user application and changes made to the EMP_HIST table by the trigger. The apply process will apply the changes made to EMP table and changes made to the EMP_HIST table separately, without firing the trigger. This is the apply process's default behavior for working with triggers.

You may want to modify the trigger firing property if the trigger is defined on tables only in the destination database and you want it to fire regardless of who made the change to the table. Or, unlike in the previous example, if EMP_HIST is not defined in replication but a trigger on the EMP table in the destination database must track changes made only by the apply process, you may want to modify the trigger firing property.

The Oracle-supplied package DBMS_DDL provides a procedure to control the trigger firing property. The procedure SET_TRIGGER_FIRING_PROPERTY can be used to specify whether the trigger always fires, fires once, or fires for changes made by the apply process (including those resulting from reapplying transactions from the error queue). The procedure is overloaded and offers two options to set the firing property.

In the following example, the trigger firing property is set to fire the trigger once, by setting the `fire_once` parameter to TRUE. The trigger will be fired only if the user application, and not the apply process, caused the triggering event. This is the default for DML and DDL triggers. If `fire_once` is set to FALSE, then the trigger will be fired regardless of who, the user application or the apply process, caused the triggering event.

```
SQL> begin
  2    dbms_ddl.set_trigger_firing_property(
  3      trig_owner => 'SCOTT',
  4      trig_name  => 'EMP_TRIG',
  5      fire_once  => TRUE);
  6  end;
  7  /
PL/SQL procedure successfully completed.
```

In the following example, the trigger firing property is set to fire only if the apply process, or the procedures to reapply transactions from the error queue, caused the triggering event. The trigger will not fire if the triggering event was a user application.

```
SQL> begin
  2     dbms_ddl.set_trigger_firing_property(
  3        trig_owner => 'SCOTT',
  4        trig_name  => 'EMP_TRIG',
  5        property   => dbms_ddl.apply_server_only,
  6        setting    => TRUE);
  7  end;
  8  /
PL/SQL procedure successfully completed.
```

The `property` parameter can be set to DBMS_DDL.FIRE_ONCE to change the trigger firing property back to fire once.

The procedure IS_TRIGGER_FIRE_ONCE in the DBMS_DDL package can be used to check the firing property of the trigger, as shown next. The procedure returns TRUE if the trigger is set to fire once, and returns FALSE if the trigger is set to always fire.

```
SQL> declare
  2     value boolean;
  3  begin
  4     value := dbms_ddl.is_trigger_fire_once (
  5                     trig_owner => 'SCOTT',
  6                     trig_name => 'EMP_TRIG');
  7     if value
  8       then
  9         dbms_output.put_line('Trigger is set to fire once');
 10       else
 11         dbms_output.put_line('Trigger is set to fire always');
 12     end if;
 13  end;
SQL> /
Trigger is set to fire once
PL/SQL procedure successfully completed.
```

The column APPLY_SERVER_ONLY in the DBA_TRIGGERS view contains YES if only the apply server causes the triggering event:

```
SQL> col apply_server_only for a20
SQL> select apply_server_only
  2    from dba_triggers
  3   where owner = 'SCOTT'
  4     and trigger_name = 'EMP_TRIG';

APPLY_SERVER_ONLY
--------------------
YES
```

Handling Column Discrepancies

In addition to the question regarding triggers, the other question that gets asked when configuring Oracle Streams replication is what happens if the source and destination tables are not identical. The column data types, number of columns, or column names might be different, or the table might not have a primary key or a unique key.

The apply engine can handle such discrepancies between the source and destination tables. The following sections discuss how the apply engine handles various types of column discrepancies.

Data Type Mismatch

The apply process performs automatic data conversion for most captured data types when it detects that the data type of the column at the destination does not match the data type in the LCR from the source database. No additional configuration is required.

Table 6-3 summarizes such data type conversions.

Fewer Columns at Destination

If the table at the destination database has fewer columns than the table at the source, then by default the apply process will raise an error and write the entire transaction to

Source Data Type	Data Type Conversion Choices at Destination
CHAR	NCHAR, VARCHAR2, NVARCHAR2, CLOB
NCHAR	CHAR, VARCHAR2, NVARCHAR2, CLOB
VARCHAR2	CHAR, NCHAR, NVARCHAR2, CLOB
NVARCHAR2	CHAR, NCHAR, VARCHAR2, CLOB
NUMBER	CHAR, NCHAR, VARCHAR2, NVARCHAR2
LONG	CLOB
LONG RAW	BLOB, DATE
RAW	BLOB, DATE
DATE	TIMESTAMP
TIMESTAMP	DATE

TABLE 6-3. *Automatic Data Type Conversion by Apply Process*

the apply error queue table. Such an error can be avoided by removing columns from the LCR that do not exist in the destination table. Such column removal can be done using an apply handler procedure, or the rule-based transformation using the DELETE_COLUMN, or the KEEP_COLUMN procedure of the DBMS_STREAMS_ADM package.

More Columns at Destination

Conversely, if the destination table has more columns than the source, the LCR will not have these extra columns from the source database. There are a couple of ways the apply process handles this situation. If the extra columns are missing from the LCR but are required in dependency computations, then an error is raised and the transaction is written to the error queue. If these extra columns are not required in dependency computations, then column default values are used while inserting new rows. If the default values are not defined, then the columns are set to NULL. It is also possible to add the extra columns to the LCR with default values by using the rule-based transformation to avoid apply errors.

Column Name Mismatch

If the column names at the destination do not match the column names at the source, the apply process raises an error and writes the entire transaction to the error queue table. It is possible to change the column name in the LCR to match the destination column name using a rule-based transformation. The procedure RENAME_COLUMN in the DBMS_STREAMS_ADM package performs such name changes.

NOTE
Rule-based transformations are discussed in detail in Chapter 9.

No Primary Key or Unique Key

Ideally, each replicated table should have a primary key. In cases where a primary key is not available, Oracle recommends that you identify a set of columns that can uniquely identify the row of the table. If available, Oracle uses the primary key, or the smallest unique key that has at least one NOT NULL column, to identify the rows in the table to apply the change. If none of these requirements can be met, then Oracle recommends that you assign a substitute key at the destination database. The substitute key can be a single column or a set of columns that will be used to uniquely identify the row in the table.

The substitute key is specified using the SET_KEY_COLUMNS procedure in the DBMS_APPLY_ADM package. The following example shows how to specify the substitute key for the SCOTT.EMP table. The procedure is overloaded and provides `column_table` parameter of type DBMS_UTILITY.NAME_ARRAY in place of `column_list` parameter of type VARCHAR2.

```
SQL> begin
  2   dbms_apply_adm.set_key_columns(
  3      object_name  =>  'SCOTT.EMP',
  4      column_list  =>  'ENAME, EMPNO'
  5      );
  6   end;
  7 /
PL/SQL procedure successfully completed.
```

In the SET_KEY_COLUMNS procedure, specifying NULL for `column_list` or `column_table` removes the existing substitute key for the table. The data dictionary view DBA_APPLY_KEY_COLUMNS lists the defined substitute keys. Also note that the substitute key is not specific to any one apply process. All apply processes will use the defined substitute key for the table.

You can specify a substitute key even if the table has a primary or unique key. In such case, the substitute key takes precedence over the other keys. Columns with LONG, LONG RAW, LOB, Oracle, or user-defined data types cannot be specified as the substitute key.

It is recommended that all columns in the substitute key be defined as NOT NULL. Also, there should be a single index created on these columns in the destination database. The columns should also have an unconditional supplemental log group defined in the source database. When no primary key, unique key, or substitute key is available, Oracle uses all columns of the table, excluding the ones with the data types just mentioned, to identify the row in the destination table. In such cases, it is recommended that the table have an unconditional supplemental logging of all columns in the source database.

Handling Transaction Dependencies

The apply engine, by default, applies dependent changes to the destination database in the same order as they are committed in the source database. Changes that are not dependent on other changes can be applied in any order based on the value set for the apply parameter `parallelism`. When it is set to 1, all changes are applied in the same order in which they are committed in the source database, and there is no transaction dependency issues. When `parallelism` is set to a value greater than 1, and the `commit_serialization` parameter is left to the default value, independent transactions can be applied in any order. The dependencies can exist between LCRs within the same transaction or between different transactions.

The apply engine always respects the dependencies between transactions that are enforced by constraints in the destination database. In this case, the values set for the apply parameters `commit_serialization` and `parallelism` do not matter. If the apply engine detects a dependency between a row LCR in one transaction and a row LCR in another transaction, then these transactions are applied in the correct order.

To compute the dependencies accurately, the apply engine uses the key columns of the table and the columns used to enforce referential integrity constraints at the destination database. These columns must exist in the LCR from the source database, and unconditional supplemental logging must be configured for these columns.

If the destination database does not enforce the referential integrity constraints, the apply engine cannot compute dependencies between transactions. If the `parallelism` parameter is also set to a value greater than 1, the multiple apply servers will apply transactions simultaneously in a random order. If you want to apply the dependent transactions in the same order in which they are committed at the source, then you need to define *virtual dependencies* in the destination database. The virtual dependencies provide the apply engine with additional information it can use in dependency computations. The virtual dependencies do not create any new objects in the data dictionary, but create dependency definitions for the apply engine. These include a parent-child relationship between two tables, or relationships between the columns of two or more tables similar to the foreign key constraints.

There are two types of virtual dependencies, as described next.

Object Dependency

The virtual object dependency defines a parent-child relationship between two tables in the destination database. Transactions against the child tables are executed only after all transactions against the parent tables, that have a lower commit SCN, are committed first. The apply process uses the object identifier in the LCR to detect dependencies between the parent and child tables. The column values in the LCR are not used to detect object dependencies. If the tables have circular dependencies, it can cause a deadlock when apply process's `parallelism` parameter is set to a value greater than 1. Such deadlocks are possible if there are two or more transactions that involve these tables.

The object dependencies are useful when the destination database does not have the relationship defined between the parent and the child table, but the user application expects this relationship when accessing data in these tables.

The CREATE_OBJECT_DEPENDENCY procedure in the DBMS_APPLY_ADM package is used to define the virtual object dependency, as shown next. This example defines the parent-child relationship between the DEPT and EMP tables in the SCOTT schema. The tables can be in different schemas.

```
SQL> begin
  2      dbms_apply_adm.create_object_dependency(
  3           object_name          => 'SCOTT.EMP',
  4           parent_object_name   => 'SCOTT.DEPT');
  5 end;
SQL> /
PL/SQL procedure successfully completed.
```

The DROP_OBJECT_DEPENDENCY procedure of the DBMS_APPLY_ADM package removes the object dependency definition. The DBA_APPLY_OBJECT_DEPENDENCIES view lists the defined object dependencies in the database. All apply processes use this information.

Value Dependency

The virtual value dependency defines a table constraint, which is similar to a unique key or column relationship between two or more tables, or to a foreign key constraint. The apply engine uses the value dependency definitions to detect dependencies between row LCRs that contain values for these columns.

The value dependencies are useful when there are no foreign key constraints defined in the destination database. Value dependencies can define the virtual foreign key relationship between two or more tables. So, if a value dependency is defined between the DEPT and EMP tables using the DEPTNO column, then different transactions involving the DEPT table and the EMP table will be executed in correct order by using the value of DEPTNO as the virtual foreign key.

The SET_VALUE_DEPENDENCY procedure in the DBMS_APPLY_ADM package is used to define or remove the value dependencies. The following example defines value dependencies between the DEPT and EMP tables in the SCOTT schema using the DEPTNO column. Multiple columns can be specified using a comma delimiter. There can more than two tables in this definition.

```
SQL> begin
  2    dbms_apply_adm.set_value_dependency(
  3        dependency_name => 'EMP_VAL_DEP',
  4        object_name     => 'SCOTT.DEPT',
  5        attribute_list  => 'DEPTNO');
  6    dbms_apply_adm.set_value_dependency(
  7        dependency_name => 'EMP_VAL_DEP',
  8        object_name     => 'SCOTT.EMP',
  9        attribute_list  => 'DEPTNO');
 10  end;
 11  /
PL/SQL procedure successfully completed.
```

The identical dependency_name value in the preceding example defines the relationship between the specified tables.

To remove the value dependency, the SET_VALUE_DEPENDENCY procedure is used with the existing dependency_name value and NULL for object_name.

There are a couple of requirements when using value dependencies. First, all the column names in the attribute list must have supplemental logging enabled at the source database. Second, the row LCRs for the objects specified in the value dependency must come from the same source database.

Message Processing by the Apply Process

By default, the apply process dequeues the messages (LCRs) and directly applies them to the destination tables. However, it offers a unique feature that provides you with a powerful mechanism to receive the LCRs in a user-defined procedure as a parameter. This flexibility offers customized processing of the LCRs to suit your business requirements. These user-defined procedures to process the LCRs are called apply handler procedures, or simply apply handlers.

Most commonly, the apply handlers are used to reformat the data in the LCR before applying it to the destination database. The reformatting can include masking out the sensitive data, transforming column names, modifying a DELETE operation to UPDATE to preserve historical data, auditing the DDL and DML actions, and so forth.

The apply process passes the LCR to the handler procedure for customized processing. Figure 6-2 shows the message processing options for an apply process.

There are several different types of apply handler procedures, as described next.

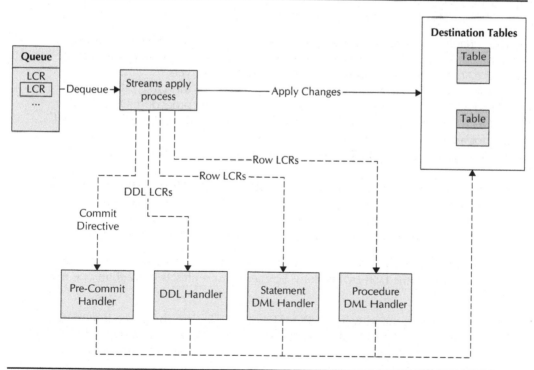

FIGURE 6-2. *Message processing options for an apply process*

DML Handler

The DML handler is a user-defined procedure that processes each row (DML) LCR that is dequeued by the apply process. The LCR contains a specific DML operation performed on a specific table. It is possible to define a number of DML handlers for an apply process. There are two types of DML handlers: procedure DML handlers and statement DML handlers. The procedure DML handler uses PL/SQL procedures to process the LCR, while the statement DML handler uses SQL statements to process the LCR. These DML handlers are described next.

Procedure DML Handler

The procedure DML handler can be used to perform any custom processing of the row LCR. You can modify the information in the LCR and execute the LCR to apply the changes. When the apply process executes the LCR via the DML handler procedure, it does not invoke the handler again.

The procedure DML handler must have the following form:

```
PROCEDURE procedure_name (
        parameter_name   IN   SYS.ANYDATA);
```

The variable `procedure_name` is the name of the user-defined handler procedure. The variable `parameter_name` is an arbitrary name for the parameter passed to the procedure. The parameter passed will be of SYS.ANYDATA type.

Multiple procedure DML handlers can be specified for the same table, each associated with a particular DML operation on the table. The procedure DML handler for an INSERT operation can process the LCR differently from how the procedure DML handler for a DELETE operation processes the LCR.

The user procedure for the handler has the following restrictions:

- The procedure should not contain COMMIT or ROLLBACK. This can violate the consistency of the transaction as such. The apply process issues these directives as the transaction is applied. Issuing the COMMIT command at the LCR level in the middle of the transaction should not be attempted.

- The procedure should not change the LCR information in such a way that re-executing the LCR by invoking `lcr.execute` affects more than one row in the table.

- If the LCR command type is UPDATE or DELETE, then the procedure must ensure that all the old values for the key columns are preserved in the LCR before re-executing it. If the key columns are not preserved, an apply error will be raised.

- If the LCR command type is INSERT, then the procedure must ensure that the new values for all the key columns are preserved in the LCR before re-executing the LCR a second time. Otherwise, duplicate rows are possible.

Following is an example of a simple procedure DML handler that masks the Social Security number in the SSNO column of the row in the EMP table before applying the LCR. The SSNO column in the destination database will always contain the masked value.

```
SQL> create or replace procedure
  2      mask_ssno_dml_handler (in_any IN SYS.ANYDATA)
  3   is
  4
  5   lcr            SYS.LCR$_ROW_RECORD;
  6   rc             PLS_INTEGER;
  7   dml_command    VARCHAR2(10);
  8   l_ssno         number;
  9   l_ssno_chg     ANYDATA;
 10
 11  begin
 12       -- Access the LCR.
 13       rc := in_any.GETOBJECT(lcr);
 14
 15       -- Get the DML command.
 16       dml_command  := lcr.GET_COMMAND_TYPE();
 17
 18       -- Set the masking value for SSNO.
 19       l_ssno := 999999999;
 20
 21       -- For INSERT change the NEW value for SSNO column.
 22       if dml_command = 'INSERT' then
 23          lcr.set_value('NEW','SSNO', ANYDATA.CONVERTNUMBER(l_ssno));
 24       end if;
 25
 26       -- For DELETE, change the OLD value for SSNO column.
 27       if dml_command = 'DELETE' then
 28          lcr.set_value('OLD','SSNO', ANYDATA.CONVERTNUMBER(l_ssno));
 29       end if;
 30
 31       -- For UPDATE, we need to check if the SSNO was changed.
 32       -- If it was, then we must set the OLD and NEW value in the LCR
 33       -- to the masking value.
 34       l_ssno_chg := null;
 35       if dml_command = 'UPDATE' then
 36          l_ssno_chg := lcr.GET_VALUE('NEW','SSNO','N');
 37          if l_ssno_chg is not null then
 38             lcr.set_value('NEW','SSNO', ANYDATA.CONVERTNUMBER(l_ssno));
 39             lcr.set_value('OLD','SSNO', ANYDATA.CONVERTNUMBER(l_ssno));
 40          end if;
 41       end if;
 42
 43       lcr.execute(true);
 44  end;
 45  /
Procedure created.
```

This procedure was executed by the Streams Administrator (STRMADMIN) to create the DML handler procedure under its schema.

Once the DML handler procedure is created successfully, it must be associated with the destination table and set up for the apply process to pass the LCR to it. The SET_DML_HANDLER procedure in the DBMS_APPLY_ADM package is used to specify the DML handler to the apply process.

The following example configures the MASK_SSNO_DML_HANDLER procedure as the DML handler for the SCOTT.EMP table. It is invoked for INSERT, UPDATE, and DELETE operations.

```
SQL> REM Set the DML Handler for the INSERT operations
SQL> begin
  2        dbms_apply_adm.set_dml_handler
  3        (object_name         => 'SCOTT.EMP',
  4         object_type         => 'TABLE',
  5         operation_name      => 'INSERT',
  6         error_handler       => FALSE,
  7         user_procedure      => 'STRMADMIN.MASK_SSNO_DML_HANDLER');
  8   end;
  9   /
PL/SQL procedure successfully completed.

SQL> REM Set the DML Handler for the UPDATE operations
SQL> begin
  2        dbms_apply_adm.set_dml_handler
  3        (object_name         => 'SCOTT.EMP',
  4         object_type         => 'TABLE',
  5         operation_name      => 'UPDATE',
  6         error_handler       => FALSE,
  7         user_procedure      => 'STRMADMIN.MASK_SSNO_DML_HANDLER');
  8   end;
  9   /
PL/SQL procedure successfully completed.

SQL> REM Set the DML Handler for the DELETE operations
SQL> begin
  2        dbms_apply_adm.set_dml_handler
  3        (object_name         => 'SCOTT.EMP',
  4         object_type         => 'TABLE',
  5         operation_name      => 'DELETE',
  6         error_handler       => FALSE,
  7         user_procedure      => 'STRMADMIN.MASK_SSNO_DML_HANDLER');
  8   end;
  9   /
PL/SQL procedure successfully completed.
```

To unset a procedure DML handler, execute the same procedure SET_DML_ HANDLER with all the same parameters but specify NULL for user_procedure.

Statement DML Handler

The statement DML handler does not use PL/SQL procedures to perform custom processing of the row LCR. It contains one or more SQL statements. Since there is no interaction with the PL/SQL engine, the statement DML handler performs better than the procedure DML handler. It is also possible to use a trigger to perform the actions that the statement DML handler might perform. However, the statement DML handler procedure will execute more efficiently.

The statement DML handler does not let you modify the values of the columns in the LCR itself. It can execute a valid DML statement on the row identified by the LCR. However, the SQL statement can insert or update a row with column values that are different from the ones in the row LCR.

One or more SQL statements can be defined for a statement DML handler. Each SQL statement has a user-defined execution sequence number. The statement executes in the ascending order of this execution number.

Multiple statement DML handlers can be specified for the same table, each associated with a particular DML operation on the table. The statement DML handler for the INSERT operation can process the LCR differently from how the statement DML handler for the DELETE operation processes the LCR.

The statement DML handler should not contain COMMIT or ROLLBACK. This can violate the consistency of the transaction as such. The apply process issues these directives as the transaction is applied.

There are two ways to create a statement DML handler:

- If the handler will have only one SQL statement to begin with, then the ADD_STMT_HANDLER procedure In the DBMS_APPLY_ADM package can be used to create the statement DML handler and associate it with the table, the DML operation, and the apply process in one step. The following example creates a statement DML handler that modifies the SSNO field while inserting rows into the SCOTT.EMP table:

```
SQL> declare
  2      stmt clob;
  3  begin
  4      stmt := 'insert into scott.emp(
  5                      empno,      ename,
  6                      jobname,    mgr,
  7                      hiredate,   sal,
  8                      comm,       deptno,     ssno)
  9                  values(
 10                      :new.empno,     :new.ename,
 11                      :new.jobname,   :new.mgr,
 12                      :new.hiredate,  :new.sal,
 13                      :new.comm,      :new.deptno,    999999999)';
```

```
14    dbms_apply_adm.add_stmt_handler(
15      object_name     => 'SCOTT.EMP',
16      operation_name => 'INSERT',
17      handler_name    => 'MODIFY_SSNO_HANDLER',
18      statement       => stmt,
19      apply_name      => 'DBXA_APP',
20      comment => 'Modifies SSNO when inserting rows into SCOTT.EMP'
21    );
22  end;
23  /
```

```
PL/SQL procedure successfully completed.
```

■ If the handler will have more than one SQL statement, then the CREATE_
STMT_HANDLER procedure in the DBMS_STREAMS_HANDLER_ADM
package can be used to create the handler first. The procedure ADD_STMT_
TO_HANDLER must be used to add the SQL statements to the existing
statement handler. Continuing with our previous example, suppose we also
want to record the timestamp, in an audit table, when a row is inserted
into the SCOTT.EMP table. The handler will now perform two actions,
and will require two SQL statements, as shown in the following example.
The `execution_sequence` parameter defined in the ADD_STMT_TO_
HANDLER procedure determines the order in which the statements will be
executed. The following example shows how the statement DML handler is
created to achieve this:

```
SQL> declare
  2    stmt_1 clob;
  3    stmt_2 clob;
  4  begin
  5    stmt_1 := 'insert into scott.emp(
  6                        empno,      ename,
  7                        jobname,    mgr,
  8                        hiredate,   sal,
  9                        comm,       deptno,     ssno)
 10              values(
 11                        :new.empno,    :new.ename,
 12                        :new.jobname,  :new.mgr,
 13                        :new.hiredate, :new.sal,
 14                        :new.comm,     :new.deptno, 999999999)';
 15
 16    stmt_2 := 'insert into scott.emp_audit(
 17                        empno,      insert_date)
 18              values(
 19                        :new.empno, sysdate)';
 20
```

```
21    -- Create a Statement Handler
22    dbms_streams_handler_adm.create_stmt_handler(
23      handler_name    => 'EMP_INSERT_HANDLER',
24      comment         => 'Statement Handler for SCOTT.EMP table'
25    );
26
27    -- Add the SQL statements to the Statement Handler
28    dbms_streams_handler_adm.add_stmt_to_handler(
29      handler_name       => 'EMP_INSERT_HANDLER',
30      statement          => stmt_1,
31      execution_sequence => 10
32    );
33    dbms_streams_handler_adm.add_stmt_to_handler(
34      handler_name       => 'EMP_INSERT_HANDLER',
35      statement          => stmt_2,
36      execution_sequence => 20
37    );
38
39    -- Assign the Statement Handler to the apply process
40    dbms_apply_adm.add_stmt_handler(
41      object_name    => 'SCOTT.EMP',
42      operation_name => 'INSERT',
43      handler_name   => 'EMP_INSERT_HANDLER',
44      apply_name     => 'DBXA_APP'
45    );
46  end;
47  /
PL/SQL procedure successfully completed.
```

DDL Handler

The DDL handler is a user-defined PL/SQL procedure that processes each DDL LCR that is dequeued by the apply process. The LCR contains a specific DDL operation performed in the source database that affects a specific table.

The DDL handler can be used to track DDL changes and create an audit trail of the DDL operations performed on the source database. Also, using a DDL handler, it is possible to allow or reject certain DDL operations in the destination database. Although not very straightforward, it is possible to check the contents of the DDL text, which contains the actual DDL command executed at the source database, and take appropriate actions in the DDL handler procedure.

If you have defined a rule-based transformation to change the schema name, table name, or column name for the replicated objects, then to replicate DDL for such objects, you will need to define a DDL handler that will change these names in the DDL LCR, including the DDL text.

The following example shows a DDL handler procedure that allows certain DDL operations to replicate based on the defined command types. All DDL commands will be logged in an audit table. For more granular control over what DDL operation gets replicated, you have to parse the actual DDL text, and possibly modify it. So, for the ALTER TABLE command type, you can filter out unwanted ALTER operations against a table.

```
SQL> create table streams_ddl_audit
  2  (
  3      timestamp                     date,
  4      source_database_name          varchar2(60),
  5      command_type                  varchar2(30),
  6      object_owner                  varchar2(30),
  7      object_name                   varchar2(30),
  8      object_type                   varchar2(20),
  9      ddl_text                      clob,
 10      logon_user                    varchar2(30),
 11      current_schema                varchar2(30),
 12      base_table_owner              varchar2(30),
 13      base_table_name               varchar2(30),
 14      streams_tag                   raw(10),
 15      transaction_id                varchar2(30),
 16      scn                           number,
 17      action                        varchar2(15)
 18  )
 19  /
Table created.
SQL> create or replace procedure ddl_handler (in_any in sys.anydata)
  2  is
  3      lcr            sys.lcr$_ddl_record;
  4      rc             pls_integer;
  5      l_command_type varchar2(30);
  6      l_action       varchar2(15);
  7      l_ddl_text     clob;
  8
  9  begin
 10    rc := in_any.getobject(lcr);
 11    -- Create temp lob for DDL Text
 12    dbms_lob.createtemporary(l_ddl_text, true);
 13    lcr.get_ddl_text(l_ddl_text);
 14    -- Get the DDL Command Type
 15    l_command_type := lcr.get_command_type();
 16    -- Check DDL command type and set action for the LCR
 17    if l_command_type in (
 18                          'TRUNCATE TABLE',
 19                          'DROP TABLE',
 20                          'DROP INDEX'
 21                          )
```

```
22      then
23          l_action := 'IGNORE';
24      else
25          l_action := 'EXECUTE';
26      end if;
27      -- Log information from the LCR in the audit table
28      insert into streams_ddl_audit
29       values ( sysdate,
30                 lcr.get_source_database_name(),
31                 lcr.get_command_type(),
32                 lcr.get_object_owner(),
33                 lcr.get_object_name(),
34                 lcr.get_object_type(),
35                 l_ddl_text,
36                 lcr.get_logon_user(),
37                 lcr.get_current_schema(),
38                 lcr.get_base_table_owner(),
39                 lcr.get_base_table_name(),
40                 lcr.get_tag(),
41                 lcr.get_transaction_id(),
42                 lcr.get_scn(),
43                 l_action
44                 );
45      -- Execute or Ignore the DDL LCR
46      if l_action =  'EXECUTE'
47      then
48        lcr.execute();
49      end if;
50      -- Release the temp lob
51      dbms_lob.freetemporary(l_ddl_text);
52
53  end;
54  /
Procedure created.
```

Once the DDL handler procedure is created, it must be associated with the apply process. This can be done using the ALTER_APPLY or the CREATE_APPLY procedure of the DBMS_APPLY_ADM package. If the apply process is already present, use the former; otherwise, use the latter to specify the DDL handler while creating the apply process. The following example shows the use of the ALTER_APPLY procedure:

```
SQL> begin
  2    dbms_apply_adm.alter_apply(
  3      apply_name  => 'DBXA_APP',
  4      ddl_handler => 'STRMADMIN.DDL_HANDLER');
  5  end;
  6  /
PL/SQL procedure successfully completed.
```

NOTE
An apply process can have only one DDL handler.

Error Handler

The error handler is a special form of a procedure DML handler. The error handler is invoked when an apply error occurs when processing a row LCR that contains a specific DML operation against a specific table. There can be multiple error handlers on the same table to handle errors resulting from different DML operations.

The error handler can be used to resolve the possible error condition and reapply the LCR, or it can simply log the error in a user-defined error-logging table and generate an alert to the support personnel. If the error handler procedure cannot resolve the error, then an apply error is raised and the transaction is rolled back and written to the apply error queue.

A table can have either an error handler or a DML handler associated with it for a particular DML operation. If a DML handler is specified, then the procedure must also handle possible errors that may occur when executing the DML operation.

In the following example, the error handler changes the UPDATE command to an INSERT when an error occurs if the row is not found in the destination table. If the error occurs due to differences in the row column values and corresponding old values in the LCR, then the procedure will simply report it as an apply error without attempting to correct it. The procedure makes use of the different Oracle errors when a row is not found (ORA-26787) and when the row has different column values (ORA-26786) to change the UPDATE operation to an INSERT. Note that unconditional supplemental logging of all columns of the table is required to be able to change the UPDATE operation to an INSERT. Also, the table in the example does not contain any columns with LONG, LONG RAW, LOB, Oracle, or user-defined data types.

```
SQL>connect strmadmin/strmadmin@DBXB.WORLD
Connected.
SQL> create or replace package error_handler_pkg
  2  as
  3    type emsg_array is table of varchar2(2000) index by binary_integer;
  4
  5  procedure update_to_insert (
  6       message            IN ANYDATA,
  7       error_stack_depth  IN NUMBER,
  8       error_numbers      IN DBMS_UTILITY.NUMBER_ARRAY,
  9       error_messages     IN EMSG_ARRAY);
 10  end error_handler_pkg;
 11  /
Package created.

SQL> create or replace package body error_handler_pkg
  2  as
  3    procedure update_to_insert (
  4       message            IN ANYDATA,
```

```
 5          error_stack_depth  IN NUMBER,
 6          error_numbers      IN DBMS_UTILITY.NUMBER_ARRAY,
 7          error_messages     IN EMSG_ARRAY)
 8   is
 9      lcr             SYS.LCR$_ROW_RECORD;
10      rc              PLS_INTEGER;
11      old_values      SYS.LCR$_ROW_LIST;
12      new_values      SYS.LCR$_ROW_LIST;
13      err_26787       number;
14      err_26786       number;
15   begin
16     -- Access the row LCR to get data.
17     rc := message.GETOBJECT(lcr);
18     err_26787 := 0;
19     err_26786 := 0;
20     -- Loop thru the error stack to mark what error occurred.
21     for i in 1..error_stack_depth
22      loop
23          if error_numbers(i) = 26787
24          then
25              if err_26787 = 0 then
26                  err_26787 := 1;
27              end if;
28          end if;
29
30          if error_numbers(i) = 26786
31          then
32              if err_26786 = 0 then
33                  err_26786 := 1;
34              end if;
35          end if;
36     end loop;
37
38     if err_26787 = 1
39     then
40       -- Row not found for UPDATE operation.
41       -- Change UPDATE to INSERT.
42       lcr.SET_COMMAND_TYPE('INSERT');
43
44       -- NOTE: It is assumed that all columns of the table
45       -- have unconditional supplemental logging defined.
46
47       -- Save existing old and new values from LCR.
48       old_values := lcr.GET_VALUES('old', 'y');
49       new_values := lcr.GET_VALUES('new', 'y');
50
51       -- Using the old values and updated new values,
52       -- prepare the LCR with correct new values for the
53       -- INSERT operation.
54       for i in 1..old_values.count
55       loop
```

```
56        for j in 1..new_values.count
57        loop
58            if old_values(i).column_name = new_values(j).column_name
59            then
60                old_values(i).data := new_values(j).data;
61            end if;
62        end loop;
63     end loop;
64     -- Set the new values in the LCR.
65     lcr.SET_VALUES('NEW', old_values);
66
67     -- Remove all old values from LCR.
68     lcr.SET_VALUES('OLD', null);
69
70     -- Execute modified LCR.
71     lcr.execute(true);
72   end if;
73   -- Row was found for UPDATE but old values did not match.
74   if err_26786 = 1
75   then
76       -- Re-Execute LCR to create error again.
77     lcr.execute(true);
78   end if;
79
80   end update_to_insert;
81 end error_handler_pkg;
82 /
Package body created.
SQL> -- Define the Error Handler to handle apply errors
SQL> -- when applying updates to SCOTT.DEPT table.
SQL> begin
  2    dbms_apply_adm.set_dml_handler(
  3    object_name     => 'SCOTT.DEPT',
  4    object_type     => 'TABLE',
  5    operation_name  => 'UPDATE',
  6    error_handler   => TRUE,
  7    user_procedure  => 'STRMADMIN.ERROR_HANDLER_PKG.update_to_insert',
  8    apply_name      => 'DBXA_APP');
  9  end;
 10  /
PL/SQL procedure successfully completed.
```

This simple procedure demonstrates one way to handle an apply error. Depending on your business requirements, you can write fairly complex procedures to correct apply errors.

Precommit Handler

The precommit handler is different from all other handlers in that it does not receive the LCRs as its parameter. The handler is invoked when the apply process receives the commit directive to commit the transaction. The commit directive is a control message that contains the COMMIT command. The handler only receives the commit SCN as its parameter. This SCN corresponds to the commit processed at the source database for the transaction.

The precommit handler can be used to audit row LCRs applied to the destination table and the time when those were applied. In such a case, a procedure DML handler or a statement DML handler inserts the LCR information in an audit table as an autonomous transaction. The precommit handler, when invoked by the apply process, can then update this information based on the commit SCN to include the commit timestamp. If required, the precommit handler procedure can also perform other processing based on the stored information in the audit table. It is also possible to use PL/SQL package variables for the DML handlers to store relevant information from the transactions to be used by the precommit handler.

The precommit handler can also be used to asynchronously refresh ON COMMIT materialized views when changes are applied to one of the master tables. This technique minimizes the delay in refreshing such materialized views. For a detailed procedure to achieve this, please contact Oracle Support.

The precommit handler procedure has the following form:

```
PROCEDURE procedure_name (
        commit_scn IN NUMBER );
```

The precommit handler procedure must use an autonomous transaction for any work that it commits, and must create named save points for rolling back changes.

Also note that use of precommit handlers may adversely affect replication performance.

What Changes Are Not Applied?

The apply process does not apply row LCRs generated from changes made to the following data types:

- BFILE

- User-defined types

- Varrays

- Nested tables

- XMLType (stored as other than CLOB)

- Oracle-supplied types: any types, spatial types, media types

The apply process will report an error when it attempts to apply a row LCR that contains columns of an unsupported data type. The apply process cannot apply DML changes to temporary tables or object tables.

The apply process does not apply the following types of DDL statements:

- ALTER MATERIALIZED VIEW
- ALTER MATERIALIZED VIEW LOG
- CREATE DATABASE LINK
- CREATE MATERIALIZED VIEW
- CREATE MATERIALIZED VIEW LOG
- CREATE SCHEMA AUTHORIZATION
- DROP DATABASE LINK
- DROP MATERIALIZED VIEW
- DROP MATERIALIZED VIEW LOG
- FLASHBACK DATABASE
- RENAME

The apply process applies all other types of DDL commands that satisfy the apply rules and were not filtered by the DDL handler procedure. If the apply process receives a DDL LCR with an unsupported command type, as listed previously, it ignores the LCR. It writes a message to the apply trace file, as shown here, followed by the entire DDL text from the LCR:

```
Apply process ignored the following DDL:
DDL Text = rename DEPT to DEPARTMENT
```

Summary

This chapter introduced you to the apply process and explained how to create it. Depending on your requirements, you can create the apply process automatically, along with the apply rules and rule set, or manually by specifying the existing rule set. The chapter also discussed how the apply rule set can be ignored altogether if there are no rule-based transformations required during the apply process. You also reviewed the data types and DDL commands that the apply process ignores.

The apply process is composed of three components; the reader server, the coordinator process, and the apply server. The reader server is responsible for dequeuing the LCRs from the apply queue and assembling them in transactions and track dependencies. The coordinator process keeps track of all assembled transactions, and passes those to apply server processes. It communicates with the apply servers. The apply server process applies the changes to the destination tables.

The apply process can handle column discrepancies between the source and destination tables. Some of these discrepancies can be addressed by using rule-based transformations that can remove extra columns from the LCR, or add new columns to the LCR as required.

The default firing property for the trigger works well with the apply process. The triggers are not fired when the apply process applies changes. However, it is possible to change the trigger firing property based on your requirements.

The apply process allows you to specify user-defined procedures to process the LCR. These apply handler procedures are a flexible and powerful mechanism to have a user-defined procedure to process the LCR. The DML handler procedure processes LCRs generated from a DML operation, and the DDL handler procedure processes LCRs for DDL operations The new statement DML handler runs more efficiently than the procedure DML handler, as it does not invoke the PL/SQL engine. The error handler procedure allows for custom processing of the apply error that can correct the error condition and reapply the LCR. The precommit handler extends the Streams capabilities to perform more customized tasks than just transform data. All these capabilities make the apply process a highly flexible, but complex, operation in Oracle Streams.

CHAPTER
7

Logical Change Records

he Logical Change Record (LCR) is a specially formatted message that represents a database change. In previous chapters, LCRs were mentioned frequently when discussing how database changes are captured, propagated, and applied. The capture process and synchronous capture process create an LCR that represents the DDL or DML changes to the database. There are two types of LCRs:

- **Row LCR**   Represents the change made to a single row (sometimes called DML LCR)

- **DDL LCR**   Represents the change made by a DDL command

Both these LCRs contain the necessary and sufficient information to apply the change to the destination database objects.

In addition to this information, it is possible to specify that additional information be captured into the LCR to be used for auditing or tracking purposes. This additional information is referred to as *extra attributes* in the LCRs. Capturing these extra attributes can be specified for the capture process and synchronous capture process.

This chapter discusses the types of LCRs, what information they contain, and how that information can be accessed and, optionally, modified via custom procedures.

Row LCRs

A row LCR represents a change made to a row of the table by a DML operation, and for this reason the row LCR is sometimes called a DML LCR. Typically each row LCR represents a change to an individual row in the table. One DML operation can affect several rows in the table, in which case an LCR is created for each of those affected rows.

If the row contains a column with a data type of LONG, LONG RAW, LOB, CLOB, or XML type stored as CLOB, then a change made to such a column may generate more than one LCR, depending on the size of the data.

Each row LCR has the following attributes:

- **command_type**   The DML command that caused the change to the row. The command can be DELETE, INSERT, UPDATE, LOB ERASE, LOB TRIM, or LOB WRITE.

- **new_values**   The column values after the change was made to the row. If the command was DELETE, then no new values are listed. If the command was UPDATE, then new values of all the columns that changed are listed. If the command was INSERT, then new values of all the columns are listed. If the synchronous capture captured the LCR, then new values for all the columns in the row are listed for UPDATE and INSERT commands.

- **object_name**   The table name that contains the changed row.

- **object_owner**   The schema name that owns the table that contains the changed row.

- **old_values**   The column values before the change was made to the row. If the command was DELETE, the existing values for all of the columns of the row are listed. If the command was UPDATE, this may contain old values for either only the changed columns or all the columns in the table, depending on the supplemental logging defined for the table. For the INSERT command, the old values are not present. If the synchronous capture process captured the LCR, then the new values for all the columns of the row are listed after the change, and there are no old values.

- **scn**   The system change number of the source database when the change took place.

- **source_database_name**   The global name of the database where the change to the row originated.

- **tag**   A raw tag value that can be used to track the LCR. The value can also be used in Streams rules to exclude the LCR from being processed.

- **transaction_id**   The identifier for the transaction associated with the DML command.

The LCR captured by the capture process also contains the following additional attributes. These are not available in LCRs captured by the synchronous capture process.

- **commit_scn**   The system change number for the transaction to which the LCR belongs

- **commit_time**   The time when the transaction for the LCR was committed in the source database

- **lob_information**   Contains LOB information for the column, such as NOT_A_LOB if the column is not of LOB type, or LOB_CHUNK if it is of LOB type

- **lob_offset**   For columns of CLOB type, contains the offset in number of characters, and for columns of BLOB type, contains the offset in number of bytes

- **lob_operation_size**   The lob operation size in number of characters for CLOB and number of bytes for BLOB

The following two additional attributes are available in the LCRs captured by both the capture process and synchronous capture process:

- **compatible**   The minimum database compatibility required to support the LCR

- **instance_number**   Relevant to Oracle RAC, the instance number of the database where the row was changed

The old_values and new_values attributes in the row LCR are very important. Oracle uses the values of these attributes to ensure data consistency and for automatic conflict detection in the apply process. Chapter 10 discusses how to handle conflicts.

DDL LCRs

A DDL LCR represents a change caused by a DDL operation that involves the replicated table. A DDL statement can alter, drop, or create an object or a dependent object such as a view on a replicated table or an index. The capture process creates the DDL LCRs if DDL changes are to be replicated.

NOTE
The synchronous capture process does not capture DDL changes, and hence does not create DDL LCRs.

Each DDL LCR has the following attributes:

- **base_table_name**   If the object affected by the DDL statement is dependent on a base table, then this is the name of the base table.

- **base_table_owner**   If the object affected by the DDL statement is dependent on a base table, then this contains the schema owner name of the base table.

- **command_type**   The DDL command that caused the change to the database object.

- **current_schema**   The default schema name used for the object, if the schema name for the object was not explicitly specified in the DDL text.

- **ddl_text**   The DDL command issued at the source database that caused the DDL change. This is the exact text of the DDL command.

- **edition_name**   The name of the edition in which the DDL change took place.

■ **logon_user**   Name of the database user under whose session the DDL statement was issued.

■ **object_owner**   The schema name that owns the database object against which the DDL command was run.

■ **object_name**   The object name against which the DDL statement was run.

■ **object_type**   The type of the database object against which the DDL statement was run.

■ **scn**   The system change number of the source database when the DDL change took place.

■ **source_database_name**   The global name of the database where the DDL change originated.

■ **tag**   A raw tag value that can be used to track the LCR. The value can also be used in Streams rules to exclude the LCR from being processed.

■ **transaction_id**   The identifier for the transaction associated with the DDL command.

The DDL LCRs captured by the capture process also contain the following additional attributes:

■ **commit_scn**   The system change number for the transaction to which the LCR belongs

■ **commit_time**   The time when the transaction for the LCR was committed in the source database

■ **compatible**   The minimum database compatibility required to support the LCR

■ **instance_number**   Relevant to Oracle RAC, the instance number of the database where the DDL command was issued

■ **source_time**   The time when the DDL change was recorded in the redo log

All the previously described attributes for the row LCR and DDL LCR are captured automatically. Oracle also provides a mechanism to include extra attributes in these LCRs. These can be used for auditing purposes, if required. The capture process or synchronous capture process can be configured to include these extra attributes in the LCRs.

Extra Attributes in LCRs

The extra attributes can be used to track additional information about the changes made at the source database. Both the capture process and synchronous capture process can capture these extra attributes when constructing the LCRs. There are six such predefined attributes that can be included in the LCRs, as defined next. You must use these names exactly as they are shown here:

- **row_id**   Relevant for the row LCR, this is the row ID of the row in the table that was changed by the DML operation. It is not part of the DDL LCR or LCRs for index-organized tables.

- **serial#**   The serial number of the session in which the DML or DDL operation took place.

- **session#**   The session number in which the DDL or DML operation took place.

- **thread#**   Relevant in Oracle RAC, the instance thread number where the DML or DDL operation took place.

- **tx_name**   The transaction name to which the DDL or DML LCR belongs. It will be blank unless specified by the user when executing the transaction.

- **username**   The name of the connected user who performed the DML or DDL operation.

The INCLUDE_EXTRA_ATTRIBUTE procedure of the DBMS_CAPTURE_ADM package is used to specify the attributes to include in the LCR. By default, these attributes are not captured in the LCRs.

The following example shows how to specify the capture of `row_id` and `username` in the LCR for a capture process named DBXA_CAP:

```
SQL> begin
  2    dbms_capture_adm.include_extra_attribute(
  3         capture_name   => 'DBXA_CAP',
  4         attribute_name => 'ROW_ID',
  5         include        => TRUE);
  6
  7    dbms_capture_adm.include_extra_attribute(
  8         capture_name   => 'DBXA_CAP',
  9         attribute_name => 'USERNAME',
 10         include        => TRUE);
 11  end;
 12  /
PL/SQL procedure successfully completed.
```

As you can see, the parameter `attribute_name` accepts only one name at a time. The `include` parameter is set to TRUE, indicating that the specified attribute is to be included in the LCR. Setting the value to FALSE indicates that the specified attribute should not be included in the LCR.

The DBA_CAPTURE_EXTRA_ATTRIBUTES view shows what attributes are included in the LCRs created by the specified capture process, as shown here:

```
SQL> select attribute_name,
  2          include
  3     from dba_capture_extra_attributes
  4    where capture_name = 'DBXA_CAP'
  5    order by attribute_name;

ATTRIBUTE_NAME                  INCLUDE
------------------------------- ----------
ROW_ID                          YES
SERIAL#                         NO
SESSION#                        NO
THREAD#                         NO
TX_NAME                         NO
USERNAME                        YES
6 rows selected.
```

The INCLUDE column in the output shows YES for the `row_id` and `username`, the two attributes we wanted to include in the LCRs. The rest of the columns are set to the default value of NO, indicating that those will not be included in the LCRs.

NOTE
Including the extra attributes in the LCRs can potentially affect replication performance because it increases the size of the LCR. Include these attributes only when absolutely required.

Accessing LCR Contents

The rules in Oracle Streams, and sometimes the custom procedures such as DML handlers, DDL handlers, and error handlers, access the contents in the LCR. Access to this information is required while evaluating a rule. Accessing the column names and their values is required when you want to track data changes, transform the data, audit certain commands, or filter out certain DML or DDL operations. Oracle Streams provides required APIs to achieve all of these tasks.

As you learned earlier, the Oracle Streams queues are of ANYDATA data type, which is an Oracle-supplied object type. The ANYDATA type can hold instances of any other Oracle data types, such as NUMBER, DATE, CLOB, and VARCHAR2, including other Oracle-supplied object types.

Type	Description
SYS.LCR$_ROW_RECORD	Represents DML changes to the row.
SYS.LCR$_DDL_RECORD	Represents DDL changes to the table.
SYS.LCR$_ROW_UNIT	Identifies the value of a column in the row LCR.
SYS.LCR$_ROW_LIST	Identifies a list of columns with values in the row LCR. This is a table of SYS.LCR$_ROW_UNIT.

TABLE 7-1. *Streams Data Types for LCRs*

ANYDATA is a self-describing data type because it contains data with a description of its type. It offers several member functions and procedures that retrieve and modify the data.

Oracle Streams also uses the additional data types listed and described in Table 7-1. These data types also have member functions and procedures to access and modify the attributes of the LCRs.

These record types are wrapped in the ANYDATA type when the LCRs are enqueued and dequeued.

Figure 7-1 shows the consolidated view of the SYS.ANYDATA type with its attributes and member functions.

Figure 7-2 shows the type model for the SYS.LCR$_ROW_RECORD type with its attributes, member functions, and procedures.

ANYDATA
- DATA
- BEGINCREATE ([IN] : dType : AnyType, [OUT] aData : ANYDATA)
- ENDCREATE : ([IN / OUT] self : ANYDATA)
- GETTYPE ([IN] self : ANYDATA, [OUT] type : AnyType)
- GETTYPENAME ([IN] self : ANYDATA, [OUT] type_name : varchar2)
- PIECEWISE ([IN / OUT] self : ANYDATA)
- GET* ( ) : PLS_INTEGER
- SET* ( )
- CONVERT* ()
- ACCESS* ()

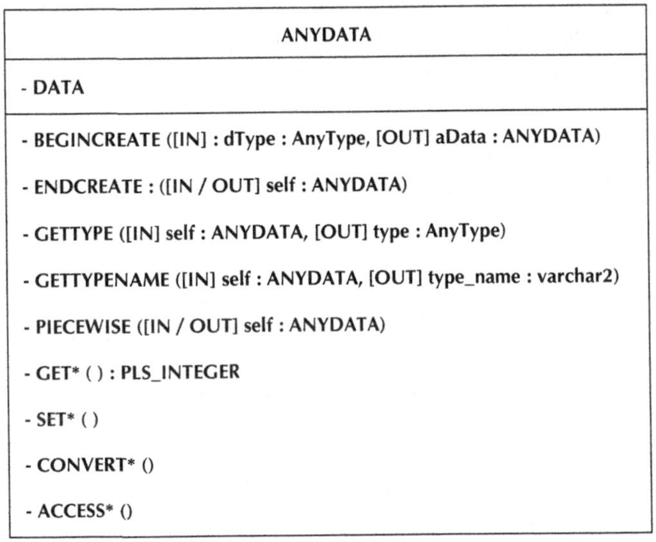

FIGURE 7-1. *ANYDATA type*

LCR$_ROW_RECORD
- SOURCE_DATABASE_NAME : VARCHAR2 - COMMAND_TYPE : VARCHAR2 - OBJECT_OWNER : VARCHAR2 - OBJECT_NAME : VARCHAR2 - TAG : RAW - TRANSACTION_ID : VARCHAR2 - SCN : NUMBER - OLD_VALUES : SYS.LCR$_ROW_LIST - NEW_VALUES : SYS.LCR$_ROW_LIST - ROW_ID : UROWID - SERIAL# : NUMBER - SESSION# : NUMBER - THREAD# : NUMBER - TRANSACTION_NAME : VARCHAR2 - USER_NAME : VARCHAR2

- CONSTRUCT ([IN] source_database_name : VARCHAR2, [IN] command_type : VARCHAR2, [IN] _object_owner :
    VARCHAR2, [IN] object_name : VARCHAR2, [IN] tag : RAW, [IN] transaction_id : VARCHAR2, [IN] scn :
    NUMBER, [IN] old_values : SYS.LCR$_ROW_LIST, [IN] new_values : SYS.LCR$_ROW_LIST) :
    LCR$_ROW_RECORD
 	
- EXECUTE ( )
 	
- ADD_COLUMN ([IN] value_type : VARCHAR2, [IN] col_name : VARCHAR2, [IN] col_value : SYS.AnyData)
 	
- CONVERT_LONG_TO_LOB_CHUNK ( )
 	
- DELETE_COLUMN ([IN] col_name : VARCHAR2, [IN] value_type : VARCHAR2)
 	
- GET_LOB_INFORMATION ([IN] value_type : VARCHAR2, [IN] col_name : VARCHAR2, [IN] use_old : VARCHAR2) : NUMBER
 	
- GET_LOB_OFFSET ([IN] value_type : VARCHAR2, [IN] column_name : VARCHAR2) : NUMBER
 	
- GET_LOB_OPERATION_SIZE ([IN] value_type : VARCHAR2, [IN] column_name : VARCHAR2) : NUMBER
 	
- GET_LONG_INFORMATION ([IN] value_type : VARCHAR2, [IN] column_name : VARCHAR2, [IN] use_old : VARCHAR2)
 	
- GET_VALUE ([IN] value_type : VARCHAR2, [IN] column_name : VARCHAR2, [IN] use_old : VARCHAR2) : ANYDATA
 	
- GET_VALUES ([IN] value_type : VARCHAR2, [IN] use_old : VARCHAR2) : SYS.LCR$_ROW_LIST
 	
- GET_XML_INFORMATION ([IN] column_name : VARCHAR2) : NUMBER
 	
- RENAME_COLUMN ([IN] from_column : VARCHAR2, [IN] to_column : VARCHAR2, [IN] value_type : VARCHAR2)
 	
- SET_LOB_INFORMATION ([IN] value_type : VARCHAR2, [IN] column_name : VARCHAR2, [IN] lob_info : NUMBER)
 	
- SET_LOB_OFFSET ([IN] value_type : VARCHAR2, [IN] column_name : VARCHAR2, [IN] lob_offset : NUMBER)
 	
- SET_LOB_OPERATION_SIZE ([IN] value_type : VARCHAR2, [IN] column_name : VARCHAR2, [IN] lob_size : NUMBER)
 	
- SET_VALUE ([IN] value_type : VARCHAR2, [IN] column_name : VARCHAR2, [IN] column_value : ANYDATA)
 	
- SET_VALUES ([IN] value_type : VARCHAR2, [IN] value_list : SYS.LCR$_ROW_LIST)
 	
- SET_XML_INFORMATION ([IN] column_name : VARCHAR2, [IN] xml_info : NUMBER)

FIGURE 7-2.   *LCR$_ROW_RECORD type*

Figure 7-3 shows the type model for the SYS.LCR$_DDL_RECORD type with its attributes, member functions, and procedures.

```
┌──────────────────────────────────────────────────────────────────┐
│                        LCR$_DDL_RECORD                             │
├──────────────────────────────────────────────────────────────────┤
│ - SOURCE_DATABASE_NAME : VARCHAR2                                  │
│ - COMMAND_TYPE : VARCHAR2                                          │
│ - OBJECT_OWNER : VARCHAR2                                          │
│ - OBJECT_NAME : VARCHAR2                                           │
│ - OBJECT_TYPE : VARCHAR2                                           │
│ - DDL_TEXT : CLOB                                                  │
│ - LOGON_USER : VARCHAR2                                            │
│ - CURRENT_SCHEMA : VARCHAR2                                        │
│ - BASE_TABLE_OWNER : VARCHAR2                                      │
│ - BASE_TABLE_NAME : VARCHAR2                                       │
│ - TAG : RAW                                                        │
│ - TRANSACTION_ID : VARCHAR2                                        │
│ - SCN : NUMBER                                                     │
│ - ROW_ID : UROWID                                                  │
│ - SERIAL# : NUMBER                                                 │
│ - SESSION# : NUMBER                                                │
│ - THREAD# : NUMBER                                                 │
│ - TRANSACTION_NAME : VARCHAR2                                      │
│ - USER_NAME : VARCHAR2                                             │
├──────────────────────────────────────────────────────────────────┤
│ - CONSTRUCT ([IN] source_database_name : VARCHAR2, [IN] command_type : │
│            VARCHAR2, [IN] _object_owner : VARCHAR2, [IN] object_name : │
│            VARCHAR2, [IN] object_type : VARCHAR2, [IN] ddl_text : CLOB, [IN] │
│            logon_user : VARCHAR2, [IN] base_table_owner : VARCHAR2, [IN] │
│            base_table_name : VARCHAR2, [IN] tag : RAW, [IN] transaction_id : │
│            VARCHAR2, [IN] scn : NUMBER) : LCR$_DDL_RECORD           │
│                                                                    │
│ - EXECUTE ( )                                                      │
│                                                                    │
│ - GET_BASE_TABLE_NAME ( ) : VARCHAR2                               │
│                                                                    │
│ - GET_BASE_TABLE_OWNER ( ) : VARCHAR2                              │
│                                                                    │
│ - GET_DDL_TEXT ([IN / OUT] ddl_text : CLOB)                        │
│                                                                    │
│ - GET_LOGON_USER ( ) : VARCHAR2                                    │
│                                                                    │
│ - GET_OBJECT_TYPE ( ) : VARCHAR2                                   │
│                                                                    │
│ - SET_BASE_TABLE_NAME ([IN] base_table_name : VARCHAR2)            │
│                                                                    │
│ - SET_BASE_TABLE_OWNER ([IN] base_table1_owner : VARCHAR2)         │
│                                                                    │
│ - SET_CURRENT_SCHEMA ([IN] current_schema : VARCHAR2)              │
│                                                                    │
│ - SET_DDL_TEXT ([IN] ddl_text : CLOB)                              │
│                                                                    │
│ - SET_LOGON_USER ([IN] logon_user : VARCHAR2)                      │
│                                                                    │
│ - SET_OBJECT_TYPE ([IN] object_type : VARCHAR2)                    │
└──────────────────────────────────────────────────────────────────┘
```

FIGURE 7-3. *LCR$_DDL_RECORD type*

LCR$_DDL_RECORD AND LCR$_ROW_RECORD COMMON SUBPROGRAMS
- GET_COMMAND_TYPE () : VARCHAR2
- GET_COMMIT_SCN( ) : NUMBER
- GET_COMPATIBLE ( ) : NUMBER
- GET_EXTRA_ATTRIBUTE ([IN] attribute_name : VARCHAR2) : ANYDATA
- GET_OBJECT_NAME ( ) : VARCHAR2
- GET_OBJECT_OWNER ( ) : VARCHAR2
- GET_SCN ( ) : NUMBER
- GET_SOURCE_DATABASE_NAME ( ) : VARCHAR2
- GET_SOURCE_TIME ( ) : DATE
- GET_TAG ( ) : RAW
- GET_TRANSACTION_ID ( ) : VARCHAR2
- IS_NULL_TAG ( ) : VARCHAR2
- SET_COMMAND_TYPE ([IN] command_type : VARCHAR2)
- SET_EXTRA_ATTRIBUTE ([IN] attribute_name : VARCHAR2, [IN] attribute_value : ANYDATA)
- SET_OBJECT_NAME ([IN] object_name : VARCHAR2)
- SET_OBJECT_OWNER ([IN] object_owner : VARCHAR2)
- SET_SOURCE_DATABASE_NAME ([IN] source_database_name : VARCHAR2)
- SET_TAG ([IN] tag : RAW)

FIGURE 7-4.   *LCR$_ROW_RECORD and LCR$_DDL_RECORD common functions*

For readability, the common functions and procedures for the LCR$_ROW_RECORD and LCR$_DDL_RECORD types are listed in Figure 7-4.

You can use the SQL*Plus describe command to list these member functions and procedures of the SYS.ANYDATA, SYS.LCR$_ROW_RECORD, and SYS.LCR$_DDL_RECORD types.

Figure 7-5 shows the various CONVERT functions available in the ANYDATA type. These are used when handling various data types in the LCR.

In the sections that follow, we will construct a simple DML and a DDL handler procedure that demonstrates how to use these functions. We will access information in the LCRs and also modify a few of the attributes.

ANYDATA – Convert Functions
- ConvertBDouble([IN] dbl BINARY_DOUBLE) : ANYDATA
- ConvertBfile([IN] b : BFILE) RETURN ANYDATA
- ConvertBFloat([IN] fl : BINARY_FLOAT) : ANYDATA
- ConvertBlob([IN] b : BLOB) : ANYDATA
- ConvertChar([IN] c: CHAR) : ANYDATA
- ConvertClob([IN] c : CLOB) : ANYDATA
- ConvertCollection([IN] col : "collection_type") : ANYDATA
- ConvertDate([IN] dat : DATE) : ANYDATA
- ConvertIntervalDS([IN] inv : INTERVAL DAY TO SECOND) : ANYDATA
- ConvertIntervalYM([IN] inv : INTERVAL YEAR TO MONTH) : ANYDATA
- ConvertNchar([IN] nc : NCHAR) : ANYDATA
- ConvertNClob([IN] nc : NCLOB) : ANYDATA
- ConvertNumber([IN] num : NUMBER) : ANYDATA
- ConvertNVarchar2([IN] nc : NVARCHAR2) : ANYDATA
- ConvertObject([IN] obj : "<object_type>") : ANYDATA
- ConvertRaw([IN] r : RAW) : ANYDATA
- ConvertRef([IN] rf : REF "<object_type>") : ANYDATA
- ConvertTimestamp([IN] ts : TIMESTAMP) : ANYDATA
- ConvertTimestampTZ([IN] ts : TIMESTAMP WITH TIMEZONE) : ANYDATA
- ConvertTimestampLTZ([IN] ts : TIMESTAMP WITH LOCAL TIMEZONE) : ANYDATA
- ConvertURowid([IN] rid : UROWID) : ANYDATA
- ConvertVarchar([IN] c : VARCHAR) : ANYDATA
- ConvertVarchar2([IN] c : VARCHAR2) : ANYDATA

FIGURE 7-5. *CONVERT functions in ANYDATA*

The user procedures, such as DML, DDL, and error handlers, which access the LCR contents, are of the following form:

```
PROCEDURE HANDLER_PROC (
        in_any   IN   SYS.ANYDATA);
```

The procedure HANDLER_PROC receives a parameter of type ANYDATA in a variable called `in_any`.

Accessing Row LCR Contents

This section presents an example that demonstrates how to retrieve and change LCR contents. You can write any other customized procedure that manipulates the LCR to address a specific business need.

Assume that we want to audit changes made to employee salaries and want to store the old and new salary values in an audit table along with other information in the LCR. The procedure will be invoked by the apply process at the destination database for the UPDATE operation against the SCOTT.EMP table. The capture process, DBXA_CAP, is already configured to include the extra attributes `row_id` and `username` in the LCR.

First, we create an audit table in the destination database under the Streams Administrator schema to store the relevant Information from the row LCR.

```
SQL>conn strmadmin/strmadmin@DBXB.WORLD
Connected.
SQL> create table salary_audit (
  2    msg_date               date default sysdate,
  3    source_database_name   varchar2(30),
  4    command_type           varchar2(30),
  5    object_owner           varchar2(30),
  6    object_name            varchar2(30),
  7    is_null_tag            varchar2(1),
  8    tag                    varchar2(30),
  9    transaction_id         varchar2(30),
 10    scn                    number,
 11    empno                  number,
 12    column_name            varchar2(30),
 13    old_value              number,
 14    new_value              number,
 15    row_id                  varchar2(30),
 16    username               varchar2(30)
 17  );
Table created.
```

Next, we create the DML handler procedure called SALARY_AUDIT_PROC under the Streams Administrator schema. Since the apply user is also the Streams Administrator, we don't have to grant execute privilege on this procedure to the apply user.

The handler procedure is listed next with inline comments explaining how the information is retrieved from the row LCR:

```
SQL> create or replace procedure salary_audit_proc (
  2          in_any IN SYS.ANYDATA
  3  )
  4  is
  5     -- Define variable lcr and rc, to access contents of row.
  6     -- LCR from sys.lcr$_row_record type and to hold the return
  7     -- code respectively.
  8     lcr                      SYS.LCR$_ROW_RECORD;
  9     rc                       PLS_INTEGER;
 10     -- Define local variables to hold values for various data
 11     -- fields from the LCR to insert into the salary_audit table.
 12     l_source_db              varchar2(30);
 13     l_command_type           varchar2(30);
 14     l_object_owner           varchar2(30);
 15     l_object_name            varchar2(30);
 16     l_is_null_tag            varchar2(1);
 17     l_tag                    varchar2(30);
 18     l_transaction_id         varchar2(30);
 19     l_scn                    number;
 20     l_empno                  number;
 21     l_column_name            varchar2(30);
 22     l_old_value              number;
 23     l_new_value              number;
 24     l_row_id                 varchar2(30);
 25     l_username               varchar2(30);
 26     l_extra_attr             ANYDATA;
 27     l_get_number             ANYDATA;
 28
 29  begin
 30     -- Access the row LCR from the parameter in_any.
 31     -- We use the GETOBJECT function of the SYS.ANYDATA type.
 32     rc := in_any.GETOBJECT(lcr);
 33     -- The contents of the LCR are now accessible using various
 34     -- member functions of the SYS.LCR$_ROW_RECORD type.
 35     -- Extract source_database_name using GET_SOURCE_DATABASE_NAME
 36     -- function.
 37     l_source_db := lcr.GET_SOURCE_DATABASE_NAME();
 38     -- Extract command_type using  GET_COMMAND_TYPE function.
 39     l_command_type := lcr.GET_COMMAND_TYPE();
 40     -- Extract object_owner using GET_OBJECT_OWNER function.
 41     l_object_owner := lcr.GET_OBJECT_OWNER();
 42     -- Extract object_name using GET_OBJECT_NAME function.
 43     l_object_name := lcr.GET_OBJECT_NAME();
 44     -- Extract is_null_tag using IS_NULL_TAG function.
 45     l_is_null_tag := lcr.IS_NULL_TAG();
 46     -- Extract tag value using GET_TAG function.
 47     l_tag := lcr.GET_TAG();
```

```
48    -- Extract transaction_id using GET_TRANSACTION_ID function.
49    l_transaction_id := lcr.GET_TRANSACTION_ID();
50    -- Extract scn using GET_SCN function.
51    l_scn := lcr.GET_SCN();
52    -- We will use the GET_VALUE function to extract the value
53    -- of the EMPNO column. This column is configured for
54    -- unconditional supplemental logging and so it will be
55    -- present in the LCR for all changes to the row.
56    -- Since the procedure is invoked for UPDATE operation,
57    -- the EMPNO will be available in the old values in the LCR.
58    -- The GET_VALUE function returns ANYDATA type.
59    -- The ACCESSNUMBER function of ANYDATA will retrieve
60    -- the number for EMPNO.
61    l_get_number := lcr.GET_VALUE('OLD','EMPNO');
62    l_empno := l_get_number.ACCESSNUMBER();
63    -- We are tracking employee salary in column called SAL.
64    -- There is no need to extract the column name from the LCR.
65    -- We just set the variable to the column name.
66    l_column_name := 'SAL';
67    -- If the SAL column was updated then we want to store the
68    -- old and new value of this column in our audit table.
69    -- If it was changed then the LCR will have its old and
70    -- new value. If it was not changed, then the LCR will not
71    -- have new values.
72    -- The parameters for the GET_VALUE function indicate that we
73    -- are looking for the NEW values of SAL column and do not
74    -- want (N) the function to return old values.
75    l_get_number := lcr.GET_VALUE('NEW','SAL');
76    l_new_value := l_get_number.ACCESSNUMBER();
77    -- If l_new_value is NOT NULL, then it means the column was
78    -- changed, and we will extract the old value.
79    if l_new_value is not null
80    then
81       l_get_number := lcr.GET_VALUE('OLD','SAL','Y');
82       l_old_value := l_get_number.ACCESSNUMBER();
83    end if;
84    -- The rowid and username are the extra attributes that we have
85    -- captured in the LCR. The SYS.ANYDATA provides a member function
86    -- called GET_EXTRA_ATTRIBUTE to access those by their names.
87    -- The function returns the value as ANYDATA. We then need to use
88    -- the ACCESSUROWID and ACCESSVARCHAR2 functions to extract their
89    -- values from the ANYDATA type.
90    l_extra_attr := lcr.GET_EXTRA_ATTRIBUTE('row_id');
91    l_row_id := l_extra_attr.ACCESSUROWID();
92    l_extra_attr := lcr.GET_EXTRA_ATTRIBUTE('username');
93    l_username := l_extra_attr.ACCESSVARCHAR2();
94    -- Now, we insert the values in our audit table, only if the
95    -- SAL column was updated.
96    if l_new_value is not null
97    then
```

```
 98        insert into salary_audit
 99         values (sysdate,
100                    l_source_db,
101                    l_command_type,
102                    l_object_owner,
103                    l_object_name,
104                    l_is_null_tag,
105                    l_tag,
106                    l_transaction_id,
107                    l_scn,
108             l_empno,
109                    l_column_name,
110                    l_old_value,
111                    l_new_value,
112                    l_row_id,
113                    l_username
114             );
115    end if;
116    -- Do not commit this row. It will be automatically done after
117    -- we execute the LCR. Please note that the LCR was handed to our
118    -- procedure by the apply process when it detected an UPDATE
119    -- operation against the SCOTT.EMP table. So, we must execute
120    -- the LCR irrespective of the change to the SAL column.
121    lcr.execute (true);
122    -- The TRUE option in the above command enables the automatic
123    -- conflict detection by the apply process.
124    -- Setting it to FALSE disables it.
125  end;
126  /
Procedure created.
SQL> show errors
No errors.
```

Now, we assign the procedure to the apply process to invoke it when the UPDATE operation is detected for the SCOTT.EMP table.

```
SQL> begin
  2      dbms_apply_adm.set_dml_handler
  3      (object_name            => 'SCOTT.EMP',
  4       object_type            => 'TABLE',
  5       operation_name         => 'UPDATE',
  6       error_handler          => FALSE,
  7       user_procedure         => 'STRMADMIN.SALARY_AUDIT_PROC',
  8       apply_name             => 'DBXA_APP');
  9  end;
 10  /
PL/SQL procedure successfully completed.
```

We are all set. After changing the salary of employee number 7566 from 2975 to 3000, not only will we see the change at the destination table, but our SALARY_AUDIT table will have the following information. The following output is produced from two separate queries against the audit table and is formatted to fit the page:

```
                                                      NUL
   EMPNO SOURCE_DB       COMMAND   OWNER     TABLE_NAME  TAG TAG
   ------ --------------- --------- -------- ------------ --- ----
    7566 DBXA.WORLD      UPDATE    SCOTT     EMP          Y
```

```
                                    OLD    NEW
   EMPNO TXN_ID            SCN COLUMN VALUE  VALUE ROW_ID            USERNAME
   ------ ---------- -------- ------ ------ ------ ------------------ --------
    7566 6.0.2049    4188833 SAL     2975   3000 AAAPqZAAEAAAACzAAD SCOTT
```

The second output shows the old and new values for the SAL column, the row ID of the row in the source table, and the username of the person who updated the row.

Accessing DDL LCR Contents

The contents of the DDL LCR are accessed in a similar way to how the contents of the row LCR are accessed, as described in the preceding section. The handler procedure to achieve this is called the DDL handler. It is described next with inline comments explaining how the information is retrieved from the DDL LCR.

The DDL handler procedure will be invoked by the apply process at the destination database for all DDL changes propagated from the source database. Our example DDL handler will record all DDL commands in a DDL audit table before executing the LCR for all DDL commands except for the CREATE INDEX command.

So, first we create an audit table under the Streams Administrator schema to store the relevant information from the DDL LCR.

```
SQL>conn strmadmin/strmadmin@DBXB.WORLD
Connected.
SQL> create table ddl_audit (
  2     msg_date                date,
  3     source_database_name    varchar2(30),
  4     command_type            varchar2(30),
  5     object_owner            varchar2(30),
  6     object_name             varchar2(30),
  7     object_type             varchar2(20),
  8     ddl_text                clob,
  9     logon_user              varchar2(30),
 10     current_schema          varchar2(30),
 11     base_table_owner        varchar2(30),
 12     base_table_name         varchar2(30),
 13     streams_tag             raw(10),
 14     transaction_id          varchar2(30),
 15     scn                     number
 16  )
 17  /
Table created.
```

Next, we create the DDL handler procedure called DDL_AUDIT_PROC under the Streams Administrator schema. Since the apply user is also the Streams Administrator, we don't have to grant execute privilege on this procedure to the apply user.

```
SQL> create or replace procedure
  2    ddl_audit_proc (in_any IN SYS.ANYDATA
  3  )
  4
  5  is
  6    lcr          SYS.LCR$_DDL_RECORD;
  7    rc               PLS_INTEGER;
  8    l_ddl_text        CLOB default empty_clob();
  9
 10  begin
 11    -- Access the DDL LCR from the parameter in_any.
 12    -- We use the GETOBJECT function of the SYS.ANYDATA type.
 13    rc := in_any.GETOBJECT(lcr);
 14    -- The contents of the DDL LCR are now accessible using various
 15    -- member functions of the SYS.LCR$_DDL_RECORD type.
 16    -- These functions are similar in behavior to the ones we saw
 17    -- earlier for accessing the row LCR contents.
 18
 19    -- To access the DDL Text in the LCR we initialize the
 20    -- LOB segment.
 21    dbms_lob.createtemporary(l_ddl_text, TRUE);
 22    -- Extract the DDL Text from the LCR into the local CLOB.
 23    lcr.GET_DDL_TEXT(l_ddl_text);
 24
 25    -- Extract information from DDL LCR to insert into the
 26    -- DDL Audit table using member functions
 27    -- of SYS.LCR$_DDL_RECORD.
 28
 29    insert into ddl_audit
 30      VALUES (SYSDATE,
 31              lcr.GET_SOURCE_DATABASE_NAME(),
 32              lcr.GET_COMMAND_TYPE(),
 33              lcr.GET_OBJECT_OWNER(),
 34              lcr.GET_OBJECT_NAME(),
 35              lcr.GET_OBJECT_TYPE(),
 36              l_ddl_text,
 37              lcr.GET_LOGON_USER(),
 38              lcr.GET_CURRENT_SCHEMA(),
 39              lcr.GET_BASE_TABLE_OWNER(),
 40              lcr.GET_BASE_TABLE_NAME(),
 41              lcr.GET_TAG(),
 42              lcr.GET_TRANSACTION_ID(),
 43              lcr.GET_SCN()
 44            );
 45
```

```
46      -- We want to ignore the DDL command that creates indexes
47      -- in the destination database.
48      if lcr.GET_COMMAND_TYPE != 'CREATE INDEX'
49      then
50          lcr.execute();
51      end if;
52
53      -- Free the temporary LOB from temp tablespace.
54      DBMS_LOB.FREETEMPORARY(l_ddl_text);
55
56  END;
57  /
Procedure created.
SQL> show errors
No errors.
```

We next assign this DDL handler procedure to the apply process, which will invoke it when it receives a DDL LCR from the source database.

```
SQL> begin
2       dbms_apply_adm.alter_apply(
3           apply_name  => 'DBXA_APP',
4           ddl_handler => 'DDL_AUDIT_PROC');
5   end;
6   /
PL/SQL procedure successfully completed.
```

Now, suppose the Streams Administrator adds a new column to the SCOTT.EMP table in the source database. When this DDL change is propagated to the destination database, the apply process will pass the corresponding LCR to our DDL handler procedure. The procedure will extract the LCR contents into the audit table before executing the LCR. The audit table will have the following information. Notice that the LOGON_USER is STRMADMIN, which is who changed the SCOTT.EMP table. The output here is produced from two separate queries against the audit table and is formatted to fit the page.

```
             LOGON      OBJECT   OBJECT   OBJECT   BASE_TABLE BASE_TABLE
COMMAND      USER       OWNER    NAME     TYPE     OWNER      NAME
-----------  ---------- -------- -------- -------- ---------- ----------
ALTER TABLE  STRMADMIN  SCOTT    EMP      TABLE    SCOTT      EMP


TRANSACTION_ID        SCN DDL_TEXT
-------------- ---------- ----------------------------------------
9.9.2022          4202354 alter table scott.emp
                          add (PHONE number)
```

The DDL_TEXT field shows the exact command entered and executed at the source database.

Modifying LCR Contents

When replicating data, sometimes there is a business requirement that sensitive data be masked or changed. Sometimes businesses simply want to update a delete flag in the replicated data rather than physically delete it, so the LCR for the DELETE operation is changed to an UPDATE operation to achieve this. Such modifications are done mainly to the row LCR contents. Modifications to the DDL LCR contents typically are very limited. If you replicated DDL changes and the tables are in a different schema at the destination, you will need to modify the schema name in the LCR as well as the DDL text if the schema name is used to qualify the table name in the DDL command at the source database.

Modifying Row LCR Contents

The DML handler example in Chapter 6 showed how to change the value for the SSNO column of the SCOTT.EMP table. Refer to that example to see how the data was modified in the LCR.

The following example shows how to modify the data type from TIMESTAMP to DATE for two columns (HIRE_DATE and BIRTH_DATE) in the EMP table. The DML handler procedure checks for the command type and performs data conversion appropriately using the function GET_VALUES and the procedure SET_VALUES.

```
SQL> create or replace procedure
  2    convert_timestamp_to_date (in_any in anydata)
  3  is
  4    lcr              SYS.LCR$_ROW_RECORD;
  5    rc               PLS_INTEGER;
  6    l_command_type   varchar2(30);
  7    l_timestamp      timestamp;
  8    l_new_values     SYS.LCR$_ROW_LIST;
  9    l_old_values     SYS.LCR$_ROW_LIST;
 10
 11  begin
 12    -- Access the row LCR.
 13    rc := in_any.GETOBJECT(lcr);
 14
 15    -- Extract the command_type
 16    l_command_type := lcr.GET_COMMAND_TYPE();
 17
 18    -- Check for the command type and perform actions.
 19    -- If the command was INSERT, then we will have only
 20    -- the new values for the table columns.
 21    if l_command_type='INSERT'
 22    then
 23      -- Extract the list of new values.
 24      l_new_values := lcr.GET_VALUES('NEW');
 25      -- Loop through the new values list.
 26      for i in 1 .. l_new_values.count
 27      loop
```

```
28          if l_new_values(i).data is not null
29          then
30            -- Check if interested columns are in the list.
31            if l_new_values(i).column_name in ('HIRE_DATE','BIRTH_DATE')
32            then
33              -- Extract the values of the interested columns.
34              rc := l_new_values(i).data.GETTIMESTAMP(l_timestamp);
35              -- Convert the Timestamp data type to Date.
36              l_new_values(i).data := ANYDATA.CONVERTDATE(to_date(trunc(l_timestamp)));
37            end if;
38          end if;
39        end loop;
40        -- Set the new values list in the LCR.
41        lcr.SET_VALUES('NEW',value_list=>l_new_values);
42        --
43        -- If the command was UPDATE then we will have
44        -- the old and new values for the table columns.
45      elsif l_command_type='UPDATE'
46      then
47        -- Extract the list of Old values.
48        l_old_values := lcr.GET_VALUES('OLD', 'Y');
49        for i in 1 .. l_old_values.count
50        -- Loop through the old values list.
51        loop
52          if l_old_values(i).data is not null
53          then
54            -- Check if interested columns are in the list.
55            if l_old_values(i).column_name in ('HIRE_DATE','BIRTH_DATE')
56            then
57              -- Extract the values of the interested columns.
58              rc := l_old_values(i).data.GETTIMESTAMP(l_timestamp);
59              -- Convert the Timestamp data type to Date.
60              l_old_values(i).data := ANYDATA.CONVERTDATE(to_date(trunc(l_timestamp)));
61            end if;
62          end if;
63        end loop;
64        -- Set the old values list in the LCR.
65        lcr.SET_VALUES('OLD',value_list=>l_old_values);
66        -- Now, extract the list of new values.
67        l_new_values := lcr.GET_VALUES('NEW', 'N');
68        -- Loop through the new values list.
69        for i in 1 .. l_new_values.count
70        loop
71          if l_new_values(i).data is not null
72          then
73            -- Check if interested columns are in the list.
74            if l_new_values(i).column_name in ('HIRE_DATE','BIRTH_DATE')
75            then
76              -- Extract the values of the interested columns.
77              rc := l_new_values(i).data.GETTIMESTAMP(l_timestamp);
78              -- Convert the Timestamp data type to Date.
79              l_new_values(i).data := ANYDATA.CONVERTDATE(to_date(trunc(l_timestamp)));
80            end if;
81          end if;
82        end loop;
83        -- Set the new values list in the LCR.
```

```
84        lcr.SET_VALUES('NEW',value_list=>l_new_values);
85        --
86        -- If the command was DELETE then we will have only
87        -- the old values for the table columns.
88   elsif l_command_type ='DELETE'
89   then
90      l_old_values := lcr.GET_VALUES('OLD', 'Y');
91      for i in 1 .. l_old_values.count
92      -- Loop through the old values list.
93      loop
94       if l_old_values(i).data is not null
95       then
96          -- Check if interested columns are in the list.
97          if l_old_values(i).column_name in ('HIRE_DATE','BIRTH_DATE')
98          then
99             -- Extract the values of the interested columns.
100            rc := l_old_values(i).data.GETTIMESTAMP(l_timestamp);
101            -- Convert the Timestamp data type to Date.
102            l_old_values(i).data := ANYDATA.CONVERTDATE(to_date(trunc(l_timestamp)));
103         end if;
104       end if;
105      end loop;
106      -- Set the old values list in the LCR.
107      lcr.SET_VALUES('OLD',value_list=>l_old_values);
108   end if;
109   -- Execute the modified LCR.
110   lcr.execute(true);
111  end;
112  /
Procedure created.
SQL> show errors
No errors.
```

Now all we need to do is specify the CONVERT_TIMESTAMP_TO_DATE procedure for the INSERT, UPDATE, and DELETE operations for the SCOTT.EMP table using the DBMS_APPLY_ADM.SET_DML_HANDLER procedure. Once done, the HIRE_DATE and BIRTH_DATE columns will be converted from TIMESTAMP to DATE data type for all DML operations against the SCOTT.EMP table.

```
SQL> begin
  2    dbms_apply_adm.set_dml_handler(
  3      object_name        => 'SCOTT.EMP',
  4      object_type        => 'TABLE',
  5      operation_name     => 'UPDATE',
  6      error_handler      => FALSE,
  7      user_procedure     => 'STRMADMIN.CONVERT_TIMESTAMP_TO_DATE',
  8      apply_name         => 'DBXA_APP');
  9    dbms_apply_adm.set_dml_handler(
 10      object_name        => 'SCOTT.EMP',
 11      object_type        => 'TABLE',
 12      operation_name     => 'INSERT',
```

```
13           error_handler       => FALSE,
14           user_procedure      => 'STRMADMIN.CONVERT_TIMESTAMP_TO_DATE',
15           apply_name          => 'DBXA_APP');
16        dbms_apply_adm.set_dml_handler(
17           object_name         => 'SCOTT.EMP',
18           object_type         => 'TABLE',
19           operation_name      => 'DELETE',
20           error_handler       => FALSE,
21           user_procedure      => 'STRMADMIN.CONVERT_TIMESTAMP_TO_DATE',
22           apply_name          => 'DBXA_APP');
23     end;
24     /
PL/SQL procedure successfully completed.
```

Modifying DDL LCR Contents

If you replicated DDL changes along with DML changes for tables, then you may
have to modify the DDL LCRs. Such modifications will be required if the schema
name and/or table name in the row LCR was modified using rule transformations. In
this case, to avoid errors, you need to write a DDL handler procedure for the apply
process that will modify the DDL LCR contents before applying it.

The following example demonstrates how to modify the current schema name,
the object owner, and the DDL text in a DDL LCR. In this example, the destination
schema name is KIRTI, and not SCOTT. We need to change the current schema and
object owner in the LCR to match the destination schema name. Also, the schema
name in the DDL text must be replaced accordingly, in case the DDL command
used the schema.table_name format, with or without double quotes around the
schema name. The table names remain the same in the source and destination.

We use the Oracle-provided regular expression function REGEXP_REPLACE to
find and replace the schema name in the DDL text. Oracle also provides REGEXP_
LIKE, REGEXP_INSTR, and REGEXP_SUBSTR functions. These functions are useful
when searching and manipulating the DDL text.

```
SQL>connect strmadmin/strmadmin@DBXB.WORLD
Connected.
SQL> create or replace procedure ddl_handler (in_any IN SYS.ANYDATA
  2  )
  3  is
  4    lcr             SYS.LCR$_DDL_RECORD;
  5    rc                    PLS_INTEGER;
  6    l_ddl_text            CLOB default empty_clob();
  7    l_ddl_text_new    CLOB default empty_clob();
  8    l_source_schema1  varchar2(30);
  9    l_source_schema2  varchar2(30);
 10    l_dest_schema1    varchar2(30);
 11    l_dest_schema2    varchar2(30);
 12
```

```
13  begin
14    -- Initialize the variables for source and destination schema names.
15    l_source_schema1 := ' '||'SCOTT';
16    l_dest_schema1   := ' '||'KIRTI';
17    l_source_schema2 := ' "'||'SCOTT'||'"';
18    l_dest_schema2   := ' "'||'KIRTI'||'"';
19
20    -- Access the DDL LCR from the parameter in_any.
21    -- We use the GETOBJECT function of the SYS.ANYDATA type.
22    rc := in_any.GETOBJECT(lcr);
23    -- The contents of the DDL LCR are now accessible using various
24    -- member functions of the SYS.LCR$_DDL_RECORD type.
25
26    -- To access the DDL Text in the LCR we initialize the
27    -- LOB segment.
28    dbms_lob.createtemporary(l_ddl_text, TRUE);
29    -- Extract the DDL Text from the LCR into the local variable.
30    lcr.GET_DDL_TEXT(l_ddl_text);
31    -- Change the current schema to match the destination schema name.
32    lcr.SET_CURRENT_SCHEMA('KIRTI');
33    -- Change the object owner to match the destination object owner.
34    lcr.SET_OBJECT_OWNER('KIRTI');
35    -- Using the Regular Expression function, replace all occurrences
36    -- of the source schema name to destination schema name in the DDL text.
37    l_ddl_text_new :=
38     regexp_replace(l_ddl_text,l_source_schema1||'\.',l_dest_schema1,1,0,'i');
39    l_ddl_text_new :=
40     regexp_replace(l_ddl_text_new,l_source_schema2||'\.',l_dest_schema2,1,0,'i');
41    -- Set the DDL text in the LCR to the new text.
42    lcr.SET_DDL_TEXT(l_ddl_text_new);
43    -- Free the temp lob for DDL text.
44    dbms_lob.freetemporary(l_ddl_text);
45    -- Execute the modified DDL LCR.
46    lcr.execute();
47  end;
48  /
Procedure created.
SQL> show errors
No errors.
```

Once the DDL handler procedure is created, we need to specify it to the apply process using the ALTER_APPLY procedure of the DBMS_APPLY_ADM package.

```
SQL> begin
  2    dbms_apply_adm.alter_apply(
  3        apply_name  => 'DBXA_APP',
  4        ddl_handler => 'DDL_HANDLER');
  5  end;
  6  /
PL/SQL procedure successfully completed.
```

The DDL handler procedure will now apply the modified DDL LCR to the destination database. The DDL changes made to tables in the SCOTT schema will be replicated to the same tables under the KIRTI schema in the destination database.

NOTE
The apply process can have only one DDL handler procedure defined, so all DDL LCR data extracts and modifications must be done in the same DDL handler procedure.

LCRs and LOB Data Types

Oracle Streams replicates tables containing LOB data types. The DML changes made to the LOB columns can result in more than one row LCR for this change. Each LCR contains chunks of the LOB data. The LOB chunk is a part of the LOB data contained in a data block. By default, the apply process applies each LCR for a LOB data change individually rather than assembling the LOB data from these LCRs and applying the changes once. So, for the same row, there could be multiple changes applied. If your application uses a number of LOB data types and those get changed frequently, then the apply process performance could be hampered.

To improve the performance of the apply process for the LOB changes, it is possible to employ a DML handler that can assemble the LOB chunks in the least number of LCRs necessary when applying changes to the LOB columns in the destination table. The number of LCRs mainly depends on the size of the LOB. The `assemble_lobs` parameter of the SET_DML_HANDLER procedure of the DBMS_APPLY_ADM package control whether the LOB chunks will be assembled before the apply process applies the LCR. Setting `assemble_lobs` to TRUE enables the LOB assembly.

NOTE
The default value for `assemble_lobs` is TRUE in Oracle Database 11g R2.

The DML handler procedure can be set up as an error handler procedure. This procedure does not perform any operations against the row LCR. It simply executes the row LCR. The following example shows such a LOB_ASSEMBLER procedure:

```
SQL> create or replace procedure LOB_ASSEMBLER(in_any IN SYS.ANYDATA)
  2  is
  3     lcr          SYS.LCR$_ROW_RECORD;
  4     rc           PLS_INTEGER;
  5  BEGIN
  6     -- Access the LCR
  7     rc := in_any.GETOBJECT(lcr);
  8     -- Apply the row LCR
  9     lcr.EXECUTE(TRUE);
 10  END;
 11  /
Procedure created.
```

Next, specify the LOB_ASSEMBLER procedure to the apply process for the tables with LOB data type and all the DML operations.

```
SQL> begin
  2      dbms_apply_adm.set_dml_handler(
  3          object_name          => 'SCOTT.EMP',
  4          object_type          => 'TABLE',
  5          operation_name       => 'INSERT',
  6          error_handler        => TRUE,
  7          assemble_lobs        => TRUE,
  8          user_procedure       => 'strmadmin.lob_assembler',
  9          apply_name           => 'DBXA_APP');
 10      dbms_apply_adm.set_dml_handler(
 11          object_name          => 'SCOTT.EMP',
 12          object_type          => 'TABLE',
 13          operation_name       => 'UPDATE',
 14          error_handler        => TRUE,
 15          assemble_lobs        => TRUE,
 16          user_procedure       => 'strmadmin.lob_assembler',
 17          apply_name           => 'DBXA_APP');
 18      dbms_apply_adm.set_dml_handler(
 19          object_name          => 'SCOTT.EMP',
 20          object_type          => 'DELETE',
 21          operation_name       => 'INSERT',
 22          error_handler        => TRUE,
 23          assemble_lobs        => TRUE,
 24          user_procedure       => 'strmadmin.lob_assembler',
 25          apply_name           => 'DBXA_APP');
 26      dbms_apply_adm.set_dml_handler(
 27          object_name          => 'SCOTT.EMP',
 28          object_type          => 'TABLE',
 29          operation_name       => 'LOB_UPDATE',
 30          error_handler        => TRUE,
 31          assemble_lobs        => TRUE,
 32          user_procedure       => 'strmadmin.lob_assembler',
 33          apply_name           => 'DBXA_APP');
 34  end;
 35  /
PL/SQL procedure successfully completed.
```

When the LOB assembly is enabled, we cannot use the SET_LOB_OFFSET, SET_LOB_INFORMATION, and SET_LOB_OPERATION_SIZE procedures of the LCR$_ROW_RECORD type on the LOB columns in the LCR. Oracle will raise an error if an attempt is made to use these.

Summary

The captured row LCRs represent the DML changes made to the tables in the source database, while the DDL LCRs represent structural changes made to the tables. Special data types SYS.LCR$_ROW_RECORD and SYS.LCR$_DDL_RECORD are used to encapsulate the LCR information that is enqueued to and dequeued from the Streams queue of an object type called SYS.ANYDATA.

The row and DDL LCRs have various attributes that contain required information to apply the LCRs to the destination database. The capture process or synchronous capture process automatically captures this information in the LCR. We can also specify additional attributes, related to the user session making changes, that can be captured in the LCR.

The special record types ANYDATA, LCR$_ROW_RECORD, and LCR$_DDL_ RECORD provide member functions and procedures that can be used to access and modify the contents in the LCR. These are implemented internally using object-oriented concepts.

This chapter demonstrated via examples how to use these member procedures and functions to modify the contents of the LCRs. Depending on your requirements, you can write customized procedures, referred to as DML handlers or DDL handlers, using these supplied functions and procedures to address other business requirements. The ability to modify the LCR in flight, using customized procedures, before it is applied to the destination is one of the powerful features of Streams replication.

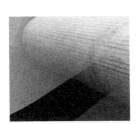

PART
III

Oracle Streams
Configuration

CHAPTER
8

Configuring Oracle
Streams for Data
Replication

he previous chapters discussed Oracle Streams architecture and its components. You now are prepared to learn how to configure Oracle Streams for data replication. Oracle Streams offers very flexible configuration methods to suit your requirements. Each of the Streams components can be created and configured individually to interact with other components to create a very simple or a highly complex replication environment.

Oracle Database 11*g* provides various APIs to configure a simple replication environment with minimum effort from you. These APIs perform all required steps automatically to create the replication environment. Oracle Enterprise Manager (OEM) Grid Control 10.2.0.5 offers Streams Replication Setup Wizard to configure Streams replication very easily. You can also configure Streams replication by developing custom scripts that use various Oracle-supplied PL/SQL packages.

Which method you should choose to configure Streams replication mainly depends on your replication requirement. In addition, you must also consider the ease of maintaining and extending the Streams environment when choosing a particular method to configure Streams replication. Knowing various different methods to configure Streams and understanding their pros and cons will help you choose the appropriate method to configure Streams replication.

This chapter explores a number of methods to configure Streams replication with different topologies using supplied PL/SQL packages. Use of OEM Grid Control to configure Streams replication is discussed in Chapter 14.

Streams Configuration Methods

Basically, there are three different methods available to configure Streams replication:

- Using the Streams Replication Setup Wizard in Oracle Enterprise Manager Grid Control

- Using Oracle-supplied procedures in the DBMS_STREAMS_ADM package (MAINTAIN_* procedures)

- Using custom scripts

Irrespective of which method you use to configure Streams replication, you must first complete a few prerequisite tasks.

Prerequisite Tasks

The prerequisite tasks that must be completed to configure Streams replication are listed here and described in detail in the sections that follow:

1. Prepare the databases:
    - ■ Configure the initialization parameters.
    - ■ Put the source database in ARCHIVELOG mode.
2. Create network connectivity between databases.
3. Create the Streams Administrator account.
4. Create database links.
5. Create directory objects (depending on the replication method chosen).

Prepare the Databases

There are a few database initialization parameters that may need to be adjusted to support Streams replication. Most of these parameters can be set and adjusted dynamically. Some of the parameters most likely will be set correctly by default, but it is a good idea to confirm their values and adjust them if necessary.

If you are not going to use the synchronous capture process to capture changes, then the source database must run in ARCHIVELOG mode. Similarly, if you are creating a downstream capture process, then the downstream database and the source database must also be running in ARCHIVELOG mode; otherwise, you will get an error when creating the capture process.

Configure the Initialization Parameters

The following database initialization parameters are relevant for various Streams configurations. Unless specified, these parameters are applicable to databases running the capture and apply processes.

- ■ **compatible**   Specifies the release with which the Oracle server must maintain compatibility. Oracle servers with different compatibility levels can participate in Streams replication. However, to use the new Streams features introduced in Oracle Database 11g Release 2, set this parameter to at least 11.2.0. Some of the APIs for configuring Streams will create rules that refer to this parameter.

- ■ **global_names**   Specifies whether a database link is required to have the same name as the database to which it connects. It is strongly recommended that you set this parameter to TRUE at each database that is participating in the Streams environment. However, it is possible to configure Streams with its value set to FALSE.

■ **log_buffer** Specifies the amount of memory to buffer the redo entries before they are written to the redo log files. It is relevant to the database running the capture process locally. Generally, you do not need to change the default value, which varies from 5MB to 32MB depending on the platform. Larger log buffer size can enable the capture process to read the changes from the memory itself, rather than accessing the online redo log files on the disk.

■ **open_links** Specifies the maximum number of open connections to a remote database that one session can have. In a Streams environment, the value for this parameter is set to 4, which is the default.

■ **parallel_max_servers** Specifies the maximum number of parallel execution and recovery processes for the database instance. It defaults to a reasonably high value depending on the value set for the `cpu_count`, `parallel_threads_per_cpu`, and `pga_aggregate_target` parameters. Streams processes use parallel servers. If there are not enough available parallel servers, then a Streams process may not be able to start after it was stopped. Be sure to set this parameter sufficiently high to support Streams and other parallel executions by the application processes.

■ **processes** Specifies the maximum number of operating system processes that can connect to the database simultaneously. When configuring Streams replication, there will be an additional background process created at the operating system level that will connect to the database. The value of this parameter must be set sufficiently high to allow for these additional processes. The default of 100 may not be sufficient to support your workload and Streams processes.

■ **sessions** Specifies the maximum number of sessions that can be created in the database. The default value is derived as (1.1 * `processes`) + 5. If this parameter is not specified, but the `processes` parameter was set sufficiently high, then the value for this parameter will be adjusted accordingly. If you specify this parameter exclusively, then be sure to set it high enough to allow for the Streams processes.

■ **shared_pool_size** Specifies the amount of memory (in bytes) used for the shared cursors, stored procedures, control structures, and so forth. The value set for this parameter matters for Streams only when `sga_target`, `memory_max_target`, `memory_target`, and `streams_pool_size` are all set to 0. In this case, Oracle allocates 10 percent of `shared_pool_size` for `streams_pool_size`.

■ **streams_pool_size** Introduced in Oracle Database 10*g*, specifies the memory allocation for the buffered queues in the system global area (SGA). In Oracle Database 11*g*, the Streams pool size can also be managed automatically by the Automatic Memory Management (AMM) or Automatic Shared Memory Management (ASMM) feature. The amount of memory allocated to the Streams pool is crucial for its performance.

If you set `memory_target` or `memory_max_target` to a nonzero value, then the AMM feature of the database will automatically manage the Streams pool.

If you set `memory_target` and `memory_max_target` to zero, and set `sga_target` to a nonzero value, then the ASMM feature of the database will manage the Streams pool.

In either case, if you set `streams_pool_size` to a nonzero value, then AMM and ASMM will treat that as the lower threshold for the Streams pool and will increase it as needed.

It is not uncommon to see `streams_pool_size` in the range of a few gigabytes where the capture process runs, and it is typically larger where the apply process runs. If you set `memory_target`, `memory_max_target`, `sga_target`, and `streams_pool_size` to zero, then 10 percent of the shared pool memory is allocated to the Streams pool.

Also note that the log-mining process by default takes 10MB from `streams_pool_size`. This is controlled by the `_sga_size` parameter of the capture process. You may have to increase this default in certain situations. In addition, 10MB from `streams_pool_size` is used by capture process parallelism and 1MB is used by apply process parallelism. So, when you increase the parallelism of these processes, remember that the memory allocation for additional parallelism is from `streams_pool_size`.

■ **timed_statistics**   Specifies if statistics related to time in various dynamic performance views are collected by the database. Its default value depends on the value set for another parameter, `statistics_level`, which defaults to TYPICAL. By default, `timed_statistics` is set to TRUE if `statistics_level` is set to TYPICAL or ALL. Changing the value of `statistics_level` to BASIC sets `timed_statistics` to FALSE, if it is not set to TRUE explicitly. It is recommended that `timed_statistics` be set to TRUE explicitly. This will enable the capture of elapsed time statistics for various Streams components along with other statistics gathered at the database level.

■ **undo_retention**   Controls how long (in seconds) the before images of the committed data are held in the undo segments. It is relevant for Streams' purposes when data pump is used to instantiate objects in the destination database. It should be set to a value larger than the time it takes to export the data for instantiation.

Configure the Initialization Parameters for Downstream Capture

In addition to the parameters listed previously, there are few parameters, as described next, that are necessary for configuring the downstream capture process. These parameters define the log file transport mechanism primarily used in the Oracle Data Guard configuration. Oracle Streams makes use of this feature when downstream capture is being configured. You can ignore these parameters if you are not configuring the downstream capture process.

Source Database   The source database needs the following parameters configured:

- **log_archive_dest_*n*** Used to define up to ten different log archive destinations, where *n* can be from 1 to 10.

  When configuring the downstream capture process, at least one `log_archive_dest_n` location must be configured to send the redo data from the source database. There are a number of attributes for this parameter, as listed here:

  - **service** Specifies the Oracle Net service name for the downstream database as defined in the `tnsnames.ora` file.

  - **async** or **sync** Specifies the redo transport mode to use. ASYNC is the default mode and has very little or no performance impact on the source database. This is similar to the maximum performance mode in the Data Guard configuration. Specifying SYNC means that the LGWR process at the source database will wait for an acknowledgement from the Log Network Server (LNS) that the redo information was received by the downstream database.

  - **noregister** Specifies that the archived log file location is not to be recorded in the control file of the downstream database. This is a required specification for configuring the downstream capture process. The downstream database is not a standby database, although Streams uses Data Guard features for redo transport.

  - **valid_for** Specifies what files the location will store. Possible value is (ONLINE_LOGFILES, PRIMARY_ROLE) or (ONLINE_LOGFILES, ALL_ROLES).

  - **template** Specifies a naming convention for the archived log file when it is copied to the downstream database. It is recommended to use TEMPLATE to distinguish the names for the archived redo logs from the source database and the logs of the downstream database. Use of `%t`, `%s`, and `%r` in the name is suggested at the source database to include the thread number, sequence number, and reincarnation number, respectively, in the filename. This attribute is not required for the real-time downstream capture process.

The following example shows how this parameter is set in the source database DBXA.WORLD to send archived log files to the downstream database DBXB.WORLD:

```
LOG_ARCHIVE_DEST_2='SERVICE=DBXB.WORLD ASYNC
        NOREGISTER VALID_FOR=(ONLINE_LOGFILES, ALL_ROLES)
        TEMPLATE=dbxa_arch_%t_%s_%r.arc'
```

It is assumed that the log_archive_dest_1 parameter is set to store archived log files of the source database and the log_archive_dest_2 parameter is available.

■ **log_archive_dest_state_*n*** Works in conjunction with the log_archive_ dest_*n* parameter, where the value of *n* matches. This parameter denotes the state of the archived destination location. By default, it will be set to ENABLE, meaning that log_archive_dest_*n* is ready to receive redo information.

Downstream Database The downstream database that runs the capture process will need the following parameters configured:

■ **log_archive_dest_*n*** When configuring at the downstream database, this parameter defines the location for the archived log file from the source database. The attributes required for this parameter are as follows:

■ **location** Specifies the operating system directory for the archived log files from the source database. The log transport service will copy these files into this directory.

■ **valid_for** Specifies what files the location will store. For the downstream database, this attribute will contain (STANDBY_LOGFILES, PRIMARY_ ROLE) or (STANDBY_LOGFILES, ALL_ROLES).

This parameter will be set as shown next in the downstream database DBXB. WORLD that receives archived files from the DBXA.WORLD database:

```
LOG_ARCHIVE_DEST_2='LOCATION=/u01/oradata/DBXA_logs
        VALID_FOR=(STANDBY_LOGFILES, PRIMARY_ROLE)'
```

The previous example assumes that log_archive_dest_1 parameter is set to store archived log files of the destination database and the log_ archive_dest_2 parameter is available.

■ **log_archive_dest_state_*n*** This parameter denotes the state of the archived destination location. By default, it will be set to ENABLE, meaning that log_archive_dest_*n* is ready to receive redo information from the source database.

Put the Source Database in ARCHIVELOG Mode

To be able to capture changes from the redo information in the source database, it must be running in ARCHIVELOG mode; otherwise, you will get an ORA-258 error when creating the capture process.

You can query the LOG_MODE column in the V$DATABASE view to confirm whether or not it is running in ARCHIVELOG mode. If not, you will need to change the log mode.

NOTE
The synchronous capture process does not require source database to be running in ARCHIVELOG mode.

It is not necessary to run the Streams destination database in ARCHIVELOG mode. However, ARCHIVELOG mode is strongly recommended, so that you can perform database point-in-time recovery in case of a media crash.

Now that you have prepared the databases, you are ready for the next prerequisite task for configuring Streams replication.

Create Network Connectivity Between Databases

Oracle Streams uses database links to propagate captured changes from the source queue to the destination queue. Therefore, the destination database must be accessible over the Oracle Net Services from the database where the source queue resides. Also, Streams requires a dedicated connection to the remote database. Typically, the tnsnames.ora file is used to define the service name and the connection information for the destination database to establish the connection over Oracle Net Services.

The following example shows the entries in the tnsnames.ora file for the source database DBXA.WORLD and the destination database DBXB.WORLD. The service_name attribute is set to the global name of the database:

```
DBXA.WORLD =
  (DESCRIPTION =
    (ADDRESS = (PROTOCOL = TCP)(HOST = linux1)(PORT = 1521))
    (CONNECT_DATA =
      (SERVER = DEDICATED)
      (SERVICE_NAME = DBXA.WORLD)
    )
  )
DBXB.WORLD =
  (DESCRIPTION =
    (ADDRESS = (PROTOCOL = TCP)(HOST = linux2)(PORT = 1521))
    (CONNECT_DATA =
      (SERVER = DEDICATED)
      (SERVICE_NAME = DBXB.WORLD)
    )
  )
```

Once these changes are made, test the connectivity to the destination database from within the source database. You may want to create a dummy database account and a private database link under this account from the source database to the destination database. Execute a remote query on the destination database and confirm that it returns the expected result.

Now, you are ready to create the Streams Administrator account in the source and destination databases.

Create the Streams Administrator Account

All databases participating in Streams replication must have a Streams Administrator account. To administer the Streams environment, the Streams Administrator account needs some special privileges that are not granted to the SYSTEM account or the DBA role. So, creating a separate Streams Administrator account is highly recommended. This account is not required to use the same username in all the databases in the Streams configuration. However, in our examples we will use the same username in all the databases, to keep things simple.

Before you create the Streams Administrator account, it is recommended that you create a default tablespace for this account in all the databases participating in Streams replication. This tablespace will contain the permanent objects created during the Streams configuration.

The following example shows the creation of the STREAMS_TBS tablespace in the source database DBXA.WORLD. It is followed by the creation of the Streams Administrator account with username STRMADMIN and all required privileges. The same steps need to be performed in the destination database DBXB.WORLD.

```
SQL> connect sys/manager@DBXA.WORLD as sysdba
Connected.
SQL>
SQL> create tablespace streams_tbs
  2    datafile '/u01/oracle/oradata/DBXA/streams_tbs_01.dbf' size 500M
  3    autoextend on next 50M maxsize 2000M
  4    extent management local
  5    segment space management auto;
Tablespace created.

SQL> connect sys/manager@DBXA.WORLD as sysdba
Connected.
SQL> create user strmadmin identified by strmadmin
  2    default tablespace streams_tbs
  3    quota unlimited on streams_tbs;

User created.
SQL> grant connect, resource, aq_administrator_role, dba to strmadmin;
Grant succeeded.
```

```
SQL> grant execute on dbms_lock to strmadmin;
Grant succeeded.
SQL> execute dbms_streams_auth.grant_admin_privilege('strmadmin');
PL/SQL procedure successfully completed.
```

Let's quickly review the privileges granted to the STRMADMIN account. It has CONNECT, RESOURCE, AQ_ADMINISTRATOR_ROLE, and DBA roles:

- The CONNECT role merely grants the `create session` privilege.

- The RESOURCE role allows the creation of database objects such as tables, procedures, trigger, sequence, and so forth.

- The AQ_ADMINISTRATOR_ROLE role allows the management of the queues used in Streams.

- The DBA role is required to allow STRMADMIN to create and manage Streams processes. Often DBAs and their managers want to know if the DBA role must be granted to the Streams Administrator. Generally, the DBAs are also the Streams Administrators, so assigning the DBA role to the Stream Administrator account should not be a major concern. However, if you require that the DBA role not be granted to the Streams Administrator account, then you have to create a separate capture and apply user with appropriate privileges. These processes perform their tasks under the security domain of this user. The DBA role can be revoked from the Streams Administrator user once Streams is configured.

The preceding example also granted execute privilege on the DBMS_LOCK package to the Streams Administrator. Although this is not required to create and maintain the Streams environment, it is required when installing the Streams Performance Advisor package (UTL_SPADV) in Streams Administrator schema; otherwise, you will encounter an error. So, it is a good idea to grant execute privilege when creating the Streams Administrator account.

Most importantly, the preceding example executed the DBMS_STREAMS_AUTH package procedure to grant administrative privileges to STRMADMIN. As the procedure name suggests, this step grants a number of privileges to the account to act as the Streams Administrator. The procedure we executed granted these privileges directly.

A variation in the invocation of the procedure, as shown next, generates a script showing all the privileges that will be granted. You could run the generated script to grant these privileges. Since the generated script is a bit lengthy for listing here, you can generate it on your own and review what privileges are required for the Streams Administrator account.

```
SQL> begin
  2      dbms_streams_auth.grant_admin_privilege(
  3         grantee           => 'strmadmin',
  4         grant_privileges  => false,
  5         file_name         => 'streams_admin_privs.sql',
  6         directory_name    => 'streams_dp_dir');
  7  end;
SQL> /

PL/SQL procedure successfully completed.
```

In this example, the script `streams_admin_privs.sql` will be created in the operating system directory defined by the `streams_dp_dir` directory object. Notice that the parameter `grant_privileges` is set to FALSE to indicate that the procedure should not grant any privileges directly to the Streams Administrator, but instead should simply create the script. You can set it to its default value of TRUE to grant the privileges directly and also to generate the script.

Create Database Links

Once the Streams Administrator account is created in all the databases involved in Streams replication, it is time to create required database links. Typically, the database links are private under the Streams Administrator account. Although it is possible to use public links, it is highly recommended that the links used by Streams be private under the Streams Administrator account, so that they won't get dropped accidentally.

So, in our example we create the database link from DBXA.WORLD to DBXB.WORLD, as well as from DBXB.WORLD to DBXA.WORLD, as shown here:

```
SQL> connect strmadmin/strmadmin@DBXA.WORLD
Connected.
SQL>
SQL> create database link DBXB
  2  connect to strmadmin identified by strmadmin
  3  using 'DBXB.WORLD';
Database link created.


SQL> connect strmadmin/strmadmin@DBXB.WORLD
Connected.
SQL> create database link DBXA
  2  connect to strmadmin identified by strmadmin
  3  using 'DBXA.WORLD';

Database link created.
```

Create Directory Objects

The database directory object is an alias for the operating system directory on the database server. Creation of directory objects is optional when configuring Streams replication.

The directory object is only required if you are using MAINTAIN_* procedures of the DBMS_STREAMS_ADM package to configure Streams. The directory object stores the export dump file created by the data pump export utility invoked by the MAINTAIN_* procedures. The Streams configuration script created by the MAINTAIN_* procedures is also stored in this directory object. The destination database requires a directory object to which the export dump file from the source database can be copied for importing.

The following example shows how to create the directory object in the source database DBXA.WORLD. Similar steps need to be executed in the destination database DBXB.WORLD.

```
SQL> connect sys/manager@DBXA.WORLD as sysdba
Connected.
SQL> create directory streams_dp_dir as '/u01/oradata/streams_dp_dir';
Directory created.
SQL> grant read, write on directory streams_dp_dir to strmadmin;
Grant succeeded.
```

At this point, all the prerequisite tasks for configuring Streams replication are complete. You should be able to configure Streams replication between the DBXA. WORLD and DBXB.WORLD databases using a method that best suits your requirements.

Streams Configuration Using MAINTAIN Procedures

The Oracle-provided DBMS_STREAMS_ADM package provides a number of procedures to configure Streams replication. These names of these procedures begin with MAINTAIN and are commonly referred to as the "MAINTAIN procedures" for configuring Streams replication.

The MAINTAIN procedures are ideal for creating simple Streams replication environments that involve two databases. The procedures can configure unidirectional or bidirectional replication with the capture process running locally in the source database or running in the downstream database. These procedures make use of the Oracle data pump utility to copy the data from the source database to the destination database. These procedures are briefly described next:

NOTE
The MAINTAIN procedures do not configure replication that uses the synchronous capture process.

- ■   **MAINTAIN_GLOBAL**   Configures the Oracle Streams replication environment at the database level. You may want to consider this procedure when replicating data in all the tables in all the schemas of the database.

- ■   **MAINTAIN_SCHEMAS**   Configures the Oracle Streams replication environment for one or more schemas in the database. Changes made to tables within these schemas will be replicated to the destination database.

- ■   **MAINTAIN_TABLES**   Configures the Oracle Streams replication environment for one or more tables in the database. Changes made to these tables will be replicated to the destination database.

- ■   **MAINTAIN_SIMPLE_TTS**   First clones a simple tablespace from the source database to the destination database, and then configures Streams replication to maintain the tablespace contents at both databases. A simple tablespace is defined as a self-contained tablespace with only one data file.

- ■   **MAINTAIN_TTS**   Uses the transportable tablespace feature in the data pump to clone a set of tablespaces from the source database to the destination database, and then configures Streams replication to maintain these tablespaces at both databases.

In addition to these MAINTAIN procedures, the DBMS_STREAMS_ADM package provides two other procedures, called PRE_INSTANTIATION_SETUP and POST_INSTANTIATION_SETUP. These procedures enable use of the Streams replication mechanism while performing a database migration or upgrade to minimize or eliminate database downtime. Generally, these procedures are not used to configure Streams replication as such. These procedures must be used together to configure Streams replication. When using these procedures, manual instantiation of the replicated object is required.

The MAINTAIN procedures have a number of parameters. These parameters control how the Streams environment will be configured and what names will be assigned to the various Streams components. Most importantly, the `instantiation` parameter controls how the data for the replicated tables will be copied to the destination using the data pump utility.

Streams Replication at the Database Level

The following example shows how to configure unidirectional Streams replication between two databases at the global or database level using the DBMS_STREAMS_ ADM.MAINTAIN_GLOBAL procedure. It is assumed that all the prerequisite steps have been completed in the source and the destination databases and that the destination database is just a skeleton database. The DBMS_STREAMS_ADM

.MAINTAIN_GLOBAL procedure is executed as the Streams Administrator user in the source database DBXA.WORLD.

```
SQL> connect strmadmin/strmadmin@DBXA.WORLD
Connected.
SQL> begin
  2    dbms_streams_adm.maintain_global (
  3    source_database             => 'DBXA.WORLD',
  4    source_directory_object     => 'STREAMS_DP_DIR',
  5    destination_database        => 'DBXB.WORLD',
  6    destination_directory_object => 'STREAMS_DP_DIR',
  7    capture_name                => 'DBXA_CAP',
  8    capture_queue_name          => 'DBXA_CAP_Q',
  9    capture_queue_table         => 'DBXA_CAP_Q_T',
 10    capture_queue_user          => 'STRMADMIN',
 11    propagation_name            => 'DBXA_TO_DBXB_PROP',
 12    apply_name                  => 'DBXA_APP',
 13    apply_queue_name            => 'DBXA_APP_Q',
 14    apply_queue_table           => 'DBXA_APP_Q_T',
 15    apply_queue_user            => 'STRMADMIN',
 16    script_name                 => 'cr_streams_global.sql',
 17    script_directory_object     => 'STREAMS_DP_DIR',
 18    dump_file_name              => NULL,
 19    log_file                    => NULL,
 20    bi_directional              => FALSE,
 21    include_ddl                 => TRUE,
 22    perform_actions             => TRUE,
 23    instantiation   => DBMS_STREAMS_ADM.INSTANTIATION_FULL
 24    );
 25  end;
 26  /

job finished

PL/SQL procedure successfully completed.
```

The example uses all the parameters available for the MAINTAIN_GLOBAL procedure. Although a number of these parameters could be left to their default value, this example uses them all to illustrate their use. The previous procedure created Streams replication at the database level with the following characteristics:

- The local capture process called DBXA_CAP in the DBXA.WORLD database.

- The capture process uses Streams queue DBXA_CAP_Q and queue table DBXA_CAP_Q_T in the source database.

- The capture user is set to STRMADMIN.

- The propagation process is DBXA_TO_DBXB_PROP in the source database.

- The apply process DBXA_APP is configured in the destination database DBXB.WORLD.

- The apply process uses Streams queue DBXA_APP_Q and queue table DBXA_APPL_Q_T in the destination database.

- The apply user is set to STRMADMIN.

- Since the STRMADMIN user has the DBA role, there is no need to grant additional privileges to perform DDL and DML operations on replicated objects.

- The `perform_actions` parameter is set to TRUE, meaning the procedure will configure the defined Streams environment. In addition, it will also create the Streams configuration script called `cr_streams_global.sql` in the directory pointed to by the `streams_dp_dir` directory object on the source database server.

- The procedure uses the DBMS_STREAMS_ADM.INSTANTIATION_FULL method for the instantiation. Since the `dump_file_name` and `log_file` parameters are set to NULL, the names for the data pump export dump file and associated log file defaulted to system-generated names.

- The parameter `include_ddl` is set to TRUE to replicate DDL changes in addition to the DML changes.

If user-defined meaningful names for the Streams components are not desired, then the following example can be used to configure Streams replication from the DBXA.WORLD database to the DBXB.WORLD database:

```
SQL> connect strmadmin/strmadmin@DBXA.WORLD
Connected.
SQL> begin
  2    dbms_streams_adm.maintain_global (
  3      source_database              => 'DBXA.WORLD',
  4      source_directory_object      => 'STREAMS_DP_DIR',
  5      destination_database         => 'DBXB.WORLD',
  6      destination_directory_object => 'STREAMS_DP_DIR',
  7      include_ddl                  => TRUE
  8    );
  9  end;
 10  /

job finished

PL/SQL procedure successfully completed.
```

This example uses only the mandatory parameters. Oracle will assign system-generated names to all the Streams components. You will need to access the DBA_CAPTURE, DBA_PROPAGATION, and DBA_APPLY views to obtain their information.

If bidirectional replication were desired at the database level, then we would have set the `bi_directional` parameter to TRUE in the previous example. In that case, it is recommended to let Oracle generate the names for the Streams components; otherwise, the same names will be used for the Streams components in both the databases, defeating the purpose of the meaningful names and causing confusion.

The example also illustrates the simplicity in using the MAINTAIN_GLOBAL procedure to configure Streams replication at the database level.

Streams Replication at the Schema Level

If you need to replicate only a few schemas from the database, then you can use the DBMS_STREAMS_ADM.MAINTAIN_SCHEMAS procedure. The following example shows how to configure unidirectional replication from the DBXA.WORLD database to the DBXB.WORLD database for the SCOTT and HR schemas. It is assumed that all the prerequisite steps have been completed in the source database and the destination database. The DBMS_STREAMS_ADM.MAINTAIN_SCHEMAS procedure is executed as the Streams Administrator user in the source database DBXA.WORLD.

```
SQL> connect strmadmin/strmadmin@DBXA.WORLD
Connected.
SQL> declare
  2     schemas    dbms_utility.uncl_array;
  3  begin
  4   schemas(1) := 'SCOTT';
  5   schemas(2) := 'HR';
  6   dbms_streams_adm.maintain_schemas (
  7     schema_names                => schemas,
  8     source_database             => 'DBXA.WORLD',
  9     source_directory_object     => 'STREAMS_DP_DIR',
 10     destination_database        => 'DBXB.WORLD',
 11     destination_directory_object => 'STREAMS_DP_DIR',
 12     capture_name                => 'DBXA_CAP',
 13     capture_queue_name          => 'DBXA_CAP_Q',
 14     capture_queue_table         => 'DBXA_CAP_Q_T',
 15     propagation_name            => 'DBXA_TO_DBXB_PROP',
 16     apply_name                  => 'DBXA_APP',
 17     apply_queue_name            => 'DBXA_APP_Q',
 18     apply_queue_table           => 'DBXA_APP_Q_T',
 19     dump_file_name              => 'schemas_expimp.dmp',
 20     log_file                    => 'schemas_expimp.log',
 21     bi_directional              => FALSE,
 22     include_ddl                 => TRUE,
```

```
23      perform_actions              => TRUE
24    );
25   end;
26   /
```

job finished

PL/SQL procedure successfully completed.

The example illustrates the use of the overloaded procedure with the `schema_names` parameter specified as an array. We could have used 'SCOTT, HR' as the value for the `schema_names` parameter. However, if the list of the schema names is long, then you can use the array to specify the schema names as shown in this example. We also specified the names for the dump file and log file for the data pump export/import operations. The instantiation method for these schemas was left to the default value DBMS_STREAMS_ADM.INSTANTIATION_SCHEMA by not specifying the `instantiation` parameter. This method for instantiation uses the dump file created by the data pump export.

In our test case, the destination database had the SCOTT schema and all the tables that matched the source database. The destination database did not have the HR schema. However, during the instantiation process, the data pump operations preserved the objects under the SCOTT schema in the destination database and only set the instantiation SCN. It created the HR schema and imported its objects, and set the instantiation SCN for them. Notice that in this example we did not create the Streams configuration script.

As a variation of the previous procedure, the following example illustrates the use of the DBMS_STREAMS_ADM.INSTANTIATION_SCHEMA_NETWORK method for instantiation. In this case, the data pump utility does not create a dump file, but performs the data import using the network link to the source database DBXA. WORLD from the destination database DBXB.WORLD. Even if this method does not create the dump file, the directory objects for the source and destination database must be specified; otherwise, an error will be reported.

Also, in this example we do not specify user-defined names for the Streams components, and use the minimum required parameters to configure schema-level unidirectional replication for DDL and DML changes using the local capture process.

```
SQL> connect strmadmin/strmadmin@DBXA.WORLD
Connected.
SQL> declare
  2     schemas  dbms_utility.uncl_array;
  3   begin
  4     schemas(1) := 'SCOTT';
  5     schemas(2) := 'HR';
  6   dbms_streams_adm.maintain_schemas (
  7     schema_names              => schemas,
```

```
 8      source_database              => 'DBXA.WORLD',
 9      source_directory_object      => 'STREAMS_DP_DIR',
10      destination_database         => 'DBXB.WORLD',
11      destination_directory_object => 'STREAMS_DP_DIR',
12      include_ddl                  => TRUE,
13      instantiation => DBMS_STREAMS_ADM.INSTANTIATION_SCHEMA_NETWORK
14    );
15  end;
16  /

PL/SQL procedure successfully completed.
```

Streams Replication at the Table Level

Table-level data replication is the most commonly used Streams replication. The MAINTAIN_TABLES procedure of the DBMS_STREAMS_ADM package is used to configure simple table-level replication as shown in the example that follows. It configures unidirectional replication from the DBXA.WORLD database to the DBXB.WORLD database for four tables using the local capture process. It is assumed that all the prerequisite steps have been completed in the source database and the destination database. The DBMS_STREAMS_ADM.MAINTAIN_TABLES procedure is executed as the Streams Administrator user in the source database DBXA.WORLD.

The example demonstrates the use of the overloaded procedure that uses an array for the table names. If you were replicating only a handful of tables, then specifying them in a single string for table_names would also suffice.

```
SQL> connect strmadmin/strmadmin@DBXA.WORLD
Connected.
SQL> declare
 2    tables    dbms_utility.uncl_array;
 3  begin
 4    tables(1) := 'SCOTT.DEPT';
 5    tables(2) := 'SCOTT.EMP';
 6    tables(3) := 'HR.SALGRADE';
 7    tables(4) := 'HR.BONUS';
 8
 9    dbms_streams_adm.maintain_tables (
10     table_names                  => tables,
11     source_database              => 'DBXA.WORLD',
12     source_directory_object      => 'STREAMS_DP_DIR',
13     destination_database         => 'DBXB.WORLD',
14     destination_directory_object => 'STREAMS_DP_DIR',
15     capture_name                 => 'DBXA_CAP',
16     capture_queue_name           => 'DBXA_CAP_Q',
17     capture_queue_table          => 'DBXA_CAP_Q_T',
```

```
18      propagation_name              => 'DBXA_TO_DBXB_PROP',
19      apply_name                    => 'DBXA_APP',
20      apply_queue_name              => 'DBXA_APP_Q',
21      apply_queue_table             => 'DBXA_APP_Q_T',
22      dump_file_name             => NULL,
23      log_file                   => NULL,
24      bi_directional             => FALSE,
25      include_ddl                => TRUE,
26      perform_actions            => TRUE,
27      instantiation  => DBMS_STREAMS_ADM.INSTANTIATION_TABLE
28      );
29  end;
30  /
job finished
job finished
PL/SQL procedure successfully completed.
```

As before, we used user-defined names for the various Streams components and used the data pump export file for instantiation. In our test case, the HR schema did not have any tables at the destination database, but had tables in the SCOTT schema. The procedure only set the instantiation SCN for tables in the SCOTT schema. It imported both the tables for the HR schema and set the instantiation SCN for those.

Streams Replication at the Tablespace Level

The DBMS_STREAMS_ADM package provides two different procedures to configure Streams replication at the tablespace level, MAINTAIN_SIMPLE_TTS and MAINTAIN_TTS. The latter provides more flexibility and options than the former.

Using these procedures is advisable when you have large tables in self-contained tablespaces. Moving data in these tables during instantiation using data pump export/import can be time consuming. The MAINTAIN procedures use the transportable tablespace feature of the data pump utility that speeds up configuring Streams in such cases.

Behind the scenes, these procedures configure replication at the table level for all supported tables in the specified tablespaces. Internally, these procedures clone the data files for the tablespaces using the CLONE_SIMPLE_TABLESPACE or CLONE_TABLESPACES procedure in the DBMS_STREAMS_ADM package. If the source and destination databases run on different platforms, then the data files will be converted to match the destination. Converted files are copied to the destination server and attached to the destination database using the ATTACH_SIMPLE_TABLESPACE or ATTACH_TABLEPSPACES procedure in the DBMS_STREAMS_ADM package. The procedures for cloning and attaching the data files use the data pump utility to perform these actions.

Using the MAINTAIN_SIMPLE_TTS Procedure

The MAINTAIN_SIMPLE_TTS procedure can be used only when configuring replication for all tables contained within one tablespace with only one data file. The data file must be stored in a non-ASM file system. If the tablespace contains more than one data file, then the procedure will terminate with an ORA-26311 error.

Before you can use this procedure, you must define a directory object in the source database that points to the operating system directory that contains the data file for the tablespace in question. If such a directory object does not exist, then the procedure terminates with an error. Similarly, you must define a directory object in the destination database to point to the directory where the source data file will be copied by the procedure. This directory must also be on a non-ASM file system.

The tablespace to replicate should not be present in the destination database. All the users who own tables in the tablespace to replicate must be defined in the destination database; otherwise, the procedure will abort and the error will be reported by the data pump import utility in the log file in the destination directory specified.

The procedure configures replication at the table level for all supported tables in the specified tablespace. There could be more than one owner with tables in the specified tablespace. The following example configures unidirectional Streams replication for all tables contained within the EXAMPLE_TS tablespace, which has only one data file. In our example, the data file for this tablespace is in the /u01/oradata/DBXA directory, so we create the directory object for this directory in the source database DBXA.WORLD:

```
SQL> create directory example_ts_dir as '/u01/oradata/DBXA';
Directory created.

SQL> grant read on directory example_ts_dir to strmadmin;
Grant succeeded
```

We want the data file to be stored in the /u02/app/oradata/DBXB directory on the destination server, so we create the directory object for this directory in the destination database DBXB.WORLD:

```
SQL> create directory example_ts_dir as '/u02/app/oradata/DBXB';
Directory created.
```

Next, we execute the MAINTAIN_SIMPLE_TTS procedure as the Streams Administrator in the source database DBXA.WORLD:

```
SQL> connect strmadmin/strmadmin@DBXA.WORLD
Connected.
SQL> begin
  2    dbms_streams_adm.maintain_simple_tts(
  3      tablespace_name          => 'EXAMPLE_TS',
  4      source_directory_object  => 'STREAMS_DP_DIR',
```

```
 5     source_database                => 'DBXA.WORLD',
 6     destination_directory_object   => 'EXAMPLE_TS_DIR',
 7     destination_database           => 'DBXB.WORLD',
 8     perform_actions                => TRUE,
 9     script_name                    => 'cr_maintain_simple_tts_uni.sql',
10     script_directory_object        => 'STREAMS_DP_DIR',
11     bi_directional                 => FALSE
12     );
13   end;
14   /
PL/SQL procedure successfully completed.
```

This example demonstrates the use of all available parameters for this procedure. Note that there is no option to capture DDL changes. By default, this procedure only captures DML changes.

Notice the use of the directory objects. The `source_directory_object` parameter points to the directory that will contain the data pump dump file for the metadata for the transportable tablespace (TTS) export and the log file for the data pump job. It will also contain the cloned data file for the tablespace in question. You must have enough space in this directory to store this file.

The `destination_directory_object parameter` points to the directory where the cloned file will be copied and attached to the destination database by the data pump import job. This directory will also contain the data pump metadata and log file. Upon completion, the procedure does not remove the cloned file from the source directory. The metadata dump file and log files are also not removed from the source and destination directories. You will have to remove those manually. Be careful to not remove the copied data file from the destination directory. It is now part of the destination database.

Also, as you can see, the procedure does not have any parameters to provide user-defined names for the Streams components. All of these will be system-generated names.

Using the MAINTAIN_TTS Procedure

The MAINTAIN_TTS procedure can be used when configuring replication for all tables stored in more than one tablespace (each of which may have more than one data file) and stored in non-ASM files systems. The MAINTAIN_TTS procedure otherwise works the same way as the MAINTAIN_SIMPLE_TTS procedure.

You will need to define directory objects for all operating system directories that contain affected data files at the source database. Yes, this can be somewhat involved work if you have a number of operating system directories containing the data files for these tablespaces.

Also, all the users who own tables in these tablespaces must be defined in the destination database. The tablespaces to replicate should not be present in the destination database.

The following example configures unidirectional Streams replication for all tables contained within the DATA_TS and EXAMPLE_TS tablespaces. The INDEX_TS tablespace contains the indexes for tables in DATA_TS, so we need to replicate that as well. The `source_directory_object` and `destination_directory_object` parameters have been defined already, as shown in the previous example.

```
SQL> connect strmadmin/strmadmin@DBXA.WORLD
Connected.
SQL> declare
  2    ts_names   dbms_streams_tablespace_adm.tablespace_set;
  3  begin
  4    ts_names(1) := 'DATA_TS';
  5    ts_names(2) := 'INDEX_TS';
  6    ts_names(3) := 'EXAMPLE_TS';
  7
  8    dbms_streams_adm.maintain_tts(
  9    tablespace_names                => ts_names,
 10    source_directory_object         => 'STREAMS_DP_DIR',
 11    destination_directory_object    => 'EXAMPLE_TS_DIR',
 12    source_database                 => 'DBXA.WORLD',
 13    destination_database            => 'DBXB.WORLD',
 14    perform_actions                 => TRUE,
 15    script_name                     => 'cr_streams_maintain_tts_uni.sql',
 16    script_directory_object         => 'STREAMS_DP_DIR',
 17    dump_file_name                  => 'maint_tts.dmp',
 18    capture_name                    => 'DBXA_CAP',
 19    capture_queue_table             => 'DBXA_CAP_Q_T',
 20    capture_queue_name              => 'DBXA_CAP_Q',
 21    capture_queue_user              => 'STRMADMIN',
 22    propagation_name                => 'DBXA_TO_DBXB_PROP',
 23    apply_name                      => 'DBXA_APP',
 24    apply_queue_table               => 'DBXA_APP_Q_T',
 25    apply_queue_name                => 'DBXA_APP_Q',
 26    apply_queue_user                => 'STRMADMIN',
 27    log_file                        => 'maintain_tts.log',
 28    bi_directional                  => FALSE,
 29    include_ddl                     => TRUE
 30    );
 31  end;
 32  /
PL/SQL procedure successfully completed.
```

One thing to note here about the `destination_directory_object` parameter is that the operating system directory it points to will store all the data files for all the tablespaces selected for replication. The procedure does not provide any option to place these data files into multiple different directories.

The directory defined for the `source_directory_object` parameter at the source database also must be large enough to hold the cloned files for these tablespaces before they are copied to the destination server.

The example demonstrates the use of all available parameters for this procedure. As you can see, we have assigned user-defined names to various Streams components for our unidirectional replication.

Configuring the Downstream Capture Process Using MAINTAIN Procedures

All the previous examples showing the use of various MAINTAIN procedures configured the capture process locally running in the source database. These procedures can also be used to configure the downstream capture process running in a database other than the source database.

Presently, these procedures can only configure the archived-log downstream capture process. Configuring the real-time downstream capture process is not possible.

The following example demonstrates schema-level Streams replication from the DBXA.WORLD database to the DBXB.WORLD database where the capture process runs in the DBXB.WORLD database to capture changes made in the DBXA.WORLD database. The DBXB.WORLD database, in this case, acts as the downstream and destination database. We have already completed all the prerequisite steps in the source DBXA.WORLD database and the destination DBXB.WORLD database.

Things to note in the this example are as follows:

■ The procedure runs in the destination database DBXB.WORLD.

■ No propagation process is required.

■ The queue and queue table names for the capture and apply processes are identical.

```
SQL> connect strmadmin/strmadmin@DBXB.WORLD
Connected.
SQL> declare
  2    schemas   dbms_utility.uncl_array;
  3  begin
  4    schemas(1) := 'SCOTT';
  5    schemas(2) := 'HR';
  6
  7    dbms_streams_adm.maintain_schemas (
  8        schema_names              => schemas,
  9        source_database           => 'DBXA.WORLD',
 10        source_directory_object   => 'STREAMS_DP_DIR',
 11        destination_database      => 'DBXB.WORLD',
```

```
12          destination_directory_object => 'STREAMS_DP_DIR',
13          capture_name              => 'DBXA_CAP',
14          capture_queue_name        => 'DBXA_CAP_Q',
15          capture_queue_table       => 'DBXA_CAP_Q_T',
16          propagation_name          => 'DBXA_TO_DBXB_PROP',
17          apply_name                => 'DBXA_APP',
18          apply_queue_name          => 'DBXA_CAP_Q',
19          apply_queue_table         => 'DBXA_CAP_Q_T',
20          dump_file_name            => NULL,
21          log_file                  => NULL,
22          bi_directional            => FALSE,
23          include_ddl               => TRUE,
24          perform_actions           => TRUE
25      );
26  end;
27  /
job finished
PL/SQL procedure successfully completed.
```

Although the propagation name is specified, the propagation process will not be created.

The following example shows how to configure Streams replication from the DBXA.WORLD database to the DBXC.WORLD database with downstream capture running in the DBXB.WORLD database. Things to note are

■ The procedure runs in the DBXB.WORLD database.

■ Propagation is defined from DBXB.WORLD to DBXC.WORLD.

■ The queue and queue table names for the capture and apply processes are different.

```
SQL> connect strmadmin/strmadmin@DBXB.WORLD
Connected.
SQL> declare
  2      schemas   dbms_utility.uncl_array;
  3  begin
  4      schemas(1) := 'SCOTT';
  5      schemas(2) := 'HR';
  6
  7      dbms_streams_adm.maintain_schemas (
  8          schema_names              => schemas,
  9          source_database           => 'DBXA.WORLD',
 10          source_directory_object   => 'STREAMS_DP_DIR',
 11          destination_database      => 'DBXC.WORLD',
 12          destination_directory_object => 'STREAMS_DP_DIR',
 13          capture_name              => 'DBXA_CAP',
```

```
14          capture_queue_name      => 'DBXA_CAP_Q',
15          capture_queue_table     => 'DBXA_CAP_Q_T',
16          propagation_name        => 'DBXB_TO_DBXC_PROP',
17          apply_name              => 'DBXA_APP',
18          apply_queue_name        => 'DBXA_APP_Q',
19          apply_queue_table       => 'DBXA_APP_Q_T',
20          dump_file_name          => NULL,
21          log_file                => NULL,
22          bi_directional          => FALSE,
23          include_ddl             => TRUE,
24          perform_actions         => TRUE
25      );
26  end;
27  /
PL/SQL procedure successfully completed.
```

Monitoring the Progress of MAINTAIN Procedures

When any of the MAINTAIN procedures is active, the following views are populated. These views can be used to monitor the progress of the procedure when it is executing the Streams configuration script.

- **DBA_RECOVERABLE_SCRIPT** Provides the current status of the recoverable script that is being executed by the procedure. When the procedure completes, the metadata about the operation is moved from this view to the DBA_RECOVERABLE_SCRIPT_HIST view.

- **DBA_RECOVERABLE_SCRIPT_PARAMS** Lists the parameters, with their values, that are in effect for the script. The contents of this view are purged after 30 days.

- **DBA_RECOVERABLE_SCRIPT_BLOCKS** Provides information about the blocks (a block is a related set of PL/SQL procedures) in the script, along with their status when the procedure is active. The contents of this view are purged after 30 days.

- **DBA_RECOVERABLE_SCRIPT_ERRORS** Provides the block number, error number, and error messages in case the procedure fails. The contents of this view are purged after 30 days.

NOTE
These views are populated only when `perform_` *`action` is set to TRUE. The views are not populated when you run the generated script manually.*

If you chose to create the script in the location defined by the `script_directory_object` parameter, you can review it to see all the steps the configuration process performs. Internally, these steps are grouped in blocks when the procedure is active. The views will refer to the block number of the script when reporting progress or any error. Also, the script will be assigned a unique identifier populated in the SCRIPT_ID column in these views.

The following script creates a view called STREAMS_BUILD_STATUS based on the DBA_RECOVERABLE_SCRIPT and DBA_RECOVERABLE_SCRIPT_BLOCKS views. This view can then be queried to check on the status and progress of the procedure.

```
connect sys as sysdba
set long 100000000
create or replace view streams_build_status
as
select to_char(rs.creation_time,'HH24:Mi:SS MM/DD/YY') CREATE_DATE,
       rs.status,
       rs.done_block_num||' of ' ||rs.total_blocks
                        ||' Steps Completed' PROGRESS,
       to_char(to_number(sysdate-rs.creation_time)*86400,9999.99)

                ELAPSED_SECONDS,
       substr(rsb.forward_block,1,5000) CURRENT_STEP,
       rs.invoking_package||'.'||rs.invoking_procedure PROCEDURE,
       rs.script_id
  from dba_recoverable_script rs,
       dba_recoverable_script_blocks rsb
 where rs.script_id = rsb.script_id
   and rsb.block_num = rs.done_block_num + 1;

create public synonym streams_build_status for streams_build_status;
grant select on streams_build_status to public;
```

When the procedure is active, you can run the following query to check on its status and progress. Here, we see that the procedure is currently executing and has completed block 13 out of 14. It has been running for 276 seconds.

```
SQL> select status,
  2          progress,
  3          elapsed_seconds elapsed,
  4          script_id
  5    from streams_build_status;

STATUS    PROGRESS                  ELAPSED  SCRIPT_ID
--------- ------------------------- -------  ---------------------------------
EXECUTING 13 of 14 Steps Completed   276.00  7CC97F3B9169704BE040A8C014006E63
```

The following query shows the current block the procedure is executing:

```
SQL> select current_step
  2    from streams_build_status;

CURRENT_STEP
--------------------------------------------------------------------
-- Start capture process DBXA$CAP
--
BEGIN

  dbms_capture_adm.start_capture(

    capture_name => '"DBXA$CAP"');

EXCEPTION WHEN OTHERS THEN
  IF sqlcode = -26666 THEN NULL;  -- CAPTURE process already running
  ELSE RAISE;
  END IF;
END;
```

Unfortunately, the block number is not listed in the generated script itself. However, the view DBA_RECOVERABLE_SCRIPT_BLOCKS can be used to view associated commands. If you did not create the script in the `script_directory_object` directory, you can use the following query to retrieve the script along with the block. You need to provide the script identifier `script_id` obtained from the STREAMS_BUILD_STATUS view.

```
SQL> set long 10000000

SQL> set pages 1000

SQL> spool maintain_script.sql

SQL> select '-- Block: ' || block_num,
  2             forward_block
  3      from dba_recoverable_script_blocks
  4     where script_id = '7CC97F3B9169704BE040A8C014006E63'
  5   order by block_num;

SQL> spool off
```

Recovering from an Error in MAINTAIN Procedures

If the MAINTAIN procedure fails due to an error, it can be restarted from the point of failure after you correct the situation that caused the error. Typically, the procedure fails if the database link is missing or the data pump job runs into an error. Sometimes the error message may not be clear and you may have to refer to the actual commands in the script to diagnose the cause of the error. Once the error is corrected, you have an option to restart the failed procedure or completely discard its actions and start over.

The DBMS_STREAMS_ADM package provides the RECOVER_OPERATION procedure. It takes the following parameters to either discard or resume the operation:

- **script_id** Identifes the script that ran into an error. The `script_id` value will be reported along with the error messages.

- **operation_mode** Directs the operation of the MAINTAIN procedures as to its disposition. It can have the following values:

  - FORWARD Resume operation from the current step

  - ROLLBACK Roll back performed operations and purge metadata about the configuration

  - PURGE Simply purge all the metadata without performing a rollback

The following example demonstrates resolution of a simple error that caused the MAINTAIN procedure to fail while configuring replication at the schema level:

```
SQL> connect strmadmin/strmadmin@DBXA.WORLD
Connected.
SQL> declare
  2    schemas       dbms_utility.uncl_array;
  3  begin
  4    schemas(1) := 'SCOTT';
  5    schemas(2) := 'HR';
  6
  7    dbms_streams_adm.maintain_schemas (
  8    schema_names               => schemas,
  9    source_database            => 'DBXA.WORLD',
 10    source_directory_object    => 'STREAMS_DP_DIR',
 11    destination_database       => 'DBXB.WORLD',
 12    destination_directory_object => 'STREAMS_DP_DIR',
 13    include_ddl                => TRUE,
 14    instantiation => DBMS_STREAMS_ADM.INSTANTIATION_SCHEMA_NETWORK
 15    );
 16  end;
 17  /
declare
*
ERROR at line 1:
ORA-23616: Failure in executing block 7 for script
7CD4E8B08BD40E08E040A8C014007723 with
ORA-39001: invalid argument value
ORA-06512: at "SYS.DBMS_RECO_SCRIPT_INVOK", line 139
ORA-06512: at "SYS.DBMS_STREAMS_RPC", line 465
ORA-06512: at "SYS.DBMS_RECOVERABLE_SCRIPT", line 659
```

```
ORA-06512: at "SYS.DBMS_RECOVERABLE_SCRIPT", line 682
ORA-06512: at "SYS.DBMS_STREAMS_MT", line 7972
ORA-06512: at "SYS.DBMS_STREAMS_ADM", line 2674
ORA-06512: at line 7
```

The error message does not clearly tell us what the problem is, but we can see that block 7 of the script identified by that long string of characters (`script_id`) ran into some problem. To see what is in block 7, we run the following query:

```
SQL> select forward_block
  2    from dba_recoverable_script_blocks
  3   where script_id = '7CD4E8B08BD40E08E040A8C014007723'
  4     and block_num = 7;
FORWARD_BLOCK
-----------------------------------------------------------
--
-- Datapump SCHEMA MODE IMPORT (NETWORK)
--
DECLARE
   h1                    NUM
......
......
```

So, the data pump import over the network link has failed. As it turns out, our problem was due to the missing database link from the destination database to the source database. After creating the database link, the job completed successfully after it was resumed, as shown here:

```
SQL> begin
  2    dbms_streams_adm.recover_operation(
  3        script_id => '7CD4E8B08BD40E08E040A8C014007723',
  4        operation_mode => 'FORWARD'
  5    );
  6  end;
  7  /
PL/SQL procedure successfully completed.
```

Advantages of MAINTAIN Procedures

There are several advantages of using the MAINTAIN procedures for simple Streams replication configurations. These procedures automate Streams configuration by performing a number of steps behind the scenes. These steps include

- Enabling supplemental logging in the source database

- Configuring the Streams buffered queues

- Configuring the Streams capture process

- Configuring the Streams propagation process

- Configuring the Streams apply process

- Performing the dump and load of the database dictionary needed for log mining

- Creating and instantiating objects at the destination database

In addition to these steps, the MAINTAIN procedures also

- Ignore unsupported objects from Streams configuration.

- Generate unique names for Streams components (queues; capture, propagation and apply processes). Unique names are important when configuring bidirectional replication using these procedures.

- Allow for correcting an error and restarting the process, which saves valuable time and avoids rework.

- Allow for monitoring the progress of the process using supplied views.

Limitations of MAINTAIN Procedures

The MAINTAIN procedures cannot be used in the following situations:

- Complex Streams environments, such as N-way replication, queue forwarding, apply forwarding, replication from a single source to multiple destinations, and so forth

- Replication of a subset of table data

- Real-time downstream replication

- Replication that uses the synchronous capture process

- Replication that requires use of a negative rule set

The MAINTAIN procedures may not be appropriate if large amounts of data must be copied to the destination database from the source database during the instantiation process. The default data pump configuration does not use parallelism to speed up this operation. It is possible to work around this issue by preloading the destination objects using data pump with parallelism.

You must also be aware of the Streams rules created by these procedures. These rules will not allow you to use the Streams tag feature to temporarily suspend the replication. This is because these procedures can also be used to create bidirectional replication, and the capture process rules are created to capture the tagged LCRs. Thus, the generated rules do not have a check for the Streams tag field. You will have to modify the generated rules to ignore LCRs with a specific Streams tag value.

The capture and apply processes are automatically started when the MAINTAIN procedure completes successfully. The parameters for these processes are set to use the default values. Sometimes these values are not adequate for the data volumes handled by these processes. You will have to review and manually modify these parameters.

Streams Configuration Using Custom Scripts

Using OEM Grid Control 10.2.0.5 or the MAINTAIN procedures to configure Streams replication is much easier than doing it with a custom script. However, if you do not have Grid Control installed, or the limitations of the MAINTAIN procedures prevent you from using them, then you have to develop your own scripts to configure Streams replication. Also, you will need to write your own script to configure replication if you want to use the synchronous capture process. Currently, the OEM and MAINTAIN procedures cannot create the synchronous capture process.

This section discusses how to configure Streams replication using custom scripts that use Oracle-provided PL/SQL procedures.

The basic tasks involved in configuring Streams replication can be summarized as follows:

1. Create Streams queues.

2. Create the apply process and apply rules.

3. Create the propagation process and propagation rules.

4. Create the capture process and capture rules.

5. Instantiate objects.

In the examples that follow, we will use the SCOTT schema to configure Streams replication. The examples will demonstrate the use, and discuss the purpose, of various Oracle-supplied PL/SQL packages used to configure the Streams environment. We will discuss the following Streams configurations:

■ Unidirectional replication with the local capture process

■ Unidirectional replication with the downstream capture process

  ■ Archived-log downstream capture process

  ■ Real-time downstream capture process

■ Bidirectional replication

- Replication from a single source to multiple destinations

- Replication using queue forwarding

- Replication using apply forwarding

- Replication using the synchronous capture process

- N-way replication (multimaster)

- Hub-and-spoke replication

The examples will involve up to three databases and up to two schemas. Most examples will use schema level Streams replication. Table level Streams replication will be configured where required, and will not involve subset rules. Refer to the section "Subset Rules" in Chapter 3 for an example that shows how to create subset rules to replicate a subset of the table data.

The three databases are DBXA.WORLD, DBXB.WORLD, and DBXC.WORLD. The two schemas are HR and SCOTT, with a few tables each.

Unidirectional Replication with the Local Capture Process

Unidirectional replication with the local capture process is by far the most widely used configuration for Streams replication. This is ideally suited for environments in which you want to offload the reporting application to a replicated database that uses the replicated data in read-only mode.

Configuring this replication environment is not very difficult. We will discuss the configuration of Streams replication at the schema level using the procedures in the DBMS_STREAMS_ADM package. The source database is DBXA.WORLD and the destination database is DBXB.WORLD.

1. Connect to the destination database and create the Streams queue and queue table:

```
SQL> conn strmadmin/strmadmin@DBXB.WORLD
Connected.
SQL> begin
  2    dbms_streams_adm.set_up_queue(
  3      queue_name   => 'DBXA_APP_Q',
  4      queue_table  => 'DBXA_APP_Q_T',
  5      queue_user   => 'STRMADMIN'
  6    );
  7  end;
  8  /

PL/SQL procedure successfully completed.
```

2. At the destination database, create the apply process and the apply rules:

```
SQL> begin
  2    dbms_streams_adm.add_schema_rules (
  3      schema_name        => 'SCOTT',
  4      streams_type       => 'APPLY',
  5      streams_name       => 'DBXA_APP',
  6      queue_name         => 'DBXA_APP_Q',
  7      include_dml        => true,
  8      include_ddl        => true,
  9      inclusion_rule     => true,
 10      include_tagged_lcr => false,
 11      source_database    => 'DBXA.WORLD',
 12      and_condition => ' :lcr.get_compatible() < dbms_streams.max_compatible()'
 13      );
 14  end;
 15  /

PL/SQL procedure successfully completed.
```

This procedure will create the specified apply process, if one does not exist. The `streams_type` parameter specifies that this is an apply process. Then it will create the positive rule set (`inclusion_rule` is set to TRUE) and attach it to the apply process. The rule set will select LCRs for changes to tables belonging to the SCOTT schema. The `include_tagged_lcr` parameter is set to FALSE to indicate that the generated apply rule condition will check for the Streams tag in the LCR to be NULL. If the tag is not NULL, then the LCR will be discarded. When the changes are applied to the destination tables, the apply process, by default, sets a tag value of hex 00 in the generated redo records. This is relevant if a capture process running in this database was to capture changes made by an apply process. This will be important in N-way replication to avoid recycling the change. Also, we added a custom rule condition to the generated rule using the `and_ condition` parameter. This condition will discard changes to unsupported tables from being applied to the destination database. Notice that this procedure does not offer an option to set the apply user. It will default to STRMADMIN, the user who ran this procedure. The created apply process will be in a disabled state and will not be started automatically.

3. Connect to the source database and create the Streams queue:

```
SQL> conn strmadmin/strmadmin@DBXA.WORLD
Connected.
SQL> set serveroutput on size unlimited
SQL> set echo on
SQL> begin
  2    dbms_streams_adm.set_up_queue(
  3      queue_name  => 'DBXA_CAP_Q',
```

```
   4       queue_table => 'DBXA_CAP_Q_T',
   5       queue_user  => 'STRMADMIN'
   6       );
   7   end;
   8   /
PL/SQL procedure successfully completed.
```

4. At the source database, create the propagation process and propagation rules:

```
SQL> begin
  2    dbms_streams_adm.add_schema_propagation_rules (
  3      schema_name            => 'SCOTT',
  4      streams_name           => 'DBXA_TO_DBXB_PROP',
  5      source_queue_name      => 'DBXA_CAP_Q',
  6      destination_queue_name => 'DBXA_APP_Q@DBXB.WORLD',
  7      include_dml            => true,
  8      include_ddl            => true,
  9      inclusion_rule         => true,
 10      include_tagged_lcr     => false,
 11      queue_to_queue         => true,
 12      source_database        => 'DBXA.WORLD',
 13      and_condition => ' :lcr.get_compatible() < dbms_streams.max_compatible()'
 14      );
 15   end;
 16   /
PL/SQL procedure successfully completed.
```

This procedure creates the propagation process if one does not exit, and adds a propagation rule to the positive rule set. The rule will select LCRs for changes made to tables belonging to the SCOTT schema. The `queue_to_queue` parameter is set to TRUE. This means that the created propagation process has its own propagation job that will not be shared with any other propagation process that may be present. Notice the Streams queue name specification for the source and destination queues.

5. At the source database, create the capture process and capture rules:

```
SQL> begin
  2    dbms_streams_adm.add_schema_rules (
  3      schema_name        => 'SCOTT',
  4      streams_type       => 'CAPTURE',
  5      streams_name       => 'DBXA_CAP',
  6      queue_name         => 'DBXA_CAP_Q',
  7      include_dml        => true,
  8      include_ddl        => true,
  9      include_tagged_lcr => false,
 10      inclusion_rule     => true,
 11      source_database    => 'DBXA.WORLD',
 12      and_condition => ' :lcr.get_compatible() < dbms_streams.max_compatible()'
 13      );
 14   end;
 15   /
PL/SQL procedure successfully completed.
```

We used the ADD_SCHEMA_RULES procedure with `streams_type` parameter set to CAPTURE. The procedure will create the specified capture process if one does not exist. Then it will create a positive rule set (`inclusion_rule` parameter is set to TRUE) and attach it to the capture process. The generated rule will capture DDL and DML changes made to tables belonging to the SCOTT schema. The `include_tagged_lcr` parameter is set to FALSE. This creates a rule condition that will only capture changes that has the Streams tag set to null. This is relevant if changes made by an apply process are to be captured in N-way replication. The created capture process will be in a disabled state and will not be started automatically.

6. Instantiate objects at the destination database:

    a. Export the schema objects from the source database and transfer the dump file to the destination database server.

        Data pump utility can be used to export (and import) the schema objects. The data pump import automatically sets the instantiation SCN for the schema objects at the destination database.

        Here is an example of the contents of the data pump export parameter file:

        ```
        directory=data_pump_dir
        schemas=SCOTT
        parallel=4
        dumpfile=schemas_%u.dmp
        logfile=schemas_expdp.log
        ```

        The generated dump files are then copied to the data pump directory on the destination database server.

    b. Import schema objects in the destination database.

        Here is an example of the contents of the data pump import parameter file:

        ```
        directory=data_pump_dir
        full=y
        parallel=4
        table_exists_action=truncate
        dumpfile=schemas_%u.dmp
        logfile=schemas_expdp.log
        ```

7. Start the apply process at the destination database:

    ```
    SQL> conn strmadmin/strmadmin@DBXB.WORLD
    Connected.
    ```

```
SQL> begin
  2    dbms_apply_adm.start_apply('DBXA_APP');
  3  end;
  4  /
PL/SQL procedure successfully completed.
```

8. Start the capture process at the source database:

```
SQL> conn strmadmin/strmadmin@DBXA.WORLD
Connected.
SQL>
SQL> begin
  2    dbms_capture_adm.start_capture('DBXA_CAP');
  3  end;
  4  /
PL/SQL procedure successfully completed.
```

9. Review the alert log of the source database.

At this point, Streams replication has been configured. However, before you test whether it works or not, it is advisable to review the alert log file for the source database. Upon startup, the capture process writes several messages to the alert log file while the LogMiner process is reading the redo logs to build the Streams data dictionary. After the data dictionary build is complete, the LogMiner will be mining current redo log files. Once you see messages similar to the following, indicating that the capture process is mining online redo logs, you can test the replication:

```
LOGMINER: Begin mining logfile for session 23 thread 1 sequence 230,
/u01/oradata/DBXA/redo01.log
LOGMINER: End   mining logfile for session 23 thread 1 sequence 230,
/u01/oradata/DBXA/redo01.log
LOGMINER: Begin mining logfile for session 23 thread 1 sequence 231,
/u01/oradata/DBXA/redo01.log
```

10. Test replication.

At this time, we can perform a DML or DDL change to one of the tables in the SCOTT schema and confirm that the same change is carried out in the destination database.

Since we configured this environment at the schema level to capture and apply DDL changes, any new tables created in the SCOTT schema at the source database will also be created in the destination database. If DDL changes were not replicated, then any structural changes to existing tables, as well as creation of new tables in the source database, may cause apply errors if these changes were not made at the destination database prior to any changes at the source database.

In the previous example, we used the procedures that implicitly create the capture, apply, and propagation processes while adding rules to them. In situations in which you just want to propagate and apply all the changes that were captured, then you can do away with the rules for the propagation and apply processes by creating these processes explicitly, as shown in this example:

```
SQL> connect strmadmin/strmadmin@DBXB.WORLD
Connected.
SQL> set serveroutput on size unlimited
SQL>
SQL> -- Create Streams queue.
SQL> begin
  2    dbms_streams_adm.set_up_queue(
  3      queue_table    => 'DBXA_APP_Q_T',
  4      queue_name     => 'DBXA_APP_Q',
  5      queue_user     => 'STRMADMIN');
  6  end;
  7  /
PL/SQL procedure successfully completed.

SQL> -- Create apply process explicitly.
SQL> -- Set apply_captured to TRUE, since the apply
SQL> -- process will apply only captured LCRs.
SQL> begin
  2    dbms_apply_adm.create_apply(
  3      queue_name       => 'DBXA_APP_Q',
  4      apply_name       => 'DBXA_APP',
  5      apply_user       => 'STRMADMIN',
  6      apply_captured   => TRUE,
  7      source_database  => 'DBXA.WORLD');
  8  end;
  9  /
PL/SQL procedure successfully completed.

SQL> -- Connect to Source Database.
SQL> connect strmadmin/strmadmin@DBXA.WORLD
Connected.
SQL>
SQL> -- Create Streams Queue.
SQL> begin
  2    dbms_streams_adm.set_up_queue(
  3      queue_table    => 'DBXA_CAP_Q_T',
  4      queue_name     => 'DBXA_CAP_Q',
  5      queue_user     => 'STRMADMIN');
  6  end;
  7  /
PL/SQL procedure successfully completed.

SQL> -- Create propagation process explicitly.
SQL> -- No propagation rules required.
SQL> begin
  2    dbms_propagation_adm.create_propagation(
  3      propagation_name    => 'DBXA_TO_DBXB_PROP',
  4      source_queue        => 'DBXA_CAP_Q',
```

```
  5     destination_queue   => 'DBXB_APP_Q',
  6     destination_dblink  => 'DBXB',
  7     queue_to_queue      => TRUE);
  8  end;
  9  /
PL/SQL procedure successfully completed.

SQL> -- Create capture process explicitly to start
SQL> -- capturing changes from current SCN.
SQL> begin
  2    dbms_capture_adm.create_capture(
  3      queue_name     => 'DBXA_CAP_Q',
  4      capture_name   => 'DBXA_CAP',
  5      rule_set_name  => NULL,
  6      start_scn      => NULL,
  7      first_scn      => NULL,
  8      source_database => 'DBXA.WORLD');
  9  end;
 10  /
PL/SQL procedure successfully completed.

SQL> -- Add Schema rules to already created capture
SQL> -- process to capture changes made to SCOTT
SQL> -- schema tables.
SQL> begin
  2    dbms_streams_adm.add_schema_rules (
  3      schema_name         => 'SCOTT',
  4      streams_type        => 'CAPTURE',
  5      streams_name        => 'DBXA_CAP',
  6      queue_name          => 'DBXA_CAP_Q',
  7      include_dml         => true,
  8      include_ddl         => true,
  9      include_tagged_lcr  => false,
 10      inclusion_rule      => true,
 11      source_database     => 'DBXA.WORLD',
 12      and_condition => ' :lcr.get_compatible() < dbms_streams.max_compatible()'
 13      );
 14  end;
 15  /

PL/SQL procedure successfully completed.
```

After this, we perform steps 6 to 10 from the previous example to instantiate the objects in the destination database, start the apply and capture processes, and test the replication.

In this example, the SCOTT schema objects did not exist in the destination database. The data pump export/import copied these objects to the destination database and set the instantiation SCN for them.

In situations where the schema objects are present and are in sync with the source, you could skip the export/import step and manually set the instantiation SCN as shown in the next code example. It needs a database link from destination to source database.

```
conn strmadmin/strmadmin@DBXA.WORLD
declare
 v_scn number;
begin
 v_scn := dbms_flashback.get_system_change_number();
 dbms_apply_adm.set_schema_instantiation_scn@DBXB.WORLD(
                source_schema_name   => 'SCOTT',
                source_database_name => 'DBXA.WORLD',
                instantiation_scn    => v_scn,
                recursive            => true);
end;
/
```

Unidirectional Replication with the Downstream Capture Process

There are two ways to configure Streams replication that use a downstream database that runs the capture process:

- **Archived-log downstream**   In this configuration, the capture process mines the archived logs from the source database to capture changes.

- **Real-time downstream**   In this configuration, the capture process mines the standby redo logs for the source database, which are defined at the destination database, to capture changes.

By design, the archived-log downstream method introduces a replication lag time since the capture process has to wait for the archived log file from the source database. If this lag time is not acceptable, then consider using the real-time downstream configuration so that the source database writes redo information to the standby redo log at the downstream database. This provides the benefit of offloading the capture process to the downstream database and also provides near-real-time capture of changes.

Configure Archived-Log Downstream Capture

The following example shows the steps required to configure Streams replication from DBXA.WORLD to DBXB.WORLD. In this example, the latter database acts as the downstream and destination database.

An important step in this configuration is the redo transport mechanism. You should get this working before you actually start the steps to configure Streams.

The source and destination databases use `log_archive_dest_1` for their own archived log files, so we use `log_archive_dest_2` to set up the redo transport:

```
SQL> connect sys/manager@DBXA.WORLD as sysdba
Connected.
SQL> alter system set log_archive_dest_2=
  2   'service=DBXB.WORLD ASYNC NOREGISTER VALID_FOR=(online_logfiles, all_roles)
  3    TEMPLATE=DBXA_arch_%t_%s_%r.arc' scope=both;

System altered.

SQL> alter system set log_archive_dest_state_2=ENABLE scope=both;
System altered.
SQL> connect sys/manager@DBXB.WORLD as sysdba
Connected.
SQL> alter system set log_archive_dest_2=
  2   'location=/u01/oradata/DBXA_logs VALID_FOR=(standby_logfiles, primary_role)'
  3    scope=both;

System altered.

SQL> alter system set log_archive_dest_state_2=ENABLE scope=both;
System altered.
```

Since the destination database is also the downstream database, we do not need to configure the propagation process. The capture and apply processes will share the Streams queue and queue table:

```
SQL> connect strmadmin/strmadmin@DBXA.WORLD
Connected.
SQL>
SQL> -- Create Streams Queue.
SQL> begin
  2   dbms_streams_adm.set_up_queue(
  3     queue_name  => 'DBXA_CAP_APP_Q',
  4     queue_table => 'DBXA_CAP_APP_Q_T',
  5     queue_user  => 'STRMADMIN'
  6   );
  7  end;
  8  /
PL/SQL procedure successfully completed.

SQL> -- Create apply process and rules.
SQL> begin
  2   dbms_streams_adm.add_schema_rules (
  3     schema_name       => 'SCOTT',
  4     streams_type      => 'APPLY',
  5     streams_name      => 'DBXA_APP',
  6     queue_name        => 'DBXA_CAP_APP_Q',
  7     include_dml       => true,
  8     include_ddl       => true,
```

```
 9      inclusion_rule        => true,
10      include_tagged_lcr    => false,
11      source_database       => 'DBXA.WORLD'
12      );
13  end;
14  /
PL/SQL procedure successfully completed.

SQL> -- No need to create propagation, since apply
SQL> -- and capture run in the same database.
SQL>
SQL> -- Explicitly create the capture process.
SQL> -- Note that use_database_link is set to TRUE.
SQL> begin
 2    dbms_capture_adm.create_capture(
 3      capture_name      => 'DBXA_CAP',
 4      queue_name        => 'DBXA_CAP_APP_Q',
 5      use_database_link => TRUE,
 6      source_database   => 'DBXA.WORLD');
 7  end;
 8  /
PL/SQL procedure successfully completed.

SQL> -- Add capture rules.
SQL> begin
 2    dbms_streams_adm.add_schema_rules (
 3      schema_name        => 'SCOTT',
 4      streams_type       => 'CAPTURE',
 5      streams_name       => 'DBXA_CAP',
 6      queue_name         => 'DBXA_CAP_APP_Q',
 7      include_dml        => true,
 8      include_ddl        => true,
 9      include_tagged_lcr => false,
10      inclusion_rule     => true,
11      source_database    => 'DBXA.WORLD'
12      );
13  end;
14  /
PL/SQL procedure successfully completed.
```

After this, we instantiate the objects in the destination database as discussed in the previous example. We start the apply process, and then start the capture process.

In the source database, we need to switch the log file so that the archived log is transferred to the downstream database. The capture process can process it and build the Streams data dictionary for the source database. Once this step is completed, we can test replication. Again, until the archived log file is transferred to and processed at the downstream database, our changes will not be applied. We can set the `archive_lag_target` parameter in the source database to automatically switch the log file at regular intervals.

In this example, the downstream database was also the destination database. Suppose the destination database was, say, DBXC.WORLD, instead of DBXB. WORLD. In that case, the apply process and its queue would have been created in DBXC.WORLD. We would have created the capture and propagation processes in DBXB.WORLD.

Configure Real-Time Downstream Capture

As with the archived-log downstream configuration, the important step in the real-time downstream capture is the redo transport mechanism. In this example, DBXA.WORLD is the source database and DBXB.WORLD is the downstream and destination database.

The following steps show how to configure the redo transport for the real-time downstream capture process:

1. On the source database, find out the size of the redo log file and the number of redo log groups:

```
SQL> conn sys/manager@DBXA.WORLD as sysdba
Connected.
SQL> select group#,
  2          bytes/1048576 MB
  3    from v$log;

   GROUP#          MB
---------- ----------
        1          50
        2          50
        3          50
```

The log file size is 50MB, and there are three log groups.

2. On the downstream database, create standby redo logs with the next higher group number. The number of standby log groups must be one higher than the number of redo log groups in the source database. Based on the previous query, we need to create four standby log groups, starting with group number 4:

```
SQL> conn sys/manager@DBXB.WORLD as sysdba
Connected.
SQL> alter database add standby logfile group 4
  2    ('/u01/oradata/DBXA/standby_logs/standby_redo04.log') size 50M;
Database altered.
```

```
SQL> alter database add standby logfile group 5
  2     ('/u01/oradata/DBXA/standby_logs/standby_redo05.log') size 50M;
Database altered.
SQL> alter database add standby logfile group 6
  2     ('/u01/oradata/DBXA/standby_logs/standby_redo06.log') size 50M;
Database altered.
SQL> alter database add standby logfile group 7
  2     ('/u01/oradata/DBXA/standby_logs/standby_redo07.log') size 50M;
Database altered.
SQL> -- Check created Standby logs
SQL> select thread#,
  2         group#,
  3         sequence#,
  4         status,
  5         archived
  6    from v$standby_log;


   THREAD#     GROUP#  SEQUENCE# STATUS     ARC
---------- ---------- ---------- ---------- ---
         0          4          0 UNASSIGNED YES
         0          5          0 UNASSIGNED YES
         0          6          0 UNASSIGNED YES
         0          7          0 UNASSIGNED YES
```

The standby log files are created, but not yet assigned for use.

NOTE
Appendix B discusses how to create standby redo logs when the source is an Oracle RAC database.

3. Configure initialization parameters for redo transport at the source and downstream databases, as discussed in the previous section.

Now, we complete the same exact steps from the previous example (archived-log downstream) to configure the Streams environment, but we stop right before the instantiation step. In this case, we must perform a couple of things before the instantiation step, as discussed next.

We need to change one of the capture process parameters. This parameter, downstream_real_time_mine, needs to be set to Y. By default, for a downstream capture it is set to N. Setting it to Y instructs the capture process to use standby redo logs for capturing changes. After this parameter is set to Y, we need to switch the log file at the source database and confirm that the standby redo log files are being used as expected.

The following steps show these two actions:

```
SQL>conn strmadmin/strmadmin@DBXB.WORLD
Connected.
SQL>
SQL> -- Modify capture Parameter
SQL> begin
  2    dbms_capture_adm.set_parameter(
  3        capture_name => 'DBXA_CAP',
  4        parameter    => 'downstream_real_time_mine',
  5        value        => 'Y');
  6    end;
  7    /

PL/SQL procedure successfully completed.

SQL> conn sys/manager@DBXA.WORLD as sysdba
Connected.

SQL> alter system archive log current;
System altered.

SQL> conn sys/manager@DBXB.WORLD as sysdba
Connected.

SQL> select thread#,
  2          group#,
  3          sequence#,
  4          archived,
  5          status
  6     from v$standby_log;

   THREAD#     GROUP#  SEQUENCE# ARC STATUS
---------- ---------- ---------- --- ----------
         1          4        289 YES ACTIVE
         0          5          0 YES UNASSIGNED
         0          6          0 YES UNASSIGNED
         0          7          0 YES UNASSIGNED
```

As we see from this output, the standby redo log is now active. We can now proceed with the instantiation of objects at the destination database, and start the apply and capture processes.

Once the alert log for the downstream database shows that LogMiner is mining the standby redo log file, we can test the replication by changing data in the SCOTT schema's table at the source, committing it, and confirming that it was replicated immediately.

Bidirectional Replication

You can think of bidirectional replication between databases as two unidirectional replications from each of the two databases to the other. So, there will be capture, propagation, and apply processes in both databases.

The important thing to consider in bidirectional replication is the potential of data conflicts, which are detected and possibly resolved at each apply process. Technically, a change can be made at about the same time in both databases to the same row of the table, causing column values to differ. The LCR that arrives at the other database will contain data that does not match the local data for the row, resulting in a conflict. So, what do we do in such a situation? Conflict resolution is discussed in Chapter 10.

As before, we will use the DBXA.WORLD and DBXB.WORLD databases and the SCOTT schema in the following example. Both databases are source and destination at the same time.

In this configuration, the instantiation SCN for the replicated objects must be set in both the databases so that each can apply changes from the other:

```
SQL> -- Connect to DBXB Database.
SQL> conn strmadmin/strmadmin@DBXB.WORLD
Connected.
SQL> -- Create Queue for apply in DBXB.
SQL> begin
  2    dbms_streams_adm.set_up_queue(
  3      queue_name  => 'DBXA_APP_Q',
  4      queue_table => 'DBXA_APP_Q_T',
  5      queue_user  => 'STRMADMIN'
  6    );
  7  end;
  8  /
PL/SQL procedure successfully completed.

SQL> -- Create Queue for capture in DBXB.
SQL> begin
  2    dbms_streams_adm.set_up_queue(
  3      queue_name  => 'DBXB_CAP_Q',
  4      queue_table => 'DBXB_CAP_Q_T',
  5      queue_user  => 'STRMADMIN'
  6    );
  7  end;
  8  /
PL/SQL procedure successfully completed.

SQL> -- Create apply process and rules in DBXB.
SQL> begin
  2    dbms_streams_adm.add_schema_rules (
  3      schema_name          => 'SCOTT',
```

```
 4      streams_type        => 'APPLY',
 5      streams_name        => 'DBXA_APP',
 6      queue_name          => 'DBXA_APP_Q',
 7      include_dml         => true,
 8      include_ddl         => true,
 9      inclusion_rule      => true,
10      include_tagged_lcr  => false,
11      source_database     => 'DBXA.WORLD'
12     );
13  end;
14  /
PL/SQL procedure successfully completed.

SQL> -- Create capture process and rules in DBXB.
SQL> begin
 2    dbms_streams_adm.add_schema_rules (
 3      schema_name         => 'SCOTT',
 4      streams_type        => 'CAPTURE',
 5      streams_name        => 'DBXB_CAP',
 6      queue_name          => 'DBXB_CAP_Q',
 7      include_dml         => true,
 8      include_ddl         => true,
 9      include_tagged_lcr  => false,
10      inclusion_rule      => true,
11      source_database     => 'DBXB.WORLD'
12     );
13  end;
14  /
PL/SQL procedure successfully completed.

SQL> -- Create propagation in DBXB to send changes to DBXA.
SQL>
SQL> begin
 2    dbms_streams_adm.add_schema_propagation_rules (
 3      schema_name             => 'SCOTT',
 4      streams_name            => 'DBXB_TO_DBXA_PROP',
 5      source_queue_name       => 'DBXB_CAP_Q',
 6      destination_queue_name  => 'DBXB_APP_Q@DBXA.WORLD',
 7      include_dml             => true,
 8      include_ddl             => true,
 9      inclusion_rule          => true,
10      include_tagged_lcr      => false,
11      queue_to_queue          => true,
12      source_database         => 'DBXB.WORLD'
13     );
14  end;
15  /
PL/SQL procedure successfully completed.
```

```
SQL> -- Connect to DBXA Database
SQL> conn strmadmin/strmadmin@DBXA.WORLD
Connected.
SQL> -- Create Queue for apply in DBXA.
SQL> begin
  2    dbms_streams_adm.set_up_queue(
  3      queue_name  => 'DBXB_APP_Q',
  4      queue_table => 'DBXB_APP_Q_T',
  5      queue_user  => 'STRMADMIN'
  6    );
  7  end;
  8  /
PL/SQL procedure successfully completed.

SQL> -- Create Queue for capture in DBXA.
SQL> begin
  2    dbms_streams_adm.set_up_queue(
  3      queue_name  => 'DBXA_CAP_Q',
  4      queue_table => 'DBXA_CAP_Q_T',
  5      queue_user  => 'STRMADMIN'
  6    );
  7  end;
  8  /
PL/SQL procedure successfully completed.

SQL> -- Create apply Process and Rules in DBXA.
SQL> begin
  2    dbms_streams_adm.add_schema_rules (
  3      schema_name          => 'SCOTT',
  4      streams_type         => 'APPLY',
  5      streams_name         => 'DBXB_APP',
  6      queue_name           => 'DBXB_APP_Q',
  7      include_dml          => true,
  8      include_ddl          => true,
  9      inclusion_rule       => true,
 10      include_tagged_lcr   => false,
 11      source_database      => 'DBXB.WORLD'
 12    );
 13  end;
 14  /
PL/SQL procedure successfully completed.

SQL> -- Create capture process and rules in DBXA.
SQL> begin
  2    dbms_streams_adm.add_schema_rules (
  3      schema_name          => 'SCOTT',
  4      streams_type         => 'CAPTURE',
  5      streams_name         => 'DBXA_CAP',
  6      queue_name           => 'DBXA_CAP_Q',
```

```
 7      include_dml           => true,
 8      include_ddl           => true,
 9      include_tagged_lcr    => false,
10      inclusion_rule        => true,
11      source_database       => 'DBXA.WORLD'
12    );
13  end;
14  /
PL/SQL procedure successfully completed.

SQL> -- Create propagation in DBXA to send changes to DBXB.
SQL> begin
 2    dbms_streams_adm.add_schema_propagation_rules (
 3      schema_name           => 'SCOTT',
 4      streams_name          => 'DBXA_TO_DBXB_PROP',
 5      source_queue_name     => 'DBXA_CAP_Q',
 6      destination_queue_name => 'DBXA_APP_Q@DBXB.WORLD',
 7      include_dml           => true,
 8      include_ddl           => true,
 9      inclusion_rule        => true,
10      include_tagged_lcr    => false,
11      queue_to_queue        => true,
12      source_database       => 'DBXA.WORLD'
13    );
14  end;
15  /
PL/SQL procedure successfully completed.
```

At this time the data in SCOTT's schema needs to be exported from DBXA database and imported into DBXB database using data pump utility. This would set up the instantiation SCN for the tables in the DBXB database. We must also set up the instantiation SCN in these tables in DBXA database so that changes from DBXB can be applied. We do this manually, as shown here:

```
SQL> -- Connect to DBXB database.
SQL> conn strmadmin/strmadmin@DBXB.WORLD
Connected.
SQL> declare
 2    v_scn number;
 3  begin
 4    v_scn := dbms_flashback.get_system_change_number();
 5    dbms_apply_adm.set_schema_instantiation_scn@DBXA.WORLD(
 6            source_schema_name    => 'SCOTT',
 7            source_database_name  => 'DBXB.WORLD',
 8            instantiation_scn     => v_scn,
 9            recursive             => true);
10  end;
11  /

PL/SQL procedure successfully completed.
```

We can now start the apply and capture processes in both databases. Once the capture processes start mining the current redo log files, we can test the replication. The changes applied by the apply process have the Streams tag value set to hex 00 by default, and the capture rules ignore such tagged LCRs by default. This mechanism avoids change recycling in bidirectional replication.

Replication from a Single Source to Multiple Destinations

Sometimes, changes from a centralized database must be replicated to more than one database. In this case you can have one capture process that enqueues the LCRs in one queue with multiple propagation processes sending the same change to multiple apply processes running at multiple destination databases. Or, you can have multiple capture and propagation processes for each of the apply destinations. This is similar to having multiple unidirectional replications with multiple capture and propagation processes running in the same source database.

There are pros and cons of both these approaches. With a single capture process and multiple propagations, the change is captured only once, but there is a chance of the source queue spilling to the disk if one or more of the destinations are not available. With the multiple capture processes approach, each capture process has to capture the same change by individually mining the same redo information, which will undoubtedly increase the complexity and management of the Streams environment.

The split and merge feature of Oracle 11g Streams replication can help us successfully implement the single capture–multiple propagation solution. The split and merge feature is automatically configured when the changes are propagated to multiple destinations from the single source queue. When there is a problem reaching one or more destinations, this feature temporarily splits the portion of replication that is encountering a problem. Once the problem is corrected, the split portion is automatically merged with the original configuration. Chapter 11 discusses split and merge in detail.

Let us review the steps in configuring replication from one source to two destinations. For our discussion, the source database is DBXA.WORLD and the destinations are DBXB.WORLD and DBXC.WORLD.

1. Configure Streams queues in DBXB.WORLD and DBXC.WORLD for the respective apply processes. Call this queue DBXA_APP_Q to apply changes from the DBXA database.

2. Configure the apply process and rules in DBXB.WORLD and DBXC.WORLD using their respective queues.

3. Configure the Streams queue in DBXA.WORLD for the capture process, say, DBXA_CAP_Q.

4. Configure the first propagation in DBXA.WORLD that uses DBXA_CAP_Q as the source to send changes to the apply queue DBXA_APP_Q in the DBXB .WORLD database.

5. Configure the second propagation in DBXA.WORLD that uses DBXA_CAP_Q as the source to send changes to the apply queue DBXA_APP_Q in the DBXC .WORLD database.

6. Configure the capture process in DBXA.WORLD using the DBXA_CAP_Q queue.

7. Perform instantiation of objects from DBXA.WORLD to DBXB.WORLD and DBXC.WORLD using data pump export and import.

8. Start the apply processes and the capture process.

Replication Using Queue Forwarding

Sometimes the destination database can't be accessed directly from the source database but data must be replicated. Such a situation can arise when there is a firewall between the database servers, or the servers are on different networks, or a similar impediment exists. Streams replication is possible in such situations, but it needs an intermediary database server that can access the source and destination databases. The intermediary acts as a relay between the source and the destination. The replication is called queue forwarding. In this case, the intermediary database does not apply the changes locally.

Setting up replication using queue forwarding is a relatively easy process. It involves creating a propagation process in the database that runs on the intermediary server. The propagation process dequeues LCRs from the source queue and enqueues them to the destination database.

For our discussion, let us assume that we want to replicate changes from the DBXA. WORLD source database to the DBXB.WORLD destination database. The changes pass through the DBXC.WORLD database that runs on the intermediary server. We need to perform the following steps to configure replication using queue forwarding:

1. Create the Streams queue for the apply process in DBXB.WORLD.

2. Create the apply process and rules in DBXB.WORLD. Be sure to set source_database to DBXA.WORLD; that is where the change originated, and not DBXC.WORLD.

3. Create the Streams queue in DBXC.WORLD.

4. Create the propagation process and rules in DBXC.WORLD that use the local queue as the source and the queue in DBXB.WORLD as the destination queue. The source_database parameter for this propagation will be DBXA.WORLD.

5. Create the Streams queue for the capture process in DBXA.WORLD.

6. Create the propagation process in DBXA.WORLD that uses the capture queue as the source and the queue in DBXC.WORLD as the destination.

7. Instantiate the objects in the DBXC.WORLD destination database transferring the data via the intermediary server. This can be achieved via data pump export and import.

8. Start the apply process and the capture process.

Replication Using Apply Forwarding

Replication using apply forwarding is similar to queue forwarding replication except that the intermediary database applies the changes locally and recaptures it to replicate to the final destination. The intermediary database becomes the destination for the change from the source database. The intermediary database can send the changes to one or more destination databases. If required, the intermediary database can also capture local changes to replicate, in addition to recapturing changes from the source database.

Continuing with our three-database example, DBXA.WORLD will send changes to the intermediary database DBXC.WORLD. The capture process running on DBXC.WORLD will capture and send those changes to the DBXB. WORLD database. The source database for the apply process on DBXB.WORLD will now be DBXC.WORLD since the change was captured after it was applied there. In addition, the capture process on DBXC.WORLD should be configured to capture tagged LCRs, because the apply process on DBXC.WORLD would have, by default, set the `apply_tag` parameter to hex '00' when applying changes from the DBXA.WORLD database.

We need to perform the following steps to configure replication using apply forwarding:

1. Create the Streams queue in the destination database DBXB.WORLD for the apply process.

2. Create the apply process and rules in DBXB.WORLD. Set `source_database` to DBXC.WORLD.

3. Create two Streams queues in the intermediary database DBXC.WORLD, one for the apply process and another for the local capture process.

4. Create the apply process and rules in DBXC.WORLD to apply changes from the source database DBXA.WORLD. Be sure to set `source_database` to DBXA.WORLD.

5. Configure the propagation process in the intermediary database DBXC. WORLD to send changes to DBXB.WORLD using the local capture queue as the source queue and the apply queue in DBXB.WORLD as the destination queue. The `source_database` parameter for the propagation will be set to DBXC.WORLD.

6. Create the capture process and rules in the intermediary database DBXC. WORLD to recapture changes from DBXA.WORLD. Be sure to set `source_database` to DBXC.WORLD. Also, set the `include_tagged_lcr` parameter to TRUE, since we are capturing the changes applied by the apply process that will have the Streams tag set to hex '00'.

7. Create the Streams queue for the DBXA.WORLD database for the capture process.

8. Create the propagation process and rules in DBXA.WORLD to send changes to DBXC.WORLD. The source queue will be the local capture queue, and the destination queue will be the apply queue in DBXC.WORLD. The `source_database` parameter will be set to DBXA.WORLD.

9. Create the capture process and rules in DBXA.WORLD to capture the local changes.

10. Instantiate the replicated objects from DBXA.WORLD to DBXC.WORLD.

11. Instantiate the replicated objects from DBXC.WORLD to DBXB.WORLD.

12. Start the apply processes and then the capture processes in these databases.

Replication Using the Synchronous Capture Process

If the source database is running under the Standard Edition of Oracle Database 11g, then synchronous capture is available to replicate data. If you have Enterprise Edition, you may not be interested in using synchronous capture because of possible performance degradation with high DML activity.

Synchronous capture does not capture DDL changes. As of Oracle Database 11g, synchronous capture must be configured at the table level. There is no option to configure it at the schema or global level.

Another thing to remember is that the LCRs created by the synchronous capture process are not considered captured LCRs. So, when we're creating the apply process, we must set the parameter `apply_captured` to FALSE. We cannot use the procedure ADD_TABLE_RULES in the DBMS_STREAMS_ADM package that creates a new apply process with rules and a rule set. This procedure sets the `apply_captured` parameter to TRUE by default and it cannot be altered. So, we must create the apply process using the DBMS_APPLY_ADM.CREATE_APPLY procedure. It, by default, sets the `apply_captured` parameter to FALSE.

The following example shows how to configure synchronous capture to replicate DML changes from DBXA.WORLD to DBXB.WORLD:

```
SQL> -- Connect to Destination Database.
SQL> conn strmadmin/strmadmin@DBXB.WORLD
Connected.
SQL>
SQL> -- Create Streams Queue.
SQL> begin
  2    dbms_streams_adm.set_up_queue(
  3      queue_name  => 'DBXA_APP_Q',
  4      queue_table => 'DBXA_APP_Q_T',
  5      queue_user  => 'STRMADMIN'
  6    );
  7  end;
  8  /
PL/SQL procedure successfully completed.

SQL> -- Create the Apply Process.
SQL> -- The APPLY_CAPTURED is set to FALSE by default.
SQL> -- But, it is included for documentation purpose.
SQL> --
SQL> begin
  2    dbms_apply_adm.create_apply(
  3      apply_name     => 'DBXA_APP',
  4      queue_name     => 'DBXA_APP_Q',
  5      apply_captured => FALSE
  6    );
  7  end;
  8  /
PL/SQL procedure successfully completed.
SQL>
SQL> begin
  2    dbms_streams_adm.add_schema_rules (
  3      schema_name     => 'SCOTT',
  4      streams_type    => 'APPLY',
  5      streams_name    => 'DBXA_APP',
  6      queue_name      => 'DBXA_APP_Q',
  7      include_dml     => true,
  8      source_database => 'DBXA.WORLD'
  9    );
 10  end;
 11  /
PL/SQL procedure successfully completed.
SQL>
SQL> -- Connect to the Source Database.
SQL>
```

```
SQL> conn strmadmin/strmadmin@DBXA.WORLD
Connected.
SQL>
SQL> -- Create Streams Queue for synchronous capture.
SQL> begin
  2   dbms_streams_adm.set_up_queue(
  3     queue_name  => 'DBXA_SYNC_CAP_Q',
  4     queue_table => 'DBXA_SYNC_CAP_Q_T',
  5     queue_user  => 'STRMADMIN'
  6    );
  7  end;
  8  /
PL/SQL procedure successfully completed.
SQL> -- Create Synchronous capture process
SQL> -- and add capture rules for replicated tables.
SQL>
SQL> begin
  2   dbms_streams_adm.add_table_rules (
  3     table_name      => 'SCOTT.DEPT',
  4     streams_type    => 'SYNC_CAPTURE',
  5     streams_name    => 'DBXA_SYNC_CAP',
  6     queue_name      => 'DBXA_SYNC_CAP_Q',
  7     include_dml     => true,
  8     inclusion_rule  => true,
  9     source_database => 'DBXA.WORLD'
 10    );
 11
 12   dbms_streams_adm.add_table_rules (
 13     table_name      => 'SCOTT.EMP',
 14     streams_type    => 'SYNC_CAPTURE',
 15     streams_name    => 'DBXA_SYNC_CAP',
 16     queue_name      => 'DBXA_SYNC_CAP_Q',
 17     include_dml     => true,
 18     inclusion_rule  => true,
 19     source_database => 'DBXA.WORLD'
 20    );
 21
 22  end;
 23  /
PL/SQL procedure successfully completed.

SQL> -- Create propagation Process and add rules.
SQL> -- We can add rules at Schema or Global level.
SQL>
SQL> begin
  2   dbms_streams_adm.add_schema_propagation_rules (
  3     schema_name             => 'SCOTT',
  4     streams_name            => 'DBXA_TO_DBXB_PROP',
```

```
  5        source_queue_name        => 'DBXA_SYNC_CAP_Q',
  6        destination_queue_name  => 'DBXA_APP_Q@DBXB.WORLD',
  7        include_dml              => true,
  8        queue_to_queue           => true,
  9        source_database          => 'DBXA.WORLD'
 10      );
 11  end;
 12  /
PL/SQL procedure successfully completed.
SQL>
SQL> -- Since the Source and Destination tables are
SQL> -- already in sync, no need to export/import data.
SQL> -- We perform the instantiation manually.
SQL>
SQL> declare
  2    v_scn number;
  3  begin
  4    v_scn := dbms_flashback.get_system_change_number();
  5    dbms_apply_adm.set_table_instantiation_scn@DBXB.WORLD(
  6             source_object_name => 'SCOTT.DEPT',
  7             source_database_name => 'DBXA.WORLD',
  8             instantiation_scn => v_scn);
  9    dbms_apply_adm.set_table_instantiation_scn@DBXB.WORLD(
 10             source_object_name => 'SCOTT.EMP',
 11             source_database_name => 'DBXA.WORLD',
 12             instantiation_scn => v_scn);
 13  end;
 14  /
PL/SQL procedure successfully completed.
```

At this time, we can start the apply process and test the replication. The synchronous capture process is enabled upon its creation and is ready to go.

Hub-and-Spoke Replication

In hub-and-spoke replication, data is replicated from a central database server, called the hub, to more than one secondary database, called spokes. The central primary database communicates with all the spoke databases. All the spoke databases communicate with the hub database only. They do not communicate with each other. The spokes can be read-only databases or read-write databases.

Configuring Streams replication between the hub and read-only spokes is identical to configuring the single source to multiple destination replication discussed earlier. Configuring Streams replication between the hub and read-write spokes can be viewed as a special case of bidirectional replication combined with apply forwarding replication. Changes made by one spoke are replicated to the hub and then to all other spokes, without causing change recycling to the original spoke. The Streams tag plays a very important role in this configuration.

We will discuss the steps involved in configuring hub-and-spoke replication with read-write spokes using three databases. The DBXA.WORLD database will act as the hub, and DBXB.WORLD and DBXC.WORLD will be the read-write spokes. In this case, we need to create the following Streams components:

■ For the hub database, one capture process, two propagation processes (one for each spoke), and two apply processes (one for each spoke)

■ Each spoke database, one capture process, one propagation process, and one apply process

Table 8-1 summarizes the names for these components. DBXA_CAP, DBXB_CAP, and DBXC_CAP capture changes in the DBXA, DBXB, and DBXC databases. DBXA_APP, DBXB_APP, and DBXC_APP apply changes from the DBXA, DBXB, and DBXC databases.

The important part for hub-and-spoke replication is to avoid recycling the change back to its source database. The hub should not send the change back to its source spoke database, but should forward the change to all other spokes. The spoke should apply the changes from other spokes that are forwarded by the hub as well changes made locally to the hub database. Consider the following points:

■ Changes from spokes that are applied to the hub must be identifiable, so that we can avoid sending the change back to its source.

We can achieve this by setting different values for the `apply_tag` parameter when creating the apply process (using the DBMS_APPLY_ADM.CREATE_APPLY procedure) in the hub database for each spoke database.

■ The capture process in the hub database must capture local changes and changes from all the spokes.

Database	Capture Process	Propagation Process	Apply Process
DBXA.WORLD (Hub)	DBXA_CAP	DBXA_TO_DBXB	DBXB_APP
		DBXA_TO_DBXC	DBXC_APP
DBXB.WORLD (Spoke)	DBXB_CAP	DBXB_TO_DBXA	DBXA_APP
DBXC.WORLD (Spoke)	DBXC_CAP	DBXC_TO_DBXA	DBXA_APP

TABLE 8-1. *Streams Components in a Hub-and-Spoke Replication*

To achieve this, the capture process must be created with `include_tagged_lcr` set to TRUE for its rules so that the capture process can capture local changes with a NULL tag value and changes from all other spokes with different tag values.

■ Propagation from hub to spoke should discard the change that originated at the same spoke.

The negative rule set for the propagation process will check for the tag value to ignore the change. Changes that originate at other spokes can then be propagated correctly.

■ The apply process at each spoke should apply changes that originated at other spokes and locally at the hub database.

This means that the apply rule should apply changes without checking for the Streams tag value, because the changes recaptured at the hub that originated at other spokes contain different tag values. By default, local changes to the hub have a NULL tag value.

■ The capture process at each spoke should only capture local changes.

The rule for the capture process should discard changes with a non-NULL tag value. So, the `include_tagged_lcr` parameter should be left to its default value of FALSE. The apply process at each spoke applies changes with different non-NULL tag values that originated at the hub or other spokes. By default, local changes will have a NULL tag value.

Table 8-2 shows the `apply_tag` setting for the apply processes in the hub database (DBXA.WORLD) as well as the negative rule condition for the propagation process. The tag will identify the source of the change, and the negative rule condition will avoid its propagation to the source. So, the captured change that originated in DBXB.WORLD with a tag value of 12 will be discarded by the DBXA_TO_DBXB propagation using the negative rule. But, this propagation will propagate the change with a tag value of 13 to DBXB.WORLD, which came from DBXC.WORLD.

Apply Process	Tag	Propagation	Propagation Negative Rule
DBXB_APP	12	DBXA_TO_DBXB	' :lcr.get_tag() = hextoraw(' '12' ') '
DBXC_APP	13	DBXA_TO_DBXC	' :lcr.get_tag() = hextoraw(' '13' ') '

TABLE 8-2. *Apply Tag Values and Negative Rule Condition*

Database	Capture Process	include_tagged_lcr
DBXA.WORLD (Hub)	DBXA_CAP	TRUE
DBXB.WORLD (Spoke)	DBXB_CAP	FALSE
DBXC.WORLD (Spoke)	DBXC_CAP	FALSE

TABLE 8-3. *Capture Process Setting*

Table 8-3 shows the `include_tagged_lcr` setting for the capture process at the hub and each spoke database. This setting will enable capture of all changes made to the hub database, but only local changes made to the spoke databases.

Finally, the instantiation of objects can be done using data pump export/import from the hub database to all the spoke databases by creating all the objects and importing data. This will also set the instantiation SCN for the imported objects in the spoke database. We must set the instantiation SCN for the objects in the hub database from each of the spokes. This can be done either manually or by importing only the metadata for these objects from the spoke databases.

Because it is possible for different users to change the same data in the hub-and-spoke database at the same time, we should set up proper conflict-resolution procedures; otherwise, the apply processes will run into errors. Chapter 10 discusses conflict handling.

Once instantiation is completed, we start the apply processes, and then the capture process, and test the setup.

N-Way Replication (Multimaster)

As the name suggests, in N-way replication there are multiple databases participating in replication. Each is a source database for the local changes, and is a destination for changes in all other databases. Each database sends local changes directly to every other database. This configuration is also called multimaster replication because there are multiple "master" databases.

In this configuration, each database has one capture process and multiple propagation and apply processes. The multiple propagation processes send changes to all other databases, and the multiple apply processes apply changes from all other databases.

Using our three-database example and the naming conventions we used in the previous example, we will have one capture process, two propagation processes, and two apply processes in each database, as listed in Table 8-4.

As before, the Streams tag field must be set appropriately to avoid change recycling. In this configuration, the change is never recaptured and forwarded to another destination, so we do not need to set the tag value for the change while applying it.

Database	Capture	Propagation	Apply
DBXA.WORLD	DBXA_CAP	DBXA_TO_DBXB	DBXA_APP
		DBXA_TO_DBXC	DBXC_APP
DBXB.WORLD	DBXB_CAP	DBXB_TO_DBXA	DBXA_APP
		DBXB_TO_DBXC	DBXC_APP
DBXC.WORLD	DBXC_CAP	DBXC_TO_DBXA	DBXA_APP
		DBXC_TO_DBXB	DBXB_APP

TABLE 8-4. *N-Way (3-Way) Replication Streams Processes*

If the apply process is created using the procedures in the DBMS_STREAMS_ADM package (ADD_*_RULES), then a tag value of hex '00' is generated in the redo log data by default. If the CREATE_APPLY procedure in the DBMS_APPLY_ADM package was used to create the apply process, then the `apply_tag` parameter should not be set. The default value will be set to hex '00'.

Similarly, if the capture process was created using the procedure in the DBMS_STREAMS_ADM package (ADD_*_RULES), then the default rule will only capture changes that have the tag value set to NULL. This avoids recycling of the change applied by the apply processes for all other databases. If the capture process was created by the CREATE_CAPTURE procedure in the DBMS_CAPTURE_ADM package, then `include_tagged_lcr` should not be set. The default value will be set to FALSE.

Finally, we will need to instantiate the objects in each database from each other database so that the instantiation SCNs are set up properly.

If the user application can change the same data about the same time on more than one database, then proper conflict-handling procedures must be configured in all databases.

Summary

Oracle Database 11g provides a number of options to configure Streams replication. Oracle-provided APIs make it very easy to configure replication for simple environments. Supplied package procedures offer the flexibility to customize the configuration. Use of customized scripts will be required when configuring complex environments. This chapter discussed the prerequisite steps for configuring Streams replication, and the various methods to configure it in a number of different topologies. Depending on your requirements, you may use one or more of these methods to configure Streams replication.

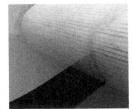

CHAPTER
9

Data Transformations

ne of the strongest features of Oracle Streams replication is data transformation. The contents in the Logical Change Record (LCR) can be modified as it flows through the replication process. The transformation of the data is done in the LCRs. Oracle calls such modifications *rule-based transformations* because they are performed after the rule evaluates to TRUE.

Such transformations are required when the source and destination objects are not identical but data must be replicated. For example, the destination table name may not be the same, the schema name may not be the same, some of the columns in source tables may not exist or may not have the same data type at the destination, and so forth. In such cases, the contents of the LCRs must be changed, or transformed, during replication. Oracle provides APIs to address a number of such transformations. It is also possible to write your own custom function that modifies the contents of an LCR to suit your requirements that are not addressed by the Oracle-provided APIs.

The Streams clients—that is, the capture, propagation, and apply processes— must have a positive rule set to define such transformations. However, the apply process might use apply handler procedures to perform such data transformations that do not require rules.

This chapter discusses various rule-based transformations using Oracle-provided procedures and explains how to configure your own data transformation functions and handler procedures.

Types of Rule-Based Transformations

There are two types of rule-based transformations:

- Declarative rule-based transformations
- Custom rule-based transformations

Declarative Rule-Based Transformations

Oracle provides a set of procedures, in the DBMS_STREAMS_ADM package, that perform most commonly used transformations. Using these procedures, you define the type of transformation required. You do not have to write any procedure to modify the LCR contents yourself.

Declarative rule-based transformations are performed internally by Oracle during the LCR enqueue and dequeue process without using any PL/SQL procedure. For this reason, these transformations run more efficiently than custom rule-based transformations. Whenever possible, you should use declarative rule-based transformations.

NOTE
*Declarative rule-based transformations are possible
with row LCRs only, and not with DDL LCRs.*

Table 9-1 lists the procedures in the DBMS_STREAMS_ADM package that perform
common declarative rule-based transformations.

Suppose you want to perform several changes at once—that is, change the
schema name, change the table name, and change the column name. In this case, it
is possible to define more than one declarative rule-based transformation associated
with one rule. These transformations will be executed in a default order. However, all
the procedures listed in Table 9-1 have a parameter, called step_number, that can
be used to change the default order. If you are not adding multiple transformations to
the rule, or do not want to change the default order of their execution, then ignore this
parameter. We will discuss the transformation execution order in a separate section in
this chapter.

Procedure	Description
ADD_COLUMN	Adds a new, or removes an existing, transformation that adds a column to a row LCR.
DELETE_COLUMN	Adds a new, or removes an existing, transformation that removes a column from a row LCR.
KEEP_COLUMNS	Introduced in Oracle 11g R2, adds a new, or removes an existing, transformation that keeps a set of columns in the row LCR. The transformation removes columns from the row LCR that are not in the specified list. When possible, use KEEP_COLUMNS instead of using DELETE_COLUMN, as the latter is not as efficient to achieve the same result.
RENAME_COLUMN	Adds a new, or removes an existing, transformation that renames a column in the row LCR.
RENAME_SCHEMA	Adds a new, or removes an existing, transformation that renames a schema in the row LCR.
RENAME_TABLE	Adds a new, or removes an existing, transformation that renames a table in the row LCR.

TABLE 9-1. *Procedures for Declarative Rule-Based Transformations*

process. Since we will be configuring the declarative rule-based transformation in the capture process, we connect to the database that runs the capture process.

```
SQL> connect strmadmin/strmadmin@DBXA.WORLD
Connected.
SQL> select rule_owner,
  2          rule_name,
  3          streams_name
  4    from dba_streams_rules
  5   where streams_type   = 'CAPTURE'
  6     and rule_set_type  = 'POSITIVE'
  7     and schema_name    = 'SCOTT'
  8     and rule_type      = 'DML';

RULE_OWNER      RULE_NAME         STREAMS_NAME
--------------  ---------------   ------------------
STRMADMIN       SCOTT375          DBXA_CAP
```

We will use rule SCOTT375 to define the declarative rule-based transformation in the capture process.

Similarly, to find the rule name for the DDL changes, we run the same query with `rule_type` set to DDL. We get the following output:

```
RULE_OWNER      RULE_NAME         STREAMS_NAME
--------------  ---------------   ------------------
STRMADMIN       SCOTT376          DBXA_CAP
```

We will use rule SCOTT376 to define a custom rule-based transformation to transform contents in the DDL LCR in the capture process.

Configuring Declarative Rule-Based Transformations

This section discusses how to configure each of the six different types of declarative rule-based transformations using the procedures available in the DBMS_STREAMS_ADM package.

Add Column Procedure

Sometimes, the destination table may require a few additional columns that aren't in the source table. If these columns are defined with default values at the destination, replicating data from the source will not encounter any problem. However, if these columns are defined as NOT NULL and no default value is set, then the apply process will encounter an error. To address this issue, we can add these additional columns to the LCR with the default data.

The ADD_COLUMN procedure of the DBMS_STREAMS_ADM package is used to add a rule-based declarative transformation to the rule that adds a column to the row LCR. The procedure is overloaded and provides two mutually exclusive parameters to set the column value: `column_value` and `column_function`. We will discuss two examples that use each of these parameters.

NOTE
Columns with a data type of BLOB, CLOB, NCLOB, LONG, LONG RAW, ROWID, BFILE, or either a user-defined or Oracle-supplied data type cannot be added to LCR using the ADD_COLUMN procedure.

Add Column Procedure: Adding a Transformation

The following example shows how to add two rule-based declarative transformations to the same rule that add two columns, PHONE and U_DATE, to the row LCRs for the SCOTT.DEPT table:

```
SQL> connect strmadmin/strmadmin@DBXA.WORLD
Connected.
SQL> begin
  2     dbms_streams_adm.add_column(
  3        rule_name      => 'SCOTT375',
  4        table_name     => 'SCOTT.DEPT',
  5        column_name    => 'PHONE',
  6        column_value   => ANYDATA.ConvertNumber(NULL),
  7        value_type     => 'NEW',
  8        step_number    => 0,
  9        operation      => 'ADD'
 10        );
 11
 12     dbms_streams_adm.add_column(
 13        rule_name      => 'SCOTT375',
 14        table_name     => 'SCOTT.DEPT',
 15        column_name    => 'U_DATE',
 16        column_function => 'SYSDATE',
 17        value_type     => 'NEW',
 18        step_number    => 0,
 19        operation      => 'ADD'
 20        );
 21  end;
 22  /
PL/SQL procedure successfully completed.
```

The `operation` parameter of the procedure is set to 'ADD'. This indicates that the transformation is to be added for the rule SCOTT375.

When there are more than one transformation of different kinds associated with the same rule, the `step_number` parameter determines the order of their execution. We set the `step_number` parameter to the default value of '0'. And since we are only adding one type of transformation (Add Column), the execution order is not important.

We use the `column_value` parameter to set the column value for the PHONE column. This parameter is of ANYDATA type. We set the value for the column to be NULL. The specification `ANYDATA.ConvertNumber(NULL)` returns a value of NULL in an ANYDATA type. We could replace NULL with any other number to set the default value for this column.

We use the `column_function` parameter to set the column value for the U_DATE column. The `column_function` and `column_value` parameters are mutually exclusive. The `column_function` parameter can be set to either SYSDATE or SYSTIMESTAMP. By setting it to SYSDATE in our example, we are adding a U_DATE column with a DATE data type.

We have set the `value_type` parameter to NEW for both the columns. This means that the columns will be added to the LCR with the new values set to our specifications. Typically, columns are added to the row LCR when inserting new rows, and the LCR will only require new values.

Add Column Procedure: Viewing Information About the Transformation

The data dictionary view DBA_STREAMS_ADD_COLUMN displays the information about the transformations created by the ADD_COLUMN procedure. The following query displays the two transformations we set up in the previous example:

```
SQL> select schema_name schema,
  2          table_name tbl,
  3          step_number step,
  4          column_name col,
  5          column_value col_value,
  6          column_type col_type,
  7          column_function col_func,
  8          value_type v_type,
  9          precedence pre
 10     from dba_streams_add_column
 11    where rule_name = 'SCOTT375';
```

SCHEMA	TBL	STEP	COL	COL_VALUE()	COL_TYPE	COL_FUNC	V_TYPE	PRE
SCOTT	DEPT	0	PHONE	ANYDATA()	SYS.NUMBER		NEW	3
SCOTT	DEPT	0	U_DATE			SYSDATE	NEW	3

Other than the PRECEDENCE (PRE) value, the rest of the information is directly from the parameters we specified when adding the transformation. The `precedence` parameter defaults to a value of 3 for the Add Column transformation execution in relation to other transformations.

Delete Column Procedure

In situations in which there are more columns in the source table than in the destination table, we have to remove the extra columns from the LCR. This mismatch in columns will certainly cause problems for the apply process at the destination while applying the change. Apply error will report ORA-26753 'Mismatched columns found in <table name>.'

The DELETE_COLUMN procedure in the DBMS_STREAMS_ADM package is used to add a declarative rule-based transformation that deletes specified columns from the LCR. Using the DELETE_COLUMN procedure is useful when the number of columns to be deleted is small. The procedure does not allow you to specify more than one column at a time. If the source table has a large number of columns and you want to delete a majority of those, then using the KEEP_COLUMN procedure would be a good choice. You will write a lot less code to achieve the same result.

Delete Column Procedure: Adding a Transformation

The following example shows how to add a rule-based declarative transformation to the SCOTT375 rule that deletes column PHONE from the LCR for the SCOTT.DEPT table:

```
SQL> connect strmadmin/strmadmin@DBXA.WORLD
Connected.
SQL> begin
  2     dbms_streams_adm.delete_column(
  3     rule_name      => 'SCOTT375',
  4     table_name     => 'SCOTT.DEPT',
  5     column_name    => 'PHONE',
  6     value_type     => '*',
  7     step_number    => 0,
  8     operation      => 'ADD'
  9     );
 10  end;
 11  /
PL/SQL procedure successfully completed.
```

The value_type parameter in this procedure can have NEW, OLD, or '*' as its value. It controls what values of the specified column will be deleted from the LCR. Specifying NEW will delete the new values, OLD will delete old values, and '*' will delete both. Choosing '*' for the value_type parameter would be appropriate if the table will have UPDATE and DELETE activity. If only the NEW, or OLD, value is removed, then the UPDATE and DELETE operations may cause the apply process to encounter an ORA-26753 error. Choosing NEW for the value_type parameter would be appropriate if the table will only have INSERT operations.

Delete Column Procedure: Viewing Information About the Transformation

The data dictionary view DBA_STREAMS_DELETE_COLUMN displays the information about the Delete Column rule-based declarative transformation we created. The following query lists the relevant information for the transformation we added in the previous example:

```
SQL> select schema_name schema,
  2          table_name tbl,
  3          step_number step,
  4          column_name col,
  5          value_type,
  6          precedence
  7     from dba_streams_delete_column
  8    where rule_name = 'SCOTT375';

SCHEMA TBL     STEP COL           VALUE_TYPE PRECEDENCE
------ -----  ------ ----------   ---------- ----------
SCOTT  DEPT       0 PHONE         *                   1
```

For the Delete Column transformation, the PRECEDENCE value is 1. This indicates the execution order of this transformation in relation to other transformations if defined for this rule.

Keep Columns Procedure

Assume you have a table with over 100 columns in the source database, but at the destination, the table only has 10 columns. To enable you to avoid coding for the deletion of all uninterested columns, Oracle Database 11*g* R2 provides an easier method to achieve this.

Instead of using the DELETE_COLUMN procedure for each column to be deleted from the LCR, the KEEP_COLUMNS procedure can be used to add, or remove, a rule-based declarative transformation that deletes all the columns not specified in the keep list.

The KEEP_COLUMNS procedure provides two ways to specify the list of columns to keep in the LCR. The `column_list` parameter can be set to a VARCHAR2 data type with a comma-delimited list of columns names. The `column_table` parameter can be set to an array of type DBMS_UTILITY.LNAME_ARRAY containing the names of the columns to keep in the LCR. You can specify one of these two parameters when adding or removing the Keep Columns transformation.

Keep Columns Procedure: Adding a Transformation

In the following example, we use the `column_table` parameter of the KEEP_COLUMNS procedure to specify the list of columns to keep in the LCR for the

SCOTT.EMP table. The destination table only has three columns in the SCOTT.EMP table. The columns not specified in the list would all be deleted from the row LCR.

```
SQL> declare
  2     keep_cols     DBMS_UTILITY.LNAME_ARRAY;
  3  begin
  4     keep_cols(1)  := 'EMPNO';
  5     keep_cols(2)  := 'ENAME';
  6     keep_cols(3)  := 'DEPTNO';
  7
  8     dbms_streams_adm.keep_columns(
  9        rule_name     => 'SCOTT375',
 10        table_name    => 'SCOTT.DEPT',
 11        column_table  => keep_cols,
 12        value_type    => '*',
 13        step_number   => 0,
 14        operation     => 'ADD'
 15     );
 16  end;
 17  /
PL/SQL procedure successfully completed.
```

The value_type parameter is set to its default value '*', meaning the LCR will contain the new and old values for the specified columns. Setting this parameter to NEW will keep the new values of the columns in the LCR. Setting this parameter to OLD will keep the old values of the columns in the LCR.

Keep Columns Procedure: Viewing Information About the Transformation

The data dictionary view DBA_STREAMS_KEEP_COLUMNS displays the information about the Keep Columns rule-based declarative transformations. The following query lists the relevant information for the transformation we added in the previous example. The view contains one row for each of the "kept" columns by the transformation. Notice the PRECEDENCE value for the Rename Column transformation is 0.

```
SQL> select schema_name,
  2         table_name,
  3         column_name,
  4         value_type,
  5         precedence
  6    from dba_streams_keep_columns
  7   where rule_name = 'SCOTT375';
```

SCHEMA_NAME	TABLE_NAME	COLUMN_NAME	VALUE_TYPE	PRECEDENCE
SCOTT	DEPT	DEPTNO	*	0
SCOTT	DEPT	EMPNO	*	0
SCOTT	DEPT	ENAME	*	0

Rename Column Procedure

Sometimes, the columns in the source and destination tables do not have identical names. Such a situation may arise if these tables were used independently by the applications and columns were added with different names. To replicate data, making the column names identical, would be one solution. However, it may not be possible due to the time-consuming task of identifying and changing all the application code that used the existing column names. In this case, the Rename Column transformation can be defined to change the name of the column in the LCR to match the destination column name.

The RENAME_COLUMN procedure in the DBMS_STREAMS_ADM package can add the declarative rule-based transformation that renames the column to the specified new name in the LCR.

Rename Column Procedure: Adding a Transformation

The following example shows how to add a rule-based declarative transformation to the SCOTT375 rule that renames the column PHONE to PHONE_NBR in the row LCR. The procedure can rename only one column at a time.

```
SQL> begin
  2      dbms_streams_adm.rename_column(
  3          rule_name          => 'SCOTT375',
  4          table_name         => 'SCOTT.DEPT',
  5          from_column_name   => 'PHONE',
  6          to_column_name     => 'PHONE_NBR',
  7          value_type         => '*',
  8          step_number        => 0,
  9          operation          => 'ADD'
 10      );
 11  end;
 12  /
PL/SQL procedure successfully completed.
```

As in the previous example, we have set `value_type` to '*'. This will cause the renaming of the column to take place for the new and old values of the column in the LCR. This will avoid errors when the LCR is applied at the destination for the UPDATE and DELETE operations.

Rename Column Procedure: Viewing Information About the Transformation

The data dictionary view DBA_STREAMS_RENAME_COLUMN displays the information about the Rename Column rule-based declarative transformations. The following query lists the relevant information for the transformation we added in the previous example. Notice the PRECEDENCE value for the Rename Column transformation is 2.

```
SQL> select schema_name schema,
  2          table_name tbl,
  3          from_column_name from_column,
  4          to_column_name to_column,
  5          value_type,
  6          precedence
  7     from dba_streams_rename_column
  8    where rule_name = 'SCOTT375';
```

SCHEMA	TBL	FROM_COLUMN	TO_COLUMN	VALUE_TYPE	PRECEDENCE
SCOTT	DEPT	PHONE	PHONE_NBR	*	2

Rename Schema Procedure

It is not uncommon to find that the replicated tables reside in a different schema at the destination. Such cases are common where the third-party application has a large number of tables but only a few of those tables are replicated in the destination database for reporting purposes. These tables are typically created in an existing schema. In such cases, the Rename Schema transformation can be defined to change the name of the schema in the LCR to match the destination schema name.

The RENAME_SCHEMA procedure in the DBMS_STREAMS_ADM package can add or remove the declarative rule-based transformation that renames the schema in the LCR during replication.

Rename Schema Procedure: Adding a Transformation

The following example shows how to add a rule-based declarative transformation to the SCOTT375 rule that renames the schema name SCOTT to TIGER. The procedure does not need the value_type parameter, as the schema name in the LCR is not stored with new and old values.

```
SQL> begin
  2    dbms_streams_adm.rename_schema(
  3      rule_name          => 'SCOTT375',
  4      from_schema_name   => 'SCOTT',
  5      to_schema_name     => 'TIGER',
  6      step_number        => 0,
  7      operation          => 'ADD'
  8    );
  9  end;
 10  /

PL/SQL procedure successfully completed.
```

Rename Schema Procedure: Viewing Information About the Transformation

The data dictionary view DBA_STREAMS_RENAME_SCHEMA displays the information about the Rename Schema rule-based declarative transformations. The following query lists the relevant information for the transformation we added in the previous example. Notice the PRECEDENCE value for the Rename Column transformation is 5.

```
SQL> select from_schema_name from_schema,
  2          to_schema_name to_schema,
  3          step_number step,
  4          precedence
  5     from dba_streams_rename_schema
  6    where rule_name = 'SCOTT375';

FROM_SCHEMA   TO_SCHEMA       STEP PRECEDENCE
------------- ------------- ------ ----------
SCOTT         TIGER              0          5
```

Rename Table Procedure

Similar to the situation in which the schema and column names are different in the source and destination databases, sometimes the table names do not match but changes to the table data must be replicated to the destination. In this case, the Rename Table transformation can be defined to change the name of the table in the LCR to match the destination table name.

The RENAME_TABLE procedure in the DBMS_STREAMS_ADM package can be used to add the rule-based declarative transformation that will rename the table in the LCR.

Rename Table Procedure: Adding a Transformation

The following example shows how to add a rule-based declarative transformation to the SCOTT375 rule that renames the table DEPT to DEPARTMENT. Both these tables are under the SCOTT schema in the source and destination databases.

```
SQL> connect strmadmin/strmadmin@DBXA.WORLD
Connected.
SQL> begin
  2    dbms_streams_adm.rename_table(
  3      rule_name       => 'SCOTT375',
  4      from_table_name => 'SCOTT.DEPT',
  5      to_table_name   => 'SCOTT.DEPARTMENT',
  6      step_number     => 0,
  7      operation       => 'ADD'
  8    );
  9  end;
 10  /
PL/SQL procedure successfully completed.
```

Since the Streams Administrator executed this procedure, specifying the schema name with the table name was required; otherwise, the procedure would have assumed the STRMADMIN as the schema for the source and destination tables.

This procedure offers multiple options, and not just renaming of the table. It is possible to rename only the table, the schema and the table, or only the schema, using appropriate values for the to_table_name parameter.

Rename Table Procedure: Viewing Information About the Transformation

The data dictionary view DBA_STREAMS_RENAME_TABLE displays the information about the Rename Table rule-based declarative transformations. The following query lists the relevant information for the transformation we added in the previous example. Notice the PRECEDENCE value for the Rename Table transformation is 4.

```
SQL> select from_schema_name from_schema,
  2         from_table_name from_table,
  3         to_schema_name to_schema,
  4         to_table_name to_table,
  5         step_number step,
  6         precedence
  7    from dba_streams_rename_table
  8   where rule_name = 'SCOTT375';
```

FROM_SCHEMA	FROM_TABLE	TO_SCHEMA	TO_TABLE	STEP	PRECEDENCE
SCOTT	DEPT	SCOTT	DEPARTMENT	0	4

Rule-Based Transformations and DDL Replication

When rule-based transformations are defined, the replication of DDL changes can potentially run into apply errors. For example, if the table is renamed to match the destination table name using the Rename Table transformation, the DDL commands against the table in the source database will fail because the DDL LCR will contain the source table name. In addition, subsequent DML operations that depend on the result of the DDL commands will cause additional apply errors.

Similarly, if the schema name or column name was changed, or columns were removed from the LCR by the rule-based transformations, then DDL commands referencing these columns will fail at the destination database.

To avoid such apply errors, the DDL LCR contents must be modified to match the corresponding actions in the rule-based transformation. In addition to changing the object name and object owner in the DDL LCR, avoiding apply errors also requires checking and modifying the actual DDL text. To perform these changes, a custom rule-based transformation must be defined. The next section discusses the custom rule-based transformations.

Configuring Custom Rule-Based Transformations

The custom rule-based transformation requires a user-defined PL/SQL function. The function has the following form:

```
FUNCTION my_function (
         my_variable IN ANYDATA )
RETURN ANYDATA;
```

The my_function is the name of a user-defined function, and the my_variable is an arbitrary name of the parameter passed to the function. The parameter will be of ANYDATA type. The function could be created as an object of its own or defined within a user-defined PL/SQL package.

After creating the function, it must be defined for the rule using the procedure SET_RULE_TRANSFORM_FUNCTION in the DBMS_STREAMS_ADM package. The procedure has two parameters, one for specifying the rule name and the other for specifying the user-defined function.

The following example defines a custom rule-based transformation for the SCOTT376 rule in the capture process. The specified function must be available or else the procedure will report an error. Only one custom rule-based transformation can be defined for a single rule.

```
SQL> begin
  2    dbms_streams_adm.set_rule_transform_function(
  3      rule_name           => 'SCOTT376',
  4      transform_function => 'STRMADMIN.TRANSFORM_DDL'
  5    );
  6  end;
  7  /
PL/SQL procedure successfully completed.
```

If the custom rule-based transformation is defined for the capture rule, then the capture user must have execute privilege on this user-defined function. If the Streams Administrator with a DBA role is the capture user, then you are all set.

If the transformation is defined for the propagation rule, then the owner of the source queue for the propagation must be granted the execute privilege on the function.

If the transformation is defined for the apply rule, then the apply user must have execute privilege on this function.

The SYS.ANYDATA object contains a number of member functions. We will use the functions available in SYS.LCR$_ROW_RECORD and SYS.LCR$_DDL_RECORD to access and modify the contents of the LCR. Chapter 7 lists the member functions of these objects and discusses how to access the LCR.

Custom Rule-Based Transformation for DDL LCRs

As discussed earlier, if the rule-based transformation changed the column name, schema name, or table name for the row LCR, then the DDL LCR should also be transformed if the DDL changes are also replicated.

For our discussion in this section, three declarative rule-based transformations for the rule SCOTT375 have been defined, as shown by the following query against the DBA_STREAMS_TRANSFORMATIONS view:

```
SQL> select rule_name rule,
  2            transform_type,
  3            declarative_type declarative,
  4            precedence
  5  from dba_streams_transformations;


RULE       TRANSFORM_TYPE               DECLARATIVE    PRECEDENCE
--------   --------------------------   -------------  ----------
SCOTT375  DECLARATIVE TRANSFORMATION   RENAME COLUMN           2
SCOTT375  DECLARATIVE TRANSFORMATION   RENAME TABLE            4
SCOTT375  DECLARATIVE TRANSFORMATION   RENAME SCHEMA           5
```

Next, we will define a custom rule-based transformation for the DDL rule SCOTT376 in the capture process by creating a PL/SQL function and then setting it up for the rule. The following function TRANSFORM_DDL will change the column name, schema name, and table name in the DDL LCR to match the destination names. It will change the schema name from SCOTT to TIGER, the table name from DEPT to DEPARTMENT, and the column name from PHONE to PHONE_NBR.

```
SQL> connect strmadmin/strmadmin@DBXA.WORLD
Connected.
SQL> create or replace function
  2    transform_ddl (in_any IN ANYDATA)
  3    return ANYDATA
  4    is
  5    lcr              SYS.LCR$_DDL_RECORD;
  6    rc               PLS_INTEGER;
  7    l_ddl_text       CLOB default empty_clob();
  8    l_ddl_text_new   CLOB default empty_clob();
  9    l_source_column  varchar2(30);
 10    l_dest_column    varchar2(30);
 11    l_source_schema  varchar2(30);
 12    l_dest_schema    varchar2(30);
```

```
13   l_source_table    varchar2(30);
14   l_dest_table      varchar2(30);
15   l_lcr_schema      varchar2(30);
16   l_lcr_owner       varchar2(30);
17   l_lcr_table       varchar2(30);
18
19  begin
20     -- Set up variables with desired values for the
21     -- source and destination column name, table name,
22     -- and schema name.
23
24     l_source_column := 'PHONE';
25     l_dest_column   := 'PHONE_NBR';
26
27     l_source_schema := 'SCOTT';
28     l_dest_schema   := 'TIGER';
29
30     l_source_table  := 'DEPT';
31     l_dest_table    := 'DEPARTMENT';
32
33     -- Access the DDL LCR from the parameter in_any.
34     rc := in_any.GETOBJECT(lcr);
35
36     -- The contents of the DDL LCR are now accessible using various
37     -- member functions of the SYS.LCR$_DDL_RECORD type.
38
39     -- Extract source table name, table owner and
40     -- schema name from the LCR.
41     l_lcr_table  := lcr.get_object_name;
42     l_lcr_owner  := lcr.get_object_owner;
43     l_lcr_schema := lcr.get_current_schema;
44
45     -- Initialize the LOB segment to access the DDL text in LCR.
46     dbms_lob.createtemporary(l_ddl_text, TRUE);
47
48     -- Extract the DDL text from the LCR into the
49     -- local CLOB l_ddl_text.
50     lcr.get_ddl_text(l_ddl_text);
51
52     -- Set the new ddl text to original text.
53     l_ddl_text_new := l_ddl_text;
54
55     -- Check for the table name in the LCR.
56     if l_lcr_table = l_source_table
57     then
58     -- ----------------------------------------------------------
59     -- Scan l_ddl_text_new contents and the incoming column name
60     -- to match the destination. We use Oracle provided regexp_replace
61     -- function to do this.
62     -- ----------------------------------------------------------
63     l_ddl_text_new:=
```

```
 64        regexp_replace(l_ddl_text_new, l_source_column||'\W',
 65                             l_dest_column||' ',1,1,'i');
 66
 67    -- ----------------------------------------------------------
 68    -- Scan l_ddl_text_new contents and replace table name.
 69    -- The table name could be followed by a ' ' or embedded within ".
 70    -- ----------------------------------------------------------
 71    l_ddl_text_new:=
 72       regexp_replace(l_ddl_text_new, l_source_table||' ',
 73                             l_dest_table||' ',1,0,'i');
 74    l_ddl_text_new:=
 75       regexp_replace(l_ddl_text_new,'"'||l_source_table||'"',
 76                             '"'||l_dest_table||'"',1,0,'i');
 77    end if;
 78
 79    -- Check for the schema name in the LCR.
 80    if l_lcr_owner = l_source_schema
 81    then
 82    -- ----------------------------------------------------------
 83    -- Change object owner and current schema in the DDL LCR.
 84    -- ----------------------------------------------------------
 85    lcr.set_object_owner(l_dest_schema);
 86    lcr.set_current_schema(l_dest_schema);
 87
 88    -- ----------------------------------------------------------
 89    -- Scan l_ddl_text_new contents and replace the schema name
 90    -- that may be present in the DDL command.
 91    -- The schema name could be followed by a '.' or embedded within ".
 92    -- ----------------------------------------------------------
 93    l_ddl_text_new:=
 94      regexp_replace(l_ddl_text_new,l_source_schema||'\.',
 95                             l_dest_schema||'.',1,0,'i');
 96
 97    l_ddl_text_new:=
 98      regexp_replace(l_ddl_text_new,'"'||l_source_schema||'\.',
 99                             '"'||l_dest_schema||'".',1,0,'i');
100    end if;
101
102    -- ------------------------------------
103    -- Put the new DDL text back in the LCR.
104    -- ------------------------------------
105    lcr.set_ddl_text(l_ddl_text_new);
106
107    -- ------------------------------------
108    -- Convert lcr back to ANYDATA and return.
109    -- ------------------------------------
110    return ANYDATA.ConvertObject(lcr);
111
112 end;
113 /
Function created.
```

After the function is created, we assign it to the DDL rule SCOTT376. Since we created the function under the Streams Administrator schema, and it is the capture user, we do not need to grant it the execute privilege on this function.

```
SQL> begin
  2    dbms_streams_adm.set_rule_transform_function(
  3      rule_name         => 'SCOTT376',
  4      transform_function => 'STRMADMIN.TRANSFORM_DDL'
  5    );
  6  end;
  7  /
PL/SQL procedure successfully completed.
```

With this custom rule-based transformation in place, the DDL operations will also be transformed correctly to match the destination schema, table, and column names. The query against the DBA_STREAMS_TRANSFORMATIONS view will list all four of our rule-based transformations:

```
SQL> select rule_name rule,
  2         transform_type,
  3         declarative_type declarative,
  4         precedence pre,
  5         user_function_name user_function
  6    from dba_streams_transformations;

RULE      TRANSFORM_TYPE               DECLARATIVE   PRE USER_FUNCTION
--------  ---------------------------  ------------- ---- ---------------------------
SCOTT375  DECLARATIVE TRANSFORMATION   RENAME COLUMN   2
SCOTT375  DECLARATIVE TRANSFORMATION   RENAME TABLE    4
SCOTT375  DECLARATIVE TRANSFORMATION   RENAME SCHEMA   5
SCOTT376  CUSTOM TRANSFORMATION                            "STRMADMIN"."TRANSFORM_DDL"
```

The value for PRECEDENCE column is NULL for the custom transformation function as listed in this example. Since there can only be one custom transformation for the rule, the values for the `precedence` and `step_number` parameters are irrelevant.

Custom Rule-Based Transformation for Row LCRs

Custom rule-based transformation for the row LCR is required when the available six options do not meet your requirements. For example, you may require that the employee's Social Security number be changed to a dummy number, or that the salary be set to zero for VPs and above when this information is replicated.

When defining and writing the custom rule-based transformation for row LCRs, be sure to take into account any changes made to the row LCRs by other declarative transactions, if any. The rule-based declarative transformations will execute first.

The following example shows such a transformation that sets the employee's Social Security number to all nines. We will add this custom rule-based transformation to the same rule SCOTT375 that already has three other transformations defined. The source schema SCOTT will change to TIGER by the existing rule-based declarative transformation. It will execute before our custom rule-based transformation.

```
SQL> create or replace function
  2    transform_ssno (in_any IN ANYDATA)
  3    return ANYDATA
  4    is
  5    lcr              SYS.LCR$_ROW_RECORD;
  6    rc               PLS_INTEGER;
  7    dml_command      varchar2(10);
  8    l_ssno           number;
  9    l_ssno_chg       ANYDATA;
 10    l_object_name    varchar2(30);
 11    l_object_owner   varchar2(30);
 12
 13  begin
 14    -- Access the LCR
 15    rc := in_any.GETOBJECT(lcr);
 16
 17    -- Set the masking value for SSNO
 18    l_ssno := 999999999;
 19
 20    -- Extract the table name and the table owner
 21    -- name from the row LCR.
 22    l_object_owner := lcr.get_object_owner;
 23    l_object_name  := lcr.get_object_name;
 24
 25    -- ------------------------------------------
 26    -- Check for the table name and the already
 27    -- transformed owner name by the declarative
 28    -- transformation.
 29    -- ------------------------------------------
 30
 31    if l_object_name = 'EMP'      and
 32       l_object_owner = 'TIGER'
 33    then
 34      -- Get the DML command
 35      dml_command  := lcr.GET_COMMAND_TYPE();
 36
 37      -- For INSERT, change the NEW value for SSNO column
 38      if dml_command = 'INSERT' then
 39         lcr.set_value('NEW','SSNO', ANYDATA.CONVERTNUMBER(l_ssno));
 40      end if;
 41
```

```
42      -- For DELETE, change the OLD value for SSNO column
43      if dml_command = 'DELETE' then
44         lcr.set_value('OLD','SSNO', ANYDATA.CONVERTNUMBER(l_ssno));
45      end if;
46
47      -- For UPDATE, we need to check if the SSNO was changed.
48      -- If it was, then we must set the OLD and NEW value in
49      -- the LCR to the masking value.
50      l_ssno_chg := null;
51      if dml_command = 'UPDATE' then
52         l_ssno_chg := lcr.GET_VALUE('NEW','SSNO','N');
53         if l_ssno_chg is not null then
54            lcr.set_value('NEW','SSNO', ANYDATA.CONVERTNUMBER(l_ssno));
55            lcr.set_value('OLD','SSNO', ANYDATA.CONVERTNUMBER(l_ssno));
56         end if;
57      end if;
58   end if;
59   -- Return LCR as ANYDATA.
60   return ANYDATA.ConvertObject(lcr);
61 end;
62 /
Function created.


SQL> begin
  2    dbms_streams_adm.set_rule_transform_function(
  3      rule_name           => 'SCOTT375',
  4      transform_function => 'STRMADMIN.TRANSFORM_SSNO'
  5    );
  6 end;
  7 /
PL/SQL procedure successfully completed.
```

The DBA_STREAMS_TRANSFORMATIONS view shows all five of our rule-based transformations defined:

```
RULE        TRANSFORM_TYPE              DECLARATIVE    PRE  USER_FUNCTION
--------    -------------------------   -------------  ---- ----------------------------
SCOTT375  DECLARATIVE TRANSFORMATION RENAME COLUMN      2
SCOTT375  DECLARATIVE TRANSFORMATION RENAME TABLE       4
SCOTT375  DECLARATIVE TRANSFORMATION RENAME SCHEMA      5
SCOTT375  CUSTOM TRANSFORMATION                              "STRMADMIN"."TRANSFORM_SSNO"
SCOTT376  CUSTOM TRANSFORMATION                              "STRMADMIN"."TRANSFORM_DDL"
```

When rule SCOTT375 evaluates to TRUE, Oracle will perform all its four transformations in the order shown in the output.

The data dictionary view DBA_STREAMS_TRANSFORM_FUNCTION lists all the custom rule-based transformations defined in the database, as shown in the following query. The CUSTOM_TYPE column shows whether the transformation returns one LCR or multiple LCRs.

```
SQL> select rule_owner,
  2          rule_name,
  3          value_type,
  4          transform_function_name,
  5          custom_type
  6    from dba_streams_transform_function;
```

RULE_OWNER	RULE_NAME	VALUE_TYPE	TRANSFORM_FUNCTION_NAME	CUSTOM_TYPE
STRMADMIN	SCOTT375	SYS.VARCHAR2	"STRMADMIN"."TRANSFORM_SSNO"	ONE TO ONE
STRMADMIN	SCOTT376	SYS.VARCHAR2	"STRMADMIN"."TRANSFORM_DDL"	ONE TO ONE

Removing Rule-Based Transformations

When a particular rule-based transformation is not needed any longer, it can be easily removed from the rule. However, you should ensure that there are no pending LCRs to be applied, and that the removal of such transformation will not cause any apply errors.

Removing Declarative Rule-Based Transformations

The procedures we used to add the declarative rule-based transformation are also used to remove these transformations. Based on the values specified for their parameters, the procedures can remove a single or multiple transformations of the same kind from the specified rule. The value of the operation parameter for these procedures must be set to REMOVE.

The NULL specification for parameters other than the rule_name parameter is treated as a wildcard. These procedures will remove transformations that satisfy the supplied non-NULL values for remaining parameters.

Removing an Add Column Transformation

The ADD_COLUMN procedure is also used to remove an existing transformation that adds a column to the LCR. If there is more than one transformation for the same rule, then the procedure removes the transformations based on the values specified for its parameters.

The following example removes all Add Column transformations for the rule SCOTT375. Notice the use of NULL as the value for the parameters.

```
SQL> begin
  2    dbms_streams_adm.add_column(
  3      rule_name    => 'SCOTT375',
```

```
 4       table_name    => NULL,
 5       column_name   => NULL,
 6       column_value  => NULL,
 7       value_type    => NULL,
 8       step_number   => NULL,
 9       operation     => 'REMOVE'
10     );
11  end;
12  /
PL/SQL procedure successfully completed.
```

The following example removes the Add Column transformation for the rule SCOTT375, table SCOTT.DEPT, and column PHONE:

```
SQL> begin
 2      dbms_streams_adm.add_column(
 3       rule_name     => 'SCOTT375',
 4       table_name    => 'SCOTT.DEPT',
 5       column_name   => 'PHONE',
 6       column_value  => NULL,
 7       value_type    => NULL,
 8       step_number   => NULL,
 9       operation     => 'REMOVE'
10     );
11  end;
12  /
PL/SQL procedure successfully completed.
```

Removing a Delete Column Transformation

The following example removes all Delete Column transformations for the rule SCOTT375. Notice the use of NULL as the value for `table_name`, `column_name`, and `step_number`.

```
SQL> begin
 2      dbms_streams_adm.delete_column(
 3       rule_name     => 'SCOTT375',
 4       table_name    => NULL,
 5       column_name   => NULL,
 6       step_number   => NULL,
 7       operation     => 'REMOVE'
 8     );
 9  end;
10  /
PL/SQL procedure successfully completed.
```

Removing a Keep Columns Transformation

Earlier, we added a Keep Columns transformation that kept the DEPTNO, EMPNO, and ENAME columns in the LCR for the SCOTT.EMP table and removed the rest. Suppose we do not want to replicate DEPTNO, and would like to remove it from the list of "kept" columns.

The following example removes the DEPTNO column from the list, and the transformation will delete DEPTNO from the LCR:

```
SQL> begin
  2    dbms_streams_adm.keep_columns(
  3      rule_name     => 'SCOTT375',
  4      table_name    => 'SCOTT.DEPT',
  5      column_list   => 'DEPTNO'
  6      value_type    => NULL,
  7      step_number   => NULL,
  8      operation     => 'REMOVE'
  9    );
 10  end;
 11  /
PL/SQL procedure successfully completed.
```

To remove the entire Keep Columns transformation for the SCOTT.EMP table from the rule SCOTT375, we would specify NULL for the `column_list`, `value_type`, and `step_number` parameters.

Removing a Rename Column Transformation

The following example removes all Rename Column transformations for the rule SCOTT375 that renames columns in the SCOTT.DEPT table. Notice the use of NULL as the value for the `from_column_name`, `to_column_name`, `value_type`, and `step_number` parameters.

```
SQL> begin
  2    dbms_streams_adm.rename_column(
  3      rule_name         => 'SCOTT375',
  4      table_name        => 'SCOTT.DEPT',
  5      from_column_name  => NULL,
  6      to_column_name    => NULL,
  7      value_type        => NULL,
  8      step_number       => NULL,
  9      operation         => 'REMOVE'
 10    );
 11  end;
 12  /
PL/SQL procedure successfully completed.
```

Removing a Rename Schema Transformation

The following example removes the existing Rename Schema transformation for the rule SCOTT375 that renamed schema SCOTT:

```
SQL> begin
  2    dbms_streams_adm.rename_schema(
  3      rule_name         => 'SCOTT375',
  4      from_schema_name  => 'SCOTT',
  5      to_schema_name    => NULL,
  6      step_number       => NULL,
  7      operation         => 'REMOVE'
  8    );
  9  end;
 10  /
PL/SQL procedure successfully completed.
```

Removing a Rename Table Transformation

The following example removes the existing Rename Table transformation for the rule SCOTT375 that renamed the table DEPT under the SCOTT schema:

```
SQL> begin
  2    dbms_streams_adm.rename_table(
  3      rule_name         => 'SCOTT375',
  4      from_table_name   => 'SCOTT.DEPT',
  5      to_table_name     => NULL,
  6      step_number       => NULL,
  7      operation         => 'REMOVE'
  8    );
  9  end;
 10  /

PL/SQL procedure successfully completed.
```

Removing Custom Rule-Based Transformations

To remove the custom rule-based transformation, we use the SET_RULE_TRANSFORM_ FUNCTION procedure of the DBMS_STREAMS_ADM package. The parameter `transform_function` needs to be set to NULL.

The following example removes the existing custom rule-based transformation from the SCOTT376 rule:

```
SQL> begin
  2    dbms_streams_adm.set_rule_transform_function(
  3      rule_name          => 'SCOTT376',
  4      transform_function => NULL
  5    );
  6  end;
  7  /
PL/SQL procedure successfully completed.
```

Table Subset Rule Transformations

The declarative and custom rule-based transformations are optional—you define them when you need them. But, if you have created subset rules to replicate a subset of the table data, then Oracle automatically creates a third type of internal transformation. This transformation will modify the LCR for an UPDATE operation to an INSERT or DELETE, depending on the condition mentioned in the subset rule. This type of transformation is called a *row migration*. Refer to the section "Subset Rules" in Chapter 3 for a complete discussion with an example that adds subset rules. The DBA_STREAMS_TRANSFORMATIONS view lists this transformation as SUBSET RULE, as shown here:

```
SQL> select rule_name,
  2          transform_type,
  3          subsetting_operation OPER,
  4          dml_condition
  5     from dba_streams_transformations
  6    where transform_type = 'SUBSET RULE';


RULE_NAME   TRANSFORM_TYPE               OPER    DML_CONDITION
----------- ---------------------------  ------  -------------------
EMP53       SUBSET RULE                  INSERT  DEPTNO IN (20,30)
EMP54       SUBSET RULE                  UPDATE  DEPTNO IN (20,30)
EMP55       SUBSET RULE                  DELETE  DEPTNO IN (20,30)
```

Transformation Execution Order

It is possible to define all three types of transformations—that is, row migration (for subset rules), declarative rule-based, and custom rule-based—for the same rule. In addition, we can also define more than one declarative rule-based transformation for a single rule. Oracle executes all these transformations in this specific order:

1. Row migration, if applicable, for subset rules

2. Declarative rule-based transformations

3. Custom rule-based transformations

When there is more than one declarative rule-based transformation for a single rule, Oracle follows a default order to perform these transformations:

1. Keep Columns

2. Delete Column

3. Rename Column

4. Add Column

5. Rename Table

6. Rename Schema

When executing the transformations in order, the results from a transformation are used by the subsequent transformation, sort of "piping" the results from one command into another.

It is possible that the LCR changed by the previous transformation will not qualify for the next transformation. For example, if the Rename Table transformation changed the SCOTT.DEPT table to TIGER.DEPARTMENT, then the Rename Schema transformation that changes SCOTT to TIGER will not be executed.

In our previous example, we listed the PRECEDENCE column from the views that showed the defined transformation. The value for PRECEDENCE ranges from 0 to 5 and aligns with the default transformation order shown previously, from 1 to 6.

If you would like to perform these transformations in a different order to address your custom requirements, then you can specify the `step_number` parameter while defining the transformation. The default value of '0' for `step_number` triggers the default execution order as indicated by the PRECEDENCE value. If there is more than one transformation with the same `step_number` value, then Oracle ignores the `step_number` parameter and uses the default order of execution for those transformations.

Use caution when changing the default execution order. It can cause errors in the apply process. Suppose you wanted to rename the schema from SCOTT to TIGER, and rename table from SCOTT.DEPT to TIGER.DEPARTMENT. If the schema name transformation is performed first, then the Rename Table transformation will not find SCOTT.DEPT to change. The LCR will have TIGER.DEPT for the table name. The schema name changed from SCOTT to TIGER. The table name SCOTT.DEPT changed to TIGER.DEPARTMENT. In this case, the Rename Table transformation will not change the table name since the LCR will contain the new name for the schema. This will result in an apply error.

NOTE
Transformations executed in an improper order will cause errors in the apply process.

Summary

Transforming data and contents of the LCR during the replication process is a very powerful and flexible feature of Oracle Streams. Sometimes such transformations are required to fulfill business and statutory requirements. These transformations can be performed during the capture, propagation, or apply process, depending on the requirements of the destination applications. The transformations are attached to a particular rule and are triggered only when the rule evaluates to TRUE.

Oracle-provided procedures address most commonly used transformations. These declarative rule-based transformations are recommended when possible. You can also write PL/SQL functions for custom rule-based transformations for actions not handled by declarative transformations. Since the declarative rule-based transformations do not use PL/SQL procedures, they run much more efficiently than the corresponding custom rule-based transformations. Custom rule-based transformations may be required when replicating DDL changes in addition to the DML changes. When there are multiple transformations defined for the same rule, Oracle executes those in a particular order. The execution order can be changed if required. Be aware that the result of one transformation becomes the input to the next transformation.

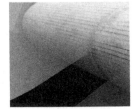

CHAPTER
10

Handling Data Conflicts

n distributed environments, where data is shared among multiple databases, the global data consistency is very important for the overall system. While each database is locally consistent, global consistency should be maintained primarily by design and administrative procedures. However, sometimes global consistency is difficult to achieve. Lack of such consistency causes data conflicts.

One of the strengths of Oracle Streams replication is automatic detection and handling of data conflicts while applying the changes. In Streams, a data conflict means the old values for the columns in the LCR do not match the existing column values in the destination table row. Such conflicts can occur when data is shared among multiple databases that individually allow changes to the shared data. The apply process detects conflicts when applying the row LCRs for the DML operations. A data conflict can occur for an INSERT, UPDATE, or DELETE operation in unidirectional, bidirectional, or N-way replication environments.

When possible, data conflicts should be avoided by the application design and Streams environment. When applications cannot be changed, and business requires that changes to the data must be replicated at multiple locations, then the Streams replication environment must handle conflicts as per the business requirements.

The most common conflict occurs when updates are made to the same table row from more than one location at about the same time. To resolve such update conflicts, Oracle Streams provides built-in conflict update handler procedures. For other data conflicts, you must write your own conflict handler procedures, called apply error handler procedures.

The apply process does not detect conflicts arising from DDL changes. Although such conflicts should be rare, you should avoid such conflicts by design.

This chapter discusses different types of data conflicts, methods to avoid them, and how to use the conflict handler procedures.

Type of Conflicts

This section assumes that you have a bidirectional or N-way replication environment that allows multiple databases to modify the same data at the same time.

In most cases of unidirectional Streams replication, no changes are expected at the destination tables. However, if changes are made to destination tables, the conflicting data could cause the apply process to report an error. If such conflicts are not resolved automatically using conflict handlers, then those conflicts will be written to the apply error queue. The entire transaction will be written to the error queue, and not just the LCR that encountered the error. Resolving apply errors is discussed in Chapter 12.

Four different types of data conflicts are possible in a Streams replication environment as described next.

Delete Conflicts

A delete conflict occurs when one transaction deletes a record while another transaction in another database either deletes or updates the same record. When these transactions reach their destination, the apply process will not find the row with the old values in the incoming LCRs to DELETE or to UPDATE.

Update Conflicts

An update conflict occurs when the apply process tries to update a row that has been updated by another UPDATE operation. The old values of the columns in the LCR will not match the current values in the row. Update conflicts generally occur when transactions in different databases change the same row at about the same time.

Uniqueness Conflicts

A uniqueness conflict occurs when the change made by the apply process violates the unique constraint defined for the destination table, such as the PRIMARY KEY or UNIQUE index. Such conflicts can occur when transactions from different databases try to insert a row with the same value for the primary key or unique index column.

Foreign Key Conflicts

Similar to the uniqueness conflict, a foreign key conflict occurs when the change made by the apply process violates the foreign key constraint defined for the destination table. Such conflicts can occur when there is more than one source database and more than one destination database.

Suppose the DBXA database sends its changes to DBXB and DBXC. The DBXB database sends its changes to DBXC and DBXA. Table ORDER_LINES has a foreign key relationship to the ORDER_MASTER table on the ORDER_NBR column. All databases have this foreign key constraint enabled. Consider a situation when a new order is created in DBXA database with a new ORDER_NBR in the ORDER_MASTER table followed by a few line items created in ORDER_LINES table. Since these changes are dependent changes, they will be applied in the correct order at DBXB and DBXC databases when they reach there. Assume that these changes have been replicated in DBXB but, due to a network issue, have not yet been replicated to DBXC.

Now, suppose a user connected to the DBXB database adds a new line item to the same order number as a simple INSERT operation. This change will be replicated to DBXA successfully since the parent order number exists in the ORDER_MASTER table, but it will fail in DBXC due to a foreign key constraint violation because the original change from DBXA has not yet created the new order in the ORDER_MASTER table in DBXC.

The apply process detects the types of conflicts described previously when it attempts to apply the LCR directly to the destination table. If there was a DML handler defined for the apply process, then conflicts are detected when the handler procedure invokes EXECUTE command for the LCR. Conflicts are also detected when a transaction in error is reapplied using the EXECUTE_ERROR or EXECUTE_ALL_ERRORS procedure from the DBMS_APPLY_ADM package. Chapter 12 discusses these procedures in detail.

How to Avoid Conflicts

Deploying methods to address data conflicts should be considered as a last resort. When possible, limit update access to the shared data from all databases participating in the replication environment. Defining primary ownership of the data in each of these databases will eliminate data conflicts. For example, application users in London will update data in the database located in London and will never update data in the database located in New York, which is for the users in New York. In this case, the users in London own data in the London database, and users in New York own the data in the New York database. If your application is homegrown and easily modifiable, such a change could be feasible. However, if implementing such a change is not economical, then you can consider other options, described next, to avoid data conflicts. You may have to employ more than one method to address data conflicts, and you may require changes at the database level and/or application level. If conflicts cannot be avoided, then you will have to implement conflict handler procedures.

Avoiding Uniqueness Conflicts

Avoiding uniqueness conflict requires that the databases use unique identifiers for the shared data that is unique across all databases, and not just unique within the local table. Sometimes this can be challenging, as it requires modifications to the database and the application. If it is a third-party application, changes to the database and the application might not be allowed.

If changes can be incorporated in the database or the application, the following methods can avoid uniqueness conflicts. Most commonly, the application uses a monotonically increasing number as a unique identifier. Generally, Oracle's sequence number generates this identifier. Sometimes it is generated by the application itself. However, those mechanisms will not guarantee uniqueness for the generated number across all databases in a replication environment. The following are ways to guarantee uniqueness across all databases in Streams replication.

Use SYS_GUID

Oracle-provided SQL operator SYS_GUID generates and returns a globally unique identifier (GUID) made up of 16 bytes with the RAW data type. The following SQL statement returns a unique identifier generated by this operator:

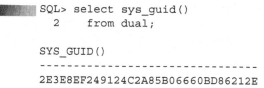

```
SQL> select sys_guid()
  2   from dual;

SYS_GUID()
--------------------------------
2E3E8EF249124C2A85B06660BD86212E
```

Oracle uses the current date and time, host server name, and process identifier to generate this unique identifier. This unique identifier can be the primary key, or part of the primary key of the tables defined in Streams replication. This identifier can be populated with a trigger when a row is inserted into the table.

Modify the Unique Identifier

If the application uses a generated sequence number in each database, then concatenating the number with either the local database name or some other variable will make the identifier unique across all databases. Sometimes users, and auditors in particular, insist on not having gaps in generated sequence numbers. Such a modification allows you to generate sequence numbers without gaps in the local database, and also makes the combined identifier unique across all databases.

Use Sequence Numbers with Ranges

If the application uses Oracle sequence numbers as the unique identifier, and gaps in such numbers is not a concern, then you can use different ranges of numbers that are unique across all databases.

If you have bidirectional replication and do not anticipate addition of another database, then you can define that one database generate only odd sequence numbers and the other database generate only even sequence numbers. This is by far the simplest and easiest way to resolve uniqueness conflict.

If you have N-way replication, or want a scalable solution to the odd/even sequence numbering scheme, then you can assign a unique starting number to the sequences in all databases and increment them by the same value, say 10. So, the databases DBXA, DBXB, and DBXC will have the sequence number starting with 1, 2, and 3, respectively, and incremented by 10. This will ensure a unique number across all three databases. This technique is scalable and no other changes will be required. So, when DBXD is added to the replication environment, it will have its sequence numbers starting with 4 and incremented by 10. Another variation of this technique uses different sequence ranges for different databases. For example:

- Database 1 uses sequence numbers from 100000000001 to 199999999999.

- Database 2 uses sequence numbers from 200000000001 to 299999999999.

- Database 3 uses sequence numbers from 300000000001 to 399999999999.

With such an implementation of sequence numbers, you can easily track the source of the record. However, there can be a downside to such tricks. The query execution plans generated by the optimizer using the histograms for the sequence columns may be suboptimal.

Avoiding Delete Conflicts

Avoiding delete conflicts in shared mode can be difficult when DELETE operations are allowed. It is recommended that, if possible, the transactions do not physically delete the row, but simply update a "delete" column marking the row as deleted. Although this has a potential for an update conflict, it can be resolved using the update conflict handler. Rows marked as deleted can then be physically removed by running a separate purge job in one database without causing any delete conflicts. The job can be run in all databases with the Streams tag set for the session to not replicate the change as a result of the DELETE operation.

Avoiding Update Conflicts

Avoiding update conflicts in a shared environment is difficult. Unlike uniqueness and delete conflicts, there isn't any possible solution to avoid update conflicts. The only way to avoid such conflicts is by not allowing concurrent updates (setting strict rules for primary ownership of data). But such a drastic measure will be almost impossible to implement. Instead, you must use update conflict handler procedures to address these conflicts.

Oracle provides prebuilt update conflict handlers that make it easy to enforce an agreed-upon resolution when update conflicts occur.

Resolving Conflicts

If the uniqueness and delete conflicts cannot be avoided, as discussed earlier, then we have to write our own procedures to resolve those conflicts. These conflict handlers can be part of the procedure DML handler or the error handler procedures. The prebuilt update conflict handlers can be used to resolve update conflicts.

The conflict handler is invoked as soon as a conflict is detected. If the conflict is not resolved by the handler procedure, then the transaction is marked as in error and written to the apply error queue. Any changes made for that transaction until the conflict was detected would be rolled back. The transaction will be considered applied. If the cause for the conflict can be corrected, then the transaction can be executed from the error queue using the EXECUTE_ERROR procedure in the DBMS_APPLY_ADM package. If there is more than one such error transaction, ensure that they are executed in the correct order.

Let us first discuss the prebuilt update conflict handlers.

Using the Prebuilt Update Conflict Handler

The Oracle-provided prebuilt update conflict handler uses one of four predefined methods to resolve the conflict. These methods are OVERWRITE, DISCARD, MAXIMUM, and MINIMUM.

The conflict handler is defined for the destination table using the SET_UPDATE_HANDLER procedure in the DBMS_APPLY_ADM package. The parameters for the procedure are listed in Table 10-1. The same procedure is used to modify or remove an existing conflict handler.

Other than `apply_database_link`, all the parameters in Table 10-1 are required input parameters. These parameters are discussed here:

- **object_name** Name of the schema and table, specified in `schema.table` format. If the schema name is not specified, the table will be assumed to be owned by the user who executed the procedure.

- **method_name** The type of the update conflict handler. One of the following methods must be specified when adding or modifying the conflict handler with the same `object_name` and `resolution_column` parameters. To remove an existing handler, specify NULL. In this case, an existing handler with the provided `object_name`, `resolution_column`, and `column_list` parameters will be removed.

  - **OVERWRITE** When the conflict occurs, the OVERWRITE method will resolve the conflict in favor of the LCR, and will apply changes from the incoming LCR to the destination row.

  - **DISCARD** When a conflict occurs, the DISCARD method will resolve the conflict in favor of the row at the destination, and will ignore the changes from the LCR.

Parameter	Data Type
object_name	VARCHAR2
method_name	VARCHAR2
resolution_column	VARCHAR2
column_list	DBMS_UTILITY.NAME_ARRAY
apply_database_link	VARCHAR2 DEFAULT NULL

TABLE 10-1. *Parameters of SET_UPDATE_HANDLER Procedure*

- **MAXIMUM** When the conflict occurs, the MAXIMUM method compares the values of the resolution column in the LCR and the resolution column in the destination row. The conflict will resolve in favor of the LCR or destination row, depending on whose value for the resolution column is larger.

- **MINIMUM** When the conflict occurs, the MINIMUM method compares the values of the resolution column in the LCR and the resolution column in the destination row. The conflict will resolve in favor of the LCR or destination row, depending on whose value for the resolution column is smaller.

- **resolution_column** Name of the column in the table. It is used to uniquely identify the handler, so it must be specified and cannot be set to NULL. It is also used to resolve the conflict for the MAXIMUM and MINIMUM methods, and must be included in the `column_list` parameter. For the OVERWRITE and DISCARD methods, the `resolution_column` parameter is not used, but it must be specified and can be any column from the `column_list` parameter.

- **column_list** List of columns from the table. The conflict handler is called when the value of any of these columns does not match the values in the LCR. If there is a conflict for columns not in this list, the conflict handler is not called. In this case, the apply process encounters an error.

- **apply_database_link** Database link name to a non-Oracle database. As of Oracle Database 11g R2, conflict handlers are not possible with non-Oracle databases. You can ignore this parameter.

The `column_list` and `resolution_column` parameters play an important role in the update conflict handler, as described next.

NOTE
If there are multiple apply processes defined in the same database, all will have access to the defined update conflict handler.

Using Column Lists

It is possible to define multiple update conflict handler methods for the same table using different column lists, but the same columns cannot be used in more than one column list. The previous procedure will generate an ORA error if an attempt is made to use the same columns in multiple column lists. Depending on what column has a conflict, Oracle will call the appropriate conflict handler.

If the conflict occurs for one or more columns in all column lists for all defined conflict handlers, then all conflict handlers will be called. If the conflict occurs for columns that are not in any column lists, and there is an error handler defined for the apply process, then the error handler will be called for the LCR. The error handler can resolve the conflict and execute the LCR. If there is no error handler defined, then the apply process will report an error and write the transaction to the apply error queue.

NOTE
The prebuilt update conflict handler does not support columns with a data type of LOB, LONG, LONG RAW, or either a user-defined or Oracle-supplied data type, so you should not include such columns in the column list.

Supplemental Logging for Columns in Column Lists

Generally, when there is more than one column in the column list, at least one conditional supplemental log group must be defined for those columns. This supplemental logging is in addition to the unconditional supplemental logging of the primary key columns.

If the column list contains one column that is constructed in the LCR by a rule-based transformation by merging multiple columns, then all those multiple columns will need supplemental logging defined. In situations where one column from the source database is split in the LCR into multiple columns that match the columns in the column list, then supplemental logging of the column that is split is not required.

Using Resolution Column

The resolution column identifies the prebuilt update conflict handler. It should be included in the column lists. If you defined the prebuilt update conflict handler with the MAXIMUM or MINIMUM method, then Oracle uses the value for the resolution column to evaluate and resolve the conflict.

When using the OVERWRITE or DISCARD method for the prebuilt update conflict handler, the resolution column is not used to resolve the conflict. In this case, it is used strictly to identify the update conflict handler, and any column from the column_list parameter can be specified as the resolution column.

Setting Up the Prebuilt Update Conflict Handler

The SET_UPDATE_CONFLICT_HANDLER procedure of the DBMS_APPLY_ADM package is used to set up the prebuilt update handler in the database. For our discussion, we will use DBXA.WORLD and DBXB.WORLD as our two databases.

Bidirectional replication is already configured for the SCOTT schema between these databases for DDL and DML changes.

We will set up the update conflict handler using the MAXIMUM method for the SCOTT.DEPT table. We will use the date and time of the change to evaluate the latest change when there is a conflict.

The following steps show how we set up the update conflict handler:

1. Since the table SCOTT.DEPT does not have a column to track the date and time of the changes made, we will add a new column, CHG_TIME, to the table in both the databases:

```
SQL> alter table scott.dept
  2     add (chg_time  timestamp with time zone);
Table altered.
```

   If the source and destination databases were located in different time zones, then using the TIMESTAMP WITH TIME ZONE as the data type for the CHG_TIME column will account for the time variations while evaluating the conflict.

2. We must also create a supplemental log group to include the CHG_TIME column in addition to the columns in the column list. For our example, we will create a supplemental log group for all columns of the SCOTT.DEPT table. This change is required in both the databases.

```
SQL> alter table scott.dept
  2     add supplemental log data (all) columns;
Table altered.
```

3. The CHG_TIME column in the SCOTT.DEPT table must be populated using the system date when a row is inserted into the table or changes are made to any of the columns of the table. If the conflict detection is restricted to certain columns of the table, then you can have the trigger fire only when those columns are modified.

```
SQL> create or replace trigger ins_upd_dept_trig
  2  before
  3   insert or update on scott.dept
  4  for each row
  5  begin
  6   if :old.chg_time is null or :old.chg_time < systimestamp
  7   then
  8      :new.chg_time := systimestamp;
  9   else
 10      :new.chg_time := :old.chg_time + 1/86400;
 11   end if;
 12  end;
 13  /
Trigger created.
```

This change is also required in both the databases. Also, we did not change the trigger firing property. By default this trigger will fire when a row is inserted or updated in the SCOTT.DEPT table of the local database. Changes made to this table by the apply process will not cause the trigger to fire.

4. We next define the update conflict handler for the SCOTT.DEPT table in the DBXA.WORLD and DBXB.WORLD databases. The update conflict handler will be called if there is a conflict for any column in the DEPT table. So, all columns of the DEPT table are listed in the column_list parameter. The resolution column is the CHG_TIME column.

Notice that the SET_UPDATE_CONFLICT_HANDLER procedure does not require the apply process name. All apply processes defined in the database can access all defined update conflict handlers.

```
SQL> connect strmadmin/strmadmin@DBXA.WORLD
Connected
SQL> declare
  2    cols dbms_utility.name_array;
  3  begin
  4    cols(1) := 'deptno';
  5    cols(2) := 'dname';
  6    cols(3) := 'loc';
  7    cols(4) := 'phone';
  8    cols(5) := 'chg_time';
  9    dbms_apply_adm.set_update_conflict_handler(
 10    object_name       => 'SCOTT.DEPT',
 11    method_name       => 'MAXIMUM',
 12    resolution_column => 'CHG_TIME',
 13    column_list       => cols
 14    );
 15  end;
 16  /
PL/SQL procedure successfully completed.


SQL> conn strmadmin/strmadmin@DBXB.WORLD
Connected.
SQL> declare
  2    cols   dbms_utility.name_array;
  3  begin
  4    cols(1) := 'deptno';
  5    cols(2) := 'dname';
  6    cols(3) := 'loc';
  7    cols(4) := 'phone';
  8    cols(5) := 'chg_time';
  9    dbms_apply_adm.set_update_conflict_handler(
```

```
10     object_name        => 'SCOTT.DEPT',
11     method_name        => 'MAXIMUM',
12     resolution_column  => 'CHG_TIME',
13     column_list        => cols
14     );
15  end;
16  /
PL/SQL procedure successfully completed.
```

The update conflict handler is now set up in both the databases in our bidirectional replication. The update handler will be called when the apply process detects a conflict for any column in the SCOTT.DEPT table. The handler will check the values from the chg_time columns in the LCR and the table row, and will apply the change if the value in the LCR is greater; otherwise, it will ignore the LCR, and the row in the DEPT table will not be changed.

Listing Defined Update Conflict Handlers

The data dictionary view DBA_APPLY_CONFLICT_COLUMNS displays information about the defined update conflict handlers. The query in the following example shows the information about the conflict handler we just added:

```
SQL> select object_owner owner,
  2         object_name,
  3         resolution_column,
  4         column_name column_list,
  5         method_name method
  6    from dba_apply_conflict_columns
  7   order by owner,
  8         object_name,
  9         resolution_column,
 10         column_list;
```

OWNER	OBJECT_NAME	RESOLUTION_COLUMN	COLUMN_LIST	METHOD
SCOTT	DEPT	CHG_TIME	CHG_TIME	MAXIMUM
SCOTT	DEPT	CHG_TIME	DEPTNO	MAXIMUM
SCOTT	DEPT	CHG_TIME	DNAME	MAXIMUM
SCOTT	DEPT	CHG_TIME	LOC	MAXIMUM
SCOTT	DEPT	CHG_TIME	PHONE	MAXIMUM

If you have defined multiple update conflict handlers in the database, be sure to order the selected contents from this view correctly so that the information about the handler can be viewed correctly. The resolution column identifies a particular update conflict handler.

Modifying Update Conflict Handlers

An existing update conflict handler can be modified using the same procedure we used to define it, SET_UPDATE_CONFLICT_HANDLER. We can change the column list, the method of the conflict handler, or both. We cannot change the resolution column name. Since the resolution column identifies a particular handler, we will have to remove the existing handler and redefine it using a new value for the resolution column.

In the following example, we change the column list from what we used to set up the conflict handler. We find out that having DEPTNO in the column list is not required. It is the primary key, and the application does not allow changes to it.

```
SQL> declare
  2      cols dbms_utility.name_array;
  3  begin
  4      cols(1) := 'dname';
  5      cols(2) := 'loc';
  6      cols(3) := 'phone';
  7      cols(4) := 'chg_time';
  8      dbms_apply_adm.set_update_conflict_handler(
  9      object_name        => 'SCOTT.DEPT',
 10      method_name        => 'MAXIMUM',
 11      resolution_column  => 'CHG_TIME',
 12      column_list        => cols
 13      );
 14  end;
 15  /
PL/SQL procedure successfully completed.
```

We can query the DBA_APPLY_CONFLICT_COLUMNS view to confirm our changes. There is no DEPTNO column listed in the column list for the update conflict handler.

OWNER	OBJECT_NAME	RESOLUTION_COLUMN	COLUMN_LIST	METHOD
SCOTT	DEPT	CHG_TIME	CHG_TIME	MAXIMUM
SCOTT	DEPT	CHG_TIME	DNAME	MAXIMUM
SCOTT	DEPT	CHG_TIME	LOC	MAXIMUM
SCOTT	DEPT	CHG_TIME	PHONE	MAXIMUM

Removing Update Conflict Handlers

We use the same procedure, SET_UPDATE_CONFLICT_HANDLER, to remove an existing update conflict handler when it is no longer needed. To remove the handler, we must specify the same resolution column that was used to define it. The handler method name must be specified as NULL. The column list must contain the resolution column name. It need not contain all the columns that were specified when the handler was defined.

In the following example, we remove the handler that was modified in the previous example:

```
SQL> declare
  2      cols dbms_utility.name_array;
  3  begin
  4      cols(1) := 'chg_time';
  5      dbms_apply_adm.set_update_conflict_handler(
  6      object_name        => 'SCOTT.DEPT',
  7      method_name        => NULL,
  8      resolution_column  => 'CHG_TIME',
  9      column_list        => cols
 10      );
 11  end;
 12  /

PL/SQL procedure successfully completed.
```

Querying the DBA_APPLY_CONFLICT_COLUMNS view confirms that the handler was removed successfully:

```
SQL> select object_owner owner,
  2          object_name,
  3          resolution_column,
  4          column_name column_list,
  5          method_name method
  6      from dba_apply_conflict_columns;

no rows selected
```

In the previous examples, we used the MAXIMUM method to resolve the update conflict. Depending on your business requirements, you may need to use other methods. However, before you use the OVERWRITE or DISCARD method in N-way replication, you should thoroughly investigate what the effect will be. Using OVERWRITE in all databases will cause data divergence that will create additional data conflicts. Using DISCARD, on the other hand, will not replicate required changes. In a unidirectional replication environment, using OVERWRITE may be beneficial in some cases because it will overwrite any local changes that may have been made to the row in the destination database.

Stopping Conflict Detection for Non-Key Columns

The apply process compares the old values for the columns in the LCR with the current values for those columns in the destination row when updating or deleting the row. This action by the apply process is called *old value comparison*. Any mismatch in this comparison is a conflict, and an appropriate conflict handler is invoked to resolve it. If there is no conflict handler defined, then the apply process marks the entire transaction in error and writes it to the error queue.

What if you do not want to check for conflicts, and simply apply the LCR if the row is found based on the key columns in the LCR? This is similar to having the OVERWRITE method to resolve conflict. By stopping the conflict detection, the UPDATE and DELETE operations will always succeed as long as the row for the key columns in the LCR is present in the destination table.

It is possible to suppress the old value comparison for non-key columns in the LCR. So, when there is no comparison of the column values, there is no conflict. The procedure COMPARE_OLD_VALUES in the DBMS_APPLY_ADM package is used to suppress the old value comparison for the listed columns. Another choice is to use a declarative rule-based transformation to remove old values of columns from the LCR.

From our previous example, the SCOTT.DEPT table has only DEPTNO as the key column. We can stop conflict detection for the rest of the columns, as shown in the following example:

```
SQL> declare
  2      cols            dbms_utility.lname_array;
  3  begin
  4      cols(1)     := 'dname';
  5      cols(2)     := 'loc';
  6      cols(3)     := 'phone';
  7      cols(4)     := 'chg_time';
  8
  9      dbms_apply_adm.compare_old_values(
 10      object_name     => 'SCOTT.DEPT',
 11      column_table    => cols,
 12      operation       => '*',
 13      compare         => FALSE
 14      );
 15  end;
 16  /
PL/SQL procedure successfully completed.
```

If we had specified TRUE for the compare parameter in the example while keeping all the other specifications unchanged, then we would have reinstated the old value comparison for these columns.

Stopping the old value comparison can be effectively used in unidirectional replication to avoid conflicts when performing UPDATE and DELETE operations. By definition, the destination data should match with the source, but if there are some unintentional changes made to the destination data, stopping conflict detection will avoid apply errors.

We can use the DBA_APPLY_TABLE_COLUMNS view to display the list columns that are excluded from the old value comparison by the apply process, as shown in the following query:

```
SQL> col compare_old_on_delete heading 'COMPARE|OLD ON|DELETE' for a10
SQL> col compare_old_on_update heading 'COMPARE|OLD ON|UPDATE' for a10
SQL> col object_owner heading 'OWNER' for a10
SQL> col object_name heading 'TABLE' for a10
SQL> col column_name heading 'COLUMN' for a10
SQL> select object_owner,
  2          object_name,
  3          column_name,
  4          compare_old_on_delete,
  5          compare_old_on_update
  6    from dba_apply_table_columns;
```

OWNER	TABLE	COLUMN	COMPARE OLD ON DELETE	COMPARE OLD ON UPDATE
SCOTT	DEPT	CHG_TIME	NO	NO
SCOTT	DEPT	DNAME	NO	NO
SCOTT	DEPT	LOC	NO	NO
SCOTT	DEPT	PHONE	NO	NO

Custom Conflict Handlers

If the prebuilt update conflict handlers do not address your business requirements, you can write PL/SQL procedures that will act as the conflict handler. Such procedures are required to address conflicts from the INSERT and DELETE operations, as there are no prebuilt conflict handlers for those.

The procedure SET_DML_HANDLER in the DBMS_APPLY_ADM package is used to specify the conflict handler for a table. One or more custom conflict handlers can be defined for the same table. Table 10-2 lists the parameters of the SET_DML_HANDLER procedure.

- **object_name**   Fully qualified name of the table for which you are setting up the conflict handler.

- **object_type**   Must be specified as TABLE.

- **operation_name**   The DML operation for which the conflict handler will be invoked. Possible values are INSERT, UPDATE, DELETE, and LOB_UPDATE. The value DEFAULT enables the handler to be invoked for conflicts in any of the DML operations.

Parameter	Data Type
object_name	VARCHAR2
object_type	VARCHAR2
operation_name	VARCHAR2
error_handler	BOOLEAN DEFAULT FALSE
user_procedure	VARCHAR2
apply_database_link	VARCHAR2 DEFAULT NULL
apply_name	VARCHAR2 DEFAULT NULL
assemble_lobs	BOOLEAN DEFAULT TRUE

TABLE 10-2. *Parameters of SET_DML_HANDLER Procedure*

- **error_handler**   When set to TRUE, the user procedure is invoked to execute the LCR for the specified table and for the specified operation. It is treated as the procedure DML handler. The procedure is responsible for handling any conflicts that may be encountered. If left to the default value, FALSE, the user procedure is invoked when the LCR encounters an error. It is treated as the procedure error handler. The procedure can then resolve the conflict and execute the LCR.

- **user_procedure**   The custom PL/SQL procedure that sets the procedure DML handler or an error handler to resolve the conflicts. The apply user must have execute privilege on this procedure. Specifying NULL will unset the procedure DML handler or error handler for the specified apply_name parameter.

- **apply_database_link**   Database link name for a non-Oracle database. Used only when applying changes to a non-Oracle database.

- **apply_name**   Name of the apply process that uses the specified user procedure for the specified object and operation. Specifying NULL will allow all apply processes in the database to use the user procedure.

- **assemble_lobs**   Defaults to TRUE in Oracle Database 11*g* R2. If there are multiple LCRs for the changes to a single LOB column, then by default these are assembled into a single LCR before the LCR is passed to the handler procedure. If set to FALSE, LOBs are not assembled into a single LCR. It is recommended to leave the default value unchanged.

If the custom conflict handler procedure does not resolve the conflict, then the apply process will roll back any applied changes and move the entire transaction into the error queue.

We can designate a prebuilt update conflict handler and a custom conflict handler for the same table. The custom conflict handler may execute the LCR using the following syntax:

```
lcr.execute(true);
```

If this execution of the LCR results in a conflict, then the prebuilt conflict handler will be invoked. The `true` value in the previous syntax is the `conflict_resolution` parameter.

Chapter 6 includes an example of a user procedure that is defined as a procedure DML handler. However, it does not contain conflict handling.

The example that follows demonstrates a custom conflict handler procedure. The procedure handles INSERT, UPDATE, and DELETE conflicts. We could have created three separate procedures to handle conflicts for these operations, but keeping them in one single procedure eliminates triplication of the common code involved in this procedure. The procedure logs the original LCR that caused the conflict in an error table for further investigation.

For this example, we have set up supplemental logging of all columns in the SCOTT.DEPT table. Also, there is a prebuilt update conflict handler defined to overwrite (using the OVERWRITE method) the destination row with changes from the source. However, this prebuilt update conflict handler will cause an apply error if the row to be updated does not exist in the destination table. Our example will fill this gap and resolve this conflict by inserting the row in the destination table. The UPDATE operation will be changed to an INSERT operation.

If the conflict occurs for the INSERT operation due to primary key constraint violation, the example simply ignores the LCR after logging it in the error table for further investigation.

For the DELETE operation, if the destination table does not contain the row to be deleted, the procedure ignores the LCR after logging it in the error table. What if the row exists but the non-key columns do not match the corresponding old values in the LCR? The apply process will detect this conflict first, before it calls our custom conflict handler. To resolve this situation, we have stopped the old value comparison for the DELETE operation against the SCOTT.DEPT table. So, there won't be any other conflict than row not found, which is handled in the procedure.

We connect to the destination database as Streams Administrator and create the error log table and our custom conflict handler package and procedure:

```
SQL> connect strmadmin/strmadmin@DBXB.WORLD
Connected.
SQL> create table strmadmin.errorlog(
  2     logdate        DATE,
  3     apply_name     VARCHAR2(30),
  4     sender         VARCHAR2(100),
```

```
    5     object_name    VARCHAR2(32),
    6     command_type   VARCHAR2(30),
    7     errnum         NUMBER,
    8     errmsg         VARCHAR2(2000),
    9     text           VARCHAR2(2000),
   10     lcr            SYS.LCR$_ROW_RECORD);
Table created.
SQL> create or replace package conflict_handlers
    2   as
    3    type emsg_array is table of varchar2(2000)
    4         index by binary_integer;
    5
    6    procedure resolve_conflicts (
    7      message            IN ANYDATA,
    8      error_stack_depth  IN NUMBER,
    9      error_numbers      IN DBMS_UTILITY.NUMBER_ARRAY,
   10      error_messages     IN EMSG_ARRAY);
   11
   12   end conflict_handlers;
   13   /
Package created.
SQL> show errors
No errors.
SQL> -- Create the package body:
SQL> create or replace package body conflict_handlers
    2   as
    3    procedure resolve_conflicts(
    4      message            IN anydata,
    5      error_stack_depth  IN number,
    6      error_numbers      IN dbms_utility.number_array,
    7      error_messages     IN emsg_array)
    8    is
    9    lcr                  sys.lcr$_row_record;
   10    ret                  pls_integer;
   11    vc                   varchar2(30);
   12    errlog_rec           errorlog%rowtype;
   13    l_anydata            anydata;
   14    l_apply_name         varchar2(30);
   15    l_err_code           number;
   16    l_err_msg            varchar2(2000);
   17    l_old_values         sys.lcr$_row_list;
   18    l_new_values         sys.lcr$_row_list;
   19    l_change_values      sys.lcr$_row_list;
   20    begin
   21    -- Access the error number from the top of the stack.
   22    errlog_rec.text := NULL ;
   23
   24    -- Check for the ORA error, and gather relevant information
   25    if error_numbers(1) = 1  -- Primary key constraint violation
   26    then
   27       l_anydata  := DBMS_STREAMS.GET_INFORMATION('CONSTRAINT_NAME');
   28       ret := l_anydata.GetVarchar2(errlog_rec.text);
   29    end if ;
   30
   31    -- Get the name of the capture process (Sender)
   32    -- and the name of the apply process.
   33    l_anydata  := dbms_streams.get_information('SENDER');
   34    ret := l_anydata.getvarchar2(errlog_rec.sender);
```

```
35      l_apply_name := dbms_streams.get_streams_name();
36
37      -- Access the LCR to gather other relevant information to log.
38      ret := message.getobject(lcr);
39      errlog_rec.errnum := error_numbers(1) ;
40      errlog_rec.errmsg := error_messages(1) ;
41      errlog_rec.object_name  := lcr.get_object_name() ;
42      errlog_rec.command_type := lcr.get_command_type() ;
43
44      -- Insert all relevant information in the errorlog table.
45      -- Commit will be automatically done. No need to commit.
46      insert into strmadmin.errorlog
47       values (
48              sysdate,
49              l_apply_name,
50              errlog_rec.sender,
51              errlog_rec.object_name,
52              errlog_rec.command_type,
53              errlog_rec.errnum,
54              errlog_rec.errmsg,
55              errlog_rec.text,
56              lcr
57        );
58
59      -- Check the Command Type and take action to resolve conflict.
60
61      if lcr.get_command_type = 'INSERT'
62         and error_numbers(1) = 1    -- Primary Key constraint violation
63      then
64            null;  -- Ignore the LCR as the row exists
65      end if;
66
67      if lcr.get_command_type = 'DELETE'
68       and error_numbers(1) = 1403    -- Row not found to delete.
69      then
70           null; -- Ignore the LCR.
71      end if;
72
73      -- Take action if row did not exist for UPDATE.
74      -- The pre-built conflict handler should handle the conflict if
75      -- the row was found with column values mismatched.
76      -- Following logic
77      if lcr.get_command_type = 'UPDATE'
78         and error_numbers(1) = 1403
79       then
80            -- Since all columns are supplementally logged, the
81            -- original LCR for UPDATE will contain all the
82            -- columns of the row with old and new values.
83            -- Save all the old and all the new values.
84            l_old_values := lcr.get_values('OLD','Y');
85            l_new_values := lcr.get_values('NEW','Y');
86
87            -- Prepare to overlay old values with changed new values
88            l_change_values:=l_old_values;
89
90            -- Loop through old and new values to combine unchanged and changed
```

```
91          -- values in the LCR.
92          for i in 1..l_new_values.count
93           loop
94               for j in 1..l_change_values.count
95                 loop
96                     if l_new_values(i).column_name = l_change_values(j).column_name
97                       then
98                             l_change_values(j).data := l_new_values(i).data;
99                       end if;
100                  end loop;
101           end loop;
102
103          -- Set the changed values in the LCR as new values.
104          lcr.set_values('NEW', l_change_values);
105          -- For insert we must remove all old columns and values.
106          lcr.set_values('OLD', NULL);
107          -- Change the LCR command type to insert the row.
108          lcr.set_command_type('INSERT');
109          -- Execute the LCR with conflict resolution set to true.
110          lcr.execute(true);
111     end if;
112
113    exception
114        when others then
115            l_err_code := sqlcode;
116            l_err_msg := substr(sqlerrm, 1 , 2000);
117            insert into strmadmin.errorlog (logdate, errnum, errmsg, text)
118                  values (sysdate, l_err_code, l_err_msg, errlog_rec.text);
119    end resolve_conflicts ;
120    end conflict_handlers;
121  /
Package body created.
SQL>
SQL> show errors
No errors.
```

Now, define the custom handler procedure for the table SCOTT.DEPT for the INSERT, UPDATE, and DELETE operations:

```
SQL> begin
  2    dbms_apply_adm.set_dml_handler(
  3    object_name     => 'SCOTT.DEPT',
  4    object_type     => 'TABLE',
  5    operation_name => 'INSERT',
  6    error_handler   => TRUE,
  7    user_procedure => 'STRMADMIN.CONFLICT_HANDLERS.RESOLVE_CONFLICTS'
  8    );
  9  end;
 10  /
PL/SQL procedure successfully completed.
SQL> begin
  2    dbms_apply_adm.set_dml_handler(
  3    object_name     => 'SCOTT.DEPT',
```

```
 4    object_type    => 'TABLE',
 5    operation_name => 'UPDATE',
 6    error_handler  => TRUE,
 7    user_procedure => 'STRMADMIN.CONFLICT_HANDLERS.RESOLVE_CONFLICTS'
 8    );
 9   end;
10   /
PL/SQL procedure successfully completed.
SQL> begin
 2    dbms_apply_adm.set_dml_handler(
 3    object_name    => 'SCOTT.DEPT',
 4    object_type    => 'TABLE',
 5    operation_name => 'DELETE',
 6    error_handler  => TRUE,
 7    user_procedure => 'STRMADMIN.CONFLICT_HANDLERS.RESOLVE_CONFLICTS'
 8    );
 9   end;
10   /
PL/SQL procedure successfully completed.
```

And, that's about it. With the custom conflict handler in place, supplemented by a prebuilt conflict handler and suppression of old value comparison for DELETE operations, our example is ready to deal with any data conflicts for the SCOTT .DEPT table. To help us investigate further, the original LCR is available in the error log table.

Summary

Automatic data conflict detection during replication is one of the strong features of Oracle Streams. Oracle-provided tools make it easy to take corrective actions when conflicts are detected. In addition, PL/SQL procedures can be written to customize the handling of conflicts to suit almost any business requirements. Generally, in a properly configured Streams replication environment, data conflicts are rare. But when conflicts do appear, there are ways to successfully address them without losing data, as discussed in this chapter.

PART
IV

Oracle Streams Management

CHAPTER
11

Managing and Monitoring
Streams Replication

our job as a Streams administrator does not end after you successfully configure the Streams replication environment. In fact, configuring Streams replication may seem like the easy part of the job after you discover what you must do to manage and monitor the Streams environment. Although this important task may seem daunting when you first read about, it is not much more difficult than the configuration task.

This chapter discusses how to manage and monitor Streams processes, and how to measure Streams replication performance using Oracle-supplied PL/SQL packages and procedures. Use of OEM Grid Control to do the same is discussed in Chapter 14.

Managing Streams Processes

After you have created all the Streams processes during the configuration of the replication environment, managing these processes is the next natural step. It mainly involves starting and stopping these processes when required, and modifying some of their parameters. The default values for these parameters may not be adequate for your requirements. During the testing phase of the replication environment, you will certainly want to experiment with these parameters to see how they affect the behavior and performance of these processes. At times, you may also be required to modify the rules and rule set associated with these processes.

The Streams processes are automatically started when you use MAINTAIN_* procedures or OEM Grid Control to configure the Streams environment. These processes are not started automatically if you create them manually or by using the ADD_*_RULES procedures.

Managing the Capture Process

The DBMS_CAPTURE_ADM package provides the required procedures to manage the capture process. This section discusses the procedures used for starting, stopping, and modifying the capture process parameters.

Starting the Capture Process

To start the capture process, we use the START_CAPTURE procedure in the DBMS_CAPTURE_ADM package. The procedure requires the name of the capture process as the only parameter. In the following example, we start the capture process DBXA_CAP in the DBXA.WORLD database:

```
SQL> connect strmadmin/strmadmin@DBXA.WORLD
Connected.
SQL> begin
  2    dbms_capture_adm.start_capture(
  3    capture_name => 'DBXA_CAP'
  4    );
  5  end;
  6  /
PL/SQL procedure successfully completed.
```

The capture process reports the startup messages in the alert log file of the database in which it is running. If you attempt to start a capture process that is already running, Oracle may report the following rather confusing message:

```
ORA-26666: cannot alter STREAMS process DBXA_CAP
ORA-06512: at "SYS.DBMS_LOGREP_UTIL", line 743
ORA-06512: at "SYS.DBMS_CAPTURE_ADM", line 38
ORA-06512: at line 2
```

Contrary to the error message, you did not try to alter anything in the capture process. There is nothing wrong with the capture process, either. Simply ignore this message.

Stopping the Capture Process

When performing database upgrades or other maintenance operations, you may be required to stop the capture process. The STOP_CAPTURE procedure of the DBMS_CAPTURE_ADM package is used to stop the capture process, as shown in the following example:

```
SQL> connect strmadmin/strmadmin@DBXA.WORLD
Connected.
SQL> begin
  2   dbms_capture_adm.stop_capture(
  3     capture_name => 'DBXA_CAP'
  4   );
  5  end;
  6  /
PL/SQL procedure successfully completed.
```

The capture process reports the shutdown messages in the alert log of the database.

In addition to the capture_name, the STOP_CAPTURE procedure has a second parameter, called force. It controls how the capture process is stopped. It takes a Boolean value of TRUE or FALSE. The default value of FALSE attempts to stop the capture and associated processes gracefully, as shown in the previous example.

If there is any problem with the LogMiner or the capture process, the capture process may not stop gracefully. Eventually, it will report a timeout error:

```
ORA-26672: timeout occurred while stopping STREAMS process DBXA_CAP
```

In this situation, you should retry stopping the capture process. If it consistently fails with the timeout error, then consider setting the force parameter to TRUE to stop the capture process, as shown in the following example:

```
SQL> begin
  2   dbms_capture_adm.stop_capture(
  3     capture_name => 'DBXA_CAP',
  4     force        => TRUE
  5   );
  6  end;
  7  /
PL/SQL procedure successfully completed.
```

Modifying Capture Process Parameters

Generally, you do not need to modify the capture process parameters. The default setting for these parameters is appropriate for most environments. However, modifying the parameter values will be required in certain cases, some of which are listed here:

■ Increase the value of the `parallelism` parameter to speed up LCR preparation.

■ Set the `trace_level` parameter as directed by Oracle Support to debug problems.

■ Set the `message_limit` parameter to limit the number of captured messages.

■ Configure the `downstream_real_time_mine` parameter to enable real-time downstream capture process.

Please refer to Chapter 4 for a detailed discussion of these parameters.

The SET_PARAMETER procedure of the DBMS_CAPTURE_ADM package modifies the current value for the specified parameter. If the parameter is changed using this procedure, Oracle sets an audit flag in an internal table to indicate that the parameter has been changed, at least once, from its default value.

The SET_PARAMETER procedure requires three parameters. The `capture_name`, `parameter`, and `value` parameters are passed to the procedure as VARCHAR2 data types.

The following example sets the capture process `parallelism` parameter to 2 from the default value of 1. Generally, the default value is adequate. It is recommended that you verify the effect of increasing the capture process `parallelism` parameter. This can be done by using Streams Performance Advisor, discussed later in this chapter.

```
SQL> conn strmadmin/strmadmin@DBXA.WORLD
Connected.
SQL> begin
  2    dbms_capture_adm.set_parameter(
  3      capture_name => 'DBXA_CAP',
  4      parameter    => 'PARALLELISM',
  5      value        => '2'
  6    );
  7  end;
  8  /
PL/SQL procedure successfully completed.
```

The view DBA_CAPTURE_PARAMETERS lists the parameters and their values currently in effect. The view also reports whether the user ever changed the parameter from its default value. Notice YES under the SET_BY_USER column in

the following query that shows the new value for the `parallelism` parameter
we just changed:

```
SQL> set pages 90
SQL> set trimspool on
SQL> col parameter for a30
SQL> col value for a10
SQL> col set_by_user heading "SET_BY_USER" for a15
SQL> select parameter,
  2          value,
  3          set_by_user
  4    from dba_capture_parameters
  5   where capture_name = 'DBXA_CAP';

PARAMETER                       VALUE      SET_BY_USER
------------------------------- ---------- ---------------
PARALLELISM                     2          YES
STARTUP_SECONDS                 0          NO
TRACE_LEVEL                     0          NO
TIME_LIMIT                      INFINITE   NO
MESSAGE_LIMIT                   INFINITE   NO
MAXIMUM_SCN                     INFINITE   NO
WRITE_ALERT_LOG                 Y          NO
DISABLE_ON_LIMIT                N          NO
DOWNSTREAM_REAL_TIME_MINE       Y          NO
MESSAGE_TRACKING_FREQUENCY      2000000    NO
SKIP_AUTOFILTERED_TABLE_DDL     Y          NO
SPLIT_THRESHOLD                 1800       NO
MERGE_THRESHOLD                 60         NO

13 rows selected.
```

Changes to some of these parameters require stopping and restarting the capture
process to take effect.

Modifying the Capture User

It is a common practice to have the Streams Administrator account as the capture
user. But this is not mandatory. The capture user can be changed if required. Such a
change may be required in environments where there is a strict separation of duties
and responsibilities, and access to the data is controlled and monitored. The DBA_
CAPTURE view lists the current capture user in the CAPTURE_USER column.

Before changing the capture user, ensure that the new capture user exists in the
database with `create session` privilege. It also needs the following privileges
granted either explicitly or via roles:

- EXECUTE privilege on the capture rule sets

- EXECUTE privilege on all rule-based transformation functions, if used with a
  positive rule set

If the rule-based transformation function invokes any packaged procedures, then the capture user must be granted EXECUTE privileges on these explicitly, and not via roles.

Oracle automatically grants the ENQUEUE privilege on the capture queue to the capture user, allowing the capture user to enqueue messages into the capture queue.

In the following example, we grant required privileges to the new capture user DBADMIN. The rule set associated with the capture process is RULESET$_14, owned by STRMADMIN. The user executing this procedure must have the DBA role granted.

```
SQL> begin
  2    dbms_rule_adm.grant_object_privilege(
  3        privilege   => SYS.DBMS_RULE_ADM.EXECUTE_ON_RULE_SET,
  4        object_name => 'STRMADMIN.RULESET$_14',
  5        grantee     => 'DBADMIN');
  6  end;
  7  /
PL/SQL procedure successfully completed.
```

Alternatively, you could also grant `execute any rule set` privilege to the capture user. Lack of execute privilege on the rule set will generate an error in the alert log file, and the capture process will not start.

Now, the ALTER_CAPTURE procedure in DBMS_CAPTURE_ADM is used to modify the capture user. The following example changes the capture user to DBADMIN. The user executing this procedure must have the DBA role granted.

```
SQL> begin
  2    dbms_capture_adm.alter_capture (
  3    capture_name => 'DBXA_CAP',
  4    capture_user => 'DBADMIN'
  5    );
  6  end;
  7  /
PL/SQL procedure successfully completed.
```

If the capture process is running when this change is made, it is stopped and restarted automatically. Oracle reports a message similar to the following in the alert log file:

```
CP01: restarting Streams Capture DBXA_CAP to reflect a parameter change
```

NOTE
Dropping the current capture user from the database with the CASCADE option also drops the capture process. No warning is issued, even if the capture process is active.

Modifying the Checkpoint Retention Time

By default, the capture process has the `checkpoint_retention_time` parameter set to 60 days. Oracle automatically purges capture checkpoint information that is older than 60 days. The checkpoint information is required if you want to restart the capture process from an SCN in the past, say, during a point-in-time recovery of the capture database. Archived logs from this point in time must also be available. So, depending on your archived log file retention time, you may want to modify the checkpoint retention time appropriately. Depending on the activity in the source database, the LogMiner tables could consume a considerable amount of disk space in the SYSAUX tablespace if the checkpoints were to be kept for a longer period of time.

The ALTER_CAPTURE procedure in the DBMS_CAPTURE_ADM package is used to modify the value of the `checkpoint_retention_time` parameter, as shown next. The value can also be specified as a fraction of a day; for example, a value of 0.5 represents 12 hours. In this case, Oracle purges checkpoint information older than 12 hours.

```
SQL> begin
  2     dbms_capture_adm.alter_capture (
  3     capture_name => 'DBXA_CAP',
  4     checkpoint_retention_time => 0.5
  5     );
  6  end;
  7  /
PL/SQL procedure successfully completed.
```

The CHECKPOINT_RETENTION_TIME column of the DBA_CAPTURE view displays the current value of the `checkpoint_retention_time` parameter for the capture process.

If you prefer to not automatically purge the checkpoint information, then you can set the `checkpoint_retention_time` parameter to INFINITE using an Oracle-provided function, as shown in the following example:

```
SQL> begin
  2     dbms_capture_adm.alter_capture (
  3     capture_name => 'DBXA_CAP',
  4     checkpoint_retention_time => DBMS_CAPTURE_ADM.INFINITE
  5     );
  6  end;
  7  /
PL/SQL procedure successfully completed.
```

NOTE
Modifying the first SCN of the capture process purges checkpoint information that is older than the new first SCN, irrespective of the value of the `checkpoint_retention_time` *parameter.*

Modifying `checkpoint_retention_time` parameter does not cause the capture process to restart.

Modifying the First SCN of an Existing Capture Process

The first SCN of an existing capture process can be changed using the ALTER_ CAPTURE procedure in the DBMS_CAPTURE_ADM package. The new first SCN must satisfy the following conditions:

- It must be greater than the current first SCN.

- If must be less than or equal to the current applied SCN if the applied SCN is non-zero.

- It must be less than or equal to the required checkpoint SCN.

When the first SCN is changed, the checkpoint and other LogMiner information below the new first SCN is purged automatically. Therefore, the start SCN for the capture process cannot be lower than the new first SCN. And, the capture process will never require the redo information prior to the new first SCN.

In the following example, we display the various SCNs from the DBA_CAPTURE view:

```
SQL> select first_scn,
  2          start_scn,
  3          applied_scn,
  4          required_checkpoint_scn
  5     from dba_capture
  6    where capture_name = 'DBXA_CAP';

 FIRST_SCN  START_SCN APPLIED_SCN REQUIRED_CHECKPOINT_SCN
---------- ---------- ----------- -----------------------
   6477573    6477573     6740415                 6739762
```

Next, we set the new value for the first SCN to 6510000, which satisfies the required conditions:

```
SQL> begin
  2    dbms_capture_adm.alter_capture(
  3      capture_name => 'DBXA_CAP',
  4      first_scn    => 6510000
  5    );
  6 end;
  7 /
PL/SQL procedure successfully completed.
```

The alert log file for the database reports the following message when the fist SCN is changed:

```
STREAMS Capture C  1: first scn changed.
scn: 0x0000.006355b0
```

Unfortunately, the message does not include the name of the capture process but only the capture number from the V$STREAMS_CAPTURE view. The same message will also be reported when the capture process purges old checkpoint information and moves the first SCN automatically. By default, this happens about every six hours when the capture process is active.

NOTE
The capture process does not mine the log files when the purge activity is in progress. This causes a temporary increase in the capture latency.

Querying the DBA_CAPTURE view for the SCNs confirms that the new first SCN is in effect:

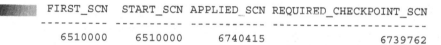
```
 FIRST_SCN   START_SCN  APPLIED_SCN REQUIRED_CHECKPOINT_SCN
---------- ---------- ----------- -----------------------
  6510000    6510000     6740415                 6739762
```

Notice that the start SCN is also changed to match the new first SCN. This is because our new first SCN, 6510000, is higher than the existing first SCN, 6477573. If it were not higher, then the start SCN would not have changed.

NOTE
The required checkpoint SCN and the applied SCN for the capture process cannot be modified.

Modifying the Start SCN of an Existing Capture Process

Typically, the start SCN of an existing capture process is modified when performing the point-in-time recovery of the destination database. The ALTER_CAPTURE procedure of the DBMS_CAPTURE_ADM package is used to modify the start SCN.

The new start SCN must be greater than or equal to the first SCN for the capture process. Also, the archived log file with the data dictionary information as of the new start SCN should be available. It is a good idea to confirm that the required log file is available before changing the start SCN. The ALTER_CAPTURE procedure does not warn you if the log file is not available. Upon starting the capture process, it will need the archived log file with the dictionary information as of the new start SCN.

Continuing from our previous example, let us say that we want to advance the start SCN to 6745000, which is larger than the current first SCN, 651000. To confirm that we have the archived log file with dictionary information as of this new SCN, we run the following query:

```
SQL> select first_scn,
  2           next_scn
  2     from dba_registered_archived_log
  3    where first_scn > 6510000
  4      and dictionary_begin = 'YES';

 FIRST_SCN   NEXT_SCN
---------- ----------
   6736514    6737362
   6744648    6745491
```

We have the required archived log files available with dictionary information. Out of these two files, the second file with FIRST_SCN of 6744648 contains the dictionary information as of our new start SCN, 6745000. So, we can safely advance the start SCN of the capture process.

First, we must stop the capture process to modify the start SCN or else Oracle will report an ORA-2666: cannot alter STREAMS process error.

```
SQL> exec dbms_capture_adm.stop_capture('DBXA_CAP');
PL/SQL procedure successfully completed.
```

Next, we execute the ALTER_CAPTURE procedure to modify the start SCN to 6745000:

```
SQL> begin
  2   dbms_capture_adm.alter_capture(
  3     capture_name => 'DBXA_CAP',
  4     start_scn    => 6745000
  5   );
  6 end;
SQL> /
PL/SQL procedure successfully completed.
```

The alert log for the database will report the following message. Unfortunately, the message does not contain the capture name or its number. Also, the new start SCN is shown in hexadecimal format.

```
knlciAlterCapture: start scn changed.
scn: 0x0000.0066eba8
```

Verify the changed start SCN value in the DBA_CAPTURE view, and restart the capture process.

Managing the Synchronous Capture Process

The synchronous capture process is enabled automatically when it is created. It cannot be started or stopped explicitly. Although the DBA_CAPTURE_PARAMETERS view lists parameters for the synchronous capture process, those cannot be changed using the SET_PARAMETER procedure of the DBMS_CAPTURE_ADM package.

Managing the Propagation Process

When the propagation process is created during the Streams configuration, the propagation queue schedule is enabled by default. There is no need to explicitly start the propagation. However, the propagation may have to be stopped and restarted when debugging problems with the network between the databases or with the Streams configuration itself. Also, the propagation job gets disabled if it encounters 16 consecutive errors while accessing the destination queue. You have to restart it manually after correcting the error.

The Oracle-provided DBMS_PROPAGATION_ADM package contains procedures to start and stop the propagation process. The DBA_PROPAGATION view provides information about the defined propagations in the database.

Starting the Propagation Process

The START_PROPAGATION procedure in the DBMS_PROPAGATION_ADM package is used to start the propagation process. The procedure has only one parameter, `propagation_name`, which must be specified. In the following example, we start the DBXA_TO_DBXB_PROP propagation process:

```
SQL> conn strmadmin/strmadmin@DBXA.WORLD
Connected.
SQL> begin
  2     dbms_propagation_adm.start_propagation(
  3     propagation_name => 'DBXA_TO_DBXB_PROP'
  4     );
  5  end;
  6  /
PL/SQL procedure successfully completed.
```

The STATUS column of the DBA_PROPAGATION view now shows ENABLED.

Stopping the Propagation Process

The STOP_PROPAGATION procedure in the DBMS_PROPAGATION_ADM package is used to stop the propagation process. The procedure has two parameters, `propagation_name` and `force`. The latter can be set to TRUE or FALSE. It defaults to FALSE if not specified. The propagation is stopped gracefully when using the default, as shown here:

```
SQL> begin
  2     dbms_propagation_adm.stop_propagation(
  3       propagation_name => 'DBXA_TO_DBXB_PROP'
  4     );
  5  end;
  6  /
PL/SQL procedure successfully completed.
```

The STATUS column of the DBA_PROPAGATION view now shows DISABLED. The accumulated statistics for the propagation process are not cleared when it is stopped using this default value. Stopping the propagation process disables the propagation queue schedule.

Occasionally, the propagation process may encounter a problem that prevents it from being stopped. In such cases, you must terminate it manually by setting the force parameter to TRUE, as shown here:

```
SQL> begin
  2     dbms_propagation_adm.stop_propagation(
  3     propagation_name => 'DBXA_TO_DBXB_PROP',
  4     force             => TRUE
  5     );
  6  end;
  7  /
PL/SQL procedure successfully completed.
```

Notice the STATUS field in the DBA_PROPAGATION view shown next. The accumulated statistics for the propagation are cleared when it is stopped by setting force to TRUE.

```
SQL> select status
  2    from dba_propagation
  3   where propagation_name = 'DBXA_TO_DBXB_PROP';

STATUS
--------
ABORTED
```

Managing the Apply Process

The DBMS_APPLY_ADM package provides required procedures to manage the apply process. This section discusses the procedures used for starting and stopping the apply process, modifying apply process parameters, and modifying the apply user.

Starting the Apply Process

The apply process is started using the START_APPLY procedure of the DBMS_APPLY_
ADM package. The procedure requires the name of the apply process, as shown in
the following example:

```
SQL> connect strmadmin/strmadmin@DBXB.WORLD
Connected.
SQL> begin
  2    dbms_apply_adm.start_apply(
  3         apply_name => 'DBXA_APP'
  4    );
  5  end;
  6  /
PL/SQL procedure successfully completed.
```

The STATUS column in the DBA_APPLY view displays ENABLED after the apply
process starts.

Similar to the capture process, if an attempt is made to start the already running
apply process, you may receive the following error messages:

```
ORA-26666: cannot alter STREAMS process DBXA_APP
ORA-06512: at "SYS.DBMS_LOGREP_UTIL", line 743
ORA-06512: at "SYS.DBMS_APPLY_ADM", line 28
ORA-06512: at line
```

Just confirm that the apply process is running, and ignore this error.

Stopping the Apply Process

At times, you may need to stop the apply process. For example, you may want to
temporarily halt replication to troubleshoot problems in the application or Streams
replication setup itself, or to perform database maintenance.

The STOP_APPLY process in DBMS_APPLY_ADM is used to stop the apply
process, as shown next. The procedure requires the name of the apply process as its
parameter. In addition, an optional parameter, `force`, can be used. It controls how
the apply process is stopped. This parameter defaults to a value of FALSE when not
specified, and the procedure stops the apply process gracefully.

```
SQL> begin
  2    dbms_apply_adm.stop_apply(
  3         apply_name => 'DBXA_APP'
  4    );
  5  end;
  6  /
PL/SQL procedure successfully completed.
```

```
SQL> select status
  2    from dba_apply
  3   where apply_name = 'DBXA_APP';

STATUS
--------
DISABLED
```

When the apply process can't stop due to some problem with it, the STOP_APPLY procedure will time out. If successive attempts to stop the apply process fail, then the apply process must be terminated by setting the force parameter to TRUE, as shown here:

```
SQL> begin
  2    dbms_apply_adm.stop_apply(
  3       apply_name => 'DBXA_APP',
  4       force       => TRUE
  5    );
  6  end;
  7  /
PL/SQL procedure successfully completed.
```

If the apply process is terminated as just shown, its status in the DBA_APPLY view shows ABORTED:

```
SQL> select status
  2    from dba_apply
  3   where apply_name = 'DBXA_APP';

STATUS
--------
ABORTED
```

Modifying Apply Process Parameters

The apply process has a number of parameters that control the functionality and behavior of the process. Often, changes to these parameters are required to improve its performance. The SET_PARAMETER procedure of DBMS_APPLY_ADM is used to change the values of the apply parameters.

In the following example, we change the disable_on_error parameter from its default value 'Y' to 'N'. This means that the apply process will not get disabled when it encounters an error. However, you are recommended to not change this parameter during the initial testing of your Streams environment. This will help you identify any problem with your setup quickly, since there will be only one error transaction to deal with.

The other parameter we change in the following example is parallelism, from its default value of 4 to 8. This creates eight apply server processes, which will help process more transactions at a time.

```
SQL> begin
  2    dbms_apply_adm.set_parameter(
  3    apply_name => 'DBXA_APP',
  4    parameter  => 'DISABLE_ON_ERROR',
  5    value      => 'N'
  6    );
  7
  8    dbms_apply_adm.set_parameter(
  9    apply_name => 'DBXA_APP',
 10    parameter  => 'PARALLELISM',
 11    value      => '8'
 12    );
 13  end;
 14  /
PL/SQL procedure successfully completed.
```

The DBA_APPLY_PARAMETERS view lists the apply parameters, and the SET_BY_USER column shows if the parameter was ever changed from its default value:

```
SQL> set pages 60
SQL> set trimspool on
SQL> col parameter for a30
SQL> col value for a22
SQL> col set_by_user heading "SET_BY_USER" for a15
SQL> select parameter,
  2         value,
  3         set_by_user
  4    from dba_apply_parameters
  5    where apply_name = 'DBXA_APP';
```

PARAMETER	VALUE	SET_BY_USER
PARALLELISM	8	YES
STARTUP_SECONDS	0	NO
TRACE_LEVEL	0	NO
TIME_LIMIT	INFINITE	NO
TRANSACTION_LIMIT	INFINITE	NO
MAXIMUM_SCN	INFINITE	NO
WRITE_ALERT_LOG	Y	NO
DISABLE_ON_LIMIT	N	NO
DISABLE_ON_ERROR	N	YES
COMMIT_SERIALIZATION	DEPENDENT_TRANSACTIONS	NO
ALLOW_DUPLICATE_ROWS	N	NO
TXN_LCR_SPILL_THRESHOLD	10000	NO
PRESERVE_ENCRYPTION	Y	NO
RTRIM_ON_IMPLICIT_CONVERSION	Y	NO
TXN_AGE_SPILL_THRESHOLD	900	NO

15 rows selected.

Oracle automatically stops and restarts the apply process, as required, when changing its parameters.

Modifying the Apply User

In most cases, the apply user is set to the Streams Administrator account. It can be changed to any other user account. The APPLY_USER column of the DBA_APPLY view lists the current apply user.

The new apply user must exist in the database and should have `create session` privilege. A number of additional privileges must be granted to the apply user for it to successfully perform rule evaluations, apply DDL and DML changes to the replicated tables, and execute user-defined handler procedures, if any. These privileges can be granted at the object level for the specific objects, or at the system level (using the ANY option). Such privileges can be granted to the apply user explicitly or via roles.

In the following example, we grant DBADMIN, our new apply user, additional privileges at the system level to apply DML changes. The user executing the following commands must have proper privileges to issue these grants to DBADMIN.

```
grant select any table to DBADMIN;
grant update any table to DBADMIN;
grant delete any table to DBADMIN;
grant insert any table to DBADMIN;
execute any rule set to DBADMIN;
execute any procedure to DBADMIN;
```

If we do not want to grant system-level privileges, then we must grant object-level privileges to DBADMIN, as shown next. The example only shows privileges for one table. We must grant these privileges for all replicated tables. In the example, we also grant an execute privilege on a user-defined apply handler procedure.

```
grant all on scott.dept to DBADMIN;
grant execute on strmadmin.apply_error_handler to DBADMIN;
```

Instead of using the GRANT ALL option to grant various privileges, you may individually grant those privileges to allow all DML operations. If the user-defined handler procedure invokes other procedures, or Oracle-supplied packages, then execute privilege on those must be granted explicitly, not via roles, to the apply user.

If the DDL changes are replicated, then the apply user needs the following privileges:

- `create table` or `create any table`

- `create index` or `create any index`

- `create procedure` or `create any procedure`

- `drop any table`

- `alter table` or `alter any table`

Most importantly, the apply user needs execute privilege on the apply rule set. Assuming the apply rule set name is RULESET$_65 and the rule set owner is STRMADMIN, the following procedure grants execute privilege on the rule set to the apply user DBADMIN. Of course, this is not required if there is no apply rule set defined for the apply process.

```
SQL> begin
  2     dbms_rule_adm.grant_object_privilege(
  3          privilege   => SYS.DBMS_RULE_ADM.EXECUTE_ON_RULE_SET,
  4          object_name => 'STRMADMIN.RULESET$_65',
  5          grantee     => 'DBADMIN');
  6   end;
  7   /
PL/SQL procedure successfully completed.
```

Alternatively, you could also grant `execute any rule set` privilege to the apply user.

Oracle automatically grants the DEQUEUE privilege on the apply queue to the apply user, allowing the apply user to dequeue messages from the apply queue.

The ALTER_APPLY procedure in the DBMS_APPLY_ADM package is used to change the apply user, as shown in the next example. The user who executes this procedure must have DBA privilege.

```
SQL> begin
  2     dbms_apply_adm.alter_apply(
  3          apply_name => 'DBXA_APP',
  4          apply_user => 'DBADMIN');
  5   end;
  6   /
PL/SQL procedure successfully completed.
```

If the apply process is running when this change is made, it is stopped and restarted automatically. Oracle reports a message similar to the following in the alert log file:

```
AP01: restarting to reflect a parameter change
```

NOTE
Dropping the current apply user from the database with the CASCADE option also drops the apply process. No warning is issued, even if the apply process is active.

Monitoring Streams Processes

After you successfully configure the Streams replication environment, the next important task is to implement steps to monitor it. Streams monitoring can be divided into two major parts: Streams process monitoring and Streams performance monitoring. Streams process monitoring includes monitoring to make sure that all required processes are running normally without encountering any errors. Streams performance monitoring includes monitoring to make sure that the replication latency is within the acceptable level.

There are a number of static data dictionary views and dynamic performance views that track related information that is used for monitoring a Streams environment. This section refers to these views in the discussion about the Streams processes and performance monitoring.

The procedures discussed in this chapter can be used to set up automated jobs to alert you when things are not working as expected. Also, Oracle Enterprise Manager Grid Control 10.2.0.5 is an excellent tool for setting up Streams monitoring and alert mechanisms. OEM Grid Control is discussed in Chapter 14.

Monitoring the Capture Process

The two important views to monitor the capture process are DBA_CAPTURE and V$STREAMS_CAPTURE. These views provide necessary information to alert you if the capture process is not performing as expected.

Monitoring the Status of the Capture Process

The STATUS column in the DBA_CAPTURE view shows the current status of the capture processes defined in the database. The STATUS column shows ENABLED for an active capture process, DISABLED for a nonrunning capture process, or ABORTED for a capture process that is terminated due to an error.

```
SQL> select capture_name,
  2          status
  3    from dba_capture;

CAPTURE_NAME    STATUS
--------------- ----------
DBXA_CAP        ENABLED
```

It is suggested that you have a routine job to check for the STATUS and issue an alert if the capture process is not active when it is supposed to be. If the STATUS shows ABORTED, then the ERROR_NUMBER and ERROR_MESSAGE columns of the DBA_CAPTURE view can provide the reason.

Monitoring the State of the Capture Process

When active, the capture process can go through a number of states depending on the task it is performing, or whether it is waiting for another task or an event to complete. The STATE column of the V$STREAMS_CAPTURE view shows the current state of the capture process. Table 11-1 lists and briefly describes the possible states of the capture process.

Depending on the environment, the capture process may not encounter some of these states. You should monitor the state of the capture process in your environment and become familiar with the different states it may report. This will enable you to diagnose a potential problem. For example, if suddenly you notice that the capture process is frequently reporting PAUSED FOR FLOW CONTROL, and sometimes for a longer duration, this may indicate that the propagation process or apply process is not keeping up with the capture process.

State	Description
ABORTING	Being terminated after encountering an error
CAPTURING CHANGES	Mining logs to capture changes
CREATING LCR	Converting a captured message to an LCR
DICTIONARY INITIALIZATION	Loading data dictionary information from a log file
ENQUEUING MESSAGE	Enqueuing an LCR to the capture queue
EVALUATING RULE	Applying rules to captured changes
INITIALIZING	In the process of starting up
PAUSED FOR FLOW CONTROL	Suspended due to too many unprocessed messages
SHUTTING DOWN	In the process of stopping
SUSPENDED FOR AUTO SPLIT/MERGE	Awaiting automatic split or merge operation to complete
WAITING FOR A SUBSCRIBER TO BE ADDED	Awaiting the subscribers to be available to dequeue messages
WAITING FOR BUFFERED QUEUE TO SHRINK	Waiting for the full buffered queue to shrink
WAITING FOR DICTIONARY REDO	Waiting to process the log file with dictionary information
WAITING FOR REDO	Waiting for the redo log file to continue

TABLE 11-1. *Different States of the Capture Process*

The following query reports the current state of the capture process and the time at which it entered that state:

```
SQL> col capture_name heading 'Capture|Name' for a10
SQL> col state heading 'State' for a25
SQL> col state_changed heading 'State|Change Time' for a20
SQL> col create_message heading 'Last Message|Create Time' for a20
SQL> select capture_name,
  2         state,
  3         to_char(state_changed_time, 'HH24:MI:SS MM/DD/YY') state_changed,
  4         to_char(capture_message_create_time, 'HH24:MI:SS MM/DD/YY') create_message
  5    from v$streams_capture
  6   order by capture_name;
Capture                              State              Last Message
Name       State                     Change Time        Create Time
---------- ------------------------- ------------------ ----------------
DBXA_CAP   PAUSED FOR FLOW CONTROL   10:28:12 02/28/10   10:27:33 02/28/10
```

Monitoring Capture Performance

The dynamic performance view V$STREAMS_CAPTURE contains valuable information about the capture process performance, including capture process latency and throughput.

Checking Capture Process Latency   The following query shows the capture process latency in enqueuing the message after it was captured. Slowness in the LogMiner process, or poorly performing custom rule-based transformation, if any, may affect capture latency. Increasing the value of the `parallelism` parameter of the capture process, or memory for LogMiner may improve the performance of the capture process.

```
SQL> col latency_seconds heading 'Latency|in|Seconds' for 9999999
SQL> col create_time heading 'Create|Time' for A20
SQL> col enqueue_time heading 'Enqueue|Time' for A20
SQL> col enqueue_message_number heading 'Message|Number' for 99999999999999
SQL>
SQL> select capture_name,
  2         (enqueue_time - enqueue_message_create_time)*86400 latency_seconds,
  3         to_char(enqueue_message_create_time, 'HH24:MI:SS MM/DD/YY') create_time,
  4         to_char(enqueue_time, 'HH24:MI:SS MM/DD/YY') enqueue_time,
  5         enqueue_message_number
  6    from v$streams_capture
  7   order by capture_name;

           Latency
Capture    in Create           Enqueue             Message
Name       Seconds Time         Time                Number
--------- ------- ------------------ ------------------ ----------------
DBXA_CAP        40 10:27:33 02/28/10  10:28:13 02/28/10        6838170
```

Checking Capture Process Throughput   The following query displays the number of redo records scanned (messages captured) and the number of messages (LCRs) created and enqueued. Note that the number of enqueued messages is greater than the number of messages created due to the commit directive for the transactions and some additional administrative messages sent to the destination.

```
SQL> col total_messages_created heading 'Messages|Created' for 999999999
SQL> col total_messages_enqueued heading 'Messages|Enqueued' for 999999999
SQL> col total_messages_captured heading 'Messages|Captured' for 999999999
SQL> select capture_name,
  2          state,
  3          total_messages_captured,
  4          total_messages_created,
  5          total_messages_enqueued
  6    from v$streams_capture
  7    order by capture_name;

Capture                                 Messages    Messages    Messages
Name        State                       Captured    Created     Enqueued
---------   ------------------------    ----------  ----------  ----------
DBXA_CAP    CREATING LCR                   54950       10029       12006
```

The following query shows the capture throughput per second since it was started. The output is from our test database, which does not have much activity.

```
SQL> col a heading 'Messages|Captured|Per Sec' for 9999999999
SQL> col b heading 'Messages|Created|Per Sec' for 9999999999
SQL> col c heading 'Messages|Enqueued|Per Sec' for 9999999999
SQL> select
  2      ceil(total_messages_captured/((sysdate - startup_time)*86400)) a,
  3      ceil(total_messages_created/((sysdate - startup_time)*86400))  b,
  4      ceil(total_messages_enqueued/((sysdate - startup_time)*86400)) c
  5    from
  6      v$streams_capture;

  Messages    Messages    Messages
  Captured    Created     Enqueued
  Per Sec     Per Sec     Per Sec
----------  ----------  ----------
         5           4           4
```

Monitoring the Propagation Process and Queues

The views DBA_PROPAGATION and DBA_QUEUE_SCHEDULES provide information to monitor the propagation process. The V$BUFFERED_PUBLISHERS and V$BUFFERED_QUEUES views provide information to monitor the buffered queues.

The STATUS field in the DBA_PROPAGATION view shows ENABLED when the propagation process is active and running. It changes to DISABLED when the propagation process is not running for whatever reason.

The FAILURES column in DBA_QUEUE_SCHEDULES tracks the number of times the propagation job fails. Such failures can occur due to connectivity issues with the destination database. When the number of failures reaches 16, the propagation is automatically disabled. Monitoring such failures, when CCA is not in effect, is important to get an early alert about an impending problem.

The following query shows the status and the number of failures of the propagation job associated with the defined propagation. The `latency` parameter of the propagation job defaults to 3 seconds, which can be changed as discussed in Chapter 5.

```
SQL> col propagation_name heading 'Propagation|Name' for a20
SQL> col latency heading 'Latency|Seconds' for 99999
SQL> col schedule_disabled heading 'Status' for a10
SQL> col failures heading 'Failures' for 999
SQL> col queue_to_queue heading 'Queue|to|Queue'
SQL> select p.propagation_name,
  2         s.latency,
  3         decode(s.schedule_disabled,
  4                 'Y', 'Disabled',
  5                 'N', 'Enabled') schedule_disabled,
  6         s.failures,
  7         p.queue_to_queue
  8    from dba_queue_schedules s, dba_propagation p
  9   where s.message_delivery_mode = 'BUFFERED'
 10     and s.schema = p.source_queue_owner
 11     and s.qname = p.source_queue_name
 12   order by propagation_name;
                                                        Queue
Propagation          Latency                            to
Name                 Seconds Status      Failures Queue
-------------------- ------- ---------- -------- -----
DBXA_TO_DBXB_PROP          3 Enabled           0 TRUE
```

The buffered queue can store messages in memory or in the queue table when they spill over from memory. Messages can spill to disk if they are not dequeued in a timely fashion, or there is not enough memory to store them. Monitoring the queues and the publisher of the messages—that is, the capture process—will help identify the cause of the message spillage.

The following query shows the total number of messages in the buffered queue, how many are in memory, and how many spilled to disk:

```
SQL> col queue_schema heading 'Queue|Schema' for a10
SQL> col queue_name heading 'Queue|Name' for a10
SQL> col msgs_in_mem heading 'Messages|In Memory' for 999999
SQL> col spill_msgs heading 'Messages|Spilled' for 999999
SQL> col num_msgs heading 'Messages|In Buffered Queue' for 999999
SQL> select queue_schema,
```

```
 2          queue_name,
 3          (num_msgs - spill_msgs) msgs_in_mem,
 4          spill_msgs,
 5          num_msgs
 6    from v$buffered_queues;
```

Queue Schema	Queue Name	Messages In Memory	Messages Spilled	Messages In Buffered Queue
STRMADMIN	DBXA_CAP_Q	9871	0	9871

The capture process publishes, or enqueues, messages in the buffered queue. From there, the messages are propagated to the destination queue. The V$BUFFERED_PUBLISHERS view tracks the number of messages enqueued, the source of the messages, memory utilization, and the state of the publisher (message sender), among a few other things.

We run the following query on our source database DBXA and destination database DBXB. Notice the values for the SENDER and SENDER QUEUE columns.

```
SQL> connect strmadmin/strmadmin@DBXA.WORLD
Connected.
SQL> col sender_name heading 'Sender' for a10
SQL> col sender_address heading 'Sender|Queue' for a10
SQL> col queue_name heading 'Queue|Name' for a10
SQL> col cnum_msgs heading 'Msgs|Enqueued' for 999999999
SQL> col memory_usage heading 'Memory|Usage' for 999999999
SQL> col publisher_state heading 'Publisher|State' for a20
SQL> select sender_name,
 2          sender_address,
 3          queue_name,
 4          cnum_msgs,
 5          memory_usage,
 6          publisher_state
 7    from v$buffered_publishers;
```

Sender	Sender Queue	Queue Name	Msgs Enqueued	Memory Usage	Publisher State
DBXA_CAP		DBXA_CAP_Q	149564	29	PUBLISHING MESSAGES

```
SQL> connect strmadmin/strmadmin@DBXB.WORLD
Connected.
SQL> /
```

Sender	Sender Queue	Queue Name	Msgs Enqueued	Memory Usage	Publisher State
DBXA_CAP	"STRMADMIN"."DBXA_CAP_Q"@DBXA.WORLD	DBXA_APP_Q	149563	5	PUBLISHING MESSAGES

In the first query for the DBXA.WORLD database, the message sender is the local capture process DBXA_CAP, which enqueued the messages to the DBXA_CAP_Q queue. These messages did not come from any other sender queue. The local queue consumed 29 percent of the Streams pool memory.

In the DBXB.WORLD database, the sender name is still DBXA_CAP, but the message sender queue belongs to the source database DBXA.WORLD. The sender queue enqueued messages to the local queue DBXA_APP_Q. The queue used 5 percent of the Streams pool memory.

The number of enqueued messages in both queues is pretty close. This means that the message transfer is working well.

The PUBLISHER_STATE column can have different values. The displayed value, PUBLISHING MESSAGES, in the previous examples is an indication of normal behavior. Any of the following values may indicate slowness or a problem with the replication process:

- IN FLOW CONTROL: TOO MANY UNBROWSED MESSAGES

- IN FLOW CONTROL: OVERSPILLED MESSAGES

- IN FLOW CONTROL: INSUFFICIENT MEMORY AND UNBROWSED MESSAGES

When the state is other than PUBLISHING MESSAGES, an automatic flow control mechanism will temporarily halt the capture of new messages and the capture process will switch into PAUSED FOR FLOW CONTROL state.

Monitoring the Apply Process

The following data dictionary views and dynamic performance views are used to monitor the apply process:

- DBA_APPLY

- DBA_APPLY_ERROR

- DBA_APPLY_PROGRESS

- V$STREAMS_APPLY_COORDINATOR

- V$STREAMS_APPLY_READER

- V$STREAMS_APPLY_SERVER

These views provide all the information required to monitor how the apply engine is functioning and to help diagnose problems.

Monitoring the Apply Process Status and Other Information

The DBA_APPLY view shows all the pertinent information about the apply process defined in the database. The STATUS column in this view shows the current status of the apply processes defined in the database. The STATUS column shows ENABLED for an active apply process, DISABLED for a nonrunning apply process, or ABORTED for an apply process that is terminated due to an error.

The following query shows some of the information from the DBA_APPLY view:

```
SQL> col apply_name heading 'Apply|Name' for a10
SQL> col status heading 'Status' for a10
SQL> col s_time heading 'Status|Change Time' for a20
SQL> col apply_captured heading 'Apply|Captured|LCR' for a10
SQL> select apply_name,
  2         status,
  3         to_char(status_change_time,'mm/dd/yy hh24:mi:ss') s_time,
  4         apply_captured
  5  from dba_apply;
```

```
                                    Apply
Apply                   Status      Captured
Name        Status      Change Time LCR
----------  ----------  -------------------- ----------
DBXA_APP    ENABLED     03/01/10 14:14:32    YES
```

The apply process DBXA_APP has been enabled since the time shown. Also, it can only apply LCRs captured in the buffered queue. It will not apply LCRs captured by the synchronous capture process in the persistent queue.

Monitoring Apply Process Latency

When it comes to apply process latency, there are essentially two latency numbers you may want to monitor. One is apply dequeue latency and the other is apply latency. Example queries in the following two sections were run back-to-back in our test database to capture information to aid our discussion.

Dequeue Latency   The dequeue latency is the time between change, which is measured from when the LCR is created in the source database to when the LCR is dequeued by the apply reader process. This information is in the V$STREAMS_APPLY_READER view.

The following query displays the dequeue latency, message creation and dequeue times, and the SCN number associated with the last dequeued LCR:

```
sql> col apply_name heading 'Apply|Name' for a10
sql> col latency heading 'Latency|In|Seconds'  for 999999999
sql> col creation heading 'Message|Creation|Time' for a17
sql> col dequeue_time heading 'Message|Dequeue|Time' for a17
sql> col dequeued_message_number heading 'Dequeued|SCN|Number' for 999999000000
sql>
sql> select apply_name,
  2        dequeue_time - dequeued_message_create_time)*86400 latency,
  3        to_char(dequeued_message_create_time,'mm/dd/yy hh24:mi:ss') creation,
  4        to_char(dequeue_time, 'mm/dd/yy hh24:mi:ss') dequeue_time,
  5        dequeued_message_number
  6   from v$streams_apply_reader;
```

Apply Name	Latency In Seconds	Message Creation Time	Message Dequeue Time	Dequeued SCN Number
DBXA_APP	14	03/02/10 09:07:08	03/02/10 09:07:22	7367898

Apply Latency   The apply latency can be tracked using the V$STREAMS_APPLY_COORDINATOR and DBA_APPLY_PROGRESS views. The former view displays the information for the LCRs captured using the capture or synchronous capture process. The latter view displays the information for the LCRs captured using only the capture process.

The following query against DBA_APPLY_PROGRESS shows the apply latency, message creation and apply times, and the last SCN associated with the last applied SCN. We see that the overall apply latency is 18 seconds, while the dequeue latency is 14 seconds, as seen in the previous example.

```
sql> col apply_name heading 'Apply|Name' for a10
sql> col latency heading 'Latency|In|Seconds'  for 999999999
sql> col creation heading 'Message|Creation|Time' for a17
sql> col apply_time heading 'Message|Apply|Time' for a17
sql> col applied_message_number heading 'Applied|SCN|Number' for 999999000000
sql>
sql> select apply_name,
  2        (apply_time-applied_message_create_time)*86400 latency,
  3        to_char(applied_message_create_time,'mm/dd/yy hh24:mi:ss') creation,
  4        to_char(apply_time,'mm/dd/yy hh24:mi:ss') apply_time,
  5        applied_message_number
  6    from dba_apply_progress;
```

Apply Name	Latency In Seconds	Message Creation Time	Message Apply Time	Applied SCN Number
DBXA_APP	18	03/02/10 09:07:04	03/02/10 09:07:22	7365315

The following query against V$STREAMS_APPLY_COORDINATOR shows the apply latency, message creation and apply times, and the last SCN associated with the last applied LCR:

```
sql> col apply_name heading 'Apply|Name' for a10
sql> col latency heading 'Latency|In|Seconds'  for 999999999
sql> col creation heading 'Message|Creation|Time' for a17
sql> col apply_time heading 'Message|Apply|Time' for a17
sql> col hwm_message_number heading 'Applied|SCN|Number' for 999999000000
sql>
sql> select apply_name,
  2         ((hwm_time - hwm_message_create_time)*86400) latency,
  3         to_char(hwm_message_create_time,'mm/dd/yy hh24:mi:ss') creation,
  4         to_char(hwm_time, 'mm/dd/yy hh24:mi:ss') apply_time,
  5         hwm_message_number
  6    from v$streams_apply_coordinator;
```

Apply Name	Latency In Seconds	Message Creation Time	Message Apply Time	Applied SCN Number
DBXA_APP	18	03/02/10 09:07:04	03/02/10 09:07:22	7365548

Notice that the latency and timing information is the same as in the previous two examples, but the applied SCN number is different. It is more recent. This is due to the fact that the information displayed by DBA_APPLY_PROGRESS comes from a static table and is slightly delayed relative to the information in the view V$STREAMS_APPLY_COORDINATOR.

Monitoring Apply Servers

The dynamic performance view V$STREAMS_APPLY_SERVER provides information about the apply servers and their current activities. The apply servers receive the LCRs from the apply coordinator and either apply those LCRs to the destination tables or pass them on to the apply handler procedures. Starting in Oracle 11*g* R2, by default, four apply servers are defined.

The following query shows the current state of the apply servers for the apply process DBXA_APP:

```
SQL> col process_name heading 'Proc|Name' for a5
SQL> col sid heading 'Sid' for 9999
SQL> col server_id heading 'Server|Id' for 9999
SQL> col event heading 'Event' for a20
SQL> col state heading 'State' for a20
SQL> col total_assigned heading 'Total|TXNS|Assigned' for 99999999
SQL> col total_messages_applied heading 'Total|LCRs|Applied' for 99999999
SQL>
SQL> select substr(s.program,instr(s.program,'(')+1,4) process_name,
```

```
 2          r.server_id,
 3          s.sid,
 4          r.state,
 5          r.total_assigned,
 6          r.total_messages_applied,
 7          s.event
 8    from v$streams_apply_server r,
 9         v$session s
10    where r.sid = s.sid
11          and r.serial# = s.serial#
12      and r.apply_name = 'DBXA_APP'
13    order by r.server_id;
```

Proc Name	Server Id	Sid	State	Total TXNS Assigned	Total LCRs Applied	Event
AS02	1	33	EXECUTE TRANSACTION	35813	476774	rdbms ipc message
AS03	2	35	EXECUTE TRANSACTION	36552	483396	rdbms ipc message
AS04	3	36	EXECUTE TRANSACTION	37443	506348	rdbms ipc message
AS05	4	40	EXECUTE TRANSACTION	33973	461152	rdbms ipc message

In this example, we have joined V$STREAMS_APPLY_SERVER with V$SESSION to get the recently posted wait event by the apply server session. It shows that the servers had waited for internal communication with the apply coordinator. The output shows all apply servers are executing transactions. It also shows the number of total transactions assigned to each server, and the total number of LCRs applied by each server since its startup.

The STATE column can have the following values:

- **ADD PARTITION** Performing an internal task to add a table partition to record information about the transaction it is currently executing.

- **DROP PARTITION** Performing an internal task to drop a table partition to purge rows that were used to record information about the transaction just completed.

- **EXECUTE TRANSACTION** Currently applying the LCR, or the apply handler procedure is being executed.

- **IDLE** Waiting for the apply coordinator to assign LCRs.

- **INITIALIZING** In the process of starting up.

- **RECORD LOW-WATERMARK** Performing an internal task that updates the information about the progress of the apply process. This is reported by the DBA_APPLY_PROGRESS and ALL_APPLY_PROGRESS views.

- **ROLLBACK TRANSACTION** Rolling back the just applied transaction.

- **TRANSACTION CLEANUP** Performing an internal task to remove LCRs from the apply queue and updating information about the completed transaction.

■ **WAIT COMMIT** Waiting to commit the just applied transaction until all other transactions with a lower commit SCN have been committed. This state is possible only when the `commit_serialization` parameter for the apply process is set to FULL, and `parallelism` is set to a value greater than 1.

■ **WAIT DEPENDENCY** Waiting to begin the transaction until another transaction on which it has dependency has been applied and committed. This state is possible only when the `parallelism` parameter for the apply process is set to a value greater than 1.

In the following query, we see some of the other states of the apply server. These are possible when running the apply process with the `parallelism` parameter set to a value greater than 1, and `commit_serialization` set to the default value DEPENDENT_TRANSACTIONS.

```
SQL> col process_name heading 'Proc|Name' for a5
SQL> col sid heading 'Sid' for 9999
SQL> col server_id heading 'Server|Id' for 9999
SQL> col event heading 'Event' for a20
SQL> col state heading 'State' for a20
SQL> col curr_txn heading 'Current|Txn|Id' for a10
SQL> col dep_txn heading 'Dependent|Txn|Id' for a10
SQL> col commitscn heading 'Current|Txn|C_SCN' for 99999999
SQL> col dep_commitscn heading 'Dependent|Txn|C_SCN' for 999999999
SQL>
SQL> select substr(s.program,instr(s.program,'(')+1,4) process_name,
  2         r.server_id,
  3         s.sid,
  4         r.state,
  5         r.xidusn||'.'||r.xidslt||'.'||r.xidsqn curr_txn,
  6         r.dep_xidusn||'.'||r.dep_xidslt||'.'||r.dep_xidsqn dep_txn,
  7         r.commitscn,
  8         r.dep_commitscn
  9    from v$streams_apply_server r,
 10         v$session s
 11   where r.sid = s.sid
 12         and r.serial# = s.serial#
 13     and r.apply_name = 'DBXA_APP'
 14    order by s.server_id;
```

Proc Name	Server Id	Sid	State	Current Txn Id	Dependent Txn Id	Current Txn C_SCN	Dependent Txn C_SCN
AS02	1	33	WAIT DEPENDENCY	8.17.5137	2.3.4973	8084203	8084201
AS03	2	35	TRANSACTION CLEANUP	3.5.4866	9.6.4974	8084198	8084196
AS04	3	36	EXECUTE TRANSACTION	7.26.4787	6.6.4958	8084206	8084193
AS05	4	40	WAIT DEPENDENCY	2.3.4973	3.5.4866	8084201	8084198

The output shows the current and dependent transaction commit SCN numbers and associated transaction IDs. So, you can figure out who is waiting on whom. For an apply server that is currently executing a transaction, server 3 in the example, the dependent transaction information is from its past state and can be ignored.

Monitoring Apply Errors

The apply process encounters errors when it cannot apply changes to the destination tables. Mainly, errors occur due to inconsistency in the data in the destination row, violation of referential integrity constraints, or missing rows in destination tables. If there is no apply handler process defined to handle and resolve such errors, the entire transaction is written to the apply error queue. If the apply parameter `disable_on_error` is changed to N, then the apply process continues to apply subsequent transactions instead of aborting upon encountering errors. Troubleshooting apply errors is discussed in Chapter 12.

The data dictionary view DBA_APPLY_ERROR contains information about all the transactions that ran into errors. The view will not return any rows when there are no apply errors. You should monitor the number of rows in this view, and issue alerts when the number is non-zero.

The following query for the apply process DBXA_APP reports one apply error in our test environment:

```
SQL> select count(*) apply_errors
  2    from dba_apply_error
  3    where apply_name = 'DBXA_APP';

APPLY_ERRORS
------------
           1
```

More information about this error is obtained using the following query:

```
SQL> col local_transaction_id heading 'Local|TxnId' for a12
SQL> col message_number heading 'LCR|Number' for 99999
SQL> col message_count heading 'LCR|Count' for 99999
SQL> col error_number heading 'Error|Number' for 9999999
SQL> col error_message heading 'Error|Message' for a40
SQL> select local_transaction_id,
  2          message_number,
  3          message_count,
  4          error_number,
  5          error_message
  6    from dba_apply_error
  7    where apply_name = 'DBXA_APP';
```

```
Local          LCR    LCR    Error Error
TxnId       Number  Count   Number Message
----------- ------ ------ -------- -----------------------------
3.19.4744        4      5    26787 ORA-26787: The row with key ("
                                   COMM", "DEPTNO", "EMPNO", "ENA
                                   ME", "HIREDATE", "JOB", "MGR",
                                    "SAL") = (1400, 30, 7654, MAR
                                   TIN, 1981-09-28:00:00:00, SALE
                                   SMAN, 7698, 1250) does not exi
                                   st in table SCOTT.EMP
                                   ORA-01403: no data found
```

The transaction in error has a total of five changes excluding the commit directive, but the fourth LCR in the transaction caused an error. The error occurred because a row with the key information listed in the error message was not found in the destination table.

Monitoring Transactions

The overall latency of Streams replication is highly dependent on the size of the transaction. The V$STREAMS_TRANSACTION view can be useful to check the size of the pending and open transactions. Querying this view on the capture and apply database will list the transactions being captured and applied. When the apply server is applying a large transaction, the apply process parallelism gets suspended for the duration of the large transaction. This will adversely affect the overall replication latency.

The following example shows a partial list of transactions waiting to be processed by the apply process DBXA_APP:

```
SQL> col xidusn heading 'Txn|Undo|Seg#' for 999999
SQL> col xidslt heading 'Txn|Undo|Slot' for 999999
SQL> col xidsqn heading 'Txn|Undo|Seq' for 999999
SQL> col cumulative_message_count heading 'Cumulative|Messages|Count' for 9999999
SQL> col total_message_count heading 'Total|Mesgs|Count' for 9999999
SQL>
SQL> select xidusn,
  2        xidslt,
  3        xidsqn,
  4        cumulative_message_count,
  5        total_message_count,
  6        first_message_time,
  7        last_message_time
  8    from v$streams_transaction
  9   where streams_name = 'DBXA_APP';
```

Txn Undo Seg#	Txn Undo Slot	Txn Undo Seq	Cumulative Messages Count	Total Mesgs Count
5	23	4344	15	15
6	29	4272	15	15
8	20	4452	15	15
9	7	4294	15	15
5	16	4328	2001	2001
6	0	4279	15	15
8	18	4461	15	15
10	5	4148	4003	4003

In this example, the total message count represents the number of LCRs in the transaction, including the commit directive, and equals the cumulative message count. If we run the query for the capture process, the total message count will show zero while the cumulative message count will increment until the commit directive is captured.

Monitoring the Alert Log File

The alert log file for the capture database will report messages when the capture process detects large and long transactions. These transactions can potentially affect replication throughput and performance. Any transaction that contains more than 10,000 changes is considered a large transaction, and a transaction that is open (no new change, commit, or rollback) for more than ten minutes since the last captured LCR is considered a long transaction. You may see messages similar to the following for the large and long transactions, respectively. The transaction ID (xid) can provide information about the transaction.

```
CP01: large txn detected (11323 LCRs), xid: 0x0006.00f.00002671

CP01: long running txn detected, xid: 0x0003.001.00002622
```

The alert log file for the apply database will report warning messages when the apply process encounters locking or contention issues. Additional information will be reported in the trace file for the apply process. The following warning message indicates that the apply process is blocked by another user process and for how long it has been blocked:

```
Sat Mar 13 14:57:25 2010
AP01: warning -- apply server 2, sid 36 waiting on user sid 61 for event (since 1200
seconds):
```

The trace file for the apply process shows the same warning and additional information that can be used to determine the cause:

```
*** 2010-03-13 14:57:25.758
AP01: warning -- apply server 2, sid 36 waiting on user sid 61 for event (since 1200
seconds):
AP01: [enq: TX - row lock contention] name|mode=54580006, usn<<16 | slot=9001d, seque
nce=1fc
```

As it turns out, in this example, the row that the apply process wanted to change was locked by another user process. The user process must commit or roll back its change before the apply process can proceed.

Split and Merge: Managing and Monitoring

In a Streams environment of a single capture process and a single propagation process that sends changes to multiple destinations, any problem with one of the destinations will adversely affect the replication to other destinations. Problems such as the apply process encountering an error and aborting, or network problems that disconnect propagation, will interrupt transmission of the LCRs to the destination queue. These undelivered messages will start to build up in the propagation queue at the source database, and will affect replication to the other destinations.

The split and merge feature of Streams addresses this problem. When Oracle detects that the destination can't be reached, it splits that destination from the Streams path to stop propagating messages to it. When such a split happens, cloned copies of the capture and propagation processes are created. The cloned processes are responsible for replicating data to the split destination when it becomes available. At this time, this arrangement behaves like a unidirectional replication. Once the backlog of queued messages gets cleared, the cloned processes are merged with the original capture and propagation processes.

The split and merge feature is enabled by default when Oracle detects multiple destinations for the same propagation queue.

In Oracle 11*g* R2, the split and merge of a destination can be achieved automatically or manually. By default, the parameters for the capture process enable automatic split and merge. If you do not want to enable this automatic feature, you have to modify the associated parameters, discussed next:

- **split_threshold** This parameter is relevant only when captured changes are sent to more than one destination. It controls the splitting of the original capture process and creation of the cloned capture process when one of the destinations becomes unreachable.

  This parameter specifies the amount of time, in seconds, that must pass after there is a break in Streams in sending changes to the destination. Once this time elapses, the cloned capture and propagation processes are created for the destination in question. The cloned capture and propagation processes will capture and send messages to this destination.

  If `split_threshold` is set to 0, then automatic splitting starts immediately upon sensing the break in reaching the destination. If it is set to INFINITE, then the automatic splitting is disabled. The default value for this parameter is 1800 seconds.

  This parameter works in conjunction with the `merge_threshold` parameter.

■ **merge_threshold** This parameter is relevant only when the captured changes are sent to more than one destination. This parameter controls the merging of the cloned capture and propagation processes with the original.

When the difference between the message creation time of the original capture process and the message creation time of the cloned capture process is less than or equal to the value (in seconds) of this parameter, then the automatic merging of these capture processes begins. Automatic merging does not begin if the difference in the message creation times is larger than the value specified for this parameter. The view DBA_STREAMS_SPLIT_MERGE shows this difference in the LAG column. The message creation time is recorded in the column CAPTURE_MESSAGE_CREATE_TIME of the V$STREAMS_CAPTURE view for the capture processes.

If the value for this parameter is set to 0, then there should not be any lag between the message creation times of the capture processes before the merging can begin. If the value is set to INFINITE, then the automatic merging begins immediately. If the value is set to any negative number, then automatic merging is disabled. You must manually merge the capture processes.

Automatic Split and Merge

To perform automatic split and merge, the `split_threshold` and `merge_threshold` parameters must be set to the values appropriate for your environment. Make sure that `split_threshold` is not set to INFINITE and `merge_threshold` is not set to a negative value.

Query the DBA_CAPTURE_PARAMETERS view to see the current values for these parameters. Oracle detects the multiple destinations for the single capture queue and creates a scheduler job. This job monitors the flow between the source and destination queues periodically. When it detects a problem with the Streams flow, it splits the unreachable destination off from the original capture process and creates cloned capture and propagation processes. The cloned components get a system-generated name.

When the split occurs, another scheduler job is created to merge the split capture and propagation processes. The merge job monitors the split environment, and when the problem is corrected, it merges the split capture and propagation processes with the original processes.

You can query the DBA_SCHEDULER_JOBS view to find information about these split and merge jobs. The JOB_NAME is system created and starts with STREAMS.

The DBA_STREAMS_SPLIT_MERGE view shows information related to the split and merge operation:

```
col original_capture_name heading 'Original|Capture|Name' for a10
col action_type heading 'Action|Type' for a10
```

```
col status_update_time heading 'Status|Update|Time' for a20
col job_next_run_date heading 'Next|Run|Date' for a20

select original_capture_name,
       action_type,
       status_update_time,
       status,
       job_next_run_date
  from dba_streams_split_merge
 order by status_update_time desc;
```

You can monitor the STATUS column in this view. It can have the following values:

■ **ABOUT TO SPLIT**   Ready to split.

■ **ABOUT TO MERGE**   Ready to merge.

■ **ERROR**   There was an error during the split or merge.

■ **MERGING**   Currently merging the processes.

■ **MERGE DONE**   Completed the merge operation.

■ **NONSPLITABLE**   Original capture cannot be split because it is disabled, aborted, or has only one destination.

■ **NOTHING TO SPLIT**   No need to split or not yet ready to split.

■ **NOTHING TO MERGE**   Not yet ready to merge.

■ **SPLITTING**   Split is in progress.

■ **SPLIT DONE**   Completed the split operation.

Other than configuring the `split_threshold` and `merge_threshold` parameters, if default values are not acceptable, there is no other configuration required for enabling automatic split and merge of the destination. It is enabled by default in Oracle 11g R2.

However, if you know the destination is going to be down for a scheduled outage (for example, for some H/W maintenance work or OS patches), you may want to manually split it off from the original Stream environment rather than wait for the automatic mechanism to kick in.

Disabling Automatic Split and Merge

To disable the automatic split and merge feature, the `merge_threshold` and `split_threshold` parameters must be set to the appropriate values using the

SET_PARAMETER procedure of the DBA_CAPTURE_ADM package, as shown in the following example. You can set either of these parameters to disable the split or merge, or set both to disable both operations.

```
begin
  dbms_capture_adm.set_parameter(
    capture_name    => 'DBXA_CAP',
    parameter       => 'MERGE_THRESHOLD',
    value           => '-9'
  );
end;
/

begin
  dbms_capture_adm.set_parameter(
    capture_name    => 'DBXA_CAP',
    parameter       => 'SPLIT_THRESHOLD',
    value           => 'INFINITE'
  );
end;
/
```

Manual Split and Merge

The DBMS_STREAMS_ADM package provides SPLIT_STREAMS and MERGE_STREAMS procedures that can be used to manually split and merge the destinations. These procedures also create scripts that you can run to perform these actions. The scripts can be modified to change their default actions to suit your requirements.

The SPLIT_STREAMS procedure can be used as shown in the following example to create the script that performs all steps required to clone the original capture and propagation processes. If the perform_actions parameter is set to TRUE, then the procedure will automatically run the generated script to split Streams environment. You can only create the script by setting the parameter to FALSE, and then run it manually. We have set it to FALSE. Also, the `auto_merge_threshold` parameter is set to NULL. This means that the merge will not take place automatically and we will need to run the MERGE_STREAMS procedure manually. To automatically run the merge process, we need to specify the names for the job schedule and the scheduled job, and set `auto_merge_threshold` to a non-zero value.

```
declare
  schedule_name varchar2(30);
  job_name varchar2(30);
begin
  schedule_name := 'auto_merge_sched';
  job_name      := 'auto_merge_job';
```

```
dbms_streams_adm.split_streams(
   propagation_name         => 'DBXA_TO_DBXC_PROP',
   cloned_propagation_name  => 'CLONE_DBXA_TO_DBXC_P',
   cloned_queue_name        => 'CLONE_DBXA_CAP_Q',
   cloned_capture_name      => 'CLONE_DBXA_CAP',
   perform_actions          => FALSE,
   script_name              => 'split_streams.sql',
   script_directory_object  => 'STREAMS_DP_DIR',
   auto_merge_threshold     => NULL,
   schedule_name            => schedule_name,
   merge_job_name           => job_name
   );
end;
/
```

After correcting the problem with the destination, the cloned capture process must be started to begin replicating data to the destination:

```
exec dbms_capture_adm.start_capture('CLONE_DBXA_CAP');
```

At this time, both the original and cloned capture processes are running. The progress of these processes should be monitored using the following query:

```
select capture_name,
       to_char(capture_message_create_time, 'mm/dd/yy hh24:mi:ss')
  from v$streams_capture;
```

When little difference exists between the message create time for the cloned capture process and the message create time for the original capture process, run the following procedure to create the script for the merging of these processes:

```
begin
   dbms_streams_adm.merge_streams(
     cloned_propagation_name => 'CLONE_DBXA_TO_DBXC_P',
     perform_actions         => FALSE,
     script_name             => 'merge_streams.sql',
     script_directory_object => 'STREAMS_DP_DIR'
   );
end;
/
```

When the script merge_streams.sql runs successfully, the original capture and propagation processes will be left running. The script will remove the cloned processes and associated components.

Streams Performance Advisor

With the introduction of Streams Performance Advisor in Oracle Database 11*g*, monitoring the overall performance of Streams to identify bottlenecks has become very easy. Oracle uses the term *Streams topology* to represent the databases and Streams components, and the message flow in the Streams replication environment.

The messages that flow between the Streams components follow different paths to reach the destination. The path begins with the capture process and ends when the message is dequeued by the apply process. On the way, the message may pass through one or more propagation processes in its path.

The DBMS_STREAMS_ADVISOR_ADM package and a set of data dictionary views are part of the Streams Performance Advisor framework. The ANALYZE_ CURRENT_PERFORMANCE procedure in this package gathers information about the Streams topology and the performance of the Streams components and various Streams paths in the Streams environment. Such information includes the capture rate, enqueue rate, and latency for the capture process; the messages send rate, latency, and network bandwidth for the propagation process; and the message apply rate, transaction apply rate, and latency for the apply process.

NOTE
The Streams Performance Advisor package does not gather information about the synchronous capture process.

The gathered performance information is visible through the following data dictionary views:

- **DBA_STREAMS_TP_COMPONENT**   Contains information about each Streams component at each database in the Streams environment

- **DBA_STREAMS_TP_COMPONENT_LINK**   Contains information about how messages flow between various Streams components

- **DBA_STREAMS_TP_COMPONENT_STAT**   Contains temporary performance statistics and session statistics about each Streams component

- **DBA_STREAMS_TP_DATABASE**   Contains information about each database that contains Streams components

- **DBA_STREAMS_TP_PATH_BOTTLENECK**   Contains temporary information about Streams components that might be slowing down the flow of messages in a Streams path

- **DBA_STREAMS_TP_PATH_STAT**   Contains temporary performance statistics about each Streams path that exists in the Streams topology

Oracle-provided package UTL_SPADV provides procedures to monitor and report Streams performance using the DBMS_STREAMS_ADVISOR_ADM package. The UTL_SPADV package is not installed by default. You must install it under the Streams Administrator schema in the database. Run the script `utlspadv.sql` in the $ORACLE_HOME/rdbms/admin directory. The script will create a number of tables and the UTL_SPADV package with the following procedures:

- **COLLECT_STATS** Gathers performance statistics for Streams components using the Streams Performance Advisor package. You can specify the number of times the advisor runs and its frequency.

- **SHOW_STATS** Produces output to show statistics gathered by COLLECT_STATS.

- **START_MONITORING** Creates and starts a monitoring job that continuously monitors Streams performance at set intervals.

- **STOP_MONITORING** Stops the monitoring job.

- **IS_MONITORING** Reports if the monitoring job is running.

- **ALTER_MONITORING** Alters the parameters of the monitoring job.

In the following example, the COLLECT_STATS procedure runs the Streams Advisor Package 20 times at every 30 seconds:

```
SQL> conn strmadmin/strmadmin@DBXA.WORLD
Connected.
SQL> begin
  2     utl_spadv.collect_stats(
  3         interval => 30,
  4         num_runs => 20
  5     );
  6  end;
  7  /

PL/SQL procedure successfully completed.
```

This procedure will complete after ten minutes based on our specification. To list the gathered statistics, we run the following procedure:

```
SQL> conn strmadmin/strmadmin@DBXA.WORLD
Connected.
SQL> set serveroutput on size unlimited
SQL> spool spadv_stats.log
SQL> begin
  2     utl_spadv.show_stats();
  3  end;
  4  /
```

Here's partial output:

```
LEGEND
<statistics>= <capture> [ <queue> <psender> <preceiver> <queue> ] <apply>
<bottleneck>
<capture>   = '|<C>' <name> <msgs captured/sec> <msgs enqueued/sec> <latency>
                    'LMR' <idl%> <flwctrl%> <topevt%> <topevt>
                    'LMP' (<parallelism>) <idl%> <flwctrl%> <topevt%> <topevt>
                    'LMB' <idl%> <flwctrl%> <topevt%> <topevt>
                    'CAP' <idl%> <flwctrl%> <topevt%> <topevt>
                    'CAP+PS' <msgs sent/sec> <bytes sent/sec> <latency> <idl%>
<flwctrl%> <topevt%> <topevt>
<apply>     = '|<A>' <name> <msgs applied/sec> <txns applied/sec> <latency>
                    'PS+PR' <idl%> <flwctrl%> <topevt%> <topevt>
                    'APR' <idl%> <flwctrl%> <topevt%> <topevt>
                    'APC' <idl%> <flwctrl%> <topevt%> <topevt>
                    'APS' (<parallelism>) <idl%> <flwctrl%> <topevt%> <topevt>
<queue>     = '|<Q>' <name> <msgs enqueued/sec> <msgs spilled/sec> <msgs in
queue>
<psender>   = '|<PS>' <name> <msgs sent/sec> <bytes sent/sec> <latency> <idl%>
<flwctrl%> <topevt%> <topevt>
<preceiver> = '|<PR>' <name> <idl%> <flwctrl%> <topevt%> <topevt>
<bottleneck>= '|<B>' <name> <sub_name> <sessionid> <serial#> <topevt%> <topevt>

OUTPUT
PATH 1 RUN_ID 11 RUN_TIME 2010-MAR-07 11:35:27 CCA Y
|<C> DBXA_CAP 3759 3524 71 LMR 0% 90% 3.3% ""   LMP (1) 6.7% 93.3% 0% "" LMB
6.7% 86.7% 6.7% "" CAP 0% 96.7% 3.3% ""  |<Q> "STRMADMIN"."DBXA_CAP_Q" 3529 0.01
9814  |<PS> =>DBXB.WORLD 3531 1.08E+06 71 0% 100% 0% ""  |<PR> DBXA.WORLD=> 0%
100% 0% ""  |<Q> "STRMADMIN"."DBXA_APP_Q" 3604 0.01 5001  |<A> DBXA_APP 3600 240
71.1 APR 0% 96.7% 3.3% ""  APC 100% 0% 0% ""  APS (4) 33.3% 0% 286.7% "Streams
apply: waiting for dependency"  |<B> DBXA_APP APS 21 3 90.% "Streams apply:
waiting for dependency"

PATH 1 RUN_ID 12 RUN_TIME 2010-MAR-07 11:35:57 CCA Y
|<C> DBXA_CAP 4219 3953 85 LMR 0% 96.7% 3.3% "" LMP (1) 3.3% 86.7% 10% "" LMB
10% 83.3% 6.7% "" CAP 0% 100% 0% ""  |<Q> "STRMADMIN"."DBXA_CAP_Q" 3948 0.01
9818  |<PS> =>DBXB.WORLD 3946 1.2E+06 86 0% 96.7% 3.3% ""  |<PR> DBXA.WORLD=>
3.3% 96.7% 0% ""  |<Q> "STRMADMIN"."DBXA_APP_Q" 3878 0.01 5001  |<A> DBXA_APP
3881 259 87 APR 3.3% 96.7% 0% ""  APC 96.7% 0% 3.3% ""  APS (4) 23.3% 0% 293.3%
"Streams apply: waiting for dependency"  |<B> DBXA_APP APS 21 3 90.% "Streams
apply: waiting for dependency"
```

The legend printed at the beginning is helpful to read this somewhat cryptic information. The bottleneck in this report is clearly identified as the apply server. It is waiting for dependency over 90 percent of the time. We also see that apply process is applying over 3600 LCRs per second, capture process is capturing over 3700 changes per second, and the propagation sender is sending over 3500 messages per second.

The detailed information collected by Streams Performance Advisor is very helpful in monitoring performance of various Streams components and identifying bottlenecks proactively.

Summary

This chapter discussed the important tasks related to managing the Streams components and monitoring the processes. Monitoring the processes for normal operations and issuing alerts when a potential problem is detected is crucial to ensure that your Streams environment is operating smoothly with minimal disruption. In the absence of OEM Grid Control, you can use the provided packaged procedures to manage and monitor all components of the Streams environment. Embedding these procedures in automated shell scripts provides the required monitoring setup. The built-in feature of split and merge virtually eliminates a potential performance impact when one of the several destinations for the single capture encounters a problem. Although split and merge can be performed manually, the automated procedures make this chore completely transparent and error free. Streams Performance Advisor and the procedures in the UTL_ SPADV package make it extremely easy to monitor the entire Streams environment. The gathered information is very helpful to proactively identify problems.

CHAPTER
12

Maintenance and Troubleshooting

nce you implement Streams replication in your environment, maintaining it and troubleshooting any problems is the next challenge. Implementing structural changes to the objects involved in replication requires careful planning and execution, particularly the decision of whether or not to replicate DDL.

Maintaining existing Streams replication involves tasks such as adding and removing replicated objects or destinations. You may also need to remove the entire Streams configuration, or only part of the configuration if multiple Streams processes were defined in the database.

When Streams processes encounter errors, troubleshooting and correcting them become a priority. Errors in the replication environment spell a mismatch of data that could cause serious application problems. Oracle-provided tools and procedures can help identify the source of the problem. The problems and errors encountered in the Streams environment can be broadly divided into two categories: configuration and stability, and performance. Both categories have unique characteristics. Problems associated with configuration and stability may result in Streams process errors, or their termination. Troubleshooting these problems requires a methodical approach. This chapter discusses the tasks involved in adding and removing objects to and from an existing Streams environment, removing all or part of a specific Streams configuration, and troubleshooting problems and handling common apply errors.

Expanding the Streams Environment

Once the Streams environment is operational and you have ironed out all known issues, it should operate flawlessly. However, there will be situations in which changes in the database structures will result in modifications to the Streams environment. In such situations, you may have to add new tables, new schemas, or a new source or destination database to an existing Streams environment, as described in this section.

Before you add tables and schemas to the Streams configuration, query the DBA_STREAMS_UNSUPPORTED view to check what tables will not be replicated.

Adding Objects to the Exiting Streams Environment

Adding tables or schemas to the existing Streams environment is relatively easy. However, which steps you should take depends on how the current replication environment is set up.

Adding Tables

If you have configured Streams replication at the table or schema level and need to add new tables to this environment, follow whichever set of steps provided next best represents your environment.

DML and DDL Operations Will Not Be Performed on the New Table at the Source Database Until After It Is Added to Streams Replication   This is the preferred method, because it enables you to perform a controlled test to confirm that replication is working before the application system begins modifying the table. Application downtime may be required, but all Streams processes can be active during the change.

Perform the following steps:

1. If the apply process has a positive rule set, then add the apply rule for the table using the ADD_TABLE_RULES procedure of the DBMS_STREAMS_ADM package.

2. If required, modify or create the apply handler process or rule-based transformation to address custom processing of the LCR or data conflicts.

3. If the propagation has a positive rule set, then add the propagation rule for the table using the ADD_TABLE_PROPAGATION_RULES procedure of the DBMS_STREAMS_ADM package.

4. If required, modify or create any rule transformation at the propagation level.

5. Add a table capture rule to the positive rule set of the capture process using the ADD_TABLE_RULES procedure of the DBMS_STREAMS_ADM package.

6. Modify or create any rule transformation if required.

7. Perform table instantiation using the Data Pump export and import procedures of the table. Data Pump is preferred because it automatically sets the instantiation SCN for the table at the destination.

8. Perform a controlled test to confirm that changes to this table are replicating as expected. Streams message tracking can be used to troubleshoot any problem or get a confirmation that all is well. Streams message tracking is discussed later in this chapter.

The Propagation or Apply Process Can Be Stopped Until After the Table Is Added to Streams Replication   Perform the following steps:

1. Stop the apply process using the STOP_APPLY procedure of the DBMS_APPLY_ ADM package. Otherwise, stop the propagation process using the STOP_ PROPAGATION procedure of the DBMS_PROPAGATION_ADM package.

2. Complete all the steps described in the previous scenario to add table rules to the Streams processes and perform instantiation.

3. If the apply process was stopped, restart it using the START_APPLY procedure in DBMS_APPLY_ADM. If the propagation process was stopped, restart it using the START_PROPAGATION procedure in DBMS_PROPAGATION_ADM.

The Capture Process Can Be Stopped Until After the Table Is Added to Streams Replication Perform the following steps:

1. Stop the capture process using the STOP_CAPTURE procedure of the DBMS_CAPTURE_ADM package.

2. Complete the steps described in the first scenario to add table rules to the Streams processes and perform instantiation.

3. Restart the capture process using the START_CAPTURE procedure in DBMS_CAPTURE_ADM.

Cannot Stop Streams Processes, or DML and DDL Operations, for a Long Time to Add the Table to Streams Replication A number of steps are required to add an active table or schema to an existing Streams replication in such a situation. It is a more involved process that requires configuration of a temporary additional Streams environment. The apply process needs to be stopped for a while and restarted.

Assume that existing replication from DBXA to DBXB is set up with capture process CAP_A running at DBXA. The propagation process PROP_A sends changes from DBXA to the apply process APP_A in the DBXB database. The Streams queue at DBXA and DBXB is QUEUE_A. To add an active table named SCOTT.EMP to this environment, perform the following steps:

1. Create a new Streams queue QUEUE_B in the DBXA and DBXB databases.

2. Create a new apply process APP_B using QUEUE_B at destination database DBXB, and add an apply rule for the table to the positive rule set of this apply process.

3. Create a new capture process CAP_B using QUEUE_B at source database DBXA, and add a capture rule for the table to the positive rule set of this capture process.

4. Create a new propagation process PROP_B using QUEUE_B at source database DBXA to send changes to QUEUE_B at destination database DBXB, and add a propagation rule for the table to this propagation process.

5. Instantiate the table SCOTT.EMP from the DBXA database to the DBXB database using Data Pump export and import procedures.

6. Start the newly created apply process APP_B and the capture process CAP_B.

7. Add a table rule for the new table SCOTT.EMP to the old capture process CAP_A at the source database.

8. Add a table rule for the new table SCOTT.EMP to the old propagation process PROP_A.

9. At source database DBXA, acquire a shared lock on the SCOTT.EMP table in the DBXA table by issuing the LOCK command:

   ```
   lock table scott.emp in share mode;
   ```

10. From another SQL session on the DBXA database, find out the current SCN from V$DATABASE or by executing the DBMS_FLASHBACK.GET_CURRENT_SCN_NUMBER procedure. This SCN must be obtained after locking the table for a short duration to make sure that no other transactions are changing the table while we get the current SCN.

11. Use the SCN obtained earlier to set the value of the `maximum_scn` parameter for the new capture process CAP_B at source database DBXA, and the old apply process APP_A at destination database DBXB. Use the SET_PARAMETER procedure of the DBMS_CAPTURE_ADM and DBMS_APPLY_ADM packages, respectively.

12. Release the shared lock on the table by issuing a COMMIT.

13. Monitor the apply process APP_A. It will be disabled when the applied SCN reaches the value of the `maximum_scn` parameter. At this time, add table SCOTT.EMP to the apply rule for the APP_A process.

14. Monitor apply process APP_B. When it is idle, stop and remove apply process APP_B, propagation process PROP_B, capture process CAP_A, and queue QUEUE_B from the source and destination databases. How to remove these components is discussed later in this chapter.

15. Set the `maximum_scn` parameter for the old apply process APP_A at destination database to INFINITE.

16. Restart the apply process APP_A at the destination database DBXB.

In summary, the preceding set of steps created a new Streams path that will be merged with the existing path at the end. There will be multiple capture, propagation, and apply processes for the time being.

To keep these tasks as simple as possible, you can possibly design your Streams environment such that it has the most selective rules for the capture process, while the propagation and apply rules are defined globally. That means all captured changes will be propagated and applied. In such environments, adding new tables to the replication environment means adding to the capture rules and performing instantiation. You do not have to modify all Streams components.

Adding Schemas

The procedure to add new schemas to an existing Streams replication at the schema level is similar to adding tables, as discussed in the previous section. The only change is the use of the ADD_SCHEMA_RULES and ADD_SCHEMA_PROPAGATION_RULES procedures of the DBMS_STREAMS_ADM package. Also, adding a schema with a fairly large number of active tables is a bit more complex than adding a few tables. It is therefore suggested that you explore and use one of the options to add tables we discussed in the previous section.

Adding a schema to an existing Streams configuration at the table level will create overlapping rules if the table under the new schema was already part of the existing replication setup. There is nothing wrong with such rules, but you need to be aware of why they exist.

Adding a Database to the Existing Streams Environment

Adding objects to the existing Streams environment is quite easy because the replication infrastructure is already defined and operational. Adding a new source or destination database might be more challenging, depending on the replication requirements.

Adding a Source Database

In environments where the replicated database is primarily used as a reporting database, you may be required to replicate additional schemas or tables from a new source database. The single replicated database can then act as a single reporting database for multiple source databases. In such cases, a new source database can be added by performing the following steps. Assume that the new source database will replicate different objects from those in the existing environment. In addition, also assume that it is a unidirectional replication.

1. Prepare the new source database for Streams. This involves changing initialization parameters as needed, making sure the database is running in ARCHIVELOG mode, and creating the Streams Administrator account with the proper privileges.

2. Create the Streams queue in the current destination database. You may also have to review and increase the allocated Streams pool size.

3. Create a new apply process in the current destination database, and add rules to the apply process for replicated objects as required.

4. Create any apply handler procedure or rule-based transformations, if required, at the apply process.

5. Create the Streams queue at the new source database.

6. Create the propagation process in the new source database using the source queue and the new destination queue.

7. Add rules to the propagation process for replicated objects as required. If needed, define any rule-based transformation.

8. Create the capture process at the new source database and add rules for the replicated objects. Define any rule-based transformation, if required.

9. Create supplemental logging for columns of the replicated tables as required. The default supplemental logging created by the ADD_*_RULES procedure of the DBMS_STREAMS_ADM package may not be sufficient.

10. Use Data Pump export and import procedures to move data for the replicated objects from the new source database to the destination database. This automatically sets the instantiation SCN at the destination database. If the objects were already present and were in sync with the source database, then you can manually set the instantiation SCN.

11. Start the new apply process at the destination database.

12. Start the capture process at the new source database.

13. Once the capture process stabilizes, test the replication.

Adding a Destination Database

An additional new destination database in an existing Streams environment can provide a new resource. Different rules and data transformations for the new environment can provide flexibility in controlling what and how data is replicated.

To add the new database, you can use either of two possible methods: create new capture and propagation processes, or use existing capture and propagation processes. For either method, you first complete the following steps in the destination database:

1. Review and modify the initialization parameters, including the Streams pool size.

2. Create the Streams Administrator account and grant required privileges.

3. Create the Streams queue for the apply process.

4. Create the apply process and add rules for the replicated objects, if required.

5. Configure any conflict handler or error handler for the apply process.

Complete the Streams configuration at the source database as outlined next, depending on the method you choose to send captured LCRs to the destination database.

Creating New Capture and Propagation Processes   This is similar to configuring a brand new replication environment. The source database already has a Streams Administrator account defined. If required, you can create a new Streams Administrator account for this new environment and grant the required privileges. You may need to review and increase the Streams pool size, as multiple capture processes will be using the same memory for staging LCRs.

Complete the following steps at the source database to configure replication to the new destination:

1. Create a new Streams queue.

2. Create a new propagation process that uses the new queue as the source to send LCRs to the queue on the destination database.

3. Add rules to the propagation process for replicated objects as required. If needed, define any rule-based transformation.

4. Create the capture process at the source database and add rules for the replicated objects. Define any rule-based transformation, if required.

5. Create supplemental logging for columns of the replicated tables as required. The default supplemental logging created by the ADD_*_RULES procedure of the DBMS_STREAMS_ADM package may not be sufficient.

6. Use Data Pump export and import procedures to move data for the replicated objects from the source database to the new destination database. This will automatically set the instantiation SCN at the destination database. If the objects were already present and were in sync with the source, then you can manually set the instantiation SCN.

7. Start the apply process at the destination database.

8. Start the new capture process at the source database.

9. Once the capture process stabilizes, test the replication.

In this method, there will be two LogMiner sessions mining the same log files for each of the capture processes.

Using Exiting Capture and Propagation Processes   In this method, the propagation process at the source database will send the LCR to two destinations. After completing the changes in the destination database as outlined earlier, complete the following steps:

1. Use Data Pump export and import procedures to move data for the replicated objects from the source database to the new destination database. This will automatically set the instantiation SCN at the destination database. If the objects were already present and were in sync with the source, then you can manually set the instantiation SCN.

2. Start the apply process at the new destination database.

3. Create a new propagation process that uses the existing Streams queue to send LCRS to the queue on the destination database.

4. Add rules to the propagation process for replicated objects as required. If needed, define any rule-based transformation.

5. Test the replication to the new destination.

By default, Oracle will use the split and merge feature of Streams since there are now two destinations for the same propagation. If you do not wish to use this feature, you need to modify the capture process parameters.

Removing Streams Configuration

Occasionally, you may need to remove the Streams configuration from the database. This is particularly true when cloning databases with Streams configuration from one environment to the other. The new environment may not need Streams replication or may need to be reconfigured differently.

If you run into the unfortunate situation of an unrecoverable error with Streams processes, Oracle Support may ask you to re-create the problematic component after dropping it. This solution is much more preferable than rebuilding the entire replication environment.

This section first describes how to remove the entire Streams configuration and then how to remove specific replicated objects and specific Streams components.

Removing Entire Streams Configuration

Removing the entire Streams configuration means all the defined Streams components are dropped from the database. The DBMS_STREAMS_ADM package provides the procedure REMOVE_STREAMS_CONFIGURATION for this purpose. The procedure should be run as SYSDBA or Streams Administrator as shown in the following example:

```
begin
  dbms_streams_adm.remove_streams_configuration();
end;
/
```

The procedure removes the entire Streams setup from the database. It requires no parameters, and it does not allow you to choose which components to remove. If there were multiple capture, propagation, and apply processes defined, all of them are removed by the procedure.

NOTE
The REMOVE_STREAMS_CONFIGURATION procedure does not remove Streams queue table and associated internal tables, indexes, and views.

Sometimes you may need to remove only particular capture, propagation, and apply processes along with their associated rules and queues. To achieve this, removing specific components associated with these processes is required, as described next.

Removing Specific Streams Configuration

It is not unusual to have multiple capture, propagation, and apply processes defined in the database. But if you want to remove only a specific set of these processes and associated Streams components, Oracle provides no one script or procedure to achieve this. The Streams processes and components involved must be removed individually. In addition to the names of these processes, you also need to know the names of the associated rule set, queue, and queue table to remove them.

Once you gather all the required information, perform the following steps:

1. Stop and drop the capture process at the source database.

2. Stop and drop the propagation process at the source database.

3. Stop and drop the apply process at the destination database.

4. Stop and drop the Streams queue at the source database.

5. Stop and drop the Streams queue at the destination database.

6. Remove the Streams queue tables used at the source and destination databases.

7. Drop the rule sets, if not already dropped, along with the Streams processes.

The next several sections describe how to remove specific components of the Streams configuration as well as dropping Streams related objects from the database.

Removing Tables or Schemas from Streams Replication

When a table or a schema does not need to be replicated, it can be removed from replication by simply adding a rule to the negative rule set of the Streams process in question. However, the objects remain defined in the replication environment. The Streams process will ignore the LCRs for those objects.

You can also remove, and drop, the associated rule from the positive rule set of the Streams process to stop replicating changes for the table or schema. If the replication was configured at the schema or global level, removing a table from such replication using a negative rule set is recommended. If the replication was configured at the table or schema level, you can simply remove the associated rule from the positive rule set.

The following example removes the SCOTT.BONUS table from the schema-level replication by adding a rule to the negative rule set of the capture process. Since we do not replicate this table to more than one destination, we are removing it from the capture process itself.

```
SQL> conn strmadmin/strmadmin@DBXA.WORLD
Connected.
SQL> begin
  2    dbms_streams_adm.add_table_rules (
  3      table_name       => 'SCOTT.BONUS',
  4      streams_type     => 'CAPTURE',
  5      streams_name     => 'DBXA_CAP',
  6      queue_name       => 'DBXA_CAP_Q',
  7      inclusion_rule   => FALSE,
  8      include_dml      => TRUE,
  9      include_ddl      => TRUE,
 10      source_database  => 'DBXA.WORLD'
 11    );
 12  end;
 13  /
PL/SQL procedure successfully completed.
```

To remove a schema from replication in a similar fashion, you would use the ADD_SCHEMA_RULES procedure.

Removing Rules

If a particular rule is not required, it can be removed from the rule set. Once the rule is removed, the rule set evaluates to FALSE for LCRs associated with objects in the rule condition. The Streams process will ignore such LCRs if the rule was part of a positive rule set. If the rule was part of a negative rule set, such LCRs will be processed.

In the following example, we remove a DDL rule associated with the SCOTT schema from the capture process in our schema-level replication. This will in effect stop replication of DDL changes.

First, we find out the rule name, rule set name, and their owner name:

```
SQL> select rule_owner,
  2           rule_name,
  3           rule_set_owner,
  4           rule_set_name
  5    from dba_streams_rules
  6   where schema_name = 'SCOTT'
  7     and streams_name = 'DBXA_CAP'
  8     and rule_type = 'DDL'
  9     and rule_set_type = 'POSITIVE';

RULE_OWNER RULE_NAME  RULE_SET_OWNE RULE_SET_NAME
---------- ---------- ------------- --------------
STRMADMIN  SCOTT8     STRMADMIN     RULESET$_9
```

Next, we remove the rule from the rule set using the REMOVE_RULE procedure in the DBMS_RULE_ADM package:

```
SQL> begin
  2    dbms_rule_adm.remove_rule(
  3      rule_name      => 'STRMADMIN.SCOTT8',
  4      rule_set_name  => 'STRMADMIN.RULESET$_9'
  5    );
  6  end;
  7  /
PL/SQL procedure successfully completed.
```

Rerunning the query to find the rule name should return no rows. The rule itself is not dropped from the database, and it will be listed by the DBA_RULES view.

Dropping Rules

A rule can be dropped from the database regardless of whether or not it is used by any rule set. However, it is a good practice to drop the rule when it is not used by any rule set.

The view DBA_RULE_SET_RULES shows the rules associated with the rule set. Continuing with our previous example, the rule STRMADMIN.SCOTT8 is not listed in this view, and can be safely dropped from the capture database:

```
SQL> select rule_set_owner,
  2         rule_set_name
  3    from dba_rule_set_rules
  4   where rule_name = 'SCOTT8'
  5     and rule_owner = 'STRMADMIN';
no rows selected
```

Now, we can drop the rule from the database using the DROP_RULE procedure of the DBMS_RULE_ADM package:

```
SQL> begin
  2    dbms_rule_adm.drop_rule(
  3      rule_name  => 'STRMADMIN.SCOTT8',
  4      force      => FALSE
  5    );
  6  end;
  7  /
PL/SQL procedure successfully completed.
```

The parameter force denotes whether or not the rule is to be dropped from the database. Setting it to TRUE drops the rule from the database even if it is defined in a rule set. In this example, the parameter force is set to FALSE, which is its default value. Since we already removed the rule from the rule set, this setting drops it from the database.

Dropping Rule Sets

A rule set can be dropped from the database using the DROP_RULE_SET procedure of the DBMS_RULE_ADM package. Assuming that the capture process has RULESET$_9, the following example drops the rule set:

```
SQL> begin
  2    dbms_rule_adm.drop_rule_set(
  3      rule_set_name => 'STRMADMIN.RULESET$_9',
  4      delete_rules  => TRUE
  5    );
  6  end;
  7  /
PL/SQL procedure successfully completed
```

The `delete_rules` parameter is set to TRUE in this example, which means that all rules defined in the rule set are also dropped. The parameter defaults to FALSE, keeping the rules in the database when the rule set is dropped.

The procedure does not warn you if the rule set was associated with any Streams process before dropping it. In our case, we removed RULESET$_9, which was the positive rule set for the capture process. The rule set name will stay associated with the capture process even after the rule set is dropped, and the DBA_CAPTURE view will report it. However, when the capture process tries to evaluate the rule set, it will abort with the ORA-1280 error, and the alert log will report errors similar to the following:

```
ORA-04067: not executed, stored procedure "STRMADMIN.RULESET$_9" does not exist
ORA-01280: Fatal LogMiner Error.
```

Before dropping a rule set, confirm that it is not used by any of the Streams processes. Check the DBA_CAPTURE, DBA_APPLY, and DBA_PROPAGATION views for the rule set name.

Dropping the Apply Process

The following example removes the apply process along with the positive and negative rule sets associated with the apply process. All the system-created rules using the procedures in the DBMS_STREAMS_ADM package will be removed from the database. Manually created rules and the apply handler procedures, if any, will not be removed.

```
SQL> conn strmadmin/strmadmin@DBXB.WORLD
Connected.
SQL> begin
  2    dbms_apply_adm.drop_apply(
  3      apply_name          => 'DBXA_APP',
  4      drop_unused_rule_sets => TRUE
  5    );
  6  end;
  7  /

PL/SQL procedure successfully completed.
```

If the rule set needs to be preserved, set the `drop_unused_rule_sets` parameter to FALSE, which is its default value. You will want to preserve the rule set if you will be re-creating the apply process.

NOTE
The apply process must be stopped before it can be dropped from the database. Otherwise, the ORA-26666 error will be reported.

Dropping the Propagation Process

The following example removes the propagation process along with the rule set associated with the process. Any custom rule transformation procedures associated with the propagation process will not be removed by this procedure.

```
SQL> conn strmadmin/strmadmin@DBXA.WORLD
Connected.
SQL> begin
  2    dbms_propagation_adm.drop_propagation(
  3      propagation_name      => 'DBXA_TO_DBXB_PROP',
  4      drop_unused_rule_sets => TRUE
  5    );
  6  end;
  7  /
PL/SQL procedure successfully completed.
```

If the rule set needs to be preserved, to use it while re-creating the propagation process, set the `drop_unused_rule_sets` parameter to FALSE, which it its default value.

It is possible to drop the propagation process when it is enabled and active. In this case, the capture process will not have a subscriber to dequeue the messages, and it will stop capturing. The STATE of the capture in the V$STREAMS_CAPTURE view will report a `WAITING FOR A SUBSCRIBER TO BE ADDED` message. The alert log will also report a message stating that the propagation sender process ended because the propagation was dropped.

Dropping the Capture Process

The following example removes the capture process along with its rule set. Any custom rule transformation procedures associated with the capture process will not be removed by this procedure.

```
SQL> begin
  2    dbms_capture_adm.drop_capture(
  3      capture_name          => 'DBXA_CAP',
```

```
4      drop_unused_rule_sets => TRUE
5    );
6  end;
7  /
PL/SQL procedure successfully completed.
```

If the rule set must be preserved, set the `drop_unused_rule_sets` parameter to FALSE, which is its default value. You may want to preserve the rule set if the capture process will be re-created to start from a particular SCN.

NOTE
The capture process must be stopped before it can be dropped from the database. Otherwise, the ORA-1338 error will be reported.

Dropping the Streams Queue

To drop the Streams queue from the database, you use the procedure REMOVE_QUEUE in the DBMS_STREAMS_ADM package. The procedure waits until currently enqueued and dequeued transactions are committed, after which it stops the queue, disabling all enqueue and dequeue activity, and then drops the queue from the database. Optionally, it can drop Streams clients that use this queue, and the queue tables associated with the queue.

In the following example, DBXA_CAP_Q is dropped from the capture database, along with the Streams client, the capture process, and the associated queue table:

```
SQL> begin
2    dbms_streams_adm.remove_queue(
3      queue_name              => 'STRMADMIN.DBXA_CAP_Q',
4      cascade                 => TRUE,
5      drop_unused_queue_table => TRUE
6    );
7  end;
8  /
PL/SQL procedure successfully completed.
```

The `cascade` parameter is set to TRUE to direct the procedure to drop the Streams client that uses this queue before dropping the queue itself. The default value of FALSE will not drop the queue if a Streams client used it. In such a case, it will report an error listing the name of the Streams client.

The `drop_unused_queue_table` parameter is set to the default value of TRUE. This means that the associated queue table will be dropped if it was empty or not used by any other queue. A value of FALSE will preserve the queue table.

Dropping Streams Queue Tables

The queue tables can be dropped using the DROP_QUEUE_TABLE procedure in the DBMS_AQADM package as shown in the following example:

```
SQL> begin
  2    dbms_aqadm.drop_queue_table (
  3      queue_table  => 'STRMADMIN.DBXA_CAP_Q_T',
  4      force        => FALSE
  5      );
  6  end;
  7  /

PL/SQL procedure successfully completed.
```

The parameter `force` is set to FALSE, which is its default value. This means that the queue table can only be dropped if it did not have any queues; otherwise, the procedure reports an error. If you set `force` to TRUE, then the procedure first drops the queue and then drops the queue table. In this case, the queue will be dropped even if a Streams client was using it, so be careful with this option.

Troubleshooting Streams Processes

At times, Streams processes may not function as expected due to problems. These problems include not having required archived log files; the listener not running at the destination database server; network glitches causing propagation to stop; too many large transactions slowing down the apply process; or the apply process reporting errors due to missing or inadequate conflict handling. Such problems can cause latency or divergence in the replicated data. This section discusses how to troubleshoot such problems.

Capture Process Troubleshooting

If the capture process is not capturing changes as expected, perform the following checks to troubleshoot and resolve the cause of the problem.

Check the Status of the Capture Process

Make sure the capture process is enabled by selecting the STATUS field from the DBA_CAPTURE view. If it is DISABLED, then the capture process is not running, and you have to start it. If the STATUS is ABORTED, then the ERROR_NUMBER and ERROR_MESSAGE fields of the DBA_CAPTURE view will provide a clue as to why the capture process was aborted. The alert log and capture process trace file will provide additional information.

One reason the capture process may abort is that the LogMiner process has aborted. The LogMiner process may abort due to lack of memory for log mining.

The capture process parameter _sga_size controls the amount of memory, in megabytes, allocated to the LogMiner process. By default, _sga_size is set to 10MB. You can increase this value using the SET_PARAMETER procedure of the DBA_CAPTURE_ADM package. The following example sets the _sga_size parameter to 50MB.

```
SQL> begin
  2     dbms_capture_adm.set_parameter(
  3        capture_name    => 'DBXA_CAP',
  4        parameter       => '_sga_size',
  5        value           => '50');
  6  end;
  7  /

PL/SQL procedure successfully completed.
```

If the replicated tables have columns with the LOB data type, it is a good idea to allocate more memory to _sga_size. Changing this underscore parameter of the capture process is supported by Oracle. The _sga_size memory is allocated from the streams_pool_size memory.

It is also possible that the capture process may abort due to bugs and generate an ORA-600 error. In such cases, you need to work with Oracle Support. Most likely, you will be asked to generate additional tracing information by setting the trace_level parameter of the capture process to a particular value provided by Oracle Support.

Check the State of the Capture Process

If an active capture process has stopped capturing changes, the STATE field of the V$STREAMS_CAPTURE view will report one of the following values. Most problems with the capture process can be identified and corrected by taking actions based on these values of the STATE field.

Paused for Flow Control   This is probably the most common reason for the capture process to stop capturing changes and enqueuing LCRs. This state indicates that an automatic flow control has been enabled to throttle down the message capture process because the propagation and apply processes can't keep up with the rate of message capture. You should check for the following:

- The propagation process is active and performing as expected.

- The apply process is actively dequeuing and applying LCRs.

- The Streams pool is configured large enough, particularly at the destination database.

The PUBLISHER_STATE column of the V$BUFFERED_PUBLISHERS view at the capture database can provide the reason why the flow control has been enabled. If the corresponding apply process at the destination database is running slowly, then flow control likely will be enabled. The apply process may run slowly if it is receiving the LCRs slowly, or the transactions are not being applied faster, for any of a number of reasons. At the destination database, the following data dictionary views provide information related to apply process performance:

■   The V$STREAMS_APPLY_READER view shows the number of LCRs dequeued along with the message creation and message dequeue times.

■   The V$STREAMS_APPLY_SERVER view shows how busy the apply server processes are, and whether they are executing transactions.

■   The V$STREAMS_TRANSACTION view shows the number of transactions along with the number of LCRs in each transaction waiting to be dequeued by the apply reader.

■   The V$SGASTAT view can be queried to check available free memory for the Streams pool. The available free memory indicates if the Streams pool was configured with adequate memory.

To minimize the occurrence of flow control, you can consider the following:

■   Allocate large enough memory for the Streams pool, particularly at the destination database.

■   Tune the apply process so that the transactions can be applied faster. Such tuning may include additional apply servers, reducing the size of the transactions, and removing unnecessary indexes and constraints at the destination database.

■   Simplify the rule conditions for propagation and apply processes. If no rule-based transformation is required, consider removing the rule sets from the propagation and apply processes.

Waiting for Redo   This state indicates that the capture process is waiting for a redo log file to be added to its LogMiner session. This means that the required archived log file is not available for the local capture process. In the case of the downstream capture process, this state indicates that the archived log file has not yet been transferred from the source database. This could be due to lack of activity at the source database, or a network glitch that prevents log file transfer to the downstream database.

Generally, additional information would be displayed with this state, as shown here:

```
WAITING FOR REDO: LAST SCN SCANNED 3180196
```

This means that the capture process has successfully processed all changes up to the displayed SCN. The displayed SCN corresponds to NEXT_SCN in the DBA_REGISTERED_ARCHIVED_LOG view. The capture process is waiting for the next log file that has a FIRST_SCN value equal to the displayed SCN. To correct this problem, the required log file must be made available to the capture process.

In case of archived-log downstream capture process, this message may indicate a problem with the file transfer mechanism. If the redo transport service was supposed to transfer the log file to the downstream database, make sure that the transport service is configured correctly. You may have to manually register the archived log file for the capture process.

If you have configured real-time downstream capture and no redo log files are registered, then you may have to force a log file switch at the source database.

Waiting for Dictionary Redo This state indicates that the capture process needs to access the archived log file that contains the data dictionary information. The message also contains the name of the file the capture process requires:

```
WAITING FOR DICTIONARY REDO: FILE /u02/DBXA/archivelog/DBXA_1_46872_711.arc
```

To correct the problem, you must make the requested log file available for the capture process. If the file is not available, you have to drop and re-create the capture process to use another archived log file that has the data dictionary information.

Waiting for A Subscriber To Be Added This state indicates that the capture queue does not have any subscribers defined or available. This state is possible in both combined capture and apply (CCA) mode and non-CCA mode when the propagation is created with the source queue name not associated with the capture process in question. Check, and correct, the queue name if it is wrong. You will have to re-create the propagation process.

Waiting for *n* Subscriber(s) Initializing This state is possible in CCA mode and indicates that the capture process is awaiting the initialization of the specified number, *n*, of apply processes. The propagation sender process will not start until then. It is possible that the destination database was down or the listener at the destination was down when the capture process was started. Check the alert log file for the ORA errors. If the listener was down, ORA-12541 will be reported. If the database was down, ORA-12564 will be reported. After waiting three minutes for the apply processes to become available, the capture process will change state to CAPTURING CHANGES and the LogMiner sessions will start. However, no LCRs will be enqueued, and messages similar to the following will be reported in the alert log file:

```
CP01: Timed out while waiting Propagation Sender to initialize
....
knlbmEnq: all subscribers are inactive - stop enqueuing
```

After starting the destination listener and/or the database, the enqueuing of LCR will resume automatically. Messages similar to the following will be reported in the alert log of the capture database:

```
Propagation Sender (CCA) DBXA_TO_DBXB_PROP for Streams Capture DBXA_CAP successfully
re-connected to Apply DBXA_APP

Propagation Sender (CCA) DBXA_TO_DBXB_PROP for Streams Capture DBXA_CAP and Apply
DBXA_APP [on destination DBXB.WORLD] with pid=27, OS id=7471 started.

knlbmEnq: some subscribers are active - resume to enqueue
```

Capturing Changes   Typically, this state indicates normal functioning of the capture process. However, this state can be misleading under certain circumstances. In CCA mode, the capture process will eventually switch to this state, as discussed in the previous section, when the destination database or the listener is not available, but it will not enqueue LCRs.

In non-CCA mode, the capture process will report this state, but LCRs may not be enqueued. Check the alert log for the capture database. It may report either a TNS-12564 or TNS-12514 error along with a few other ORA errors. Make sure that the destination database and the listener are running. The destination queue may not be reachable. You may have to bounce the capture process after restarting the destination database and/or the listener.

Propagation Process Troubleshooting

When the propagation process is not working, the destination queue does not receive the LCRs. In most cases, a network error, listener issue, or outage of the destination database causes propagation problems. Therefore, you should first check the accessibility and connectivity to the destination database. You can use the TNSPING command, or a remote SQL session over a database link after making sure that the listener for the destination database is operational. If tnsping does not work, then you may have to use operating system utilities to diagnose any network issues.

If your Streams environment was just created, it is possible that the propagation process is not using the correct source queue and destination queue names. Check the source and destination queues for the propagation in question. The following

query can be used to verify the source and destination queue names for the
propagation in question:

```
SQL> select a.source_queue_owner ||'.'||
  2             a.source_queue_name ||'@'||
  3             b.global_name  source_queue_name,
  4             a.destination_queue_owner ||'.'||
  5             a.destination_queue_name  ||'@'||
  6             a.destination_dblink destination_queue_name
  7    from dba_propagation a,
  8         global_name b
  9   where a.propagation_name = 'DBXA_TO_DBXB_PROP';

SOURCE_QUEUE_NAME                 DESTINATION_QUEUE_NAME
-------------------------------   -------------------------------
STRMADMIN.DBXA_CAP_Q@DBXA.WORLD   STRMADMIN.DBXA_APP_Q@DBXB.WORLD
```

If the queue names are not correct for the propagation, then you have to drop
and re-create the propagation process using the correct queue names.

If your Streams environment has been operational, then it is possible that the
propagation process is either disabled or aborted for some reason.

In non-CCA mode, when the propagation is disabled or aborted, the ERROR_
MESSAGE and ERROR_DATE fields in the DBA_PROPAGATION view will be
populated. The error message can provide clues as to why propagation has failed. The
propagation process will be aborted after the propagation schedule encounters 16
consecutive errors when connecting to the destination queue. The following queries
can be used to check the status of the propagation process and the number of failures:

```
SQL> select status
  2    from dba_propagation
  3   where propagation_name = 'DBXA_TO_DBXB_PROP';

STATUS
--------
ABORTED

SQL> col disabled heading 'Prop Sched Disabled?'  for a20
SQL> select decode(schedule_disabled, 'Y','Yes','No') disabled,
  2             failures
  3    from dba_queue_schedules
  4   where qname = 'DBXA_CAP_Q'
  5     and message_delivery_mode = 'BUFFERED'
  6  /

Prop Sched Disabled?   FAILURES
--------------------   ----------
Yes                          16
```

After you make sure that the destination listener and database are up and running and that there are no other network problems in reaching the destination database from where the propagation is running, you need to restart the propagation process. The failures count, if non-zero, will not reset to zero until the next successful transmission of the LCR to the destination queue.

In CCA mode, the propagation sender process, which is part of the capture process, stops when the destination database becomes unavailable. The only indication of a problem is the following error message written to the alert log file of the capture database:

```
knlbmEnq: all subscribers are inactive - stop enqueuing
```

Along with this error message, there will be a TNS-12564 error reported.

If you do not have any mechanism to alert you of the destination database failure, this error may go unnoticed because the DBA_PROPAGATION view will still show the propagation as ENABLED, and the STATE of the capture process will be CAPTURING CHANGES. However, there will not be any enqueuing of the LCRs. Propagation of the LCRs will resume automatically when the destination database becomes accessible. Messages similar to the following will appear in the alert log file:

```
Propagation Sender (CCA) DBXA_TO_DBXB_PROP for Streams Capture DBXA_CAP successfully
re-connected to Apply DBXA_APP

knlbmEnq: some subscribers are active - resume to enqueue
```

Apply Process Troubleshooting

If the apply process is not applying changes as expected, perform the following steps to troubleshoot and resolve the cause of the problem:

Check the Status of Apply Process

When the apply process is functioning normally, the STATUS column of the DBA_ APPLY view reports ENABLED.

If the status is DISABLED or ABORTED, then, of course, the LCRs are not applied to destination tables. If the apply process is disabled, then you must start it again and verify that the status changes to ENABLED. If the apply process is aborted, then you need to find out why it was aborted before attempting to start it. The following query can be used to get the time at which the apply process aborted. The error number and message can provide a clue as to why the process aborted.

```
SQL> select status_change_time,
  2         error_number,
  3         error_message
  4    from dba_apply
  5   where status = 'ABORTED'
  6     and apply_name = 'DBXA_APP';
```

```
STATUS_CHANGE_TIME    ERROR_NUMBER ERROR_MESSAGE
------------------- ------------ ------------------------------
03/13/2010 15:32:31          26714 ORA-26714: User error encounte
                                    red while applying
```

In this example, it is clear from the error message that the apply process aborted when applying a change. In this case, the DBA_APPLY_ERROR view can provide additional details about why there was an error. How to troubleshoot such an error is discussed a bit later in this section.

Check the Apply Process Configuration

The apply process can apply LCRs that were staged in a buffer queue or a persistent disk queue. However, the same apply process cannot be used to process LCRs from both these queues. If the LCR is captured using a synchronous capture process, then the apply process must be configured differently from how it is configured for the LCRs captured by an asynchronous capture process. The LCRs in the latter are called *captured LCRs*, and an apply process must be configured to process captured LCRs.

The following query shows how to check the configuration of the apply process for the type of LCRs in question:

```
SQL> col apply_captured heading 'LCRs Applied' for a30
SQL> select decode(apply_captured,
  2                  'YES', 'From Buffered Queue',
  3                  'NO', 'From Persistent Queue'
  4               ) apply_captured
  5    from dba_apply
  6   where apply_name = 'DBXA_APP';

LCRs Applied
------------------------
From Buffered Queue
```

If the apply process is not applying the LCRs from the proper queue, then depending on the capture process type, you will have to drop and re-create the apply process.

Check the Latency of the Apply Process

Sometimes the apply process may be slow in applying the recent change that you wanted to see at the destination. Check the apply process latency using the V$STREAMS_APPLY_READER view, as discussed in Chapter 11. There are a number of factors that can adversely affect apply latency. If the latency is at an unacceptable level, you may want to consider increasing the apply process parallelism or pursuing other tuning efforts to speed up the apply process. These may include reducing the number of indexes on destination tables, reducing the transaction size at the source database, modifying the Oracle Net parameters in a WAN environment (more about this in Appendix A), removing unnecessary referential integrity constraints from destination tables, and so forth.

Check the Receipt of Messages by the Apply Queue

Of course, the apply process cannot apply the changes unless the LCRs reach the intended apply queue. You can monitor the V$STREAMS_APPLY_READER view to confirm that it is dequeuing messages correctly. If it is not, then the problem lies with the rules and the configuration of the capture and propagation processes. Make sure that these processes are defined correctly using correct rules and correct queues. These processes must be enabled and functioning normally. Check the spelling of the schema, table, and database names that appear in the rules involved. If these processes or rules are not configured correctly, you will have to drop and re-create them.

If the LCRs are getting dequeued correctly from the apply queue but you don't see the change being applied, and there are no apply errors reported in the DBA_APPLY_ERROR view, then the problem could be in the apply rules or the apply handler, if defined. Again, confirm that the apply rules are defined correctly without any spelling mistakes.

Check the Custom Apply Handler Procedure

The apply handlers process the LCRs dequeued from the apply queue. If the apply process is not applying changes as expected, and there are handlers defined, then the problem could be with the handler procedures. Depending on the handler functionality, the procedure may or may not apply the LCRs. You may have to review the procedure code and correct it if it is rejecting the wrong LCRs. The following query lists the apply handlers and their types:

```
SQL> col owner for a6
SQL> col tbl heading 'TABLE' for a5
SQL> col opr_name for a8
SQL> col user_procedure for a21
SQL> col handler_name for a18
SQL> set echo on
SQL> select object_owner owner,
  2         object_name tbl,
  3         operation_name opr_name,
  4         user_procedure,
  5         handler_name,
  6         handler_type
  7    from dba_apply_dml_handlers
  8   where apply_name = 'DBXA_APP';
```

OWNER	TABLE	OPR_NAME	USER_PROCEDURE	HANDLER_NAME	HANDLER_TYPE
SCOTT	EMP	INSERT		EMP_INSERT_HANDLER	STMT HANDLER
SCOTT	DEPT	INSERT	"SCOTT"."DML_HANDLER"		PROCEDURE HANDLER
SCOTT	DEPT	UPDATE	"SCOTT"."DML_HANDLER"		PROCEDURE HANDLER
SCOTT	DEPT	DELETE	"SCOTT"."DML_HANDLER"		PROCEDURE HANDLER

Check the Apply User Privileges

Most often, the Streams Administrator with DBA privilege is the apply user, and that user won't encounter problems while applying DML and DDL changes to destination tables, or executing any apply handler process, if defined.

If the apply user does not have proper privileges to apply the change, then the apply process will report an ORA-942 error and the transaction will be written to the apply error queue. The DBA_APPLY_ERROR view will show additional information about the transaction and the error. For the DDL change, ORA-942 will be reported in the alert log file and the trace file for the apply server. To correct this problem, you need to grant proper privileges to the apply user and reapply the error transaction. The privileges can be granted explicitly or via a role.

If there is a custom apply handler defined, and if the apply user was not granted execute privilege on this user procedure, then the apply process will report ORA-6550 and PLS-201 errors in the alert log. The transaction will be written to the apply error queue and will be visible via the DBA_APPLY_ERROR view. After you grant to the apply user the execute privilege, either explicitly or via a role, on the user procedure, you can reapply the error transaction.

If there is a custom rule-based transformation defined, and the apply user is not granted the execute privilege on the user function or procedure, then the apply process will abort without reporting this error in DBA_APPLY_ERROR. The alert log will report ORA-6550 and PLS-201 errors. The propagation receiver process will report the same errors along with additional Information about the LCR in its trace file. You must grant to the apply user the execute privilege, either explicitly or via a role, on the transformation function or procedure before you restart the apply process, or else the apply process will abort again. Note that you will not lose the transaction that encountered the error. After granting the execute privilege to the apply user, you can restart the apply process and it will process the LCR.

Check for Apply Server Contention

In Oracle Database 11*g* R2, by default there will be four apply servers started for the apply process. In addition, the apply parameter `commit_serialization` defaults to DEPENDENT_TRANSACTIONS (which is the same as NONE in earlier releases). This configuration helps improve the performance of the apply process when applying multiple independent transactions. Oracle automatically detects dependent transactions and applies them in proper order. However, when applying independent transactions, it is possible that one apply server may have to wait for a resource used by another apply server, resulting in contention for the resource. Contention can result when the row that the apply server wants to change is locked by an end-user session. This is called *logical contention*. In this case, the apply server waits until the contention is resolved, when the locking session issues a commit or rollback. Contention can also occur when multiple apply servers try to access the same Interested Transaction List (ITL) to lock different rows in the same block. This is called *physical contention*. The server process will keep trying until it succeeds in acquiring access to the block.

An apply server that encounters contention that is not caused by another apply server of the same apply process will wait for the contention to resolve. This causes latency in applying the change. In the case of logical contention, the trace file for the apply process will report messages similar to the following:

```
AP01: [enq: TX - row lock contention] name|mode=54580006, usn<<16 | slot=2000b,
sequence=697
*** 2010-03-19 20:23:40.500
AP01: warning -- apply server 1, sid 16 waiting on user sid 22 for event (since
300 seconds):
AP01: [enq: TX - row lock contention] name|mode=54580006, usn<<16 | slot=2000b,
sequence=697
```

These messages will be repeated every 300 seconds until the contention is resolved. You can track down what session 22 is doing, so that you can take corrective action. At least you now know why the apply process is not moving. The STATE of the apply server in the V$STREAMS_APPLY_SERVER view will be stuck at EXECUTE TRANSACTION until the contention is removed.

On the other hand, if the contention is caused by another apply server of the same apply process, then one of these apply servers will roll back the changes it has applied. This situation can arise if the apply handler process obtains conflicting locks and blocks another apply server of the same apply process. Such contention is automatically resolved by Oracle, and messages similar to the following will be written to the alert log file:

```
AP01: apply server 4 blocked on server 4:
AP01: [enq: TX - row lock contention] name|mode=54580006, usn<<16 | slot=2000b,
sequence=697

AP01: apply server 4 rolled back
```

The view V$STREAMS_APPLY_COORDINATOR reports such rollback information in the column TOTAL_ROLLBACKS. To minimize or eliminate such contention, you may have to reduce apply server parallelism.

If too many apply server processes frequently report WAITING in the STATE column of the V$STREAMS_APPLY_SERVER view while only one server process is executing a transaction, then there is no gain in performance by using apply server parallelism. Such a situation is possible when there are large transactions involved or there is an issue with data integrity constraints. Chapter 13 discusses how to handle large transactions.

Check for Apply Errors

When the apply process encounters an error while applying an LCR, Oracle rolls back any applied changes in the transaction and writes the entire transaction to an apply error queue table on disk. The DBA_APPLY_ERROR view shows information about the transaction in error. The Oracle error number and message provide a clue as to why the error occurred.

Ideally, the DBA_APPLY_ERROR view should report zero rows. When there are errors, each row in this view corresponds to one transaction that may contain one or more LCRs. The LCRs may represent changes to one or more tables. Any unresolved apply error means the data in one or more tables has diverged from the source database. You should monitor the number of rows in the DBA_APPLY_ERROR view and correct any errors in a timely fashion to avoid data divergence. How to correct some of the common apply errors is discussed a bit later in the chapter.

Table 12-1 lists and describes the columns in the DBA_APPLY_ERROR view.

Column Name	Description
APPLY_NAME	Name of the apply process at the local database that encountered the error
QUEUE_NAME	Name of the queue from which the transaction was dequeued
QUEUE_OWNER	Name of the queue owner
LOCAL_TRANSACTION_ID	Transaction ID that encountered the error in the local database
SOURCE_DATABASE	Global name of the source database where the transaction originated
SOURCE_TRANSACTION_ID	Transaction ID at the source database
SOURCE_COMMIT_SCN	SCN at the source database when the transaction was committed
MESSAGE_NUMBER	Serial number for the LCR in the transaction that caused the error
ERROR_NUMBER	Oracle error number for the error
ERROR_MESSAGE	Oracle error message for the error
RECIPIENT_ID	User ID for the original user that applied the transaction
RECIPIENT_NAME	Name of the original user that applied the transaction
MESSAGE_COUNT	Total number of LCRs in the error transaction
ERROR_CREATION_TIME	Timestamp of when the error occurred
SOURCE_COMMIT_POSITION	Reserved for internal use

TABLE 12-1.   *Columns of DBA_APPLY_ERROR View*

Starting from Oracle Database 11g, the error message has been enhanced to provide information that can help speed up error correction. Also, reviewing the data in the LCR that caused the error can be of immense help in identifying the cause of the error, and can also help in correcting the data. Oracle provides procedures to display the contents of the LCRs in the error transaction.

Displaying Error Transaction Information I recommend that as a part of configuring Streams, you create the procedures that are used to display detailed information about the LCRs and transactions that caused the apply error. Oracle provides the required PL/SQL procedures, which are listed in the section "Displaying Detailed Information About Apply Errors" of Chapter 26, "Monitoring Oracle Streams Apply Processes," in *Oracle Streams Concepts and Administration, 11g Release 2 (11.2)*. I suggest that you create these procedures under the Streams Administrator schema in all databases running apply processes. Run the scripts listed under Step 2, Step 3, Step 4, and Step 5 in order. The PRINT_ERRORS procedure will print the contents of all LCRs from all the error transactions. The PRINT_TRANSACTION procedure will print the same for the supplied local transaction ID. The output from these procedures can be overwhelming to read if the transaction had a large number of LCRs.

NOTE
The Oracle-provided script in Step 2 does not print column data for certain data types, such as NVARCHAR, NCHAR, and so forth. You will need to modify the script to print column data for these data types.

I recommend that you create the following procedure in addition to those just described. Run it as the last step. The PRINT_ERROR_LCR procedure will only print the contents of the LCR that caused the error. It will print all such LCRs from all error transactions in the apply error queue.

```
CREATE OR REPLACE PROCEDURE print_error_lcr IS
  CURSOR c IS
    SELECT LOCAL_TRANSACTION_ID,
           SOURCE_DATABASE,
           MESSAGE_NUMBER,
           ERROR_NUMBER,
           ERROR_MESSAGE
      FROM DBA_APPLY_ERROR
      ORDER BY SOURCE_DATABASE, SOURCE_COMMIT_SCN;
  i      NUMBER;
  txnid  VARCHAR2(30);
  source VARCHAR2(128);
  msgnbr NUMBER;
  errnum NUMBER := 0;
```

```
   errno  NUMBER;
   errmsg VARCHAR2(255);
   lcr    SYS.AnyData;
   r      NUMBER;
BEGIN
  FOR r IN c LOOP
    errnum := errnum + 1;
    msgnbr := r.MESSAGE_NUMBER;
    txnid  := r.LOCAL_TRANSACTION_ID;
    source := r.SOURCE_DATABASE;
    errmsg := r.ERROR_MESSAGE;
    errno  := r.ERROR_NUMBER;
    DBMS_OUTPUT.PUT_LINE('**************************************************');
    DBMS_OUTPUT.PUT_LINE('----- ERROR #' || errnum);
    DBMS_OUTPUT.PUT_LINE('----- Local Transaction ID: ' || txnid);
    DBMS_OUTPUT.PUT_LINE('----- Source Database: ' || source);
    DBMS_OUTPUT.PUT_LINE('-----LCR with Error: ' || msgnbr);
    DBMS_OUTPUT.PUT_LINE('----Error Number: '||errno);
    DBMS_OUTPUT.PUT_LINE('----Message Text: '||errmsg);
    DBMS_OUTPUT.PUT_LINE('--message: ' || msgnbr);
        lcr := DBMS_APPLY_ADM.GET_ERROR_MESSAGE(msgnbr, txnid);
        print_lcr(lcr);
  END LOOP;
END print_error_lcr;
/
```

The following examples show how to run these procedures:

```
SQL> connect strmadmin/strmadmin@DBXB.WORLD
SQL> set serveroutput on size unlimited

SQL> spool apply_error_details.log
-- Print contents of all LCRs in all error transactions
SQL> exec print_errors;

-- Print contents of all LCRs in one error transaction
-- Requires Local Transaction ID from DBA_APPLY_ERROR
SQL> exec print_transaction (ltxnid => '10.3.2347');

-- Print contents of the LCR from all error transactions
-- that caused error.
SQL> exec print_error_lcr;

SQL> spool off
```

OEM Grid Control 10.2.0.5 (discussed in Chapter 14) provides an easy interface to manage apply errors. If there are only a few such errors, you can diagnose the problematic transaction and associated tables and mismatched records using Grid Control. However, if you have, for some unknown reason, many apply errors, then the previously described diagnosis using scripts will be a better choice. You can customize these scripts easily to find the cause of the errors so that you can arrive at solutions faster.

Identifying Common Apply Errors   In a properly configured Streams environment, you should not encounter apply errors. However, when errors do occur, there are a few errors that are more common than others. The following list discusses these more common errors and how to correct and avoid them:

■ **ORA-26687 Instantiation SCN Not Set**   This error occurs when the instantiation SCN for the destination table is not set. The view DBA_APPLY_ INSTANTIATED_OBJECTS lists all the objects that are set up with the instantiation SCN. The objects may not have proper instantiation SCNs if you created the objects at the destination database without preparing them for instantiation at the source database.

The error message will list the object that is missing. The instantiation SCN for the missing object can be set using one of the following methods:

■ Export the objects from the source database and import them into the destination. Use the CONSISTENT option for `exp`, and the STREAMS_ INSTANTIATION option for `imp`.

■ Use Data Pump export and import procedures.

■ Manually use the applicable procedure in the DBMS_APPLY_ADM package (SET_TABLE_INSTANTIATION_SCN, SET_SCHEMA_INSTANTIATION_SCN, or SET_GLOBAL_INSTANTIATION_SCN).

■ **ORA-01403 No Data Found**   This error occurs in two situations. First, when the apply process does not find the row to delete or update. Second, when the apply process finds the row to update or delete, but the row columns do not match the old values in the LCR. Starting from Oracle Database 11g, Oracle has modified reporting of such errors with additional information and new ORA errors to clearly distinguish between these two situations. The ORA-26786 and ORA-26787 errors will be reported as described next.

■ **ORA-26786 Row Has Conflicting Columns**   This error occurs when the apply process tries to update or delete rows but some of the row column values do not match the old values of the corresponding columns in the LCR. This means that the destination table row has diverged from the source. The error message will be self-explanatory and will contain the list of the columns that do not match, as shown in the following example. The LOC column in the SCOTT.DEPT table at the destination database has a different value than the old value for the LOC column in the LCR.

```
ORA-26786: A row with key ("DEPTNO") = (20) exists but has conflicting  column(s)"LOC"
in table SCOTT.DEPTORA-01403: no data found
```

You can print the LCR that caused the error to see the old values of the columns. Depending on the replication configuration, you can resolve this error in one of several ways:

- Update the row to the old values that the LCR expects, and re-execute the transaction in error. Be careful that you do not replicate this change if there was another capture process set up to replicate changes to this table to other destinations. Use the Streams tag feature to avoid capturing this change.

- Update the row in the destination table to match the source, and delete the apply error, if the error transaction only has one LCR. If the transaction affected other tables, then consider the previous option.

- Suppress the default comparison of old and new values of all non-key columns and re-execute the transaction. However, this option will not work if the table contains LONG or LOB columns.

- Define a temporary DML or error handler procedure that resolves column discrepancies in an acceptable way, and re-execute the error transaction. If the temporary handler procedure is very specific for only the LCR in error, you may want to stop the apply process when correcting this error, or else other errors may get ignored.

To avoid this error in the future, you can deploy an error handler, a conflict handler, or a DML handler for the apply process. In unidirectional replication, you can also consider suppressing old value comparisons.

- **ORA-26787 Row Does Not Exist** This error occurs when the apply process fails to find the row to update or delete using the key columns in the LCR, or the defined apply columns that act as key columns. The error message will be self-explanatory and will contain the key columns, as shown here:

```
ORA-26787: The row with key ("DEPTNO") = (40) does not exist in table SCOTT.DEPT
ORA-01403: no data found
```

To correct this error, you can take one of the following steps:

- If possible, create the row in the destination table using the old values from the LCR for the columns, and re-execute the error transaction.

- If this was a DELETE operation, and if there was only one LCR in the transaction, then you may simply delete the transaction from the error queue.

- If this was an UPDATE operation, then you can use a conflict handler or error handler procedure to resolve the column discrepancies or to change it to an INSERT operation.

■ **ORA-26688 Missing Key In LCR** This error occurs when the LCR does not contain enough information to apply it to the destination table. To compute transaction dependencies, the apply process requires the values of the primary columns of the destination table. If there is no primary key defined, then the values of the apply key columns must be present in the LCR. In addition, when apply server parallelism is greater than 1, then the apply process requires values for any indexed column at the destination table.

When the supplemental logging of required columns is not specified at the source database, then the LCR does not contain the values for the required columns. In this case, review the supplemental logging at the source database by querying DBA_LOG_GROUPS and DBA_LOG_GROUP_COLUMNS.

To correct this error, you can define a procedure DML handler that modifies the LCR to include required information, and then re-execute the transaction. To avoid this error in the future, define supplemental logging of all required columns at the source database.

Dispose of Error Transactions

The transactions in the error queue will be persistent; they will not be removed automatically. You can either re-execute the transactions after correcting the data that caused the error, or manually delete them. The DBMS_APPLY_ADM package provides procedures to perform those actions, as described next.

Re-executing the Error Transaction You can execute either one transaction in error or all transactions in error by using the EXECUTE_ERROR procedure or EXECUTE_ALL_ERRORS procedure, respectively, of the DBMS_APPLY_ADM package.

If you want to re-execute an individual error transaction, use the EXECUTE_ERROR procedure, as shown here:

```
SQL> begin
  2    dbms_apply_adm.execute_error(
  3        local_transaction_id  => '5.11.1723',
  4        execute_as_user       => FALSE,
  5        user_procedure        => NULL
  6    );
  7 end;
  8 /
PL/SQL procedure successfully completed.
```

The `execute_as_user` parameter is set to the default value of FALSE, meaning that the transaction will be executed under the security domain of the original apply user. If set to TRUE, the current user will act as the apply user and will need proper privileges to execute the transaction. The `user_procedure` parameter is also left to the default value of NULL. You can specify a handler procedure that can manipulate the LCR to resolve the error. Both these parameters can be ignored if you do not want to use these options.

If you want to re-execute all the error transactions, then you can use the EXECUTE_ALL_ERRORS procedure, as shown here:

```
SQL> begin
  2     dbms_apply_adm.execute_all_errors(
  3        apply_name       => 'DBXA_APP',
  4        execute_as_user => FALSE
  5     );
  6  end;
  7  /
PL/SQL procedure successfully completed.
```

If there is more than one apply process in the destination database, then the `apply_name` parameter must be specified. The `execute_as_user` parameter has the same meaning as discussed previously. If there is only one apply process, then both these parameters can be omitted.

If there is more than one error transaction, and you want to execute only some of those transactions individually using the EXECUTE_ERROR procedure, then you should exercise caution. The transactions could be dependent on other transactions in error. If the dependency order is not followed, you may create new errors. The DBA_APPLY_ERROR view provides the source commit SCN and the error creation time. Use this information to determine the order in which you should re-execute the transactions.

The EXECUTE_ALL_ERRORS procedure re-executes all error transactions in proper order.

Deleting the Error Transaction   When you are certain that the transaction in the apply error queue is no longer required, you can delete it manually. Use extreme caution when deleting transactions from the error queue.

The DELETE_ERROR or DELETE_ALL_ERRORS procedure in the DBMS_APPLY_ ADM package can be used to delete one transaction or all transactions, respectively, from the error queue, as shown in the following examples:

```
SQL> begin
  2     dbms_apply_adm.delete_error(
  3        local_transaction_id   => '2.25.1718'
  4     );
  5  end;
SQL> /
PL/SQL procedure successfully completed.
```

```
SQL> begin
  2    dbms_apply_adm.delete_all_errors(
  3      apply_name      =>   'DBXA_APP'
  4    );
  5  end;
  6  /
PL/SQL procedure successfully completed.
```

If more than one apply process is defined in the database, then you must specify the apply process to delete related error transactions; otherwise, error transactions for all apply processes will be removed from the error queue.

Streams Message Tracking

The most frustrating moment in Streams replication comes when you do not see the change you made at the source database replicated to the destination database. You make sure all processes are up and running, the change is committed, and no error is reported by the apply process, yet the change doesn't appear in the destination database. So, how do you troubleshoot this problem? Do you open a Service Request (SR) for help from Oracle Support?

Before going the SR route, there is something very easy you can try that most likely will help you find the root cause of the problem. The DBMS_STREAMS_ADM package contains a procedure called SET_MESSAGE_TRACKING. The procedure sets a tracking label in the LCR for the changes captured. If not specified, the default name Streams_tracking is used. The LCR will then be tracked as it flows through the various components of Streams. By default, the dynamic performance view V$STREAMS_MESSAGE_TRACKING will be populated with relevant information about the LCR. This information includes the component names and types that processed the LCR.

Monitoring the contents of the V$STREAMS_MESSAGE_TRACKING view will show how the LCR propagated through the Streams flow and where it stopped, or got ignored. You can then check the associated rule set that may have rejected the LCR due to lack of proper rule condition, misspelled table name, or the handler process that somehow did not execute the LCR.

For troubleshooting purposes, the tracking label should be set for the session before performing the DML or DDL change that is to be tracked.

The following example shows how to track an LCR. Streams is configured at the schema level for the SCOTT schema in the source database DBXA.WORLD and the destination database DBXB.WORLD.

```
SQL>conn strmadmin/strmadmin@DBXA.WORLD
Connected.
-- Set tracking label and actions to populate
-- v$streams_message_tracking view.
SQL> begin
  2    dbms_streams_adm.set_message_tracking(
  3      tracking_label => 'TRACK_LCRS',
```

```
  4    actions         => DBMS_STREAMS_ADM.ACTION_MEMORY
  5    );
  6  end;
  7  /
PL/SQL procedure successfully completed.


-- Check tracking label for session.
SQL> col tracking_label for a15
SQL> select dbms_streams_adm.get_message_tracking() tracking_label
  2    from dual;

TRACKING_LABEL
---------------
TRACK_LCRS

-- Update a row in SCOTT.DEPT table.
SQL> update scott.dept set loc = 'PARIS' where deptno=10;
1 row updated.
SQL> commit;
Commit completed.
```

Now, let us see the tracking information from the V$STREAMS_MESSAGE_TRACKING view. The ACTION and ACTION_DETAILS columns are combined to show what the Streams component did with the LCR.

```
-- List tracking information
SQL>@show_tracking.sql
SQL> set lines 130
SQL> set trimspool on
SQL> col component_name for a17
SQL> col component_type for a20
SQL> col a_d heading 'ACTION/DETAILS' for a40
SQL> col command_type heading 'CMD' for a6
SQL> select component_name,
  2         component_type,
  3         action||'/'|| action_details  a_d,
  4         command_type
  5    from v$streams_message_tracking
  6   where tracking_label = 'TRACK_LCRS'
  7   order by xid, timestamp;


COMPONENT_NAME   COMPONENT_TYPE       ACTION/DETAILS                           CMD
---------------- -------------------- ---------------------------------------- ------
DBXA_CAP         CAPTURE              Created/                                 UPDATE
DBXA_CAP         CAPTURE              Enqueue/                                 UPDATE
DBXA_TO_DBXB_PROP PROPAGATION SENDER  Dequeued/                                UPDATE
DBXA_TO_DBXB_PROP PROPAGATION SENDER  Rule evaluation/positive rule set: "STRM UPDATE
                                      ADMIN"."SCOTT4"
DBXA_TO_DBXB_PROP PROPAGATION SENDER  Rule evaluation/Rule evaluation complete UPDATE
                                      d
DBXA_TO_DBXB_PROP PROPAGATION SENDER  Propagation Sender sent/                 UPDATE
DBXA_CAP         CAPTURE              Created/                                 COMMIT
DBXA_CAP         CAPTURE              Enqueue/                                 COMMIT
```

```
DBXA_TO_DBXB_PROP PROPAGATION SENDER    Dequeued/                          COMMIT
DBXA_TO_DBXB_PROP PROPAGATION SENDER    Rule evaluation/positive rule set: "STRM COMMIT
                                        ADMIN"."SCOTT4"
DBXA_TO_DBXB_PROP PROPAGATION SENDER    Rule evaluation/Rule evaluation complete COMMIT
                                        d
DBXA_TO_DBXB_PROP PROPAGATION SENDER    Propagation Sender sent/           COMMIT
```

Running the same query in the destination database DBXB.WORLD shows that these changes were properly dequeued and applied:

```
COMPONENT_NAME    COMPONENT_TYPE       ACTION/DETAILS                        CMD
----------------  -------------------- ------------------------------------- ------
DBXA_TO_DBXB_PROP PROPAGATION RECEIVER Propagation receiver enqueue/Received fr UPDATE
                                       om propagation sender
DBXA_TO_DBXB_PROP PROPAGATION RECEIVER Rule evaluation/positive rule set: "STRM UPDATE
                                       ADMIN"."SCOTT1"
DBXA_TO_DBXB_PROP PROPAGATION RECEIVER Rule evaluation/Rule evaluation complete UPDATE
                                       d
DBXA_TO_DBXB_PROP PROPAGATION RECEIVER Propagation receiver enqueue/enqueue to  UPDATE
                                       buffered queue (CCA)
DBXA_APP          APPLY READER         Dequeued/buffered queue(CCA)          UPDATE
DBXA_TO_DBXB_PROP PROPAGATION RECEIVER Propagation receiver enqueue/Received fr COMMIT
                                       om propagation sender
DBXA_TO_DBXB_PROP PROPAGATION RECEIVER Rule evaluation/positive rule set: "STRM COMMIT
                                       ADMIN"."SCOTT1"
DBXA_TO_DBXB_PROP PROPAGATION RECEIVER Rule evaluation/Rule evaluation complete COMMIT
                                       d
DBXA_TO_DBXB_PROP PROPAGATION RECEIVER Propagation receiver enqueue/enqueue to  COMMIT
                                       buffered queue (CCA)
DBXA_APP          APPLY READER         Dequeued/buffered queue(CCA)          COMMIT
DBXA_APP          APPLY SERVER         Static statement/                     UPDATE
DBXA_APP          APPLY SERVER         Commit/Commit LCR                     COMMIT
```

The last two lines in this example confirm that the UPDATE and COMMIT operations were processed by the apply server.

Now, suppose that the STRMADMIN.SCOTT1 rule was removed from the apply rule set. This will cause no apply errors, but the LCR will be ignored as the rule evaluation will fail. We will see no changes applied to SCOTT's tables. The tracking information will look like the following:

```
COMPONENT_NAME    COMPONENT_TYPE       ACTION/DETAILS                        CMD
----------------  -------------------- ------------------------------------- ------
DBXA_TO_DBXB_PROP PROPAGATION RECEIVER Propagation receiver enqueue/Received fr UPDATE
                                       om propagation sender
DBXA_TO_DBXB_PROP PROPAGATION RECEIVER Rule evaluation filtering/positive rule  UPDATE
                                       set name: "STRMADMIN"."RULESET$_3"
DBXA_TO_DBXB_PROP PROPAGATION RECEIVER Rule evaluation/Rule evaluation complete UPDATE
                                       d
DBXA_TO_DBXB_PROP PROPAGATION RECEIVER Propagation receiver enqueue/Received fr COMMIT
                                       om propagation sender
DBXA_TO_DBXB_PROP PROPAGATION RECEIVER Rule evaluation filtering/positive rule  COMMIT
                                       set name: "STRMADMIN"."RULESET$_3"
DBXA_TO_DBXB_PROP PROPAGATION RECEIVER Rule evaluation/Rule evaluation complete COMMIT
                                       d

6 rows selected.
```

The action details indicate that the LCRs for UPDATE and COMMIT were filtered out by the rule set evaluation performed by the propagation receiver, and the LCRs never made it to the apply reader. Correcting the rule set for the proper rule will fix this problem.

The previous examples showed the contents of only a few columns from the V$STREAMS_MESSAGE_TRACKING view. You can also include the source database, object owner, object name, and transaction ID.

The message tracking information is available only via the V$STREAMS_MESSAGE_TRACKING view.

By default, Oracle automatically tracks every 2,000,000th LCR and reports the information in the V$STREAMS_MESSAGE_TRACKING view. This automatic tracking is controlled by the message_tracking_frequency parameter of the capture process. If tracking the LCRs via an interactive session is not possible, then you can lower the value of this parameter to track more LCRs to troubleshoot the problem. Be sure to change the value to reduce the tracking frequency.

Streams Health Check Report

Oracle provides a script to generate a Streams Health Check (HC) report. The report provides comprehensive information about the Streams environment in the database. The report lists configuration problems, if any, and provides Streams process performance statistics. This information can be readily used to identify current and potential problems in Streams configuration and performance of the components. Routinely generating and reviewing this report will provide you with a good understanding of how your replication environment functions under different workloads.

Appendix C discusses how to install and run the Streams Health Check script. It also discusses how to use the report and interpret the reported information.

Data Comparison and Convergence

Oracle Database 11g provides a new package called DBMS_COMPARISON. Although this package is not used by Streams replication as such, you can use it to compare shared database objects at two databases. After comparing the database objects, any differences in the objects can be converged so that the objects are consistent and in sync at these databases. In a Streams replication environment, if the tables get out of sync for whatever reason, the procedures in this package can be used synchronize those tables without performing expensive data movement using export/import, or rebuilding Streams.

The DBMS_COMPARISON package contains a number of procedures and functions that help identify and converge the differences. These are listed and described in Table 12-2.

Function or Procedure	Description
COMPARE function	Performs the specified comparison
CONVERGE procedure	Executes DML changes to synchronize the portion of the database object that was compared in the specified scan
CREATE_COMPARISON procedure	Creates a comparison
DROP_COMPARISON procedure	Drops a comparison
PURGE_COMPARISON procedure	Purges the comparison results, or a subset of the comparison results, for a comparison
RECHECK function	Rechecks the differences in a specified scan for a comparison

TABLE 12-2. *Procedures and Functions in DBMS_COMPARISON Package*

To compare a database object that is shared at two different databases, perform these steps:

1. Run the CREATE_COMPARISON procedure to create a comparison. The comparison identifies the database objects to compare and specifies parameters for the comparison.

2. Run the COMPARE function to compare the database object at the two databases and identify differences. This function returns TRUE when no differences are found and FALSE when differences are found. This function also populates the data dictionary views with comparison results. Separate comparison results are generated for each execution of the COMPARE function.

3. If you want to examine the comparison results, query the following DBA data dictionary views (there are USER versions of these views):

   ■ DBA_COMPARISON_SCAN

   ■ DBA_COMPARISON_SCAN_SUMMARY

   ■ DBA_COMPARISON_SCAN_VALUES

   ■ DBA_COMPARISON_ROW_DIF

4. If there are differences, and you want to synchronize the database objects at the two databases, then run the CONVERGE procedure in this package.

5. Run the RECHECK function, which rechecks the differences in a specified scan. This should not find any difference.

The created comparison can be run periodically using the COMPARE function to identify any changes or divergence in the shared objects. Each such run can perform one or more scans of the objects. Each scan is assigned a unique scan ID. The scanning is performed for a range of rows in the objects. Such ranges are called *buckets*. The COMPARE function scans each bucket and larger buckets. Larger buckets can be split into smaller ones, resulting in parent and children scans. The parent scan ID will be used for managing the results of the comparison. The COMPARE function runs efficiently with a large number of buckets.

The rest of this section provides an example that shows how to use the DBMS_COMPARISON package to detect data differences and converge the source and destination tables so that the destination table matches the source table. In this example, the source schema is SCOTT and the destination schema is also SCOTT. The shared table is EMPMASTER. The table has the same primary key constraint at the source database, DBXA.WORLD, and the destination database, DBXB.WORLD.

Creating the Comparison

The CREATE_COMPARISON procedure creates a comparison for the supplied schema name, table name, and remote database link. The comparison name is user defined. The max_num_buckets parameter should be set high (to a few million) for large tables for improved performance.

```
SQL> begin
  2      dbms_comparison.create_comparison(
  3          comparison_name      => 'COMPARE_EMPMASTER',
  4          schema_name          => 'SCOTT',
  5          remote_schema_name   => 'SCOTT',
  6          object_name          => 'EMPMASTER',
  7          dblink_name          => 'DBXB',
  8          max_num_buckets      => 10000000
  9          );
 10      end;
 11  /
PL/SQL procedure successfully completed.
```

Running the Comparison

In this step, we run the just created comparison, COMPARE_EMPMASTER, using the DBMS_COMPARISON.COMPARE function to find any differences in the shared table.

The procedure will report a scan ID for this task. We do need to remember this scan ID for the following steps.

```
SQL> SET SERVEROUTPUT ON SIZE UNLIMITED
SQL> declare
  2     consistent BOOLEAN;
  3     scan_info DBMS_COMPARISON.COMPARISON_TYPE;
  4   begin
  5    consistent := dbms_comparison.compare(
  6                   comparison_name => 'COMPARE_EMPMASTER',
  7                   scan_info       => scan_info,
  8                   perform_row_dif => TRUE);
  9     dbms_output.put_line('Scan ID is: '||scan_info.scan_id);
 10     if consistent = TRUE then
 11      dbms_output.put_line ('No differences were found');
 12     else
 13       dbms_output.put_line('Differences were found');
 14     end if;
 15   end;
 16   /
Scan ID is: 29819
Differences were found
PL/SQL procedure successfully completed.
```

Listing the Comparison

This step is optional. The following SQL script shows how many differences were found between the local (source) and remote (destination) tables. We need to provide the scan ID (29819) that was assigned to the comparison when it ran in the previous step.

```
SQL> col current_dif_count heading 'DIFFERENCES' for 9999999
  1   select c.owner,
  2          c.comparison_name,
  3          c.schema_name,
  4          c.object_name,
  5          s.current_dif_count
  6     from dba_comparison c,
  7          dba_comparison_scan_summary s
  8    where c.comparison_name = s.comparison_name
  9      and c.owner = s.owner
 10      and s.scan_id = 29819;
```

OWNER	COMPARISON_NAME	SCHEMA_NAME	OBJECT_NAME	DIFFERENCES
STRMADMIN	COMPARE_EMPMASTER	SCOTT	EMPMASTER	57554

Converging from the Local Table to the RemoteTable

The CONVERGE procedure executes the DML changes to synchronize the portions of the tables that were compared in the specified scan ID. You have the option to choose to make the "remote" table match the "local" table, or vice versa. You need to provide the comparison name and the scan ID for the comparison.

The following example illustrates converging the "local" table to the "remote" table as defined in the `converge_options` parameter. The output shows the results of this process as to how many rows in the "remote" table were deleted and how many rows were either inserted or updated to match the "local" table.

```
SQL> declare
  2    scan_info DBMS_COMPARISON.COMPARISON_TYPE;
  3  begin
  4    dbms_comparison.converge(
  5      comparison_name  => 'COMPARE_EMPMASTER',
  6      scan_id          => 29819,
  7      scan_info        => scan_info,
  8      converge_options => DBMS_COMPARISON.CMP_CONVERGE_LOCAL_WINS);
  9      dbms_output.put_line('Local Rows Merged: '||scan_info.loc_rows_merged);
 10      dbms_output.put_line('Remote Rows Merged: '||scan_info.rmt_rows_merged);
 11      dbms_output.put_line('Local Rows Deleted: '||scan_info.loc_rows_deleted);
 12      dbms_output.put_line('Remote Rows Deleted: '||scan_info.rmt_rows_deleted);
 13  end;
 14  /
Local Rows Merged: 0
Remote Rows Merged: 57517
Local Rows Deleted: 0
Remote Rows Deleted: 37
PL/SQL procedure successfully completed.
```

Rechecking the Comparison

The RECHECK function rechecks the differences in a specified scan for a comparison. This function performs one of the following actions:

- If the specified scan completed successfully the last time it ran, then this function checks the previously identified differences in the scan.

- If the specified scan completed partially, then this function continues to check the database object from the point where the previous scan ended.

NOTE
The RECHECK function does not identify new differences in the database objects that have appeared since the specified scan was run. To identify new differences, run the COMPARE function.

The following example shows how to use this function. The scan for the scan ID 29819 completed successfully and the function did not report any differences.

```
SQL> declare
  2    consistent BOOLEAN;
  3  begin
  4    consistent := DBMS_COMPARISON.RECHECK(
  5                    comparison_name => 'COMPARE_EMPMASTER',
  6                    scan_id => 29819
  7                  );
  8    if consistent = TRUE then
 10      dbms_output.put_line('No differences were found.');
 11    else
 12      dbms_output.put_line('Differences were found.');
 13    end if;
 14  end;
 15  /
No differences were found.
PL/SQL procedure successfully completed.
```

Purging the Comparison

The PURGE_COMPARISON procedure purges scanned information for a supplied comparison name. If the supplied scan ID is NULL, then the procedure purges data for all scans; otherwise, it purges data for the supplied scan ID. It is suggested that after converging data to resynchronize local and remote tables, you purge the comparison. You can run the comparison again when you want to check for any new differences in the data.

```
SQL> begin
  2    dbms_comparison.purge_comparison(
  3           comparison_name => 'COMPARE_EMPMASTER',
  4           scan_id         => 29819,
  5           purge_time      => NULL);
  6  end;
  7  /

PL/SQL procedure successfully completed.
```

Dropping the Comparison

The DROP_COMPARISON procedure deletes the specified comparison, including any scanned information for comparison, if available. You will need to create the comparison again using the CREATE_COMPARE procedure to be able to find differences in the table data. You should drop and re-create the comparison when the table and index structures change.

```
SQL> begin
  2    dbms_comparison.drop_comparison(
  3            comparison_name => 'COMPARE_EMPMASTER');
  4  end;
  5  /
PL/SQL procedure successfully completed.
```

Summary

Once the Streams replication is functional in your environment, the setup may need some maintenance as the application or business requirements change. For example, you may have to add new objects to replicate or perhaps remove some of the existing objects from the replication. Sometimes you may have to create multiple Streams processes in the same environment. You can achieve all these tasks without having to re-create or remove Streams entirely from the database. This chapter discussed how to perform such addition and removal of components to and from the Streams environment using the Oracle-supplied procedures.

In addition to the maintenance tasks, this chapter also discussed several techniques for troubleshooting each of the Streams processes. It discussed the common errors encountered by each of the Streams components and provided techniques to solve these errors. Extreme caution is needed to handle transactions in error. The decision to remove such error transactions must be handled carefully to preserve data integrity.

The new Streams features (namely Streams Performance Advisor, message tracking, and data comparison) that are available in Oracle Database 11g can greatly help you to diagnose the bottlenecks and synchronize table data in the replication environment.

CHAPTER
13

Streams Performance
Considerations

racle has implemented numerous enhancements in Oracle 11*g* R1 and R2 to improve Streams replication performance. For a simple replication environment with a single source database and a single destination database, you may not have to modify any of the default settings. However, a number of things, such as, insufficient resources, incorrect configuration of various database and Streams processes parameters, transaction size and duration, and application design can adversely affect Streams performance and become bottlenecks in a complex and high-volume environment. Fortunately, there are several actions you can take to improve the Streams performance.

This chapter discusses what can contribute to poor replication performance, and some of the techniques you can use to improve performance.

Streams Queue Spilling

The Streams capture process enqueues the LCRs to the buffered queue in the Streams pool memory. By default, the LCRs are expected to be consumed, or dequeued, within 300 seconds. Unfortunately, this time duration is not configurable. If the LCRs are not dequeued within this time, then they are written to the disk queue spill table. This is called *queue spilling*.

Queue spilling can also happen if there is shortage of memory space in the Streams pool. Such shortage can result when a large number of LCRs are waiting acknowledgment from the apply process. These LCRs cannot be purged until after the acknowledgement is received.

The spilling of LCRs adversely affects the replication performance. The Streams pool advisory view, V$STREAMS_POOL_ADVICE, can shed some light on the estimated number of spilled LCRs, the estimated time it will take to write them to disk, and the estimated time to read them back to process (*unspill*):

```
SQL> col streams_pool_size_factor format 999.99 heading 'Stream|Pool Size|Factor'
SQL> col streams_pool_size_for_estimate heading 'Stream|Pool Size|Estimate'
SQL> col estd_spill_count    heading 'Spill|Count|Estimated'
SQL> col estd_spill_time     heading 'Spill|Time|Estimated'
SQL> col estd_unspill_count  heading 'UnSpill|Count|Estimated'
SQL> col estd_unspill_time   heading 'UnSpill|Time|Estimated'
SQL>
SQL> select streams_pool_size_factor,
  2          streams_pool_size_for_estimate,
  3          estd_spill_count,
  4          estd_spill_time,
  5          estd_unspill_count,
  6          estd_unspill_time
  7  from v$streams_pool_advice;
```

Stream Pool Size Factor	Stream Pool Size Estimate	Spill Count Estimated	Spill Time Estimated	UnSpill Count Estimated	UnSpill Time Estimated
.80	160	0	0	0	0
.90	180	0	0	0	0
1.00	**200**	**0**	**0**	**0**	**0**
1.10	220	0	0	0	0
1.20	240	0	0	0	0
1.30	260	0	0	0	0
. . . . .					
. . . . .					

In this example, the Streams Pool Size Estimate lists the amount of memory, in megabytes, currently allocated against the Streams Pool Size Factor of 1.00. The report shows estimated spillage for different sizes of the Streams pool memory. We see that no spillage is estimated even if we were to reduce the Stream pool size to 160MB from the currently allocated 200MB. When the spill count is non-zero, then increase the Streams pool size to the higher value for which the estimated spill count is zero.

NOTE
Queue spilling does not occur at the source database or destination database when CCA is in effect.

When the propagation and apply processes are working efficiently, and adequate memory is allocated to the Streams pool, queue spilling can be minimized or completely eliminated.

Even if Automatic Shared Memory Management (ASMM) or Automatic Memory Management (AMM) is in use, it is recommended that you set the `streams_pool_size` explicitly to a value greater than 200MB to begin with. You may have to increase it after monitoring the V$STREAMS_POOL_ADVICE view during peak workloads.

Apply Spilling

The apply process can spill the transaction to the apply spill tables under two conditions: when the LCR is in the queue for a certain amount of time, and when the transaction exceeds a certain number of LCRs. Such spilling is called *apply spilling*.

The apply process will write all the LCRs in the transaction into the apply spill table on disk if those LCRs are not processed within the time specified by the apply parameter `txn_age_spill_threshold`, which defaults to 900 seconds. If the apply process is slow and there is an LCR in the apply queue for more than this time, then the entire transaction will be spilled to disk to make room for new LCRs that are being dequeued.

The apply process will also spill the transaction if the number of LCRs in the transaction exceeds the value set for the apply parameter `txn_lcr_spill_threshold`. The default is 10,000 LCRs. In this case, the transaction spills to the disk in batches. The number of LCRs in the first batch equals the value of this parameter. If the reader process detects more messages for the same transaction, then each subsequent batch will have up to either 100 messages or the number specified for this parameter, whichever is less. When the commit directive is received by the apply process, spilled LCRs will be read from the disk table and applied, and the final batch of LCRs will be applied from the apply queue itself.

In both the previous cases, the spilled LCRs are written to apply spill tables (SYS.STREAMS$_APPLY_SPILL_*) and not the queue spill tables.

If your application has a large number of transactions with more than 10,000 LCRs, then, to minimize the apply spilling, you may want to increase the value for the apply parameter `txn_lcr_spill_threshold`. Also, if most of the transactions take more than 15 minutes to execute, you may want to increase the value for `txn_age_spill_threshold`. Increasing the value of these parameters may also require that you increase the memory allocated to the Streams pool size by the `streams_pool_size` parameter.

If possible, consider reducing the size of transactions at the source to improve the performance of the apply process, instead of increasing values for the apply parameters. If the transaction size cannot be changed, then investigate if certain DML operations could be performed at the source and destination databases, bypassing the replication, as discussed in the next section.

Handling Large Transactions

Large transactions, with thousands of LCRs, are the Achilles' heel of Streams replication. There are a couple of issues to consider with large transactions. By design, the Streams apply process does not begin applying the LCRs to the destination tables until it receives the commit directive for the transaction. This is true for all transactions, but it is more noticeable for large transactions. If a large transaction takes, say, 30 minutes to complete at the source database, it will actually begin executing at the destination after 30 minutes and may take another 30 minutes to complete. Depending on the transaction size, the apply process may first spill it to the disk queue, as just discussed, slowing it down even further.

Also, the apply parallelism will be automatically suspended when one of the apply server processes is executing the large transaction. Other independent transactions that could have been applied otherwise will wait until the large transaction completes. This will adversely affect the overall replication performance.

So, what exactly is a large transaction? The capture process considers a transaction to be "large" if it has more then 10,000 LCRs. It will write a message, every 10 minutes, to the alert log file of the capture database when it detects a large transaction, as shown next. The message contains the transaction ID that can be used to identify the session and the SQL statement involved. There will be a message when the transaction commits or rolls back.

```
Wed May 19 08:33:11 2010
CP01: large txn detected (13698 LCRs), xid: 0x0006.00f.00002671
Wed May 19 08:43:10 2010
CP01: large txn detected (16084 LCRs), xid: 0x0006.00f.00002671
Wed May 19 08:53:11 2010
CP01: large txn detected (18470 LCRs), xid: 0x0006.00f.00002671
Wed May 19 08:55:39 2010
CP01: large txn committed, xid: 0x0006.00f.00002671
```

You can also query the view V$STREAMS_TRANSACTION at the source and destination databases to monitor the large transaction. The view shows you the number of LCRs in the transaction, as shown in the following query from the capture database:

```
SQL> select xidusn,
  2          xidslt,
  3          xidsqn,
  4          cumulative_message_count,
  5          total_message_count
  6   from v$streams_transaction;
XIDUSN   XIDSLT   XIDSQN  CUMULATIVE_MESSAGE_COUNT  TOTAL_MESSAGE_COUNT
------   -------  ------- ------------------------- -------------------
     6        15    9841                     14164                   0
```

The CUMULATIVE_MESSAGE_COUNT column lists the number of LCRs in the transaction when the query ran. The TOTAL_MESSAGE_COUNT column remains at 0 because the transaction is still open. The transaction ID can be used to find the SQL statement either from the session that may be currently active in the source database or from mining the redo log file separately.

The apply process, on the other hand, does not identify a large transaction based on the number of LCRs. If the transaction can't be stored in the buffered queue, it will be spilled to the disk, as discussed earlier. Oracle recommends keeping the size of transactions to around 1000 (or fewer) LCRs.

If possible, you should review the application to see if large transactions can be avoided. The application may have to commit more often. Depending on what the transactions do, it may also be possible to execute them independently at the source and destination databases, bypassing replication. For example, a large transaction involving mass updates, data purge, or other seasonal activity affecting a large number of records may be run simultaneously at the source and destination databases using the Streams tag to suppress their replication. You may also consider setting up procedural replication, wherein the PL/SQL procedure that performs such mass changes can be replicated, instead of replicating the DML changes made by the procedure.

Streams Tag

At the source database, you can set the Streams tag field to prevent capturing changes made during the current session, particularly by large transactions that can be executed independently at the destination database.

Setting the tag field to a value that is not currently used in the Streams rules prevents the capture process from capturing the change for replication. The capture rule for the table must have a condition to check for the tag field. If replication is set up using a MAINTAIN_* procedure, then the default rule does not have such a condition. In this case, you have to modify the rule to check for the tag field, typically by adding the following condition to the DML rule in the positive rule set for the table:

```
:dml.is_null_tag = 'Y'
```

It is assumed the captured LCRs will have a NULL value for the Streams tag. So, when the Streams tag is set to a non-NULL value for the session, the rule will evaluate to FALSE and the LCR will be ignored.

The following steps show how to set and reset the Streams tag for the session. The connected user must have the execute privilege on the DBMS_STREAMS_ADM package or must be granted the EXECUTE_CATALOG_ROLE.

To set the Streams tag:

```
execute dbms_streams_adm.set_tag(hextoraw ('1D') );
```

To reset the Streams tag:

```
execute dbms_streams_adm.set_tag (NULL);
```

You must set the Streams tag before the start of the large transaction in the session. The value is persistent across multiple transactions in the same session until the session exits or the tag is reset to NULL as just shown.

You can run the following procedure to see the current value of the Streams tag:

```
set serveroutput on
declare
    raw_tag raw(2048);
begin
    raw_tag := dbms_streams_adm.get_tag();
    dbms_output.put_line('Tag Value = ' || rawtohex(raw_tag));
end;
/
```

NOTE
The SET_TAG procedure and the GET_TAG function are also available in the DBMS_STREAMS package. However, these methods may be deprecated in a future release of Oracle Database from DBMS_STREAMS package. Oracle recommends using DBMS_STREAMS_ADM package for these methods.

This example assumes that the Streams tag was left to the default value of NULL for the capture process and was not set to any other value for controlling selective processing of LCRs, such as in N-way or queue forwarding replication environments.

Setting a non-NULL value for the simple uni- or bidirectional Streams environment to bypass replication is fairly easy. However, in a hub-and-spoke configuration, it could be a bit complex because you are working with LCRs for which tags have special use and meaning. In such cases, it might be worth considering proper negative rules to ignore LCRs from replication.

Procedural Replication

Procedural replication is a technique that replicates the call to a stored procedure rather than the actual DML changes performed by the procedure. This technique is most useful when performing DML operations that affect a large number of rows in a single transaction. Procedure replication requires a special setup in the source and destination databases. This setup creates packages and procedures that are used in the procedural replication. These procedures are not installed automatically. You have to contact Oracle Support to get the required scripts. Instructions will be provided on how to run these scripts in the source and destination databases.

The user procedure that actually performs the mass changes has some restrictions when setting it up for procedural replication. The user procedure must run as an anonymous block, and it should not commit its work. It will also not have any out parameters. You will also need to implement some mechanism to prevent concurrent DML activity on tables modified by the replicated procedure.

When the procedural replication is configured, a PL/SQL wrapper procedure executes the user procedure that will be replicated. It actually generates a DDL statement that will execute the user procedure in the destination database, rather than the DML activity generated by the user procedure. The execution of the user procedure in the source and destination databases will take place as a single transaction.

Handling Long-Running Transactions

Similar to when it detects a large transaction, the capture process writes messages to the alert log file when it detects a long-running transaction, as shown in the following example. A transaction is considered "long" when the commit, or rollback, is not received within ten minutes from the last captured LCR for the transaction. The message contains the transaction ID, which can be used to identify the session and SQL statement involved.

```
Wed May 19 14:30:02 2010
CP01: long running txn detected, xid: 0x000a.008.00001f75
```

So, how does this affect replication performance? Since a long-running transaction is an open transaction, the LCRs can't be applied to the destination until a commit is received. These LCRs take up space in the buffered queue. They may also be spilled to the disk tables after they age out. Both conditions will affect the replication latency.

You can query the V$STREAMS_TRANSACTION view, as discussed in the previous section, to monitor a long-running transaction. When the query is run in the destination database, the columns CUMULATIVE_MESSAGE_COUNT and TOTAL_MESSAGE_COUNT will report an identical number for the LCRs in the transaction. The transaction ID can be used to find the SQL statement either from the session that may be currently active in the source database or from mining the redo log file separately.

Log Mining Activity

The capture process caches log mining information in memory within the Streams pool. The memory size is controlled by the _sga_size parameter of the capture process, which defaults to 10MB. This memory may not be sufficient in cases where there is high DDL activity in the database and there are LOB or LONG columns in the tables with high DML activity. The LogMiner information may spill from the memory to the internal log miner tables. Such spilling can slow down log mining activity and increase the capture latency. The log miner spillage can be detected by running the following query:

```
select capture_name,
       name,
       value
  from v$streams_capture,
       v$logmnr_stats
 where logminer_id = session_id
   and name = 'bytes paged out';
```

Ideally, the value for the the number of bytes paged out should be zero. If not, then the log miner memory must be increased to avoid log miner spilling. Increasing the value set for the _sga_size parameter will increase the log miner memory, as shown in the following example where it is set to 40MB:

```
begin
   dbms_capture_adm.set_parameter(
     capture_name  => 'DBXA_CAP',
     parameter     => '_SGA_SIZE',
     value         => '40');
end;
/
```

You may also have to increase the _sga_size parameter if ORA-01431 or ORA-01280 is reported in the alert log for the database running the capture process. Please also note that if you increase the value of the parallelism parameter for the capture process, each additional preparer process uses _sga_size amount of memory.

Capture Process Considerations

There are a couple of things you should be aware of that may offer an opportunity to improve the efficiency of the capture process: parallelism and checkpoint information.

Parallelism

The capture process parameter parallelism is set to 1 by default. It is possible to increase its value to have multiple preparer server processes. With multiple preparer processes, it is possible to improve internal operations that scan redo information and perform some of the rule evaluations. The default value is adequate for most environments. You may want to carefully conduct tests to see if increasing the value of the parallelism parameter is of any benefit in your environment. You can use the following SQL query to check the capture latency during testing of the effect of changes to capture parallelism:

```
select capture_name,
       ((sysdate - capture_message_create_time)*86400) latency_seconds,
       ((sysdate - capture_time)*86400)                 last_status,
       to_char(capture_time, 'hh24:mi:ss mm/dd/yy')     capture_time,
       to_char(capture_message_create_time, 'hh24:mi:ss mm/dd/yy') create_time
from v$streams_capture;
```

In most cases, increasing the apply parallelism, rather than capture parallelism, is beneficial.

Checkpoint Information

The frequency of checkpoints and the retention of the checkpoint information can have some implications for the capture process. The checkpoint information is stored in the SYSTEM.LOGMNR_RESTART_CKPT$ table. How much information is inserted into this table during a checkpoint depends on the number of active sessions and number of capture processes in the database. Each capture process has its own checkpoint information.

The size of the LOGMNR_RESTART_CKPT$ table depends on how long the information is kept and how often it is captured. When the checkpoint information for a capture process exceeds the duration set by the checkpoint_retention_time parameter, it is purged. This internal maintenance operation can take some time, depending on the amount of information to purge. During this operation, the capture process does not mine the redo information. The more information to purge, the longer it will take for the capture process to resume its normal operation. This will cause the capture latency to increase momentarily, while the capture process status reports normal operation.

Generally, the default checkpoint frequency is adequate for most environments. But you can change it to have fewer or more checkpoints. In the following example, the checkpoint frequency is changed from the default of 1000MB. The checkpoint will occur after mining 1500MB of new redo information.

```
begin
   dbms_capture_adm.set_parameter(
      capture_name     => 'DBXA_CAP',
      parameter_name   => '_CHECKPOINT_FREQUENCY',
      value            => '1500');
end;
/
```

Changing the default value of the `checkpoint_retention_time` parameter from its rather long default, 60 days, to a reasonable value of 7 days is recommended, as shown in this example:

```
begin
   dbms_capture_adm.alter_capture(
      capture_name               => 'DBXA_CAP',
      checkpoint_retention_time  =>  7);
end;
/
```

Periodically, you should shrink the LOGMNR_RESTART_CKPT$ table, based on the number of rows and number of blocks occupied, as shown in the following example. An automated job can be set up to stop the capture process, shrink the table, and restart the capture process.

```
alter table system.logmnr_restart_ckpt$ enable row movement;
alter table system.logmnr_restart_ckpt$ shrink space;
alter table system.logmnr_restart_ckpt$ disable row movement;
```

Propagation Process Considerations

When combined capture and apply (CCA) mode is in effect, the capture process performs the job of the propagation sender, and the apply process performs the job of the propagation receiver. By design, this mechanism improves the replication performance considerably, and you do not have to worry about propagation performance at all.

Using queue-to-queue propagation instead of queue-to-database link propagation is recommended. This is true irrespective of whether CCA or non-CCA mode is being used. Queue-to-queue propagation has its own propagation job to propagate messages from the source to the destination queue. Also, queue-to-queue propagation offers the failover capability in a RAC environment, so that the propagation from the source to the destination establishes automatically when the Streams process is switched to a different node due to node failure or other problems.

In non-CCA mode, if there has been a considerable amount of queue spilling, the internal queue spill table will have grown large. After processing the spilled messages, the table may still occupy a large amount of space. To improve Streams performance, you need to reclaim the space, as shown next. The queue table name is DBXA_CAP_Q_T.

```
alter table AQ$_DBXA_CAP_Q_T_P enable row movement;
alter table AQ$_DBXA_CAP_Q_T_P shrink space;
alter table AQ$_DBXA_CAP_Q_T_P disable row movement;
```

If there is no need to modify the contents of the LCRs using rule transformation during the propagation—that is, all the LCRs are propagated to the destination queue—then you do not need any positive rule set associated with the propagation process. If a positive rule is defined, then you can remove it as shown here:

```
begin
  dbms_propagation_adm.alter_propagation(
    propagation_name => 'DBXA_TO_DBXB_PROP',
    remove_rule_set  =>  true);
end;
/
```

Without the positive rule set, the propagation process does not perform any rule evaluation and will propagate the LCRs efficiently to the destination queue.

Apply Process Considerations

The cause of poor replication performance is often a poorly performing apply process. Oracle has been improving the internal workings of the apply process over the past releases. Some of these improvements include applying changes to the destination tables without actually invoking the SQL engine, defaulting the apply process to run with parallelism set to 4, and applying independent transactions simultaneously. These improvements make the apply process in Oracle Database 11g R2 highly efficient. However, there are a few other things you can explore to improve the performance of the apply process, as discussed in this section.

Tuning Apply Process Parameters

There are some apply process parameters that can affect the performance of the apply process. Changes to their values should be considered based on the type of the workload, available resources (CPU and memory), and the replication latency requirements.

commit_serialization

The default value of this parameter changed to DEPENDENT_TRANSACTIONS in Oracle 11*g* R2 from NONE in the previous releases. This means that the apply process in Oracle 11*g* R2, by default, serializes the commits for the dependent transactions to match the commit order at the source database. In other words, the apply process will commit independent transactions in any order. If the workload is composed mainly of independent transactions, the apply process performance significantly improves with the default value.

parallelism

You may consider increasing the apply parallelism to match the workload at the source database. If the view V$STREAMS_TRANSACTION at the destination reports a large number of rows with the apply servers staying mostly busy (not in IDLE state) then you can try increasing the parallelism. You may want to test different values for parallelism based on available CPU resources. Typically, the value for this parameter is a multiple of four for high workloads.

When the parallelism is set to a value greater than 1, you should also modify the `initrans` value for the SYS.STREAMS$_APPLY_PROGRESS table to be equal to or greater than the value set for parallelism. This will minimize the ITL contention when multiple apply slave processes update this table. Also, change the `pctfree` value to be at least 10 or more.

Similarly, you should also modify the `initrans` value for each of the replicated tables and its indexes to reduce the ITL contention.

The default value for parallelism is set to 4. When running the apply process with parallelism set to more than 1, it can affect the values for the apply process parameters `_hash_table_size` and `_txn_buffer_size`.

_hash_table_size

This parameter specifies the size (in bytes) of the dependency hash table used internally by the apply process to compute transaction dependencies. The default value is 1,000,000.

In a mixed workload (INSERT, UPDATE, DELETE) or a workload of mostly UPDATE operations, the apply server slaves can report a large number of dependency waits when replicated tables have several referential integrity constraints. The dependency waits can trigger a rollback of the transaction processed by the apply server slaves so that the dependent transactions are applied in the correct order. This can adversely affect the apply process performance. To minimize or eliminate such waits by improving the dependency calculations, you may have to increase the size of the dependency hash table. The value is typically increased to 10,000,000 or even to 20,000,000. Do not increase it beyond 25,000,000.

In the following example, the value for this parameter is set to 20,000,000:

```
begin
   dbms_apply_adm.set_parameter(
      apply_name      => 'DBXA_APP',
      parameter_name  => '_HASH_TABLE_SIZE'
      value           => '20000000');
end;
/
```

_txn_buffer_size
The transactions are fetched by the apply coordinator process from the apply reader to allocate to the apply server slaves. The coordinator can prefetch the transactions before they can be allocated to the apply server slaves. The number of transactions that the coordinator can prefetch is set by the _txn_buffer_size parameter. The value for this parameter is derived as 80 times the parallelism for the apply process. The minimum value is 320, with default parallelism of 4. In Oracle Database 11g, it is recommended that you do not set this parameter explicitly. It is automatically adjusted.

Handling LOB Data Types
When replicating changes made to tables that contain LOB data type columns, Oracle creates multiple LCRs that contain the chunks of the LOB data. The apply process then applies each of these LOB LCRs individually to the row in the destination table. By default, the apply process does not assemble the LOB before applying the LCR to the entire row.

The apply performance can be improved when applying LOBs, by defining a dummy DML error handler for the apply process. The handler does not perform any actions other than simply executing the LCR. This is a workaround to get the apply process to assemble all the LOB chunks in the least number of LCRs when applying them to the destination row.

The following example shows the dummy DML error handler:

```
SQL> connect strmadmin/strmadmin@DBXB.WORLD
Connected.
SQL>
SQL> create or replace type emsg_array is table of varchar2(100)
  2  /
```

```
Type created.
SQL> create or replace procedure lob_error_handler(
  2                  lcr_anydata        IN sys.anydata,
  3                  error_stack_depth IN number,
  4                  error_numbers      IN dbms_Utility.number_array,
  5                  error_messages     IN emsg_array)
  6  authid current_user
  7  is
  8    lcr    sys.lcr$_row_record;
  9    rc     pls_integer;
 10  begin
 11    rc := lcr_anydata.GetObject(lcr);
 12    lcr.execute(true);
 13  end;
 14  /
Procedure created.
```

Now, we register the LOB error handler procedure with the apply process for each table that contains columns with the LOB data type for the specified DML operations:

```
SQL> begin
  2    dbms_apply_adm.set_dml_handler(
  3    object_name              => 'SCOTT.EMP_DETAILES',
  4    object_type              => 'TABLE',
  5    operation_name           => 'UPDATE',
  6    error_handler            => TRUE,
  7    user_procedure           => 'STRMADMIN.LOB_ERROR_HANDLER',
  8    apply_database_link      => NULL,
  9    apply_name               => 'DBXA_APP',
 10    assemble_lobs            => TRUE);
 11  end;
 12  /
PL/SQL procedure successfully completed.

SQL> begin
  2    dbms_apply_adm.set_dml_handler(
  3    object_name              => 'SCOTT.EMP_DETAILES',
  4    object_type              => 'TABLE',
  5    operation_name           => 'DELETE',
  6    error_handler            => TRUE,
  7    user_procedure           => 'STRMADMIN.LOB_ERROR_HANDLER',
  8    apply_database_link      => NULL,
  9    apply_name               => 'DBXA_APP',
 10    assemble_lobs            => TRUE);
 11  end;
 12  /
PL/SQL procedure successfully completed.
```

```
SQL> begin
  2      dbms_apply_adm.set_dml_handler(
  3      object_name            => 'SCOTT.EMP_DETAILES',
  4      object_type            => 'TABLE',
  5      operation_name         => 'LOB_UPDATE',
  6      error_handler          => TRUE,
  7      user_procedure         => 'STRMADMIN.LOB_ERROR_HANDLER',
  8      apply_database_link    => NULL,
  9      apply_name             => 'DBXA_APP',
 10      assemble_lobs          => TRUE);
 11  end;
 12  /
PL/SQL procedure successfully completed.
```

Apply Rule Set

Similar to the propagation process, if there is no need to modify the contents of the LCRs using rule transformation during the apply process, then you do not need any positive rule set associated with the apply process. If there is a positive rule set defined, then you can remove it as shown next. With no rule set to evaluate, there is less work for the apply process.

```
begin
   dbms_apply_adm.alter_apply(
      apply_name        => 'DBXA_APP',
      remove_rule_set   => true);
end;
/
```

Detecting Conflicts

If the destination table is used strictly in read-only mode, and no DML or DDL activity is allowed, then consider disabling the conflict detection for the non-key columns of such tables for the UPDATE and DELETE operations. You can turn off the old value comparison for the UPDATE and DELETE operations using the COMPARE_OLD_VALUES procedure of the DBMS_APPLY_ADM package. This will improve the apply process performance when applying these changes.

When performing DELETE operations at the source that affect a large number of rows, you can reduce the size of the LCR by keeping only the key columns in the LCR and removing all the rest. You can use the KEEP_COLUMNS or DELETE_COLUMN procedure of the DBMS_STREAMS_ADM package to achieve this. You also need to turn off old value comparison for the columns that will not be in the LCR. So, with the LCRs that only contain the key values to delete a row, the Streams pool can accommodate a large number of LCRs without causing possible queue spillage due to lack of memory to hold the LCRs.

Bug Fixes

Since its introduction in Oracle 9.2.0.4, Streams has had its share of bugs and other troubles. Oracle Support has created a document on the My Oracle Support web site that specifically tracks all patches and bug fixes issued for Streams. MOS note 437838.1 describes all the bug fixes and patches available for Streams. There are a few bug fixes that address the most commonly reported performance problems and other problems. You should review this note and patch the Oracle Home directory with all recommended patches for your platform. Also, it is a good idea to review and install all applicable patch set updates (PSUs).

Summary

Since its introduction in Oracle 9.2.0.4, Oracle Streams has been enhanced and improved to offer better performance along with new features. With features such as the capability to mine redo information from the log buffer, the capability for the capture process to send LCRs directly to the apply process in CCA mode, automatic split and merge, revised default settings for Streams parameters, and enhanced internal mechanisms for the apply process, the Streams replication performance has improved considerably in Oracle Database 11g R2. For most simple replication environments, the default settings deliver excellent performance.

The replication performance can be further improved by using other mechanisms as well. Depending on the application and the type of the transactions, you may be able to execute those transactions differently or minimize them by making changes to the application. The transactions spilling to the queue spill table, or apply spill table, on disk can be minimized or eliminated by allocating enough memory to the Streams pool and by adjusting the apply process parameters.

Applying changes to the LOB data can be improved by employing a DML error handler procedure for the apply process that assembles LOB chunks before applying the multiple LCRs. Removing a positive rule set when rule transformation is not required can also help improve the throughput of the propagation and apply processes. By cleverly removing unwanted columns from the LCR, and suppressing the conflict detection when applying updates and deletes to read-only tables at the destination, the apply performance can be further improved. And, lastly, keeping current with the available bug fixes that may address commonly reported issues affecting performance is very important to make sure that your Streams environment runs as expected and delivers the results you want.

CHAPTER
14

Oracle Enterprise Manager Grid Control for Streams Replication

racle Enterprise Manager (OEM) Grid Control simplifies Streams configuration, management, and monitoring. The provided Streams replication wizards can configure different types of commonly used replication environments. The OEM pages provide an easy-to-use interface for managing various Streams components, including process parameters, rules, handlers, and errors. Streams monitoring can be performed at the database level for the Streams components, or across the replication path from the source database to the destination database (end to end). The predefined Streams alerts are available and enabled based on the process status, errors, and replication latency.

This chapter discusses how to use the Streams Replication Setup wizard to configure schema-level replication. It also discusses some of the tasks in Streams management and monitoring. This chapter covers just a sample of the use cases that are possible with OEM.

The examples and images shown in this chapter are from the OEM Grid Control 10.2.0.5 release. This is the minimum recommended release of Grid Control for Streams replication. Prior releases of OEM also have Streams topics, but the 10.2.0.5 release contains enhancements for Streams management.

It is also recommended that you apply patch number 9133343 to the Oracle Management Server (OMS). This patch addresses some issues related to Streams in OEM. MOS note 1078864.1 discusses the latest patch set updates (10.2.0.5.3) to the OMS and the Oracle Agent.

Streams Configuration Wizards

Configuring Streams replication using the wizards is simple. The wizards help you to configure replication between two databases for specific tables, schemas, or the entire database. You can also configure the replication at the granularity of tablespaces, where all tables in specified tablespaces are replicated and the initial instantiation is performed using transportable tablespaces.

When using the wizards to configure replication for one or more schemas, you can exclude tables that you don't want to replicate. The wizards will set up the proper rules and rule set automatically.

The replication wizards can also help you configure a downstream capture process. The steps will include configuration of the redo log transport as well. Also, you can simply generate the Streams configuration script using the wizard and run it manually. The script will be created in the directory object specified.

To access the Streams wizards, log into OEM Grid Control and navigate to the Databases Home page. Select the database where you want to set up the Streams environment. For a RAC database, select one database instance. Next, click the Data Movement tab (see Figure 14-1).

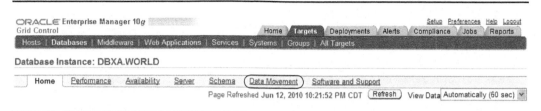

FIGURE 14-1. *Data Movement tab*

The Data Movement page (see Figure 14-2) shows the Streams main menu. From this menu, you can launch the Streams Setup wizard or the Manage Replication wizard.

To launch the Streams Setup wizard, click the Setup menu item. If you haven't already logged into the source database as Streams Administrator, you are presented with the Database Login page (see Figure 14-3). Log in as Normal using the Streams Administrator username and password.

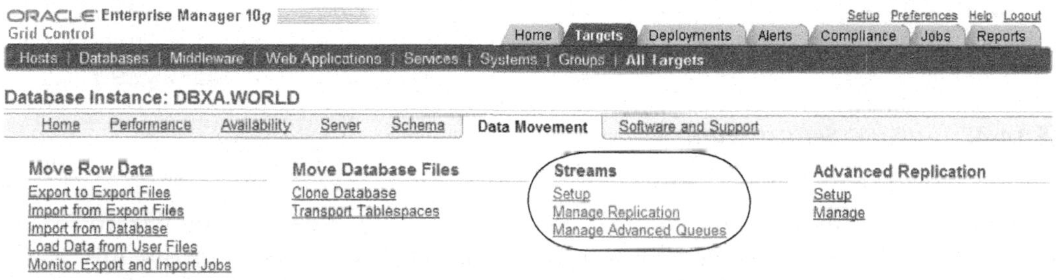

FIGURE 14-2. *Streams menu*

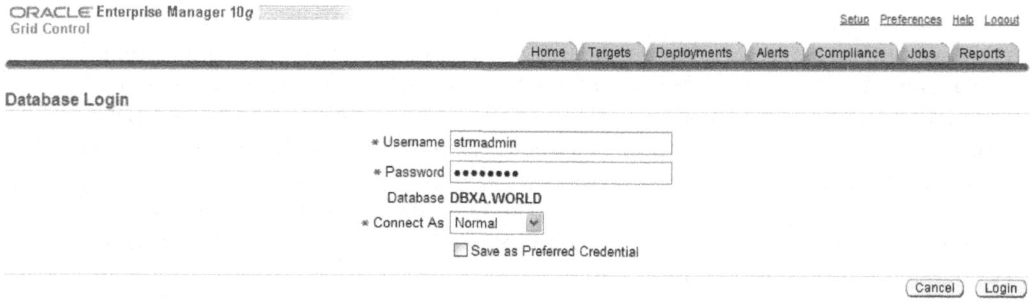

FIGURE 14-3. *Database Login page*

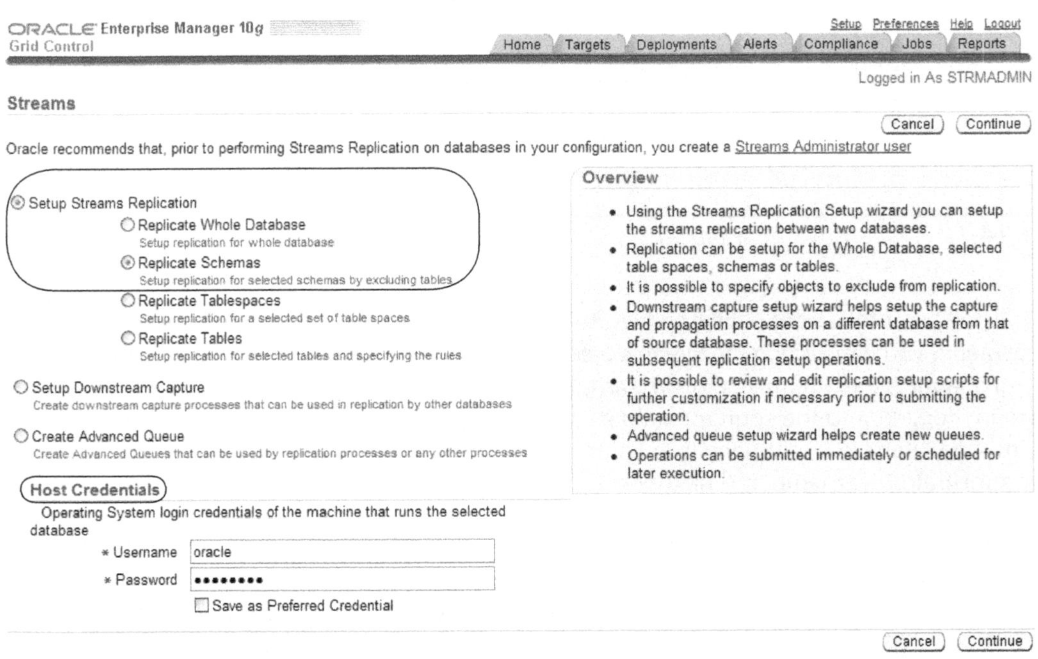

FIGURE 14-4. *Streams Setup wizard*

After successfully logging into the source database, the Streams Setup wizard page will be displayed (see Figure 14-4). Using this page, you can set up Streams replication at the schema, table, tablespace, or database level between two databases.

Creating Schema-Level Replication

This section presents the steps to configure Streams replication for the SCOTT schema. As displayed in Figure 14-4, select the Setup Streams Replication option for creating the local capture process, and then select the Replicate Schemas option. In the Host Credentials section, enter a login ID that has administrator privileges for the database. In this example, we log in as user oracle. Click the Continue button to start the Streams Replication Setup wizard.

As described next, there are five steps in the Streams Replication Setup wizard. Internally, the wizard uses the same mechanism used by the MAINTAIN procedures to configure Streams (discussed in Chapter 8).

Step 1: Object Selection

The first step of the wizard sets up the source database options based on the replication option selected. For schema replication, we select schemas to replicate. Figure 14-5 shows our selection of the SCOTT schema. Note that you also have the option to enter a schema name in the Search area and click Go to filter your results set.

To ignore specific tables from schema-level replication, you can expand the Exclude Tables option and add the table names. When done, click the Next button to go to Step 2.

Step 2: Destination Options

The second wizard step configures the destination database (see Figure 14-6). You can type in the destination database name or choose it by clicking the flashlight (search) icon. Enter the Streams Administrator username and password for the destination database, and then click the Next button to go to Step 3.

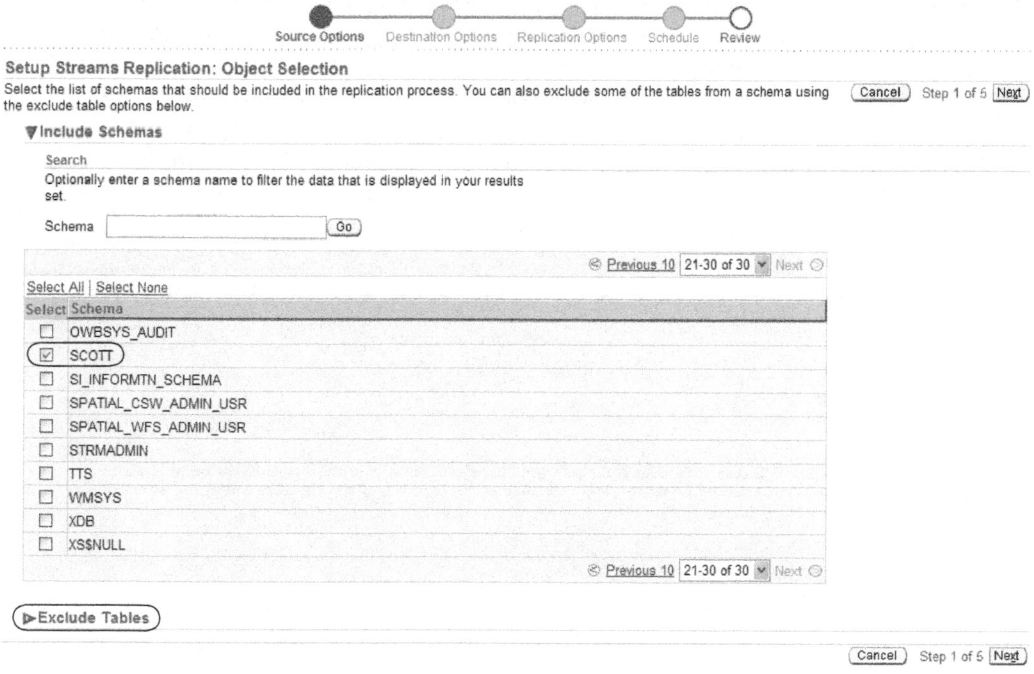

FIGURE 14-5. *Selecting the list of schemas to include in replication*

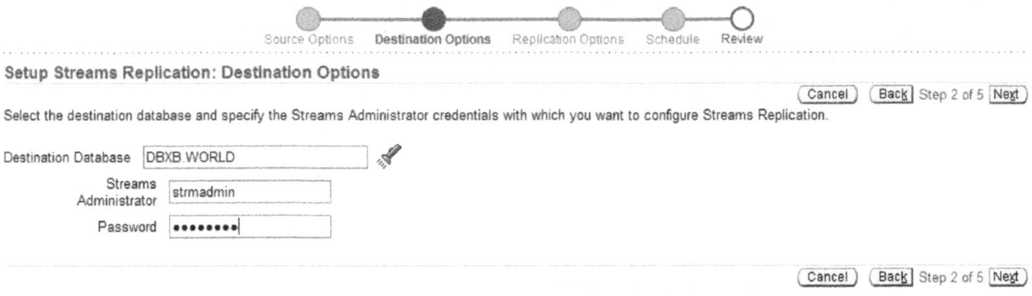

FIGURE 14-6. *Selecting the destination database*

Step 3: Replication Options

In the third wizard step, the replication options are configured. Data Pump export and import will be used to transport data from the source database at a defined point in time and instantiate the objects at the destination database. By default, the Setup wizard chooses directory paths to store the exported dump file. You can overwrite the directory paths.

Alternatively, as shown in Figure 14-7, you can specify the existing directory objects by checking the Specify Directory Objects check box and entering the directory object name for the source and destination databases. This example specifies STREAMS_DP_DIR as our directory objects, as shown in Figure 14-7.

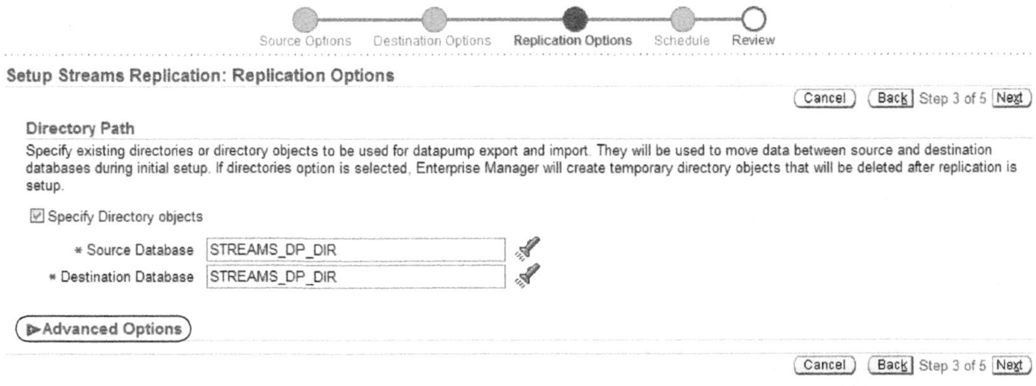

FIGURE 14-7. *Specifying directory objects to use in Data Pump export and import*

By default, the Setup wizard configures unidirectional replication from the source to the destination database using local capture and assigns system-generated names to the Streams components. For other replication options, such as to specify bidirectional replication, specify downstream replication, or specify user-defined names for the Streams components, expand the Advanced Options menu on the page (see Figure 14-8).

By default, the wizard chooses replication of the DML and DDL operations. If you do not want to replicate DDL, then uncheck the Capture, Propagate, and Apply Data Definition Language (DDL) Changes option.

FIGURE 14-8. *Advanced replication options*

In the Processes section under Advanced Options, you can choose either the local capture process or downstream capture process, and specify the archive log destination name to send the archived log files from the source database to the destination database. Figure 14-8 shows our selection of Local Capture. We have also assigned user-defined names for the capture, propagation, and apply processes. If the names are left blank, Oracle will assign system-generated names.

At this stage, we have provided all required information to set up Streams replication from DBXA to DBXB for the SCOTT schema. The DML and DDL changes will be replicated. Click Next to go to Step 4.

Step 4: Schedule Job

The fourth wizard step controls when to run the job to perform the actual setup tasks. Oracle executes the job via the job scheduler. You can either run the job immediately or schedule it to begin later at a specified time. However, if you select Immediately, as shown in Figure 14-9, the job does not begin until it is submitted in the final step of the wizard. If you schedule the job to run at a later time, the time and time zone information will be from the repository database.

Click Next to go to the fifth and final step.

Step 5: Review

The fifth and final step allows (see Figure 14-10) you to review the selections from the previous steps. If you need to make a change, you can go back and change your selections by clicking the Back button.

FIGURE 14-9. *Scheduling when to run replication setup*

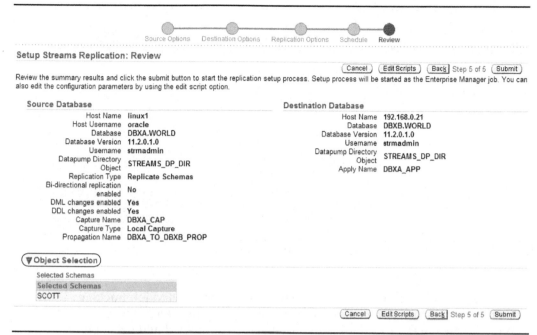

FIGURE 14-10. *Reviewing the replication setup*

Clicking the Edit Scripts button displays the generated script and enables you to modify configuration parameters if needed. Be careful when changing this script, though. You can select all of the text and save it (copy and paste) in a file to review later.

You can also expand the Object Selection menu to verify the objects selected for replication.

Finally, you click the Submit button to schedule the setup job to run. A confirmation page (see Figure 14-11) shows the submitted job name.

Logged in As STRMADMIN

Confirmation

A job has been submitted to setup Streams Replication. The status of the job can be monitored by clicking on the job id.   (OK)

Stream Setup Job_1275095150890

(OK)

FIGURE 14-11. *Replication job confirmation*

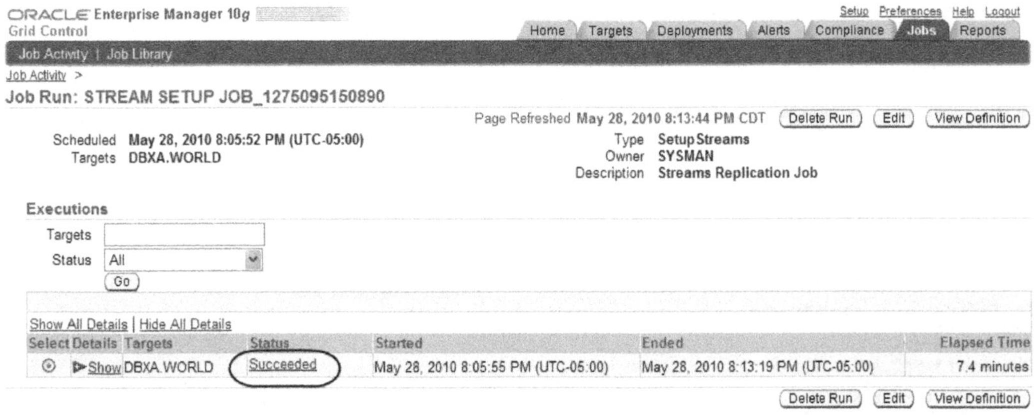

FIGURE 14-12. *Successful replication setup job completion*

You can track the progress of the job using the normal OEM job tracking mechanism. Once the job completes successfully (see Figure 14-12), the replication from the source database to destination database is operational and the capture, propagation, and apply processes are active.

Note that the Streams Setup wizard uses default values for all the parameters of the Streams processes. You may need to review and change those values depending on your requirements.

Monitoring and Managing the Streams Replication Environment

OEM Grid Control can also be used to monitor and manage the Streams replication environment. Using OEM is easy and intuitive to monitor information about the Streams components, statistics, process parameters, performance, and so forth. It also makes it easy to manage Streams processes, rules, handler procedures, and error handling. OEM has predefined Streams alerts that warn about problems with Streams processes and components.

The entry point for managing and monitoring Streams replication is the Streams management page. You should be logged into the database as Streams Administrator. You can access the Streams management page either by clicking the Manage Replication link on the Data Movement page (refer to Figure 14-2) or by clicking the number to the right of Streams Components under the High Availability section on the Databases Home page, as shown in Figure 14-13.

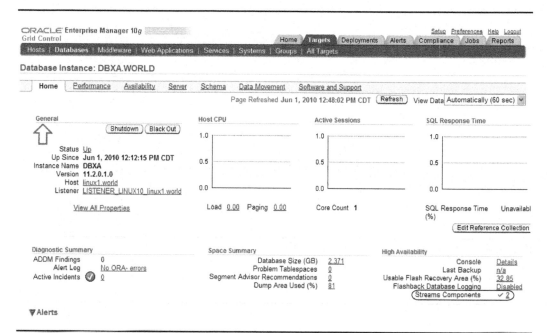

FIGURE 14-13. *Accessing the Streams Management page*

NOTE
Typically, more than one way exists to navigate to the OEM pages discussed in this chapter.

The default view for the Streams management page shows the Overview subpage. Click the Streams tab to get to the Streams subpage for the defined Streams components. Figure 14-14 shows the Streams subpage for our source database DBXA.WORLD. From here you can manage and monitor the Streams components in the current database.

The Action pull-down menu on the Streams management subpage provides options to perform various actions applicable to the selected component in the connected database. All available actions are shown in Figure 14-15.

Information about Streams components is available in several OEM pages. Managing these components requires navigation through multiple pages. Choosing an option from the Action pull-down menu is one of the entry points to these pages. The following sections review the View Details option for the Streams component.

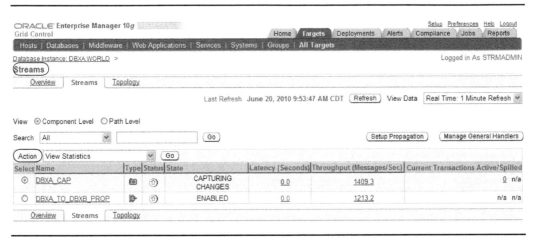

FIGURE 14-14. *Streams Management subpage*

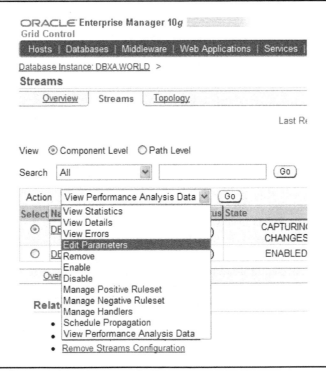

FIGURE 14-15. *Streams Management Action menu*

Monitoring the Capture Process

To view detailed information about the capture process, log into the capture database as Streams Administrator and navigate to the Streams subpage (refer to Figure 14-14). Select the capture process, choose the View Details option from the Action pull-down menu, and then click the Go button. The page showing information about the capture process will appear, as shown in Figure 14-16. The displayed information includes the status of the capture process, the capture process type, the queue name, the rule set, the rule type, various SCNs, and so forth. The information mainly comes from the DBA_CAPTURE view.

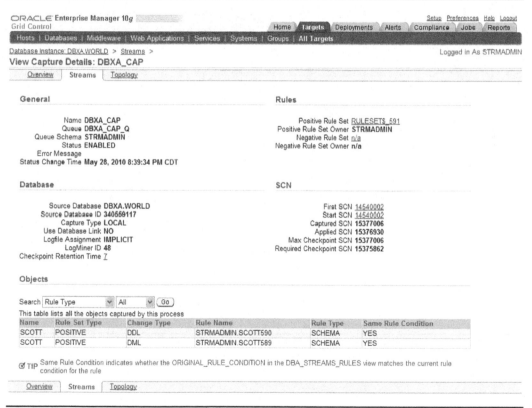

FIGURE 14-16. *Monitoring Streams capture process details*

Monitoring the Propagation Process

Log into the database running the propagation process as Streams Administrator and navigate to the Streams subpage (refer to Figure 14-14). Select the propagation process, choose the View Details option from the Action pull-down menu, and then click the Go button. The page showing information about the propagation process will appear, as shown in Figure 14-17. The displayed information includes the source queue and destination queue names, the source and destination databases, the rule set, the rule type, and so forth. This information mainly comes from the DBA_PROPAGATION view.

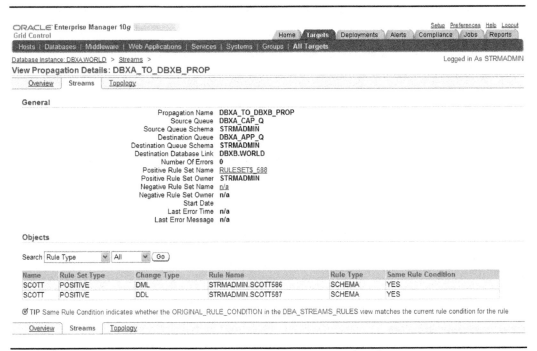

FIGURE 14-17. *Monitoring Streams propagation process details*

Monitoring the Apply Process

OEM makes it very easy to monitor the status and performance of the apply process and its components. Log into the database running the apply process as Streams Administrator and navigate to the Streams subpage, as shown in Figure 14-18.

For each apply process displayed on this page, the Status and State columns indicate whether or not the apply process is active. This page also shows the number of currently active transactions waiting to be processed and the number of spilled transactions. You can click the numbers in the Current Transactions Active/Spilled column to get more information about these transactions. If there are apply errors, then the Status icon displays a warning sign, as shown in Figure 14-18. You can click the Status icon to drill down to the list of apply errors.

Select the apply process, choose the View Details option from the Action pull-down menu, and then click the Go button. The page showing information about the apply process will appear, as shown in Figure 14-19. The displayed information includes the status of the apply process, the queue name, the rule set, the rule type, the type of LCRs applied, and so forth. In addition, this page shows whether any handlers are defined and the apply tag number. This tag number will be recorded in the redo log file for the changes made by the apply process. If the Streams configuration is performed using

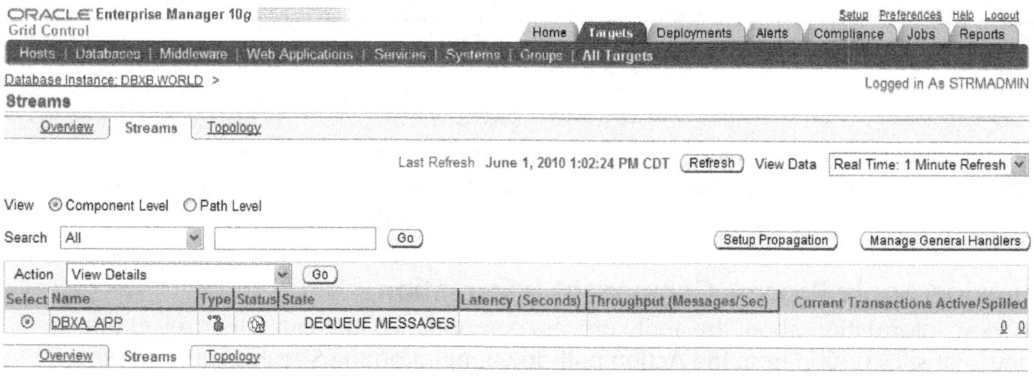

FIGURE 14-18. *Streams Management subpage for the destination database*

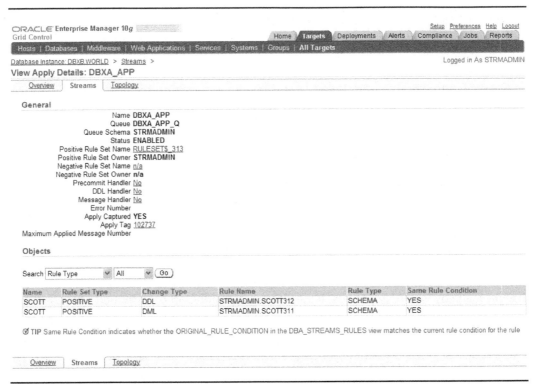

FIGURE 14-19. *Monitoring Streams apply process details*

OEM Streams Replication Setup wizard, this tag number is assigned automatically. You can change it by clicking the tag number and entering a new one on the page displayed. The information displayed comes mainly from the DBA_APPLY view.

Viewing Apply Process Component Information

To view information about the apply process components, you can either select the View Statistics option from the Action pull-down menu on the Streams subpage or simply click the name of the apply process (refer to Figure 14-18). You will see the View Apply Statistics page, similar to the example shown in Figure 14-20, where the reader process details and statistics are displayed. Any spilled transactions are listed at the bottom of the page. The information on this page mainly comes from the V$STREAMS_APPLY_READER and DBA_APPLY_SPILL_TXN views.

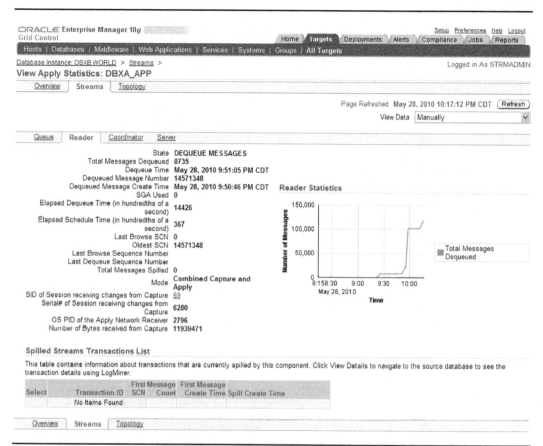

FIGURE 14-20. *Viewing reader statistics for apply process components*

To view detail information about the coordinator process, click the Coordinator tab. A page similar to Figure 14-21 will be displayed. The information displayed on the page comes from the V$STREAMS_APPLY_COORDINATOR and V$STREAMS_TRANSACTION views.

To view detailed information about apply server processes, click the Server tab. A page similar to Figure 14-22 will be displayed. The information displayed on the page includes the contents of the V$STREAMS_APPLY_SERVER view. The table has a row for each of the apply server processes. For each server process, the number of

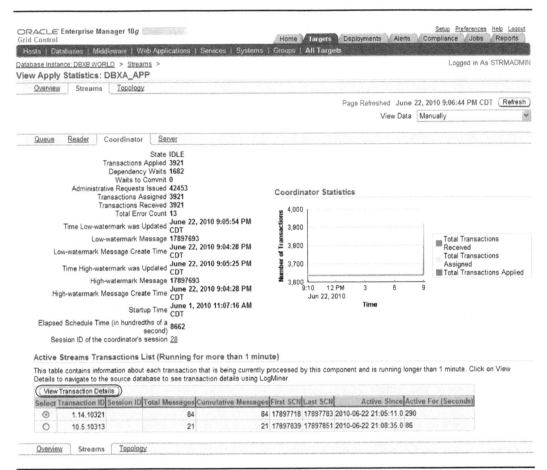

FIGURE 14-21. *Viewing coordinator statistics for apply process components*

transactions assigned and the total number of messages (LCRs) applied are displayed. The current state of the server is also displayed. The example in Figure 14-22 shows that out of four servers, two are idle, one is busy executing a transaction, and one is waiting for this transaction to commit, as it depends on the currently executing transaction. You can also drill down further to see the transaction details by selecting it and clicking the View Details button. A LogMiner session will be launched from the source database, showing you the details of the transaction.

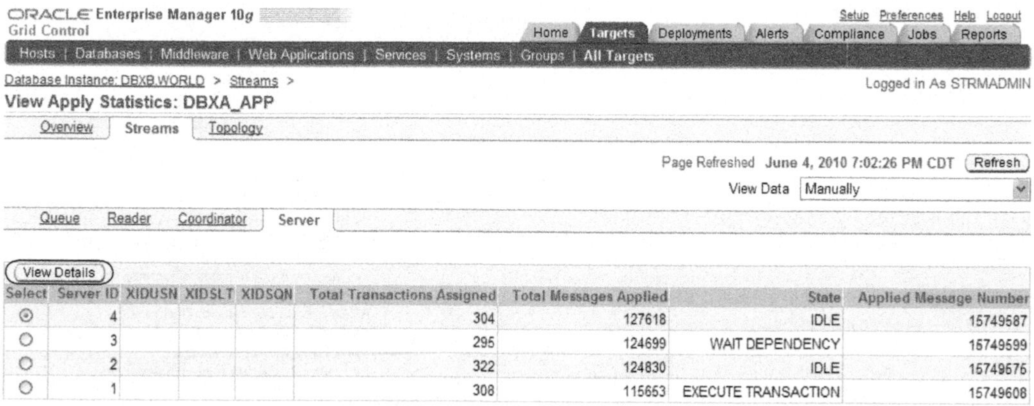

FIGURE 14-22. *Viewing server statistics for apply process components*

The Active Streams Transactions List section (refer to Figure 14-21) lists transactions that are currently executing for more than one minute. Clicking the View Transaction Details button launches a LogMiner session at the source database, as described in the following section. You may be presented with the Database Login page to connect to the source database. The LogMiner page will have the query filled in to view the data in the selected transaction.

Displaying Transaction Details: LogMiner Session

OEM Grid Control 10.2.0.5 offers a unique new feature, the ability to launch a LogMiner session at the source database to obtain detailed information about the transactions. The OEM pages showing transaction information have a drill-down button option to initiate the LogMiner session. The displayed LogMiner page automatically contains the required data to browse the transaction. You can also enter the relevant data for your specific log-mining requirement.

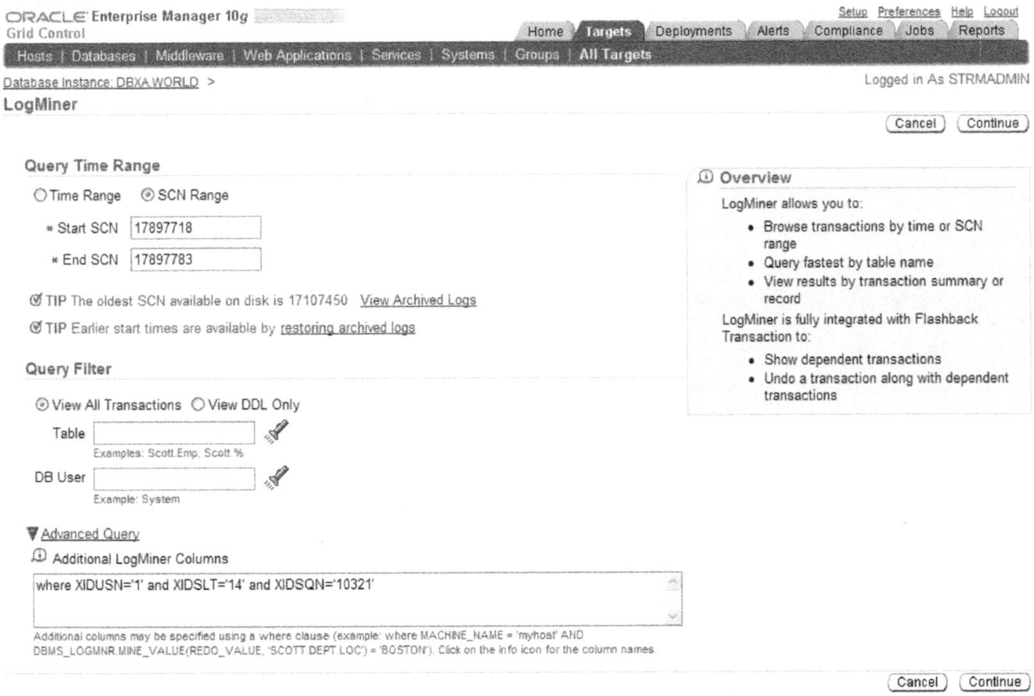

FIGURE 14-23. *LogMiner session*

Figure 14-23 shows the LogMiner page displayed after clicking the View Transaction Details button shown in Figure 14-21.

Clicking the Continue button on the LogMiner page shows the results from the LogMiner session for the selected transaction. Figure 14-24 shows the SQL redo records for the transaction. These are filtered using the Redo Record option of the View By pull-down menu. Other selections will display the operation type, the affected schema and table names, and the SQL for the undo operation.

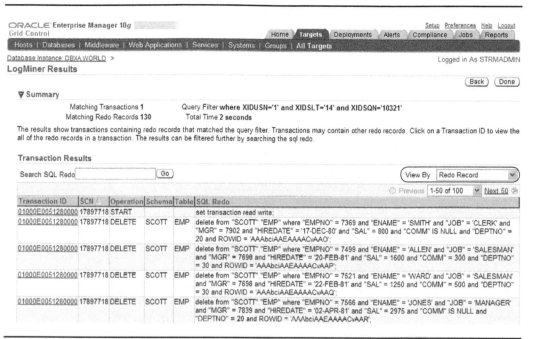

FIGURE 14-24. *LogMiner results*

Displaying Overview of Streams Components

The Streams Overview subpage of the Streams Management page in OEM Grid
Control summarizes information about Streams replication in the current database
(Streams Components) and across the database (Streams Paths). The Streams path is
the flow of the message from the source database to the destination database.

The Overview subpage, shown in Figure 14-25, is the entry point for Streams
Management, as described earlier. This page provides a simple way to check the
status of the Streams components and their performance. It also serves as a baseline
to monitor any abrupt changes in the throughput or message flow. Under the Streams
Summary (Current Database) section, each Streams component type in the current
database is listed with a status indicator followed by the number of components. In
the example shown in Figure 14-25, for the DBXA database, there is only a single
capture and a single propagation defined. Both these components are up and running,
as indicated by the check mark. Clicking the number for a component takes you to
the corresponding component subpage.

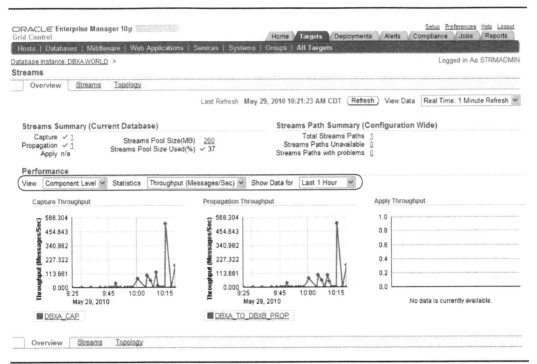

FIGURE 14-25. *Streams Overview subpage*

The Overview subpage also displays the allocated memory, in megabytes, for the Streams pool size and the percentage of the memory used by all the components. The check mark next to the Streams Pool Size Used(%) metric indicates that the percentage used is within an acceptable range for the Streams pool size alert threshold. Clicking the number for Streams Pool Size(MB) will take you to the Initialization Parameters editing page, where the Streams pool size can be modified.

The Streams Path Summary (Configuration Wide) section of the Overview subpage lists the number of Streams paths from the source to the destination, along with the number of paths unavailable and paths currently encountering problems. You can drill down to the pages for these paths by clicking the number displayed.

The Performance section displays charts showing performance of the Streams components. There are two possible performance views: Component Level and Path Level. The view can be changed using the View pull-down menu. Figure 14-25 shows the Component Level view. It is changed from the default Path Level view. The Statistics pull-down menu enables you to choose to display either Latency in seconds or Throughput (Messages/Sec), and the Show Data For pull-down menu enables you to display data for a predefined duration of Last 1 Hour, Last 12 Hours, or Last 1 Day.

The Path Level view displays charts for latency and throughput for the top five paths monitored with Grid Control.

Displaying Streams Paths and Performance Analysis Data

The Streams path begins when the LCR is enqueued into a queue at the source database, and the path ends when the LCR is dequeued by the apply process. The Streams path may flow through a number of queues and propagations before reaching the destination. So, a single Streams path can consist of a number of source-destination component pairs before reaching the apply process. Streams Performance Advisor tracks the message flow in the Streams environment as it follows the path to its destination.

To display the Streams paths for the Streams components, navigate to the Streams subpage of the Streams Management page (refer to Figure 14-14). Select the Path Level View option, as shown in Figure 14-26. It shows the Streams paths for the unidirectional replication from the DBXA database to the DBXB database.

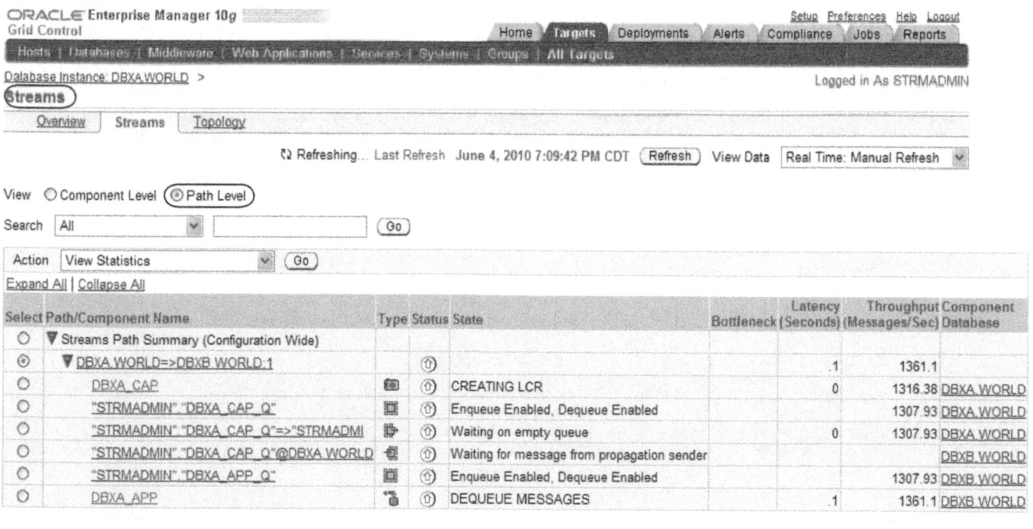

FIGURE 14-26. *Streams paths*

The Path Level view also indicates that a component is a bottleneck by displaying an icon in the Bottleneck column. If the component is a bottleneck, then check its Status column. If the component is disabled, then you can enable it. If an enabled component is a bottleneck, then check whether you can modify that component to improve its performance.

To display the performance data for a component, select the component, choose View Performance Analysis Data from the Action pull-down menu, and then click the Go button. You will see a View Details page for the capture process similar to the page shown in Figure 14-27. The Component Level Statistics table displays statistics for the selected component. This example shows the statistics for the capture process. It includes the rate for capturing and enqueuing LCRs per second, and the capture latency in seconds.

If applicable for the selected component, the Session Level Statistics table shows performance information for its subcomponents. For the capture process, there will be information for LogMiner reader, preparer, and builder processes. The page shows their idle time percentage and top wait events.

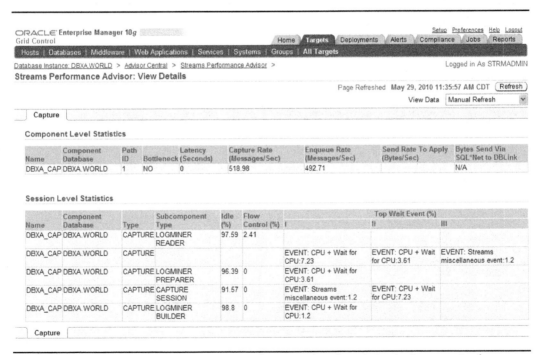

FIGURE 14-27. *Viewing component- and session-level statistics in Streams Performance Advisor*

Managing Streams Processes

The Streams process management tasks include starting and stopping the processes, changing process parameters, checking for and assigning handler procedures, viewing and modifying rules, and so on. All these tasks can be accomplished easily using the OEM pages.

The entry point to managing Streams processes is the Streams Management subpage, as shown earlier in Figure 14-14. The Action pull-down menu for the selected Streams component provides the navigation path to different tasks to manage the process.

This section reviews a couple of tasks for the capture process. The same procedures are applicable to other Streams processes.

Changing Process Parameters

As previously mentioned, the parameters for Streams processes are set with default values when Streams replication is configured using the OEM Streams Setup wizard or the MAINTAIN procedures. We can review and change these parameters using OEM very easily. Navigate to the Streams subpage on the Streams Management page (refer to Figure 14-14). If you are currently logged into the capture database, then select the capture process, choose Edit Parameters in the Action pull-down menu, and click the Go button. You will see a page similar to Figure 14-28, in which the capture process running in the DBXA database was selected. Figure 14-28 shows the capture process parameters.

You can review the current values for the capture process parameters and modify those as needed. The column Set by User displays YES after you apply the change for a particular parameter. A value of NO means the parameter was never changed from its default value. Clicking the Restore Default Values button restores default values for all the parameters. In this example, we did not change values for any of these parameters. However, we did change the Checkpoint Retention Time for the capture process from the default 60 days to 7 days. For the capture process, you can also adjust the Start SCN. Refer to Chapter 4 for more details as to when the SCN value needs to be changed.

To modify the apply process parameters, you would follow the same steps after connecting to the destination database and selecting the apply process on the Streams subpage.

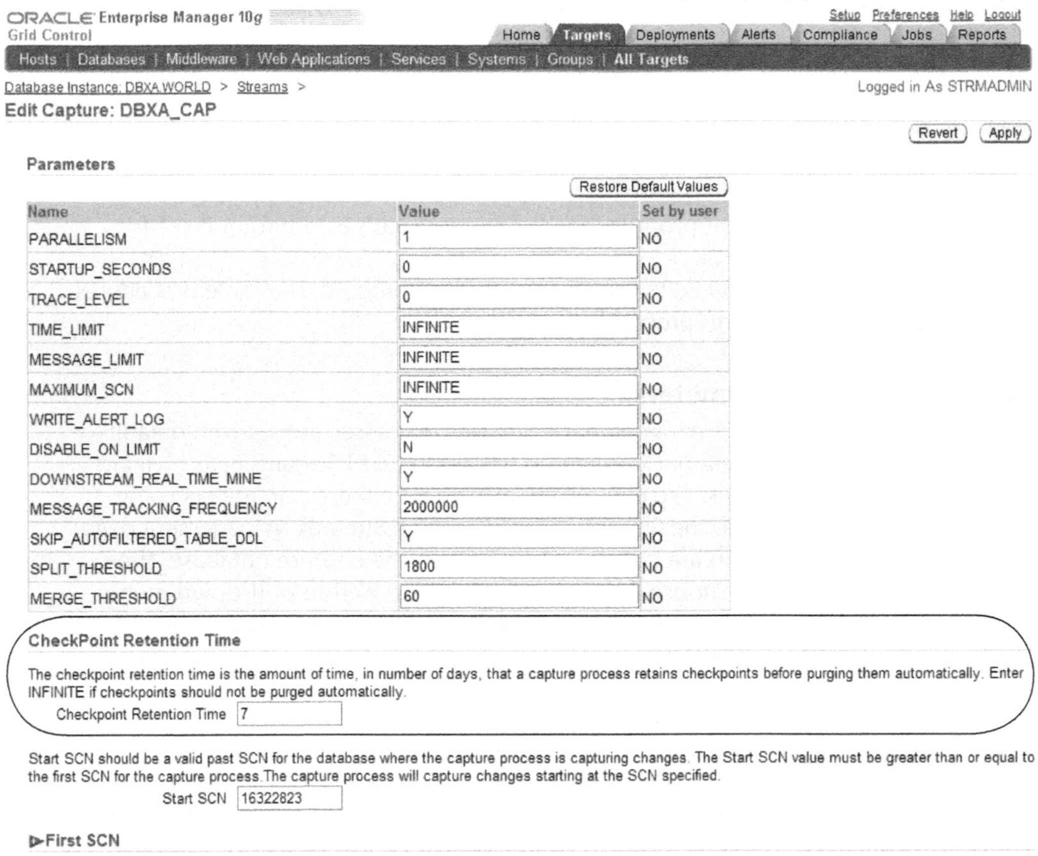

FIGURE 14-28. *Editing capture process parameters*

Managing Rules and Rule Sets

OEM simplifies viewing and modifying the rules in the positive and negative rule sets associated with the Streams processes. You can also define, or remove, rule-based transformations associated with a particular rule.

The Manage Rule Set page (see Figure 14-29) can be accessed in several ways. For example, you can select Manage Positive Ruleset or Manage Negative Ruleset from the Action pull-down menu (refer to Figure 14-15) on the Streams Management subpage of a selected Streams component. You can also click the rule set name when viewing the Streams process details (for example, as shown earlier in Figure 14-16 for the capture process).

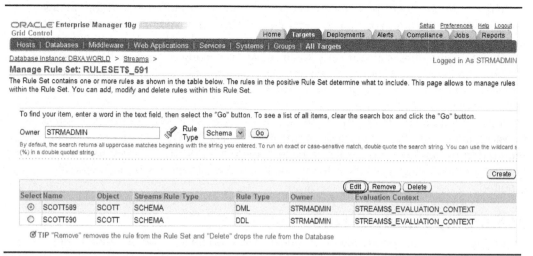

FIGURE 14-29. *Rule set management*

Figure 14-29 shows the details for a positive rule set for the capture process. The selected rule owner is STRMADMIN for the rule type of Schema. The rule set has two rules—one each for capturing DML and DDL changes for the SCOTT schema.

After selecting a particular rule, click the Edit button to open the Edit Rule page, as shown in Figure 14-30 for the DML rule SCOTT589. To remove the rule from the rule set, click the Remove button; however, the rule will remain in the database. To remove the rule from the rule set and the database, click the Delete button.

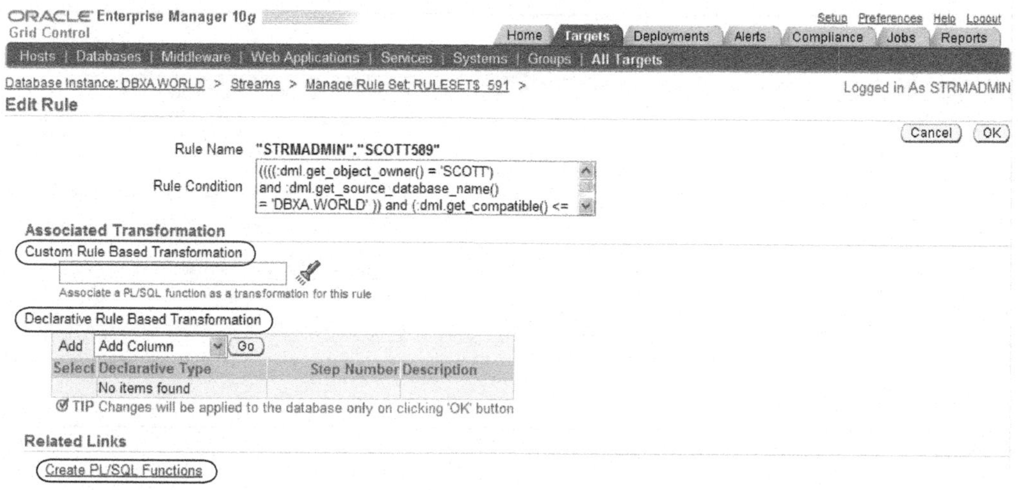

FIGURE 14-30. *Edit Rule*

The Edit Rule page displays the rule condition, and any rule-based transformations associated with the rule. You can edit the rule condition in the editing window. This is much easier than using the command-line interface to modify the rule condition. Be sure that the parentheses are properly balanced when making changes to the rule.

You can assign a custom rule-based transformation function to the rule, if one already exists. If not, clicking the link Create PL/SQL Functions at the bottom of the page will help you create one.

You can add a declarative rule-based transformation to the rule. Select the desired transformation from the Add pull-down menu and click the Go button. Provide the required information on the displayed page. If there are rule-based transformations defined for the rule, they will be listed on the page. You can modify or delete them as required.

Managing Apply Errors

The apply process can encounter errors due to data problems or configuration issues. The presence of an apply error is indicated by an Apply Error Alert reported at the bottom of the Databases Home page. Also, there will be a warning symbol on the Status icon in the Streams subpage for the apply process. Moving the cursor over the icon will pop up a message box showing the number of errors, as shown in Figure 14-31.

Clicking the Status icon displays the Apply Errors page, which lists more information about the errors, as shown in Figure 14-32. The descriptive error message provides enough clues as to the cause of the error. The information presented on this page comes from the DBA_APPLY_ERROR view. The Message Number and Message Count columns present, respectively, the LCR number in the transaction that ran into an error and the total number of LCRs in the transaction. In our example, the LCR with an error has the message number 2. The transaction also has two LCRs.

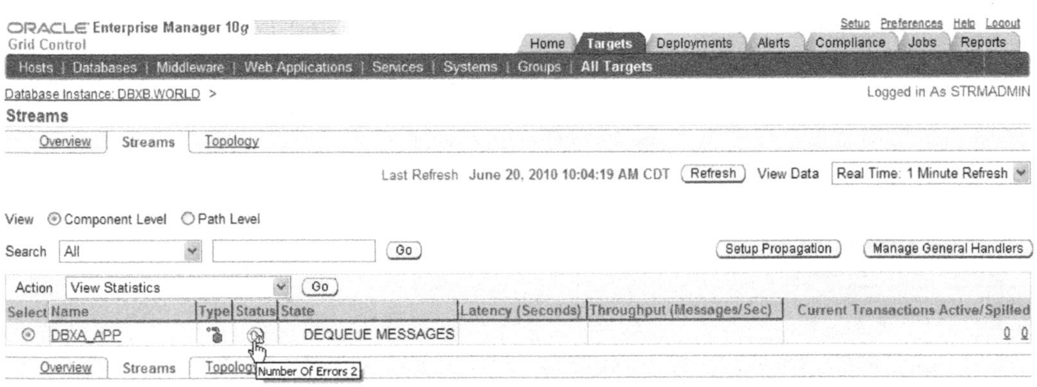

FIGURE 14-31. *Streams Management page for the apply process*

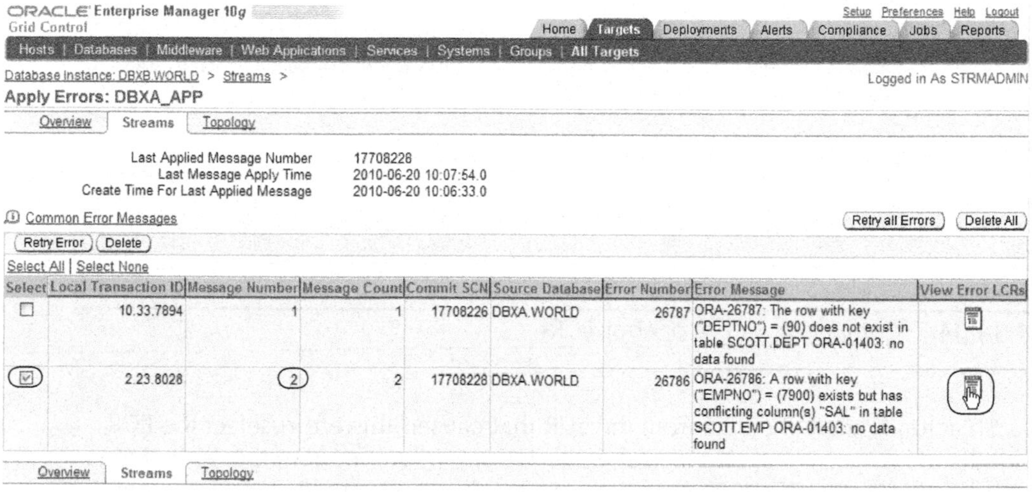

FIGURE 14-32. *Apply errors*

It is possible to retry one or more error transactions after correcting the cause of the errors, by clicking the Retry Error or Retry All Errors button. You could also delete one or more transactions. Ensure that deleting the transaction is the proper way to address the error situation. A transaction may affect multiple tables and may contain dependent data required by other dependent transactions in the error queue.

To view the LCRs in the error transaction, select the transaction and then click the icon in the View Error LCRs column, as shown in Figure 14-32. A View Error LCRs page opens (see Figure 14-33), which shows basic information about the LCRs, including the schema name, object name, type of operation, and type of LCR.

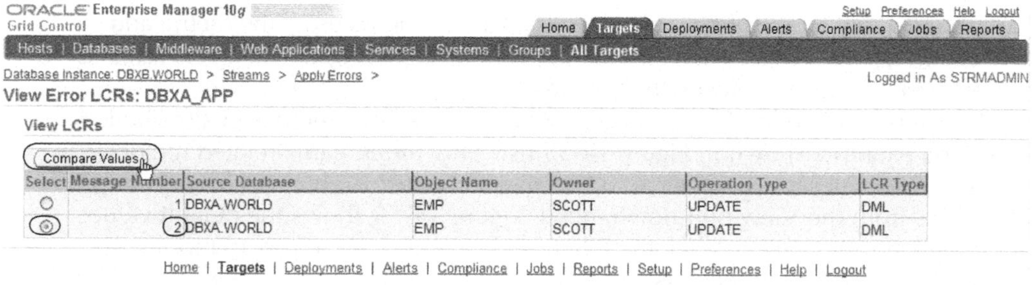

FIGURE 14-33. *Error LCRs*

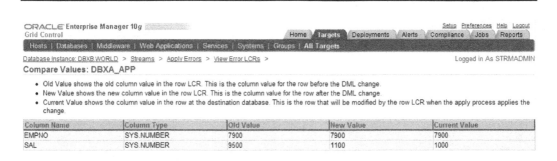

FIGURE 14-34.   *Comparing values of error LCRs*

To actually view the data from the LCR that caused this error, select the LCR with the Message Number that matches the Message Number from the Apply Errors page (see Figure 14-32). It is message number 2 in our example. Then, click the Compare Values button.

The Compare Values page (see Figure 14-34) displays the old and new values for the columns in the LCR. The information provided on this page clearly explains why the error occurred, enabling you to correct the error.

In our example, the SAL column value in the LCR did not match the SAL column value in the destination row. Updating the SAL column value in the destination row to the old value in the LCR and then retrying the transaction is one option to correct this error. Since there are no other tables involved in the transactions, we can also update the SAL column to the new value, and then remove this transaction from the error queue. However, we need to make sure that such a direct update to the destination row will not cause other issues, particularly if there is a capture process at the destination.

Streams Metrics and Alerts

Oracle Streams has its own metrics and alerts in OEM. These are enabled by default. You can view and modify the warning and critical thresholds using the Metric and Policy Setting page, which is accessible from various OEM pages. The link is listed in the Related Links section toward the bottom of the page.

The Metric and Policy Settings page displays all available metrics in alphabetical order. The example shown in Figure 14-35 lists only the Streams-related metrics after removing the rest from the captured image. This list is obtained by selecting All Metrics from the View pull-down menu. Figure 14-35 shows the default values for the thresholds. You can click the Edit icon at the end of the row to modify the thresholds per your requirements.

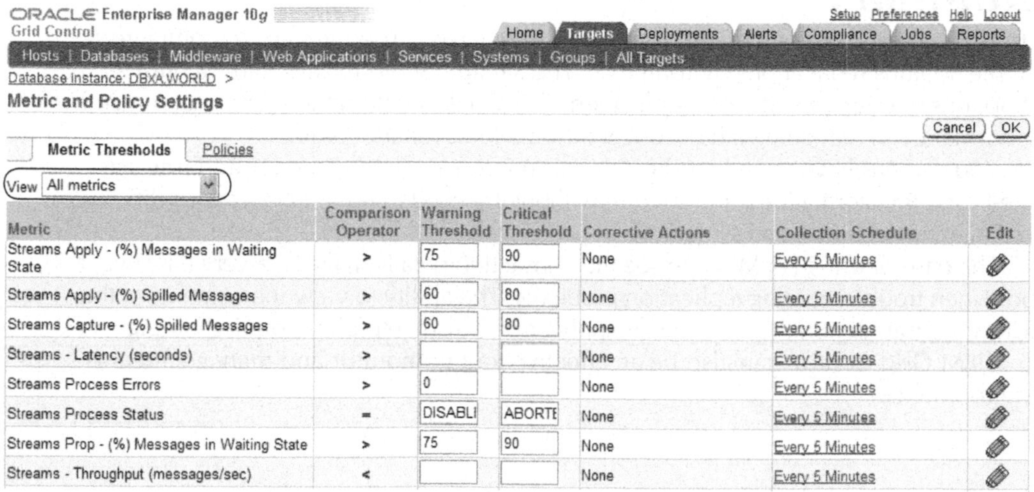

FIGURE 14-35.   *Streams metrics*

The predefined Streams alerts are listed in Table 14-1. When an alert is triggered, based on the associated metric, it is reported in the Alerts section, a link to which is located at the bottom of the Databases Home page.

The Streams alerts do not need to be managed because they are for informational purposes only. If the Streams environment is monitored regularly by other means to resolve problems as they appear, there is no need to monitor Streams alerts. You can even disable the Streams alerts altogether.

Alert Name	Alert Message
Apply Aborts Alert	Streams apply process <apply_name> aborted with ORA-<error_number>
Apply Error Alert	Streams error queue for apply process <apply_name> contains new transaction with ORA-<error_number>
Capture Aborts Alert	Streams capture process <capture_name> aborted with ORA-<error_number>
Propagation Aborts Alert	Streams propagation process <source_queue>, <destination_queue>, <database_link> aborted after 16 failures

TABLE 14-1.   *Streams Alerts*

Summary

Oracle Enterprise Manager Grid Control offers an easy-to-use interface to configure simple Streams replication environments. The Streams Setup wizard offers a number of options to configure Streams replication. OEM makes it possible to monitor Streams performance in real time with historical information available online.

You can easily view and modify Streams process parameters, rules and rule sets, rule-based transformations, and so forth without the need to remember various different packages, procedures, and syntax.

The ease of using LogMiner to see the transaction details makes it a very effective tool when troubleshooting replication problems. The ability to view the contents of the LCRs for a transaction that ran into an apply error is also helpful in troubleshooting.

OEM Grid Control can also be an effective tool to monitor and manage Streams environments.

PART
V

Appendixes

APPENDIX
A

Oracle Streams
Best Practices

or a successful implementation of Oracle Streams for data replication, Oracle recommends that you follow certain guidelines or best practices. This appendix discusses these best practices.

Oracle Patches

Make sure that all the Oracle databases involved in Streams replication have the latest critical software patches applied for their platforms. Consult the My Oracle Support (MOS) website to acquire currently available patches. Consult MOS note 437838.1 for the recommended Streams-specific patches. Apply all the applicable patch set updates (PSUs) for your platform and environment.

If you use OEM Grid Control 10.2.0.5 to manage your Streams environment, then consult MOS Note 1078864.1 for applicable patches and PSUs for the Oracle Agent and Oracle Management Server.

If you use the downstream capture process, consult MOS for any issues related to the redo log transport mechanism.

Thoroughly test the Streams replication environment after applying any patches.

ARCHIVELOG Mode and Archived Log Files

If you are only using the synchronous capture process, then it is possible to run the source database in NOARCHIVELOG mode. Otherwise, the source database must be running in ARCHIVELOG mode.

Configure a local archive destination for the archived log files. This applies even when using the Flash Recovery Area (FRA). Do not place archived log files only in the FRA, as it is a fixed-size storage area and log files may get purged when there is space pressure.

In one-way Streams replication, running the destination database in ARCHIVELOG mode is not required, though it is recommended to facilitate media recovery.

Tablespace for Streams

Create a dedicated tablespace for Streams-specific objects to allow for better space management. Use of Automatic Segment Space Management (ASSM) is strongly recommended because it facilitates shrinking of object segments.

For the local capture process, the tablespace should be created in the source and destination databases. For the downstream capture process, the tablespace should be created in the downstream database running the capture process and in the destination database.

Streams Administrator User Account

Create a separate database user account to act as a Streams Administrator to configure and maintain the Streams replication environment. Do not use the SYS or SYSTEM account for this purpose.

A separate Streams Administrator account will facilitate separation of duties, when and if required. Assign the Streams tablespace as the default tablespace for this account.

Streams Administrator Privileges

All the required privileges to configure and maintain the Streams environment are granted to the Streams Administrator user, say, STRMADMIN, by the GRANT_ADMIN_ PRIVILEGE procedure in the DBMS_STREAMS_AUTH package, as shown here:

```
execute DBMS_STREAMS_AUTH.GRANT_ADMIN_PRIVILEGE('STRMADMIN');
```

In addition, the Streams Administrator requires the DBA role during the Streams configuration steps. Chapter 8 has more details about privileges granted to the Streams Administrator.

Database Initialization Parameters

Configure the key initialization parameters for the databases in Streams replication. These parameters are described in Chapter 8.

It is recommended that the `streams_pool_size` parameter be set explicitly, even when using ASMM or AMM. The recommended minimum value for this parameter is 256MB. Monitor the V$STREAMS_POOL_ADVICE view and adjust the value for this parameter. When configuring the downstream capture process, the `streams_pool_size` parameter is not required at the source database.

Database Links

Make sure that all Streams databases are accessible over Oracle Net. Create private database links in the Streams Administrator schema.

Use the global name of the destination database as the database link name from the source database.

For the downstream capture process, create a database link pointing to the source database from the downstream database, in addition to the database link pointing to the destination database.

Validate all database links by logging in as Streams Administrator and selecting information from the remote database—for example, select the name of the database pointed to by the database link.

Network Tuning

For propagating changes over a significant distance, it is suggested to tune the Oracle Net and TCP/IP parameters. This network tuning is applicable to both the local and downstream capture process configurations, and is highly recommended in a WAN environment. The network tuning involves changing operating system parameters, network device queue sizes, and Oracle Net parameters.

Operating System Parameters

The parameters listed here are for the Linux operating system. Check with your system administrator for comparable parameters for other operating systems.

Set the maximum value for the network core write and receive memory buffer:

```
net.core.rmem_max = 16777216
net.core.wmem_max = 16777216
```

Set the minimum, default, and maximum values for the TPC/IP read and write buffers:

```
net.ipv4.tcp_rmem = 4096   87380   16777216
net.ipv4.tcp_wmem = 4096   65536   16777216
```

These parameters are set in the /etc/sysctl.conf file, which requires root access to change. Once the file is modified, issue the command sysctl -p to make the changes effective. There is no need to reboot the server. It is a good idea to save a copy of the file before you make your changes.

Network Device Queue Size

The size of the queue between the network subsystem and the device driver for the network interface card can also be modified. However, you should consult with system and network administrators before modifying the queue sizes. Improper queue sizes may affect overall TCP throughput.

The network device queue sizes are important for TCP, because losses on local queues cause TCP to fall into congestion control, limiting the TCP sending rates.

For the Linux operating system, there are two queues:

- **Interface Transmit Queue**   The queue size is configured by the network interface option txqueuelen.

- **Network Receive Queue**   The queue size is configured by the kernel parameter netdev_max_backlog.

The default value of 100 for txqueuelen is inadequate for long-distance, high-throughput networks. For example, a 1GB network with a latency of 100 ms would benefit from `txqueuelen` set at 10000. These parameters can be changed as follows for the `eth0` network:

```
echo 20000 > /proc/sys/net/core/netdev_max_backlog
echo 1 > /proc/sys/net/ipv4/route/flush
ifconfig eth0 txqueuelen 10000
```

Oracle Net Parameters

In addition to the operating system parameters, there are a couple of Oracle Net parameters that Oracle recommends modifying to improve propagation performance over the network.

Session Data Unit Size

Under typical database configuration, Oracle Net encapsulates data into buffers the size of the **session data unit (SDU)** before sending the data across the network. Oracle Net sends each buffer when it is filled or flushed, or when an application tries to read data. Adjusting the size of the SDU buffers relative to the amount of data provided to Oracle Net to send at any one time can improve performance, network utilization, and memory consumption.

When large amounts of data are being propagated from the source database to the destination database, increasing the SDU size can improve performance and network throughput. It is recommended to set SDU to 32767.

At the source database, specify the SDU parameter in the `tnsnames.ora` file for the connect descriptor for the destination database, as shown here:

```
DBXB.WORLD =
  (DESCRIPTION =
    (SDU = 32767)
    (ADDRESS = (PROTOCOL = TCP)(HOST = linux2)(PORT = 1521))
    (CONNECT_DATA =
       (SERVER = DEDICATED)
       (SERVICE_NAME = DBXB.WORLD)
    )
  )
```

At the destination database, specify the SDU parameter in the `listener.ora` file as shown next for listener name LISTENER:

```
SID_LIST_LISTENER =
(SID_LIST=
  (SID_DESC=
    (SDU=32767)
    (SID_NAME=DBXB)
    (GLOBAL_DBNAME=DBXB.WORLD)
  )
)
```

TCP Socket Buffer Size

Reliable network protocols, such as TCP/IP, buffer data into send and receive buffers while sending and receiving to or from lower- and upper-layer protocols. The sizes of these buffers affect network performance by influencing flow control decisions.

The `recv_buf_size` and `send_buf_size` parameters specify sizes of socket buffers associated with an Oracle Net connection. To ensure the continuous flow of data and better utilization of network bandwidth for the propagation of LCRs, specify the buffer size for receive and send operations with the `recv_buf_size` and `send_buf_size` parameters.

The optimal socket buffer size is three times the Bandwidth-Delay Product (BDP). The BDP is computed based on the bandwidth of the network link, and the network Round Trip Time (RTT). The RTT is the time required for the network communication to travel from the source database to the destination database and back. RTT is measured in milliseconds.

You can ask your network administrator for the RTT value for your network link, and the network bandwidth. Assuming 1Gb network bandwidth and a RTT of 30 ms, the BDP can be computed as shown here:

BDP = Network Bandwidth in Bytes * RTT
 = 1,000,000,000 bits * 0.030 second
 = 30,000,000 bits
 = 30,000,000 / 8 bytes
 = 3,750,000 bytes/second

From this example, the optimal buffer size can be computed as follows:

Socket Buffer Size = 3 * BDP
 = 3 * 3,750,000
 = 11,250,000 bytes

Although the socket buffer size can be set at the operating system level, setting it at the Oracle Net level is recommended so that other TCP sessions will not use additional memory.

At the source database, set the `send_buf_size` and `recv_buf_size` parameters in the `tnsnames.ora` file for the connect descriptor for the destination database as shown here:

```
DBXB.WORLD =
  (DESCRIPTION =
  (SDU = 32767)
  (SEND_BUF_SIZE = 11250000)
  (RECV_BUF_SIZE = 11250000)
  (ADDRESS = (PROTOCOL = TCP)(HOST = linux2)(PORT = 1521))
  (CONNECT_DATA =
     (SERVER = DEDICATED)
     (SERVICE_NAME = DBXB.WORLD)
  )
  )
```

At the destination database, the `send_buf_size` and `recv_buf_size` parameters can be set in the `listener.ora` or `sqlnet.ora` file as follows:

```
# listener.ora
LISTENER =
(DESCRIPTION =
 (SEND_BUF_SIZE = 11250000)
 (RECV_BUF_SIZE = 11250000)
 (ADDRESS = (PROTOCOL=tcp)(HOST=linux2)(PORT=1521))
)


# sqlnet.ora
SEND_BUF_SIZE = 11250000
RECV_BUF_SIZE = 11250000
```

Heartbeat Table

A "heartbeat" table in a Streams environment is a small replicated table against which periodic DML activity is performed at the source.

The Streams capture process requests a LogMiner checkpoint after mining 1000MB of redo information. During the checkpoint, the metadata for Streams is maintained if there are active transactions.

Implementing a heartbeat table is recommended; particularly when there is low DML activity for a considerable amount of time. Periodic DML activity against the heartbeat table ensures that there are open transactions occurring regularly in the source database. Such activity will provide additional opportunities for the metadata to be updated often. Also, the APPLIED_SCN column of the DBA_CAPTURE view is updated periodically when there is DML activity in the database that gets replicated.

Generally, the heartbeat table has two columns to store the source database name, or some other identifier, and a timestamp. It is often created in the Streams Administrator schema. You may insert a row into the table to begin with, and then update the timestamp at a set interval using a job scheduler.

You can also consider a heartbeat table with two columns at the source and three columns at the destination. The third column will store the local timestamp when the row is inserted at the destination. In this case, instead of updating the row at the source, you will periodically insert a row. The apply process can then have a DML handler procedure to add the third timestamp column. The timestamp columns can help you quickly determine the approximate latency, and the rows in the table can provide historical information. With DDL replication set up for the heartbeat table, you can truncate the data when it is not required. Use of a DML handler is suggested, in case there is no positive rule set associated with the apply process; otherwise, you can use the ADD_COLUMN procedure of the DBMS_STREAMS_ADM package.

DDL Replication

When replicating DDL changes, do not use the system-generated names for constraints and indexes. Any changes to these objects may fail at the destination database because object names may not match.

The tablespace name for the replicated objects should also be kept identical between Streams databases. If this is not possible, then use a DDL handler to modify the DDL text to handle such differences.

Establish Performance Goals

In almost all replication environments, it is expected that the replicated data will be available as fast as possible after the changes are committed at the source database. In reality, there are a number of factors that may affect the speed of replication. You should define the goals, often referred to as a Service Level Agreement (SLA), for replication depending on the application workload and the replication environment.

You should establish goals for the following:

- Throughput rate
- Replication latency (lag time)

Use the Streams Performance Advisor utility (UTL_SPADV) to gather Streams performance data, as discussed in Chapter 11. The collected information will show the throughput rate and replication latency for the capture, propagation, and apply processes. If goals for these are met, then there is no need to take any actions. The Streams Performance Advisor output also identifies the bottlenecks to help you concentrate your troubleshooting efforts. Often, large batch processes run during the nighttime hours. This may cause an increase in the replication latency and decrease in throughput rate as compared to the mostly OLTP operations that run during the daytime. The SLAs should account for any such variations.

APPENDIX
B

Oracle Streams
Replication in a
RAC Environment

he Streams setup in a RAC environment is not much different from the Streams setup in a single-instance database. Because of multiple nodes and instances in a RAC environment, some additional configuration details must be dealt with, as described in the following sections.

Archived Logs

The capture process can be configured as a local capture or as a downstream capture in the RAC environment. When required, the capture process needs to mine all the archived logs, so the instance that is running the capture process needs to have access to archived log threads from all the other instances on a shared file system. When you're using Streams, Oracle recommends that you not store the archived logs in the Flash Recovery Area (FRA). The FRA is a fixed-sized storage area, and the archived logs will be removed from FRA when the amount of space available becomes low, even when the capture process needs these logs to restart. You can define `log_archive_dest_<n>` parameter as an additional location where the capture process can independently access the archived log files.

Streams Queues

As discussed in Chapter 5, the Streams queue table contains the information regarding the queues used by the Streams components. When the source and/or destination database is running in a RAC environment, we can specify one of the instances as the primary instance for the queue table. This instance acts as the primary "owner" of the queue table. It is possible to specify the primary and secondary instances for the ownership of a queue table.

The ALTER_QUEUE_TABLE procedure of the DBMS_AQADM package allows us to specify the primary and secondary instances for the queue table. If this procedure is not used to indicate the primary instance as the owner of the queue table, then the instance from where the queue is created becomes the primary instance of the queue table. The ALTER_QUEUE_TABLE procedure can only define two instances for ownership of the queue table.

When the primary instance becomes unavailable, for whatever reason, the ownership of the queue table transfers to the secondary instance. If the secondary instance was not defined, or is not available, then any other instance, if available, that responds will become the owner of the queue table.

When the source database is a RAC database, the capture and propagation processes will always run on the instance that owns the queue table. When the primary instance becomes unavailable, the capture process automatically restarts on the instance that becomes the owner of the queue table. When the primary instance becomes available, the capture process automatically switches back.

When the destination database is a RAC database, a similar setup for the Streams queue will enable the apply process to run on the surviving instance of the database that owns the Streams queue.

The propagation process of the source database always connects to the instance of the destination database that owns the queue table of the destination Streams queue.

Queue-to-Queue Propagation

Chapter 5 discussed the queue-to-database link propagation and queue-to-queue propagation methods. In a RAC environment, the queue-to-queue propagation method has a unique feature: it uses the service name to connect to the destination queue. The queue service is automatically created when a buffered queue is created in a RAC environment.

The following example shows such a service at the destination database. The service creation date will match the queue creation date.

```
SQL> select name,
  3          network_name,
  4          creation_date
  5     from dba_services
  6    where name in (select owner ||'.'|| name
  7                     from dba_queues);

NAME                        NETWORK_NAME                  CREATION_DATE
------------------------    ----------------------------  --------------------
STRMADMIN.DBXA_APP_Q SYS$STRMADMIN.DBXA_APP_Q.DBXB DEC 26 2009 11:11:01
```

The automatically created queue service is managed by Oracle. There is no need for you to manage it.

The service for the queue-to-queue propagation always runs in the instance that owns the Streams queue. So, a transparent failover of the propagation process is possible when the RAC instance fails. In this case, the queue ownership switches to the secondary instance, if defined, or to any other surviving instance. When the primary instance becomes available, the service and the propagation switch back automatically.

On the other hand, the queue-to-database link propagation connects to the instance-specific database link that refers to the owner instance of the destination queue. If this instance crashes and the propagation tries to connect to another instance, you might get an ORA-25303 error: "Buffered operation allowed only on the owner instance."

Checking Queue Table and Streams Process Locations

The following query shows the instance number that currently owns the Streams queue and its defined primary and secondary instances:

```
SQL> select queue_table,
  2          owner_instance,
  3          primary_instance,
  4          secondary_instance
  5    from dba_queue_tables
  6   where owner = 'STRMADMIN';

QUEUE_TABLE     OWNER_INSTANCE PRIMARY_INSTANCE SECONDARY_INSTANCE
--------------- -------------- ---------------- ------------------
DBXA_CAP_Q_T                 3                2                  3
```

The following query shows the instance currently running the capture process:

```
SQL> select inst_id,
  2          sid,
  3          serial#,
  4          state
  5    from gv$streams_capture
  6   where capture_name = 'DBXA_CAP';

INST_ID        SID    SERIAL# STATE
------- ---------- ---------- ------------------
      3       1017        149 CAPTURING CHANGES
```

From these examples, we can see that the capture process is running in instance 3, which is defined as the secondary instance for the queue table in the database. In this case, the primary instance 2 evidently is not available, and the capture process has switched to instance 3.

Creating Standby Redo Log Groups for Downstream Capture

Chapter 8 discussed the configuration of the downstream capture process. The following steps show how to configure the redo transport for the real-time downstream capture process when the source database is a RAC database.

1. On the source database, find out the size of the redo log file and the number of redo log groups per thread. We can query the V$LOG view for this information for all instances (threads):

```
-- Connect to Source Database
SQL> connect sys/manager@DBXA.WORLD as sysdba
Connected.
SQL> select group#,
  2         thread#,
  3         bytes/1048576 MB
  4    from v$log;

    GROUP#    THREAD#           MB
---------- ---------- -----------
         1          1           50
         2          1           50
         3          2           50
         4          2           50
```

The log file size is 50MB, and there are two threads (for a two-node RAC database), each with two log groups. The total number of log groups is four in this case. We need to have three standby log groups per thread with the log file of size 50MB.

2. On the downstream database, create standby redo logs with the next higher group number. The number of the standby log groups should be one higher than the number of redo log groups in each instance of the database. So, we need three standby log groups per thread with the log file of size of 50MB.

The total number of standby logs will be (number of log groups + 1) * number of threads. In this example, we need (2 + 1) * 2 = 6 standby log groups. There will be three standby log groups per thread starting with group number 5, as shown in the following example. We are creating only one log member per group.

```
SQL> -- Connect to Downstream Database
SQL> connect sys/manager@DBXB.WORLD as sysdba
Connected.
SQL> alter database add standby logfile thread 1 group 5
  2    ('/u01/oradata/DBXA/standby_logs/standby_redo05.log') size 50M;
Database altered.
SQL> alter database add standby logfile thread 1 group 6
  2    ('/u01/oradata/DBXA/standby_logs/standby_redo06.log') size 50M;
Database altered.
SQL> alter database add standby logfile thread 1 group 7
  2    ('/u01/oradata/DBXA/standby_logs/standby_redo07.log') size 50M;
Database altered.
```

```
SQL> alter database add standby logfile thread 2 group 8
  2    ('/u01/oradata/DBXA/standby_logs/standby_redo08.log') size 50M;
Database altered.
SQL> alter database add standby logfile thread 2 group 9
  2    ('/u01/oradata/DBXA/standby_logs/standby_redo09.log') size 50M;
Database altered.
SQL> alter database add standby logfile thread 2 group 10
  2    ('/u01/oradata/DBXA/standby_logs/standby_redo10.log') size 50M;
Database altered.

SQL> -- Check created Standby logs
SQL> select thread#,
  2         group#,
  3         sequence#,
  4         status,
  5         archived
  6    from v$standby_log;

   THREAD#     GROUP#  SEQUENCE# STATUS     ARC
---------- ---------- ---------- ---------- ---
         1          5          0 UNASSIGNED YES
         1          6          0 UNASSIGNED YES
         1          7          0 UNASSIGNED YES
         2          8          0 UNASSIGNED YES
         2          9          0 UNASSIGNED YES
         2         10          0 UNASSIGNED YES
```

The standby log files are created, but not yet assigned for use.

APPENDIX
C

Streams Health
Check Report

he Oracle-provided Streams Health Check script produces a comprehensive report of the Streams environment in the database. The script for your version of the database can be downloaded from the My Oracle Support website. MOS note 27367.1 has links to download the script.

Oracle Support will ask for the Health Check (HC) report from all Streams databases when you open a service request for any Streams-related issue. Depending on your Streams environment, the generated report may be very detailed. It may also take some time to run the script.

The HC report provides complete information about the Streams environment in the database. You can use this information to confirm that the Streams setup has been done correctly. The information is also very useful to diagnose the cause of problems in Streams replication. The HC report includes performance statistics for the Streams components.

The HC script does not alter the configuration or change any database settings. The script only reports the Streams configuration and operation of Streams replication when it is run. The HC script uses default values to issue warnings. If those defaults are not suitable for your environment, you may want to change them.

The HC report is too lengthy to include here as an example. It is suggested that you create one for your setup, as described next, and then review it by following the discussion in the "How to Use Health Check Report" section, which focuses on only a few sections of the report that alert you about potential problems.

How to Run the Streams Health Check Script

Make sure you run the correct script for your version of the database. The script does not spool the output to a file. You can either include the SPOOL command in the script or set it manually in the SQL session. It does turn the spooling off at the end.

The default output is in HTML format. Using this format is recommended because it makes it easy to navigate to the various parts of the report when viewing it via a web browser. You can turn off the HTML format by changing `set markup HTML ON` to `set markup HTML OFF` in the first few lines of the script. Oracle Support will need the report in HTML format, though. By default, the HC script connects to the local database using the `connect / as sysdba` command.

```
$ sqlplus /nolog
SQL> spool streams_hc_report_DBXA.html
SQL> @streams_hc_11GR2.sql
SQL> exit;
```

When to Run the Streams Health Check Script

Ideally, you should run the HC script right after completing the Streams setup, and review the report for configuration issues, if any. Don't wait until Oracle Support asks you to run the script!

You should also run the HC script during peak load on the database. This will capture statistical information that can be used to diagnose any issues with Streams processes. The HC script itself triggers additional checks depending on some of the performance data.

Of course, when you suspect replication is not working as expected, you should run the HC script first and review the HC report for any obvious issues. The HC script should be run in all Streams databases simultaneously to capture relevant statistics and information for Streams components.

It is a good idea to run the HC script routinely (once a week or so), to record the latest information about your replication environment. In situations in which you have to re-create the entire environment or only some of the Streams components, you will find all the needed information in the HC report.

The HC script is a collection of several different SQL and PL/SQL scripts. You can create your own custom version of the HC script to gather only the important information for your configuration.

How to Use the Health Check Report

The HC report has three main sections—Configuration, Analysis, and Statistics. Each section in turn has several links to different subsections in the report. The headings for these subsections are self-explanatory as to what information they display. Also, the following lines that appear on several pages facilitate easy navigation to the subsections in the report:

```
Configuration: Database Queue Capture Propagation Apply XStream
Analysis: History Rules Notifications Configuration Performance Wait Analysis Topology
Statistics: Streams Statistics Queue Capture Propagation Apply Apply_Errors XStream
Outbound XStream Inbound
```

Configuration

The Configuration section contains information about the database, the instance, key initialization parameters for Streams, and all the details about the Streams components defined in the database. These include their current status, state, tracked SCNs, parameters, rule transformations, handler procedures, and so on. Some of the information reported is critical in diagnosing replication problems, as discussed next.

The name of the archived log file that the capture process will access when it is restarted is listed under the following heading:

++ Minimum Archive Log Necessary to Restart Capture ++

All the subsequent archived log files should also be available for the capture process. This is critical information. If you do not use RMAN for archived log backup and removal using the RETENTION POLICY setting, then the preceding information can be used to determine which archived log files can be safely purged.

Other important information reported in this section includes the supplemental logging and the objects prepared for instantiation in the source database. Improper supplemental logging can cause apply errors. The displayed information can be easily used to verify supplemental logging at the source database. If the objects are not prepared for instantiation, that can also cause apply errors. Check for this information under these headings:

```
++ TABLES PREPARED FOR CAPTURE ++
++ SCHEMAS PREPARED FOR CAPTURE ++
++ DATABASE PREPARED FOR CAPTURE ++
++ TABLES WITH SUPPLEMENTAL LOGGING ++
++ TABLE LEVEL SUPPLEMENTAL LOG GROUPS ENABLED FOR CAPTURE ++
```

NOTE
In a downstream capture environment, run the HC script in the source database to get supplemental logging information.

For the Streams processes, the rule set, rules, and rule condition are listed. Checking the rules and rule condition is important when you suspect the change is not replicated.

The registered archived log files for the capture process are also listed under the following heading:

++ Registered Log Files for Capture ++

The information includes whether or not the file contains a data dictionary. This can be a long list of files, particularly when the `checkpoint_retention_time` parameter for the capture process is set to a high value, or left at the default value of 60 days.

Analysis

The Analysis section shows statistical information for Streams queues and processes for the last 24 hours in hourly snapshots. This information is useful to see the number of messages that are captured, enqueued, propagated, and applied.

The HC script performs a detailed analysis of the Streams environment and notifies you of possible problem areas. The findings are grouped in the Summary subsection and reported under the following headings toward the end of the report:

```
++ Notifications ++
++ SYS Checks
++ init.ora checks ++
++ Configuration checks ++
++ Performance Checks ++
++ STREAMS Process Wait Analysis ++
```

Under the Notifications heading, you will see messages only when there is a problem with the Streams processes or components. In that case, a descriptive message tells you exactly what the problem is. These notification messages are triggered based on values of certain parameters. The threshold values for those parameters are hard-coded into the HC script. If the default values are not suitable, then you can modify them in the HC script. These are defined after the following line in the HC script:

```
prompt   ++ <a name="Notification">Notifications</a> ++
```

In the SYS Checks subsection, notification message will be reported when the Streams pool utilization exceeds the default value of 95 percent. Again, this threshold can be adjusted in the script. There will be a message if there is a problem with buffer queue recovery. Ideally, there should be no messages reported in this subsection.

In the init.ora checks subsection, you will see messages if the key initialization parameters are not set correctly.

The Configuration Checks subsection of the HC report contains output from a number of checks performed by the script. These checks include the following:

- Propagation Latency

- Database Names in Rules

- Overlapping Rules

- Queue Name Length

- Queue Table Name Length

- Database Registry Status

- Shared Streams Queue for Apply and Capture

- Supplemental Logging Checks

Ideally, there should not be any messages reported by these checks. This will confirm that your Streams setup does not have any obvious issues.

In addition to these messages, there will be a few suggestions printed if rule sets are defined for propagation and apply processes. For cases in which everything captured is replicated without any rule transformations, then consider removing the rule set from the Streams process. This can help improve the performance of the process since there won't be rule evaluations performed.

In the Performance Checks subsection, warning messages will be reported when the HC script detects problems with Streams processes and queue performance. Such warnings are issued for

- Capture Latency

- Apply Reader Latency

- Apply Coordinator Latency

- Number of Unconsumed Messages in Queues

- Percentage of Spilled Messages

- LogMiner Spilling Messages

- Complex Rules

The thresholds for these warning are hard-coded into the HC scripts. You can change them to suit your requirements.

The STREAMS Process Wait Analysis subsection contains the past 30 minutes of information about the wait events encountered by the Streams processes. The wait events can provide a clue of any bottlenecks that may be adversely affecting the Streams process performance.

NOTE
The Configuration Checks subsection of the HC report should be reviewed for potential problems after creating or altering the Streams setup.

Statistics

The Statistics section contains the detailed performance data for all the Streams components. This information is dynamic as of the time the HC script was run, and includes data for the Streams components that are enabled and active.

Most of the information in this section can be used to track the performance of the Streams components.

Information under the following headings is of particular interest because it points to potential and current problems:

```
++ LOGMINER STATISTICS ++
++ APPLY SPILLED TRANSACTIONS ++
++ ERROR QUEUE ++
```

The LOGMINER STATISTICS subsection for the capture process lists values for the critical statistics. The bytes paged out statistics should ideally have a value of zero. Any non-zero value indicates that the LogMiner process is spilling redo information to disk. This will adversely affect capture process latency. Increasing the value for the _sga_size parameter for the capture process will reduce or eliminate page outs.

The APPLY SPILLED TRANSACTIONS subsection lists the transactions that have been spilled to the disk error queue. Spilled transactions will cause apply latency to increase. You may have to investigate transaction sizes and adjust the txn_lcr_spill_threshold and txn_age_spill_threshold apply parameters, as well as the streams_pool_size parameter in the destination database.

The ERROR QUEUE subsection lists information about the transactions that are in the apply error queue on disk. The information is sorted in order of the source commit SCN and shows the LCR number in the transaction that caused the error as well the number of LCRs in the error transaction. A large number of apply errors has an impact on the SYSAUX tablespace and will adversely affect apply process performance when reapplying the error transactions and during its cleanup afterward.

Other Information

The HC report contains additional information that is not linked to any of the particular sections described previously. This information contains the following sections (not a complete list):

- Defined Comparisons and Comparison Information

- Constraints on Tables Configured in Streams

- List Indexes on Tables

- List Unsupported Tables in Streams

- Streams Dictionary Information

- LogMiner Database Map

- LogMiner Statistics

- LogMiner Session Statistics

- LogMiner Cache Objects
- LCR Cache Information
- Streams Pool Memory Information
- Queue Memory and Flow Control Values
- Defined Jobs in Database
- Current Long Running Transactions
- Streams Pool Advice
- Streams Alerts History, Most Recent Streams Alerts (Max=10) Occurring Within Last 10 Days
- Initialization Parameters

APPENDIX
D

Data Dictionary Views for
Streams Replication

here are a number of data dictionary views that display information about Streams processes and configuration. The following list briefly describes several of these DBA and V$ views that you may access. Not all DBA views have corresponding ALL and USER versions. In a RAC environment, please use the GV$ version of the V$ view.

Views for Configuration and Administrative Tasks

- **DBA_STREAMS_ADD_COLUMN** This view lists the columns added to the row LCR by rule transformation procedure DBMS_STREAMS_ADM. ADD_COLUMN.

- **DBA_STREAMS_ADMINISTRATOR** This view displays information about the users who have been granted privileges by the procedures in the DBMS_STREAMS_AUTH package. It displays whether a user has local or remote Streams administrative privileges.

- **DBA_STREAMS_COLUMNS** This view contains information about the columns that are not supported by the Streams replication.

- **DBA_STREAMS_DELETE_COLUMN** This view lists the columns removed from the row LCR by rule transformation procedure DBMS_STREAMS_ADM .DELETE_COLUMN.

- **DBA_STREAMS_KEEP_COLUMNS** This view displays information about the columns that are kept in the row LCR in the rule transformation associated with the rule.

- **DBA_STREAMS_NEWLY_SUPPORTED** This view lists all the tables that are newly supported by the capture process starting from the specified database compatibility level. These tables were not supported in lower releases.

- **DBA_STREAMS_RENAME_COLUMN** This view lists the columns renamed in the row LCR by rule transformation procedure DBMS_STREAMS_ADM. RENAME_COLUMN.

- **DBA_STREAMS_RENAME_SCHEMA** This view lists the schemas that are renamed in the row LCR by rule transformation procedure DBMS_ STREAMS_ADM.RENAME_SCHEMA.

- **DBA_STREAMS_RENAME_TABLE** This view lists the tables that are renamed in the row LCR by rule transformation procedure DBMS_STREAMS_ADM. RENAME_TABLE.

■ **DBA_STREAMS_TP_COMPONENT**   This view lists all of the Streams components at each database.

■ **DBA_STREAMS_TP_COMPONENT_LINK**   This view displays information about how messages flow between Streams components.

■ **DBA_STREAMS_TP_COMPONENT_STAT**   This view displays temporary performance statistics and session statistics about each of the Streams components.

■ **DBA_STREAMS_TP_DATABASE**   This view displays the database information that contains the Streams components.

■ **DBA_STREAMS_TP_PATH_BOTTLENECK**   This view has temporary information about the Streams components that might be causing a slowdown for messages in the Streams path.

■ **DBA_STREAMS_TP_PATH_STAT**   This view displays temporary performance statistics about each Streams path that is defined in the Streams topology.

■ **DBA_STREAMS_UNSUPPORTED**   This view contains information about all tables that are not supported by Streams in the current database.

■ **V$STREAMS_POOL_ADVICE**   This view displays information about the estimated count of spilled or unspilled messages and the associated time spent in the spill or the unspill activity for different Streams pool sizes. The sizes range from 10 percent to 200 percent of the current Streams pool size, in equal intervals. The value of the interval depends on the current size of the Streams pool.

Views for Capture Process

■ **DBA_CAPTURE**   This view provides all the information about the capture process configuration and running statistics.

■ **DBA_CAPTURE_EXTRA_ATTRIBUTES**   This view lists the extra attributes that are included in the LCR by all the capture processes in the database.

■ **DBA_CAPTURE_PARAMETERS**   This view lists all the parameters for all the capture processes in the database.

■ **DBA_HIST_STREAMS_CAPTURE**   This view contains information about the capture process. It is intended to be used with the Automatic Workload Repository (AWR) as it contains snapshots from the V$_STREAMS_CAPTURE view.

■ **DBA_SYNC_CAPTURE**   This view displays information about all synchronous capture processes in the database.

■ **DBA_SYNC_CAPTURE_TABLES**   This view lists all the tables that are captured by the synchronous capture process.

■ **V$STREAMS_CAPTURE**   This view contains comprehensive information about the active capture processes in the database.

Views for Apply Process

■ **DBA_APPLY**   This view provides all the information about the apply process configuration and running statistics.

■ **DBA_APPLY_ERROR**   This view contains information about the error transactions generated by all the apply processes in the database.

■ **DBA_APPLY_KEY_COLUMNS**   This view displays information about the substitute key columns for the tables. Substitute key columns are set using the DBMS_APPLY_ADM.SET_KEY_COLUMNS procedure.

■ **DBA_APPLY_OBJECT_DEPENDENCIES**   This view lists the object dependencies for all the apply processes in the database.

■ **DBA_APPLY_PARAMETERS**   This view contains information about all the apply process parameters.

■ **DBA_APPLY_PROGRESS**   This view displays information about the progress of the apply process that dequeues the messages from the queue. It only shows information about the messages that were queued by the capture process.

■ **DBA_APPLY_SPILL_TXN**   This view displays information about the transactions spilled from memory to hard disk by all apply processes in the database.

■ **DBA_APPLY_TABLE_COLUMNS**   This view displays, for all tables in the database, information about the non-key table columns for which Oracle Streams apply processes do not detect conflicts for updates and deletes.

■ **DBA_APPLY_VALUE_DEPENDENCIES**   This view displays information about the value dependencies for all apply processes in the database.

■ **V$STREAMS_APPLY_COORDINATOR**   This view displays information about each apply process coordinator.

■ **V$STREAMS_APPLY_READER**   This view displays information about each apply reader.

■ **V$STREAMS_APPLY_SERVER**   This view displays information about each apply server and its activities.

Views for Propagation Process

- **DBA_PROPAGATION**   This view contains all the information about the Streams propagation process.

- **DBA_QUEUE_SCHEDULES**   This view displays all propagation schedules in the database.

- **V$PROPAGATION_RECEIVER**   This view displays information about buffer queue propagation schedules on the receiving (destination) side. The values are reset to zero when the database (or instance in a RAC environment) restarts, when propagation migrates to another instance, or when an unscheduled propagation is attempted.

- **V$PROPAGATION_SENDER**   This view displays information about buffer queue propagation schedules on the sending (source) side. The values are reset to zero when the database (or instance in a RAC environment) restarts, when propagation migrates to another instance, or when an unscheduled propagation is attempted.

Views for Rules and Rule Sets

- **DBA_EVALUATION_CONTEXTS**   This view displays all rule evaluation contexts in the database.

- **DBA_EVALUATION_CONTEXT_TABLES**   This view displays the tables in all rule evaluation contexts in the database.

- **DBA_EVALUATION_CONTEXT_VARS**   This view displays the variables in all rule evaluation contexts in the database.

- **DBA_RULES**   This view displays all the rules for Streams components in the database.

- **DBA_RULE_SETS**   This view displays all the rule sets for Streams components in the database.

- **DBA_RULE_SET_RULES**   This view displays the rules in all rule sets in the database.

- **DBA_STREAMS_GLOBAL_RULES**   This view displays information about the global rules created for all Streams capture processes, propagation processes, and apply processes in the database.

- **DBA_STREAMS_RULES**   This view lists the rules used by all the Streams components in the database.

Oracle Streams 11g Data Replication

- **DBA_STREAMS_SCHEMA_RULES**   This view displays information about the Schema rules created for all Streams components.

- **DBA_STREAMS_TABLE_RULES**   This view displays information about the table rules created for all Streams capture processes, propagation processes, and apply processes in the database.

- **V$RULE**   This view displays rule statistics. This view has a row for every rule loaded into shared memory.

- **V$RULE_SET**   This view displays rule set statistics. This view has a row for every rule set loaded into shared memory.

- **V$RULE_SET_AGGREGATE_STATS**   This view displays statistics aggregated over all evaluations on all rule sets. This view has a row for each type of statistic.

Views for Instantiation

- **DBA_APPLY_INSTANTIATED_GLOBAL**   This view displays information about the source databases for which an instantiation SCN has been set in the local database.

- **DBA_APPLY_INSTANTIATED_OBJECTS**   This view displays information about source objects for which an instantiation SCN has been set in the local database.

- **DBA_APPLY_INSTANTIATED_SCHEMAS**   This view displays information about source schemas for which an instantiation SCN has been set in the local database.

- **DBA_CAPTURE_PREPARED_DATABASE**   This view displays information about when the local database was prepared for instantiation.

- **DBA_CAPTURE_PREPARED_SCHEMAS**   This view displays information about all schemas prepared for instantiation at the local database.

- **DBA_CAPTURE_PREPARED_TABLES**   This view displays information about all tables prepared for instantiation at the local database.

- **DBA_SYNC_CAPTURE_PREPARED_TABS**   This view displays information about all tables in the database that are prepared for synchronous capture instantiation.

Views for Supplemental Logging

- **DBA_CAPTURE_PREPARED_DATABASE** This view displays information about when the local database was prepared for instantiation.

- **DBA_CAPTURE_PREPARED_SCHEMAS** This view displays information about all schemas prepared for instantiation at the local database.

- **DBA_CAPTURE_PREPARED_TABLES** This view displays information about all tables prepared for instantiation at the local database.

- **DBA_LOG_GROUPS** This view displays log group definitions on all tables in the database.

- **DBA_LOG_GROUP_COLUMNS** This view displays all columns in the database that are specified in log groups.

- **V$DATABASE** This view displays information about the database. The columns SUPPLEMENTAL_LOG_DATA_* show the level of supplemental logging. Also, the column FORCE_LOGGING indicates if NOLOGGING operations are suppressed.

Views for Handlers

- **DBA_APPLY** The column DDL_HANDLER in this view lists the name of the DDL handler assigned to the apply process.

- **DBA_APPLY_DML_HANDLERS** This view contains information about all DML handlers on all tables in the database.

- **DBA_STREAMS_STMTS** This view displays information about the statements in all statement DML handlers in the database.

- **DBA_STREAMS_STMT_HANDLERS** This view displays information about all statement DML handlers in the database.

Views for Conflict Handlers

- **DBA_APPLY_CONFLICT_COLUMNS** This view contains information about the conflict handlers on all tables in the database.

- **DBA_APPLY_TABLE_COLUMNS** This view displays, for all tables in the database, information about the non-key table columns for which Oracle Streams apply processes do not detect conflicts for updates and deletes.

Views for Transformations

- **DBA_STREAMS_TRANSFORMATIONS**   This view displays information about all Streams transformations available in the database, in order of execution.

- **DBA_STREAMS_TRANSFORM_FUNCTION**   This view displays information about all rule-based transformation functions in the database.

Views for LogMiner

- **DBA_LOGMNR_LOG**   This view displays all archived logs registered with active LogMiner persistent sessions in the database.

- **DBA_LOGMNR_SESSION**   This view displays all active LogMiner persistent sessions in the database.

Views for Archived Log/Redo Log Files

- **DBA_REGISTERED_ARCHIVED_LOG**   This view displays information about all registered archived log files in the database.

- **V$ARCHIVED_LOG**   This view displays archived log information from the control file, including archive log names.

- **V$LOG**   This view displays log file information from the control file.

- **V$LOGFILE**   This view contains information about redo log files.

- **V$LOG_HISTORY**   This view contains log history information from the control file.

View for Transactions

- **V$STREAMS_TRANSACTION**   This view displays information about transactions that are being processed by capture processes or apply processes. This view can be used to identify long running transactions and to determine how many LCRs are being processed in each transaction. This view only contains information about captured LCRs. This view only shows information about LCRs that are being processed because they satisfied the rule sets for the Streams process at the time of the query.

- For capture processes, this view only shows information about changes in transactions that the capture process has converted to LCRs. It does not show information about all the active transactions present in the redo log.

- For apply processes, this view only shows information about LCRs that the apply process has dequeued. It does not show information about LCRs in the apply process's queue.

Views for Queues and Queue Tables

- **DBA_QUEUE_SCHEDULES**   This view displays all propagation schedules in the database.

- **DBA_QUEUE_SUBSCRIBERS**   This view displays all subscribers on all queues in the database.

- **DBA_QUEUE_TABLES**   This view displays information about the owner instance for a queue table. A queue table can contain multiple queues. In this case, each queue in a queue table has the same owner instance as the queue table.

- **DBA_QUEUES**   This view displays the operational characteristics of every queue in a database.

- **V$BUFFERED_PUBLISHERS**   This view displays performance information about all the publishers in the database instance who enqueue messages to the buffered queue. There is one row for each publisher. The information contains statistical data on message queuing along with the current state of the publisher. Typically, the publisher is the capture process.

- **V$BUFFERED_QUEUES**   This view displays performance information about all buffered queues in the database instance.

- **V$BUFFERED_SUBSCRIBERS**   This view displays performance information about all the subscribers in the database instance who dequeue messages from the buffered queue. There is one row for each subscriber. Typically, the subscriber is the apply process.

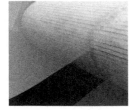

APPENDIX
E

References

ollowing is a list of all the Oracle Corporation material that I used as references for writing this book. Any omission from this list is purely unintentional.

The following eight references can be accessed from the Oracle Database Online Documentation 11*g* Release 2 (11.2) portal at www.oracle.com/pls/db112/portal.portal_db?selected=15&frame=.

■ Oracle Database 2 Day + Data Replication and Integration Guide 11*g* Release 2 (11.2)

■ Oracle Streams Concepts and Administration 11*g* Release 2 (11.2)

■ Oracle Streams Replication Administrator's Guide 11*g* Release 2 (11.2)

■ Oracle Streams Extended Examples 11*g* Release 2 (11.2)

■ Oracle Streams Advanced Queuing User's Guide 11*g* Release 2 (11.2)

■ Oracle Database PL/SQL Packages and Types Reference 11*g* Release 2 (11.2)

■ Oracle Database Reference 11*g* Release 2 (11.2)

■ Oracle Database Net Services Administrator's Guide 11*g* Release 2 (11.2)

The first three references in the list below can be accessed from the Oracle Database 11*g* Features: Data Replication and Integration portal at www.oracle.com/technetwork/database/features/data-integration/index.html. The last two references can be accessed directly using the specified URLs.

■ Oracle Database 11*g* Streams Features Overview

■ Oracle Database 11*g*: Oracle Streams (Technical White Paper)

■ Grid Control 10.2.0.5: Streams Management

■ Oracle Streams Configuration Best Practices: Oracle Database 10*g* Release 10.2, www.oracle.com/technetwork/database/features/availability/maa-10gr2-streams-configuration-132039.pdf.

■ Oracle Streams Performance Tuning Best Practices: Oracle Database 10*g* Release 10.2, www.oracle.com/technetwork/database/features/availability/maa-wp-10gr2-streams-performance-130059.pdf.

Index

D

S

T

U

GET YOUR FREE SUBSCRIPTION TO *ORACLE MAGAZINE*

Oracle Magazine is essential gear for today's information technology professionals. Stay informed and increase your productivity with every issue of *Oracle Magazine*. Inside each free bimonthly issue you'll get:

- Up-to-date information on Oracle Database, Oracle Application Server, Web development, enterprise grid computing, database technology, and business trends
- Third-party news and announcements
- Technical articles on Oracle and partner products, technologies, and operating environments
- Development and administration tips
- Real-world customer stories

If there are other Oracle users at your location who would like to receive their own subscription to *Oracle Magazine*, please photocopy this form and pass it along.

ORACLE
M A G A Z I N E

Three easy ways to subscribe:

① Web
Visit our Web site at **oracle.com/oraclemagazine**
You'll find a subscription form there, plus much more

② Fax
Complete the questionnaire on the back of this card
and fax the questionnaire side only to **+1.847.763.9638**

③ Mail
Complete the questionnaire on the back of this card
and mail it to **P.O. Box 1263, Skokie, IL 60076-8263**

Want your own FREE subscription?

To receive a free subscription to *Oracle Magazine*, you must fill out the entire card, sign it, and date it (incomplete cards cannot be processed or acknowledged). You can also fax your application to **+1.847.763.9638. Or subscribe at our Web site at oracle.com/oraclemagazine**

O **Yes, please send me a FREE subscription** *Oracle Magazine*.   O No.

O From time to time, Oracle Publishing allows our partners exclusive access to our e-mail addresses for special promotions and announcements. To be included in this program, please check this circle. If you do not wish to be included, you will only receive notices about your subscription via e-mail.

O Oracle Publishing allows sharing of our postal mailing list with selected third parties. If you prefer your mailing address not to be included in this program, please check this circle.

If at any time you would like to be removed from either mailing list, please contact Customer Service at +1.847.763.9635 or send an e-mail to oracle@halldata.com. If you opt in to the sharing of information, Oracle may also provide you with e-mail related to Oracle products, services, and events. If you want to completely unsubscribe from any e-mail communication from Oracle, please send an e-mail to: unsubscribe@oracle-mail.com with the following in the subject line: REMOVE [your e-mail address]. For complete information on Oracle Publishing's privacy practices, please visit oracle.com/html/privacy/html

X

signature (required) _____ date _____

name _____ title _____

company _____ e-mail address _____

street/p.o. box _____

city/state/zip or postal code _____ telephone _____

country _____ fax _____

Would you like to receive your free subscription in digital format instead of print if it becomes available? O Yes O No

---

YOU MUST ANSWER ALL 10 QUESTIONS BELOW.

① WHAT IS THE PRIMARY BUSINESS ACTIVITY OF YOUR FIRM AT THIS LOCATION? (check one only)

- □ 01 Aerospace and Defense Manufacturing
- □ 02 Application Service Provider
- □ 03 Automotive Manufacturing
- □ 04 Chemicals
- □ 05 Media and Entertainment
- □ 06 Construction/Engineering
- □ 07 Consumer Sector/Consumer Packaged Goods
- □ 08 Education
- □ 09 Financial Services/Insurance
- □ 10 Health Care
- □ 11 High Technology Manufacturing, OEM
- □ 12 Industrial Manufacturing
- □ 13 Independent Software Vendor
- □ 14 Life Sciences (biotech, pharmaceuticals)
- □ 15 Natural Resources
- □ 16 Oil and Gas
- □ 17 Professional Services
- □ 18 Public Sector (government)
- □ 19 Research
- □ 20 Retail/Wholesale/Distribution
- □ 21 Systems Integrator, VAR/VAD
- □ 22 Telecommunications
- □ 23 Travel and Transportation
- □ 24 Utilities (electric, gas, sanitation, water)
- □ 98 Other Business and Services _____

② WHICH OF THE FOLLOWING BEST DESCRIBES YOUR PRIMARY JOB FUNCTION? (check one only)

CORPORATE MANAGEMENT/STAFF
- □ 01 Executive Management (President, Chair, CEO, CFO, Owner, Partner, Principal)
- □ 02 Finance/Administrative Management (VP/Director/ Manager/Controller, Purchasing, Administration)
- □ 03 Sales/Marketing Management (VP/Director/Manager)
- □ 04 Computer Systems/Operations Management (CIO/VP/Director/Manager MIS/IS/IT, Ops)

IS/IT STAFF
- □ 05 Application Development/Programming Management
- □ 06 Application Development/Programming Staff
- □ 07 Consulting
- □ 08 DBA/Systems Administrator
- □ 09 Education/Training
- □ 10 Technical Support Director/Manager
- □ 11 Other Technical Management/Staff
- □ 98 Other

③ WHAT IS YOUR CURRENT PRIMARY OPERATING PLATFORM (check all that apply)

- □ 01 Digital Equipment Corp UNIX/VAX/VMS
- □ 02 HP UNIX
- □ 03 IBM AIX
- □ 04 IBM UNIX
- □ 05 Linux (Red Hat)
- □ 06 Linux (SUSE)
- □ 07 Linux (Oracle Enterprise)
- □ 08 Linux (other)
- □ 09 Macintosh
- □ 10 MVS
- □ 11 Netware
- □ 12 Network Computing
- □ 13 SCO UNIX
- □ 14 Sun Solaris/SunOS
- □ 15 Windows
- □ 16 Other UNIX
- □ 98 Other
- 99 □ None of the Above

④ DO YOU EVALUATE, SPECIFY, RECOMMEND, OR AUTHORIZE THE PURCHASE OF ANY OF THE FOLLOWING? (check all that apply)

- □ 01 Hardware
- □ 02 Business Applications (ERP, CRM, etc.)
- □ 03 Application Development Tools
- □ 04 Database Products
- □ 05 Internet or Intranet Products
- □ 06 Other Software
- □ 07 Middleware Products
- 99 □ None of the Above

⑤ IN YOUR JOB, DO YOU USE OR PLAN TO PURCHASE ANY OF THE FOLLOWING PRODUCTS? (check all that apply)

SOFTWARE
- □ 01 CAD/CAE/CAM
- □ 02 Collaboration Software
- □ 03 Communications
- □ 04 Database Management
- □ 05 File Management
- □ 06 Finance
- □ 07 Java
- □ 08 Multimedia Authoring
- □ 09 Networking
- □ 10 Programming
- □ 11 Project Management
- □ 12 Scientific and Engineering
- □ 13 Systems Management
- □ 14 Workflow

HARDWARE
- □ 15 Macintosh
- □ 16 Mainframe
- □ 17 Massively Parallel Processing

- □ 18 Minicomputer
- □ 19 Intel x86(32)
- □ 20 Intel x86(64)
- □ 21 Network Computer
- □ 22 Symmetric Multiprocessing
- □ 23 Workstation Services

SERVICES
- □ 24 Consulting
- □ 25 Education/Training
- □ 26 Maintenance
- □ 27 Online Database
- □ 28 Support
- □ 29 Technology-Based Training
- □ 30 Other
- 99 □ None of the Above

⑥ WHAT IS YOUR COMPANY'S SIZE? (check one only)

- □ 01 More than 25,000 Employees
- □ 02 10,001 to 25,000 Employees
- □ 03 5,001 to 10,000 Employees
- □ 04 1,001 to 5,000 Employees
- □ 05 101 to 1,000 Employees
- □ 06 Fewer than 100 Employees

⑦ DURING THE NEXT 12 MONTHS, HOW MUCH DO YOU ANTICIPATE YOUR ORGANIZATION WILL SPEND ON COMPUTER HARDWARE, SOFTWARE, PERIPHERALS, AND SERVICES FOR YOUR LOCATION? (check one only)

- □ 01 Less than $10,000
- □ 02 $10,000 to $49,999
- □ 03 $50,000 to $99,999
- □ 04 $100,000 to $499,999
- □ 05 $500,000 to $999,999
- □ 06 $1,000,000 and Over

⑧ WHAT IS YOUR COMPANY'S YEARLY SALES REVENUE? (check one only)

- □ 01 $500, 000, 000 and above
- □ 02 $100, 000, 000 to $500, 000, 000
- □ 03 $50, 000, 000 to $100, 000, 000
- □ 04 $5, 000, 000 to $50, 000, 000
- □ 05 $1, 000, 000 to $5, 000, 000

⑨ WHAT LANGUAGES AND FRAMEWORKS DO YOU USE? (check all that apply)

- □ 01 Ajax
- □ 02 C
- □ 03 C++
- □ 04 C#
- □ 13 Python
- □ 14 Ruby/Rails
- □ 15 Spring
- □ 16 Struts
- □ 05 Hibernate
- □ 06 J++/J#
- □ 07 Java
- □ 08 JSP
- □ 09 .NET
- □ 10 Perl
- □ 11 PHP
- □ 12 PL/SQL
- □ 17 SQL
- □ 18 Visual Basic
- □ 98 Other

⑩ WHAT ORACLE PRODUCTS ARE IN USE AT YOUR SITE? (check all that apply)

ORACLE DATABASE
- □ 01 Oracle Database 11*g*
- □ 02 Oracle Database 10*g*
- □ 03 Oracle9*i* Database
- □ 04 Oracle Embedded Database (Oracle Lite, Times Ten, Berkeley DB)
- □ 05 Other Oracle Database Release

ORACLE FUSION MIDDLEWARE
- □ 06 Oracle Application Server
- □ 07 Oracle Portal
- □ 08 Oracle Enterprise Manager
- □ 09 Oracle BPEL Process Manager
- □ 10 Oracle Identity Management
- □ 11 Oracle SOA Suite
- □ 12 Oracle Data Hubs

ORACLE DEVELOPMENT TOOLS
- □ 13 Oracle JDeveloper
- □ 14 Oracle Forms
- □ 15 Oracle Reports
- □ 16 Oracle Designer
- □ 17 Oracle Discoverer
- □ 18 Oracle BI Beans
- □ 19 Oracle Warehouse Builder
- □ 20 Oracle WebCenter
- □ 21 Oracle Application Express

ORACLE APPLICATIONS
- □ 22 Oracle E-Business Suite
- □ 23 PeopleSoft Enterprise
- □ 24 JD Edwards EnterpriseOne
- □ 25 JD Edwards World
- □ 26 Oracle Fusion
- □ 27 Hyperion
- □ 28 Siebel CRM

ORACLE SERVICES
- □ 28 Oracle E-Business Suite On Demand
- □ 29 Oracle Technology On Demand
- □ 30 Siebel CRM On Demand
- □ 31 Oracle Consulting
- □ 32 Oracle Education
- □ 33 Oracle Support
- □ 98 Other
- 99 □ None of the Above

CPSIA information can be obtained
at www.ICGtesting.com
Printed in the USA
LVOW02s1700080217

523626LV00005B/254/P